AnтHоny

USA

JAMES DixoN

Body & Soul

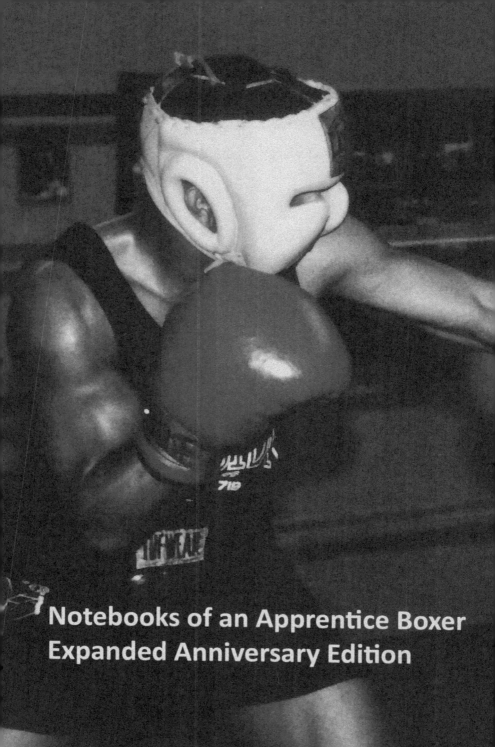

Notebooks of an Apprentice Boxer
Expanded Anniversary Edition

OXFORD
UNIVERSITY PRESS

Oxford University Press is a department of the University of Oxford. It furthers
the University's objective of excellence in research, scholarship, and education
by publishing worldwide. Oxford is a registered trade mark of Oxford University
Press in the UK and certain other countries.

Published in the United States of America by Oxford University Press
198 Madison Avenue, New York, NY 10016, United States of America.

© Oxford University Press 2022

Originally published by Oxford University Press in 2004

CIP data is on file at the Library of Congress
ISBN 978–0–19–046569–8

9 8 7 6 5 4 3 2 1

Printed by LSC Communications, United States of America

In loving memory of **DeeDee Armour**
who is now coaching in that great big gym
in the heavens

Contents

When Social Science
Meets the Sweet Science

Preface to the Expanded Anniversary Edition

> It is good for the ethnographer sometimes to put aside camera, note book and pencil, and to join in himself in what is going on. He can take part in the natives' games, he can follow them on their visits and walks, sit down and listen and share in their conversations. I am not certain if this is equally easy for everyone . . . but though the degree of success varies, the attempt is possible for everyone. Out of such plunges into the life of the natives . . . I have carried away a distinct feeling that their behavior, their manner of being, in all sorts of tribal transactions, became more transparent and easily understandable than it had been before.
> —Bronislaw Malinowski, *Argonauts of the Western Pacific*, 1922

This expanded anniversary edition of *Body and Soul* marks the twentieth year since the publication of the original French edition and the thirtieth year since I climbed into the ring to fight in the Chicago Golden Gloves tournament under the colors of the Woodlawn Boys Club, buoyed by the ardent shouts of my gym mates and emboldened by the calm voice and sage advice of coach DeeDee in my corner. In the new postface that follows the narrative of the epiphanic stretch of my pugilistic journey, culminating in that fateful encounter in the squared circle, I draw out the inspiration, design, and implications of my sociological vivisection of prizefighting. I retrace the entwined biographical and intellectual pathways that led me to apprentice in the trade. I expound on the analytic framework and theoretical agenda that animate my account of the forging of the boxer in the black American ghetto. I also offer a concise genealogy and anatomy of *habitus*, the key concept of Pierre Bourdieu's that is both the object and the tool of my analysis, and I explicate how it helps us capture the practical logic that guides human action.[1] I amplify this extended analytic revisit by retracing how the regulars of the Woodlawn Boys Club have fared on the pugilistic circuit and the social front in the decades since the gym closed, and what their

---

1. Pierre Bourdieu, *Le Sens pratique* (Paris: Minuit,1980, trans. *The Logic of Practice*, Cambridge: Polity Press, 1990).

trajectories in and out of the ring teach us about the social and symbolic structures of prizefighting. In this brief preface, I would like to consider the following seemingly simple, but in truth intricate, question: *What happens when social science meets the Sweet science?*[2] There are two parts to the answer. The first is what sociology teaches us about boxing, the second is what boxing teaches us about sociology.

What does social inquiry into the workaday world of pugilists disclose about their trade that we would not otherwise know from the profusion of artistic and journalistic accounts? Probing beyond prefabricated images of the heroic champion stepping into the limelight, *Body and Soul* focuses on ordinary boxers in their quotidian environment of the gym, with its drab and smelly ambiance.[3] It captures the dualities that organize the prizefighter's existence: material interest and sensuous desire, individualism and solidarity, affection and exploitation, the routine and the charismatic, the masculine and the feminine, abstinence and jouissance, the sacred and the profane. It paints the portrait of devoted artisans of the virile body who patiently hone an honorific craft, share a protected and protective sociability, and seek recognition and redemption within the closed brotherhood of the ring. Entering into what Harold Garfinkel calls "the demonics of social action" reveals that the subject of boxing is not the lone individual waltzing near-naked between the ropes but the dense web of social, moral, and symbolic relations constitutive of the gym as a place of worship of the skilled masculine body. The gym functions at once as a sanctuary against the dangers of the street, a scaffolding for the silent pedagogy of expert organisms in motion, and a school of discipline in which occupational ethic is literally inscribed onto the flesh.

So much to say that forging boxers is a fundamentally collective and spiritual enterprise, rather than an individual and strictly material endeavor, and that it is driven, not by distant monetary incentives ("club

2. The expression "Sweet science" was coined in the early nineteenth century by the British popular journalist and sportswriter Pierce Egan (in his learned and exquisitely illustrated multivolume study *Boxiana, or Sketches of Ancient and Modern Pugilism* [1813–1829]). It purported to stress the skill and knowledge of fighters, at a time when boxing matches were both illegal and wildly popular; see David Snowdon, *Writing the Prizefight: Pierce Egan's Boxiana World* (London: Peter Lang, 2013). It fell into a long spell of disuse before being revived by A. J. Liebling in his classic 1956 collection, *The Sweet Science*; see A. J. Liebling: *The Sweet Science and Other Writings,* ed. Pete Hamill (New York: Library of America, 2008).
3. For a visual account of this peculiar atmosphere, see the documentary by Frederick Wiseman, *Boxing Gym* (2010).

fighters" compete infrequently and earn paltry purses), as by the more tangible 'promise of *ontological transcendence*, the day-by-day gradual machining of a new social being out of the old so as to escape the common determinations that otherwise consign the gym's recruits to public insignificance. Prizefighting allows its practitioners to live, for a time, in a state of *social suspension*, where it seems that they are not condemned to remaining what they are, that a world of opportunities remains open to them, that they can escape banality and anonymity. To sum up, I could borrow the words that Émile Durkheim uses to characterize religion, and say that pugilism is a system of material and moral "forces *sui generis*, which elevate the individual above himself, which transport him into another world from that in which his profane existence is passed, affording him a life that is very different, more exalted and more intense."[4]

Now the converse question: What does boxing teach us about sociology? Pugilism throws a stiff challenge to the conventional models of social science, which depict the agent either as a maximizing computing machine (as with variants of rational choice theory descended from Jeremy Bentham) or a symbolic animal spinning webs of meaning (found in phenomenological and hermeneutic approaches influenced by Immanuel Kant). Both models share this flaw that they *disincarnate action*, scotomizing the inconvenient but stubborn fact that humans are sensory and suffering creatures, fated to die, and that they know it. The rational actor and his symbolic cousin are equally mutilated and mutilating on account of excluding desire, sensual infatuation, and visceral attraction as driving forces of social existence. In short, normal social science typically gives us "an excellent skeleton" of social life, as Malinowski put it a century ago, "but it lacks flesh and blood."[5]

Pugilism forces us to confront this flaw and points at once to the need for, and the possibility of, a *sociology of passion* as a modality of our relationship to the social world. A passion is a powerful and compelling emotion or feeling (such as love or hate), an ardent sexual yearning, or a fondness and enthusiasm that one finds difficult to contain. The

4. Émile Durkheim, "Le problème religieux et la dualité de la nature humaine" (1913), reprinted in *Textes, 2, Religion, morale, anomie* (Paris: Minuit, 1975), 23–59.
5. Bronislaw Malinowski, *Argonauts of the Western Pacific: An Account of Native Enterprise and Adventure in the Archipelagoes of Melanesian New Guinea* (New York: Routledge, [1922] 2002), 7. For an elaboration of this position, see Loïc Wacquant, "For a Sociology of Flesh and Blood," *Qualitative Sociology* 38, no. 1 (2015): 1–11.

medieval Latin *passio* originally denoted sinful desire, physical suffering, and martyrdom. What more appropriate term to designate the pre-reflexive, visceral affection that moves the boxer to give himself over to his craft body and soul (*religiossime*), in spite of his better judgment about its potentially destructive consequences? Prizefighters are well aware of the physical toll and risks they take, and, to express their sense of exploitation, they compare themselves to prostitutes, slaves, and stallions. Yet they do not enter and persevere in their gruesome avocation because they are constrained to ("Can't nobody put a gun to your head and make you fight, Louie"); they box because they love the game. But—and this is the catch and the enigma that the present book strives to resolve—theirs is not a free and self-governed predilection. Rather, it is a coerced, captive, perhaps even malicious affection, born of pervasive material necessity and severe social limitation.

Boxers choose to box because they love it, but they do not choose to love to box. Their craving to invest their time, energy, and proficient organism into the fistic trade, the *libido pugilistica* that propels them in the gym and into the ring, is itself the product, *embodied*, of domination, and it binds them to the very structures of class inequality, caste exclusion, and plebeian masculinity from which they are striving to escape. And, somewhere, somehow, the fighter knows this: "I got kinda *tricked* into the sport and I kinda fell in love with it," quips one lowly pug to explain why he put on the gloves as a youngster and then went on to "turn pro." Thus, his love is profoundly ambivalent, bittersweet, and strained. It is a passion in the etymological sense of the term.

Recall now these sagacious words of Blaise Pascal's: "Man finds nothing so intolerable as to be in a state of complete rest, without passions, without occupation, without diversion, without effort. Then he feels his nothingness, his abandon, his inadequacy, his dependency, his helplessness, his emptiness."[6] By embracing the fistic cosmos, and being embraced by it in return, the boxer begets his passion. And he escapes nothingness, helplessness, and emptiness. He makes a world in which what he does makes a difference, where he is known and acknowledged—in short, where he exists. His passion is his making and his unmaking, but no matter the outcome, he is right *at the point of production*. Come to think of it, there is a little bit of the boxer in all of us, and a lot of us in the boxer.

Paris and Berkeley, December 2020

---

6. Blaise Pascal, *Pensées* (Paris: Gallimard, 2010 [1670]), parag. 622, "Boredom."

The Taste and Ache of Action

Preface to the U.S. Edition

Nihil humanum alienum est.

—Baruch Spinoza

This book is both a kind of sociological-pugilistic *Bildungsroman* retracing a personal *experience* of initiation into a bodily craft that is as notorious for its heroic symbolism—Muhammad Ali is no doubt, ahead even of Pelé, the most famed and celebrated man walking the planet—as it is mysterious in its prosaic reality, and a scientific *experiment.* It aims to provide a demonstration in action of the fruitfulness of an approach that takes seriously, at the theoretical, methodological, and rhetorical levels, the fact that the social agent is before anything else a being of flesh, nerves, and senses (in the twofold meaning of sensual and signifying), a "suffering being" (*leidenschaftliches Wesen,* as the young Marx put it in his *Manuscripts of 1844*) who partakes of the universe that makes him, and that he in turn contributes to making, with every fiber of his body and his heart. Sociology must endeavor to clasp and restitute this carnal dimension of existence, which is particularly salient in the case of the boxer but is in truth shared in various degrees of visibility by all women and men, through a methodical and meticulous work of detection and documentation, deciphering and writing liable to capture and to convey the taste and the ache of action, the sound and the fury of the social world that the established approaches of the social sciences typically mute when they do not suppress them altogether.

To accomplish that, there is nothing better than initiatory immersion and even *moral and sensual conversion* to the cosmos under investigation, construed as a technique of observation and analysis that, on the express condition that it be theoretically armed, makes it possible for the sociologist to appropriate in and through practice the cognitive, aesthetic, ethical, and conative schemata that those who inhabit that cosmos engage in their everyday deeds. If it is true, as Pierre Bourdieu contends, that "we learn by body" and that "the social order inscribes itself in bodies through this permanent confrontation, more or less dramatic, but which always grants a large role to affectivity," then it is imperative that the sociologist submit himself to the fire of action *in situ;* that to the greatest extent possible he put his own organism, sensibility, and incarnate intelligence at the epicenter of the array of material and symbolic forces that he intends to dissect; that he strive to acquire the appetites and the competencies that make the diligent agent in the universe under consideration, so as better to plumb the inner depths of this "relation of presence to the world, and being in the world, in the sense of belonging to the world, being possessed by it, in which neither the agent nor the object is posited as such,"[1] and that nonetheless defines them both as such and joins them by a thousand complicitous ties that are all the stronger for being invisible. So much to say that boxers have a great deal to teach us here, about prizefighting of course, but also and above all about ourselves.

It would however be artificial and misleading to present the research of which this book offers a first account in a predominantly narrative mode (as prelude and stepping-stone to a second, more explicitly theoretical work) as animated by the will to prove the value of carnal sociology and to concretely put its validity to the test. For in reality it is the opposite that occurred: it is the need to understand and fully master a transformative experience that I had neither desired nor anticipated, and that long remained confusing and obscure to me, that drove me to thematize the necessity of a sociology not only *of* the body, in the sense of object, but also *from* the body, that is, deploying the body as tool of inquiry and vector of knowledge.

I landed in the Woodlawn boxing gym by default and by accident. At the time, I was seeking an observation point from which to scrutinize, listen to, and touch up-close the everyday reality of the black

---

1. Pierre Bourdieu, *Pascalian Meditations* (Cambridge: Polity Press, [1997] 2000), 141, my translation.

American ghetto, which I had undertaken to study at the invitation of, and in close collaboration with, the eminent African-American sociologist William Julius Wilson,[2] but of which I did not have the slightest practical apperception, having grown up in a middle-class family in a small village in southern France. From the outset, it seemed to me impossible, for reasons both ethical and epistemological, to write about the South Side of Chicago without getting at least a rough sociological grasp of it at ground level, considering that its grinding poverty was spread out beneath my balcony (literally, since the University of Chicago had assigned me the very last available apartment of its student-housing stock, the one that nobody had wanted precisely because it was located right on the demarcation line of the black neighborhood of Woodlawn, on a border marked out every fifty yards by white emergency telephones used to call out the cars of the university's private police in case of need). And because the normal sociology of the relations between class, caste, and state in the U.S. metropolis seemed to me riddled with false concepts that obscure the reality of the ghetto by projecting onto it the racial (and racist) common sense of the national society, beginning with the tale of the "underclass," a bastard neologism that conveniently allowed scholars to absolve white domination and the ineptitude of the authorities on the social and urban fronts by focusing attention on the ecology of poor neighborhoods and the alleged "antisocial" behavior of their residents.[3]

After several months spent in a vain quest for a place where I could insert myself to observe the local scene, a French friend who practiced judo took me to the gym on 63rd Street, a mere two blocks from my abode but on a different planet, as it were. I signed up immediately, out of curiosity and because that was obviously the only acceptable way to hang around there and to get to meet young men from the neighborhood. And right after my first boxing training session I started an ethnographic diary, without imagining for a second that I would attend the gym with increasing assiduity for three and a half years and, in the process, amass some twenty-three hundred pages of raw notes by religiously

2. Our collaboration, which lasted for four years, commenced as Wilson was finishing his major book of the 1980s, *The Truly Disadvantaged* (Chicago: University of Chicago Press, 1987).
3. Loïc Wacquant, *"L"underclass'* urbaine dans l'imaginaire social et scientifique américain," in *L'Exclusion. L'État des savoirs* (Paris: La Découverte, 1996), 248–262.

consigning to paper for hours every evening detailed descriptions of the events, interactions, and conversations of the day. For once I had entered the Woodlawn Boys Club, I found myself confronted with a triple challenge, in spite of myself.

The first challenge was brute and even brutal: Would I be capable of *learning this roughest and most demanding of sports,* of mastering its rudiments so as to carve out for myself a small place in the simultaneously fraternal and competitive world of the Sweet science of bruising, to weave with the members of the gym relationships of mutual respect and trust and thereby, eventually, carry out my field investigation of the ghetto? The answer was several months in coming. After difficult and painful beginnings, during which my technical ineptitude was equalled only by my feeling of frustration and sometimes discouragement (those who would later become my dearest ring buddies were then unanimous in betting that I would give up at any moment), I managed to improve my physical constitution, toughen my morale, and acquire the gestures and imbibe the tactics of the pugilist. I learned the ropes on the floor and then proved myself between the ropes by "gloving up" regularly with the boxers of the gym, amateur and professional, before entering Chicago's great Golden Gloves tournament with the fervent support of the entire club, and even later seriously envisaged "turning pro." I accrued a practical knowledge and refined my judgment of the Manly art to the point where the old trainer DeeDee asked me one day to replace him as "cornerman" for a major bout fought by Curtis, Woodlawn's star boxer, taking place overseas. DeeDee was also fond of forecasting that, down the road, I would open my own boxing gym: "An' you gonna be a *helluva coach* one day, Louie, I know that."

I had no sooner overcome this initial barrier and fulfilled the minimum condition necessary to lodge myself durably in the milieu than I was called back to a second challenge, that of my original project: Could I grasp and explain social relations in the black ghetto based on my embeddedness in that particular location? My long-term immersion in that little boxing gym and my intensive participation in the exchanges it supported day-to-day have allowed me—in my eyes at least, but the reader can judge for herself on the evidence—to reconstruct root and branch my understanding of what a ghetto is in general, and my analysis of the structure and functioning of Chicago's black ghetto in post-Fordist and post-Keynesian America at the end of the twentieth century in particular, as well as to better discern what distinguishes this *terra non grata* from the neighborhoods of relegation of other advanced societies.[4] For starters, I recused the false idea, deeply rooted in the American sociology of the relations between racial division and urban marginality since the earliest works of the Chicago School, that the ghetto is a "disorganized" universe, characterized by lack, want, and absence. The gym enabled me to link theoretical work with ongoing empirical observation and thereby to effectively question the "Orientalizing" vision of the ghetto and its denizens, and to restore to the heart of its study the power relations that characterize it as such, that is, as instrument of economic extraction and social ostracization of a group stripped of ethnic honor, a manner of "ethnoracial prison" in which America's urban pariahs are forcibly confined.[5]

There remained the third challenge, the most formidable of all, which I would never in a million years have imagined to be facing one day when I walked in through the gates of the Woodlawn Boys Club, and to which this work provides a first, partial and provisional, answer (as are all scientific investigations, even when they disguise themselves as narrative): How to account anthropologically for a practice that is so intensely corporeal, a culture that is thoroughly kinetic, a universe in which the most essential is transmitted, acquired, and deployed beneath language and consciousness—in short, for an *institution made man* (or men) situated at the extreme practical and theoretical edge of practice? To put it another way: having understood what the craft (*métier*) of boxing is, in the sense of occupation and social state but also ministry and mystery (according to the etymology of the word *mestier*), "by body," with my fists and my guts, by being myself caught, captured and captivated by it, would I know how to retranslate this comprehension of the senses into sociological language and find expressive forms

---

4. For a preliminary formulation of this work, see *Urban Outcasts: A Comparative Sociology of Advanced Marginality* (Cambridge: Polity Press, 2008); see also "Elias in the Dark Ghetto," *Amsterdams Sociologisch Tidjschrift* 24, 3/4 (December 1997): 340–348; and "Inside the Zone: The Social Art of the Hustler in the Black American Ghetto," *Theory, Culture, and Society* 15, 2 (May 1998 [1992]): 1–36, reprinted in Pierre Bourdieu et al., *The Weight of the World: A Study in Social Suffering* (Cambridge: Polity Press, [1993] 1999), 140–167.

5. Loïc Wacquant, "Three Pernicious Premises in the Study of the American Ghetto," *International Journal of Urban and Regional Research* 21, 2 (June 1997): 341–353; "'A Black City within the White': Revisiting America's Dark Ghetto," *Black Renaissance* 2, 1 (fall–winter 1998): 141–151; and "The New 'Peculiar Institution': On the Prison as Surrogate Ghetto," *Theoretical Criminology* 4, 3 (2000): 377–389.

suitable to communicating it without in the process annihilating its most distinctive properties?

The organization of this book according to the principle of communicating vessels, the proportion of analysis and narrative, of the conceptual and the depictive, gradually reversing through the pages (so that a profane reader can work her way backward, returning to the sociology from the "lived experience," albeit a lived experience that has been sociologically constructed), the braiding of genres and modes of writing, but also the strategic use of photographs and personal notations taken from my notebooks, all answer the concern to make the reader enter into the daily moral and sensual world of the ordinary boxer, to make her palpitate along with the author so as to give her *both* the reasoned understanding of the social mechanisms and existential forces that determine him *and* the particular *aisthesis* that illuminates his intimacy as fighter.[6] By entering into the manufacture of the boxer, by elucidating "the coordination of these three elements, the body, the individual consciousness, and the collectivity" that mold him and make him vibrate day to day, "it is life itself, it is all of man"[7] that we discover. And that we discover inside ourselves.

6. The interested reader will find complementary materials on this theme in Loïc Wacquant, "The Prizefighter's Three Bodies," *Ethnos* 63, 3 (November 1998): 325–352; "Whores, Slaves, and Stallions: Languages of Exploitation and Accommodation among Professional Fighters," *Body and Society* 7, 2/3 (June 2001): 181–194; and "Chicago Fade: Putting the Researcher's Body Back Into Play," *City* 13, 4 (2009), 510–516.

7. Marcel Mauss, "Allocution à la société de psychologie" (1923), reprinted in *Oeuvres*, vol. 3, *Cohésion sociale et divisions de la sociologie* (Paris: Éditions de Minuit, 1969), 281.

Body & Soul

Any group of persons—prisoners, primitives, pilots, or patients—develop a life of their own that becomes meaningful, reasonable and normal once you get close to it.

—Erving Goffman, *Asylums* (1962)

Subjective difficulties. Danger of superficial observation. Do not "believe." Do not think that you know something because you have seen it; do not pass any moral judgement. Do not be surprised. Do not get angry. Try to live in the native society. Choose testimonies carefully. . . . Objectivity shall be sought in exposition as well as in observation. Tell what you know, all that you know, and nothing but what you know.

—Marcel Mauss, *Manuel d'ethnographie* (1947)

Prologue

I n August 1988, following a combination of chance circumstances,[1] I enrolled in a boxing gym in a neighborhood of Chicago's black ghetto. I had never practiced that sport or even considered trying it. Aside from the superficial notions and stereotyped images that everyone can gain of boxing through the media, movies, and literature,[2] I had never had any contact with the pugilistic world. I thus found myself in the situation of the perfect novice.

1. This combination was set off by my friend Olivier Hermine, to whom I am forever grateful for having taken me to the Woodlawn Boys Club. I would like to thank Pierre Bourdieu for having supported me from the outset in an enterprise which, because it requires putting one's physical person on the line, could not have been brought to fruition without constant moral sustenance. His encouragement, his advice, and his visit to the Boys Club helped me, in my moments of doubt (and exhaustion), find the strength to persist in my investigations. My gratitude also goes to all those, colleagues, relatives, and friends, too numerous to be named here, who succored, stimulated, and comforted me during and after this research: they know who they are and what I owe them. Thanks are due also to Thierry Discepolo, for the boundless energy and patience with which he worked on the production the original French manuscript. Finally, it goes without saying that this book would not exist without the generosity and fraternal trust of my "gym buddies" from Woodlawn and of our mentor, DeeDee: I hope that they will see in it the sign of my eternal esteem and affection.
2. To keep to the great names of contemporary U.S. literature, Arthur Krystal ("Ifs, Ands, Butts: The Literary Sensibility at Ringside," *Harper's* 274 (June 1987): 63–67) mentions among others Ernest Hemingway, Jack London, Dashiell Hammett, Nelson Algren, James Farrell, Ring Lardner, Norman Mailer, and Ralph Ellison,

For three years I trained alongside local boxers, both amateur and professional, at the rate of three to six sessions a week, assiduously applying myself to every phase of their rigorous preparation, from shadowboxing in front of mirrors to sparring in the ring. Much to my own surprise, and to the surprise of those close to me, I gradually got taken in by the game, to the point where I ended up spending all my afternoons at the Woodlawn gym and "gloving up" with the professionals from the club on a regular basis, before climbing through the ropes for my first official fight in the Chicago Golden Gloves. In the intoxication of immersion, I even thought for a while of aborting my academic career to "turn pro" and thereby remain with my friends from the gym and its coach, DeeDee Armour, who had become a second father for me.[3]

Following in their wake, I attended some thirty tournaments and boxing "cards" held in various nightclubs, movie theaters, and sports arenas in the city and its suburbs, in the capacity of gym-mate and fan, sparring partner and confidant, "cornerman" and photographer, which earned me access to all the stages and backstages of the theater of bruising. I also accompanied the boxers from my gym "on the road," going to fights organized in other Midwestern towns and in the glittering (but seedy) casinos of Atlantic City. And I gradually absorbed the

---

joined lately by one of very few women, novelist Joyce Carol Oates, to whom we owe the beautiful *On Boxing* (Garden City, N.Y.: Doubleday, 1987).

3. As is attested by this note, among many others of the same ilk, written in my field notebook in August 1990: "Today I had such a ball being in the gym, talking and laughing with DeeDee and Curtis sitting in the back room and just *living and breathing* there, among them, soaking up the atmosphere of the gym like a human sponge, that I was suddenly suffocated by a wave of anguish at the idea of having to leave soon for Harvard [where I had just been elected at the Society of Fellows]. I feel so much pleasure simply *participating* that *observation* becomes secondary and, frankly, I'm at the point where I tell myself that I'd gladly give up my studies and my research and all the rest to be able to stay here and box, to remain 'one of the boys.' I know that's completely crazy and surely unrealistic but, at this very moment, I find the idea of migrating to Harvard, of going to present a paper at the ASA [American Sociological Association] meetings, of writing articles, reading books, attending lectures, and participating in the *tutti frutti* of academe totally devoid of meaning and downright depressing, so dreary and dead compared to the pure and vivacious carnal joy that this goddamn gym provides me (you've got to see the scenes between DeeDee and Curtis, they're worthy of Marcel Pagnol) that I would like to quit everything, drop out, to stay in Chicago. It's really crazy. PB [Pierre Bourdieu] was saying the other day that he's afraid that I'm 'letting myself be seduced by my object' but, boy, *if he only knew:* I'm already way beyond seduction!"

categories of pugilistic judgment under DeeDee's guidance, gabbing endlessly with him at the gym and dissecting fights on television at his place at night, the two of us sitting side by side on his bed in the kitchen of his little apartment.

The friendship and trust accorded to me by the regulars of Woodlawn were such that I was able not only to blend in among them in the gym but also to accompany them in their everyday peregrinations outside of it, in search of a job or an apartment, hunting for bargains in ghetto stores, in their hassles with their wives, the local welfare office, or the police, as well as cruising with their "homies" from the fearsome housing projects nearby. My ring colleagues allowed me to share in their joys and sorrows, their dreams and their setbacks, their picnics, evenings out dancing, and family excursions. They took me with them to pray in their churches, to get a "fade" at their barber shop, to play pool in their favorite tavern, to listen to rap until I had gotten my fill of it, and even to applaud Minister Louis Farrakhan at a political-religious meeting of the Nation of Islam—where I found myself the only European non-believer among ten thousand entranced African-American faithful. I lived through three funerals, two weddings,[4] four births, and a baptism with them, and I witnessed, at their side, with unfathomable sadness, the closing of the Woodlawn gym, condemned in February 1992 and razed a year later as part of an urban "renewal" operation.

Nightly after each training session I consigned my notes to my field notebooks for several hours, initially to help me overcome a profound feeling of awkwardness and physical unease, a feeling no doubt exacerbated by the fact of being the only white member of a gym frequented nearly exclusively by black athletes at the time of my entry. Together with the observations, pictures, and recordings made at the fights in which members of my gym performed, these notes provide the materials for the texts that follow.[5]

4. One will find an ethnography of the matrimonial festivities of Anthony and Mark in my article, "Un mariage dans le ghetto," *Actes de la recherche en sciences sociales* 113 (June 1996): 63–84.
5. These ethnographic observations made day-to-day in and around the gym were complemented and triangulated at the end of the research journey by the systematic collection of the life stories of the main members of the Woodlawn Boys Club, over one hundred in-depth interviews with professional pugilists then active in Illinois as well as with their trainers and managers, and by the dissection

From the outset it was clear that, to have any chance of escaping from the preconstructed object of collective mythology, a sociology of boxing has to renounce the facile recourse to the *prefabricated exoticism* of the public and publicized side of the institution—the fights, great or small, the heroism of the social ascent of the excluded ("Marvelous Marvin Hagler: From Ghetto to Glory," eloquently proclaimed a poster taped onto one of the walls of the Woodlawn Boys Club), the exceptional lives and careers of champions. It must instead grasp boxing through its least known and least spectacular side: the drab and obsessive routine of the gym workout, of the endless and thankless preparation, inseparably physical and moral, that preludes the all-too-brief appearances in the limelight, the minute and mundane rites of daily life in the gym that produce and reproduce the belief feeding this very peculiar corporeal, material, and symbolic economy that is the pugilistic world. In short, to avoid the excess knowledge of spontaneous sociology that the evocation of fights never fails to conjure, one must not step into the ring by proxy with the extra-ordinary figure of the "champ" but "hit the bags" alongside anonymous boxers in their habitual setting of the gym.

The other virtue of an approach based on participant observation (which, in this case, is better characterized as an "observant participation") in a run-of-the-mill gym is that the materials thus produced do not suffer from the "ecological fallacy" that affects most available studies and accounts of the Manly art. Thus none of the statements reported here were expressly solicited, and the behaviors described are those of the boxer in his "natural habitat,"[6] not the dramatized and highly codified (re)presentation that he likes to give of himself in public, and that journalistic reports and novels retranslate and magnify according to their specific canons.

---

of the "native" literature (specialized magazines and newsletters, biographies and autobiographies) and its scholarly derivatives (literary and historiographical writings). I also trained in three other professional gyms in Chicago and visited another dozen clubs in the United States and in Europe over a period of four years. After my departure from Chicago, I was a member of boxing gyms in Boston, New York City, and Oakland, California.

6. On the ecological fallacy, read Aaron Cicourel, "Interviews, Surveys, and the Problem of Ecological Validity," *The American Sociologist* 17, 1 (February 1982): 11–20, and the kindred methodological remarks of Howard Becker, "Studying Practioners of Vice and Crime," in *Pathways to Data*, ed. Robert Wesley Habenstein (Chicago: Aldine, 1970), 30–49.

Breaking with the moralizing discourse—that indifferently feeds both celebration and denigration—produced by the "gaze from afar" of an outside observer standing at a distance from or above the specific universe, this book seeks to suggest how boxing "makes sense" as soon as one takes pains to get close enough to it to grasp it *with one's body,* in a quasi-experimental situation. It is for this reason composed of three texts of deliberately disparate statuses and styles, which juxtapose sociological analysis, ethnographic description, and literary evocation in order to convey at once percept and concept, the hidden determinations and the lived experiences, the external factors and the internal sensations that intermingle to make the boxer's world. In short, the book aims to *display and demonstrate* in the same move the social and sensual logic that informs boxing as a bodily craft in the contemporary black American ghetto.

The first text unravels the skein of the troubled relations tying the street to the ring and deciphers the inculcation of the Manly art as a work of gymnic, perceptual, emotional, and mental conversion effected in a practical and collective mode, on the basis of an implicit and mimetic pedagogy that patiently recalibrates all the parameters of the boxer's existence one by one. It is based on an article written during the summer of 1989, a year after I joined the Woodlawn club, when getting my nose broken during a sparring session had forced me into a period of inactivity propicious to a reflexive return on my novitiate in progress.[7] I had to resist the temptation to totally revise this early writing effort, as prelude to a more comprehensive analysis of the "manufacturing" of the boxer which is the theme of another book-in-progress,[8] especially by investing in it all the results of subsequent works that grew out of two additional years of intensive immersion. I strove instead to enrich the data, to deepen the backdrop, and to clarify the original analyses while preserving their overall economy. For it seemed to me that the empirical lacunae and analytic seminaïveté of this text by an apprentice

7. Loïc Wacquant, "Corps et âme: notes ethnographiques d'un apprenti-boxeur," *Actes de la recherche en sciences sociales* 80 (November 1989): 33–67. It was in writing this article that I understood to what extent the gym constitutes a "strategic research site" (as Robert Merton would say) and decided to make the craft of the boxer a second object of study, parallel to my investigations of social life in the ghetto.
8. *The Passion of the Pugilist* will address in a more in-depth manner, among other topics, the dialectic of desire and domination in the social genesis of the boxer's vocation, the structure and functioning of the pugilistic economy, the work of the trainer as virile mothering, native beliefs about sex and women, and confrontation in the ring as a homoerotic ritual of masculinization.

sociologist had in its favor an ethnographic freshness and a candor of tone that might help the reader to better slip into the skin of the boxer.

The second part of this book, first drafted in 1993 and then revised and completed seven years later with the help of audio and video tapes recorded at the time, describes in minute detail the day leading to a boxing "card" at a tavern in a working-class neighborhood of Chicago's far South Side, from the preparations for the official weigh-in early in the morning at the gym until the return from the postfight festivities late in the night. The unity of time, place, and action makes it possible to set into relief the mutual interweaving of the social ingredients and networks that the first text necessarily had to separate: interest and desire, affection and exploitation, the masculine and the feminine, the sacred and the profane, abstinence and jouissance, the routine and the unexpected, the virile code of honor and the brutal dictates of material constraints.

The third part of this book is, if I may be permitted an expression that borders on the oxymoronic, a "sociological novella." Written at the request of Michel Le Bris for a special issue of the French literary journal *Gulliver* devoted to "Writing Sports,"[9] it follows step-by-step the author's preparation for and performance at the 1990 Chicago Golden Gloves, the biggest amateur tournament in the Midwest, in a narrative mode that aims to erase the traces of the work of sociological construction (to the point where Le Bris thought, wrongly, that he was warranted to characterize it in his preface as a "narrative, all sociology suspended") while preserving the insights and results of that work.[10] The blending of these genres ordinarily kept safely segregated, sociology, ethnography (in the strict sense of the term), and novella, aims to enable the reader to better grasp pugilistic things "in the concrete, as they are" and to see boxers in motion, "as in mechanics one sees masses and systems, or as in the sea we see octopi and anemones. We catch sight of numbers of men, of mobile forces, and which float through their environment and their sentiments."[11]

9. Loïc Wacquant, " 'Busy' Louie aux Golden Gloves," *Gulliver* 6 (April–June 1991): 12–33.

10. This text furthermore poses in practical terms the question of writing in the social sciences and of the difference between sociology and fiction, a question that has much preoccupied anthropologists over the last decade, since, shortly after its publication, this article earned me the offer by a leading Parisian publishing house of a contract for . . . my "novel."

11. Marcel Mauss, "Essai sur le don. Forme et raisons de l'échange dans les sociétés archaïques," in *Sociologie et anthropologie* (Paris: Presses Universitaires de France, 1950, orig. 1925), 276, my translation. *The Gift* (New York: Norton, 1990), 80.

In closing, it is instructive to point out the main factors that made this research possible, the most decisive of which was no doubt the "opportunistic" character of my insertion.[12] In point of fact, I did not enter the boxing club with the express aim of dissecting the pugilistic world. My original intention was to use the gym as a "window" onto the ghetto so as to observe the social strategies of young men in the neighborhood—my initial object of study—and it was not until after sixteen months of assiduous attendance, and after I had been inducted as a bona fide member of the inner circle of the Boys Club, that I decided, with the approval of those concerned, to make the craft of the boxer an object of study in its own right. There is no doubt that I would never have been able to gain the trust and to benefit from the collaboration of the Woodlawn regulars if I had joined the gym with the explicit and avowed aim of studying it, for that very intention would have irrevocably modified my status and role within the social and symbolic system under consideration.

Next, I had the good fortune of having practiced several competitive sports during my adolescence in the Languedoc region of southern France (soccer, basketball, rugby, tennis) so that at the time of my entry at the Boys Club I had at my disposal a small sporting capital to start with that was to prove indispensable for my successfully enduring the pugilistic trial by fire. The hazards of geography also determined that I would enroll in a "traditionalist" gym, ruled with an iron fist by a coach of international stature and enjoying an enviable renown in the city since its opening in 1977, such that I was able to learn how to box according to the rules of the art, through contact with competent trainers and fighters.[13] It is likely that I would not have persisted in my endeavor

12. Jeffrey M. Riemer, "Varieties of Opportunistic Research," *Urban Life* 4, 5 (January 1977): 467–77.

13. The Woodlawn gym was at that time one of 52 boxing clubs officially listed in the state of Illinois and one of the four major so-called professional gyms in Chicago (that is, gyms where "pro" boxers train, who are paid for their performances between the ropes, aside from the amateurs who populate all gyms). Most of the prominent boxers from the 1980s in Chicago passed through the Woodlawn Boys Club at one time or another, and the gym was one of the major suppliers of fighters for boxing cards held throughout the region up until its closing. After the end of his career between the ropes, Muhammad Ali, who owns a house a few miles from the gym in the upscale neighborhood of Hyde Park–Kenwood, an island of white opulence lost in the midst of the ocean of black poverty that is the South Side, used to come train there—his appearance never failed to provoke spectacular outbreaks of popular jubilation on the block.

or, worse, that I would have suffered grievous damage had I done my apprenticeship in one of the anomic gyms run by the city's Park District.

Being the only white member in the club (at the time of entry and for most of my sojourn there) could have constituted a serious obstacle to my integration and thus amputated my capacity to penetrate the social world of the boxer, if not for the conjugated action of three compensating factors. First of all, the egalitarian ethos and pronounced color-blindness of pugilistic culture are such that everyone is fully accepted into it so long as he submits to the common discipline and "pays his dues" in the ring. Next, my French nationality granted me a sort of stat-utory exteriority with respect to the structure of relations of exploitation, contempt, misunderstanding, and mutual mistrust that oppose blacks and whites in America. I benefited from the historical capital of sympathy that France enjoys in the African-American population owing to the wel-come its soldiers received there during the two world wars (where, for the first time in their lives, they were treated as human beings and not as members of an out-caste)[14] and from the simple fact of not having the *hexis* of the average white American, which continually marks, if against his or her own best intentions, the impenetrable border between the communities. Eddie, the assistant trainer at Woodlawn, explains:

I got respect for you, Louie, for you comin' in d'gym and just bein' one of d'guys and bein' just like everybody else in d'gym. . . . Ain't too many Caucasians who do that with us blacks. . . .

My wife and I, we've lived in Hyde Park [the University of Chicago neighborhood, eighty percent white at the time] for five years now and we never met no Caucasians, never. When they get close to you on d'street, they be lookin' at you scared like you gonna jump on'em or somethin'. So my wife an' I, we never talked to no Caucasians in Hyde Park. [Emotion makes the pitch of his voice go up and his delivery quicken.] Most Caucasians, if you get close to'em or try to talk to'em, *they back off an' look atchyou like you got a ring in your nose,* y'know. Stare atchyou [he rolls his eyes with a fierce look] and

14. On the "historical affection" of black Americans for France and its origins in the lived experience of a mixedness that was then taboo and violently repressed in the United States, see Tyler Stovall, *Paris Noir: African Americans in the City of Light* (Boston: Houghton-Mifflin, 1996).

you can see somethin's wrong. But you, you don't be doin' that, you be *so relaxed* in d'gym and when you come with us to d'fights. . . .

Man! you be so relaxed it's har' to tell you're Caucasian. [Your girlfriend] Liz an' you, *d'only way one can tell you ain't black is by the way you talk an' by you bein' a Frenchman* of course. But you be down there in d'gym, you talk with'em guys, you be like d'other guys. You ain't tense and worried that you're with us. You're loose, you get along with d'guys and they like you too . . . See, I respects people who respects me. So I respects you. Louie, *you're part of d'team down there.* I was tellin' somebody down at my work, "We got the Fightin' Frenchman on our team!" [He roars in obvious delight.] Yep, you're part of d'gym, like everybody else.[15]

Finally, my total "surrender" to the exigencies of the field,[16] and especially the fact that I regularly put the gloves on with them, earned me the esteem of my club-mates, as attested by the term of address *"brother Louie"* and the collection of affectionate nicknames they bestowed upon me over the months: "Busy Louie," my ring moniker, but also "Bad Dude," "The French Bomber," "The French Hammer" (in reference to my dancing skills and not my punching power), and "The Black Frenchman." Aside from the tokens of solidarity offered day-to-day outside the gym through services rendered and varied interventions with the public and private bureaucracies that govern their lives, the fact of having pursued my initiation to the point of "doing" the Golden Gloves greatly contributed to establishing my status in the club and to sealing my legitimacy as an apprentice boxer in the eyes of the athletes and trainers from the other gyms, who, after my official performance between the ropes, spontaneously recognized me as "one of DeeDee's boys."

15. After my return from a visit back home in France for the Christmas holidays, the same Eddie beckoned me in a loud voice, in front of all the regulars: "Hey, Louie, did you tell your family that you're trainin' in d'gym with professional boxers? Did you tell your family that *you're one of d'guys, that we treat you like you're a black guy?"*
16. Kurt Wolf defines the concept of "surrender" in ethnography as implying "total involvement [in which] a person's received notions are suspended, everything is pertinent, [which implies] identification [and] the risk of being hurt." Kurt Wolf, "Surrender and Community Study: The Study of Loma," in *Reflections on Community Studies,* eds. Arthur J. Vidich and Joseph Bensman (New York: Wiley, 1964), 237. See also 233–263, esp. 238–240. Read also Hortense Powdermaker, *Stranger and Friend: The Way of an Anthropologist* (New York: Norton, 1966), esp. pp. 287–296.

The tools of the trade in the workshop

The Street and the Ring

Just as one cannot understand what an instituted religion such as Catholicism is without studying in detail the structure and functioning of the organization that supports it, in this case the Roman Church, one cannot elucidate the meaning and roots of boxing in contemporary American society—at least in the lower regions of social space, where it continues to defy an extinction periodically announced as its imminent and inevitable fate—without canvassing the fabric of the social and symbolic relations woven in and around the training gym, the hub and hidden engine of the pugilistic universe.

A gym is a complex and polysemous institution, overloaded with functions and representations that do not readily reveal themselves to the outside observer, even one acquainted with the nature of the place. On the surface, though, what could be more banal and more self-evident than a boxing gym? One could indeed take word for word the following vignette of the famed Stillman's Gym in the New York City of the fifties, composed by George Plimpton, to describe just about any gym in America today, so powerful are the invariants that govern their design:

> A dark stairway led up into a gloomy vault-like room, rather like
> the hold of an old galleon. One heard the sound before one's eyes
> acclimatized: the *slap-slap* of the ropes being skipped, the thud of
> leather into the big heavy bags that squeaked from their chains as
> they swung, the rattle of the speed bags, the muffled sounds of gym

shoes on the canvas of the rings (there were two rings), the snuffle of the fighters breathing out through their noses, and, every three minutes, the sharp clang of the ring bell. The atmosphere brought to mind a fetid jungle twilight.[1]

The gym, as we shall see, is the forge where the pugilist molds himself into shape; the workshop wherein is manufactured the body-weapon and shield that he intends to launch into confrontation in the ring; the crucible wherein the technical skills and strategic knowledge whose delicate assemblage makes the accomplished fighter are honed; and finally, the furnace wherein is stoked the flame of pugilistic desire and the collective belief in the validity of indigenous values without which no one would dare risk himself for very long between the ropes. But the boxing gym is not just that, and its ostensible technical mission—to transmit a particular sporting competence—must not conceal the extrapugilistic functions it fulfills for those who come there to commune in the plebian cult of virility that is the Manly art. Above all, the gym protects one from the street and acts as a buffer against the insecurity of the neighborhood and the pressures of everyday life. In the manner of a *sanctuary,* it offers a cosseted space, closed and reserved, where one can, among like-minded others, shelter oneself from the ordinary miseries of an all-too-ordinary life and from the spells that the culture and economy of the street hold in store for young men trapped into this place scorned and abandoned by all that is the dark ghetto. The

1. George Plimpton, *Shadowbox* (New York: Putnam, 1977), 38. This description is valid for all of the urban United States and most industrialized countries: boxing gyms around the world are made up more or less of the same ingredients and look so much alike that they could be mistaken for one another. This is readily apparent in comparing, for example, the descriptions of the obscure New Oakland Boxing Club in northern California with that of the celebrated Kronk Gym in Detroit provided by Ralph Wiley, *Serenity: A Boxing Memoir* (New York: Holt, 1989), 28–29 and 153–166; of the Rosario Gym in East Harlem by William Plummer, *Buttercups and Strong Boys: A Sojourn at the Golden Gloves* (New York: Viking Books, 1989), 51–85; and of the Cabbagetown Boxing Gym in the suburbs of Toronto by Stephen Brunt, *Mean Business: The Rise and Fall of Shawn O'Sullivan* (Markham, Canada: Penguin Books, 1987), 43–69. The book by photographer Martine Barrat, *Do or Die* (New York: Viking Books, Preface by Martin Scorcese, 1993), provides a faithful visual transcription of the atmosphere of a boxing gym in New York that evokes the luscious portrait that Ronald Fried paints of Stillman's Gym in its Golden Age in *Corner Men: Great Boxing Trainers* (New York: Four Walls Eight Windows, 1991), 32–53.

gym is also a *school of morality,* in Durkheim's sense of the term,[2] that is to say a machinery designed to fabricate the spirit of discipline, group attachment, respect for others as for self, and autonomy of will that are indispensable to the blossoming of the pugilistic vocation. Finally, the boxing gym is the vector of a *debanalization of everyday life* in that it turns bodily routine and remolding into a bridge to a distinctive sensorial and emotional universe in which adventure, masculine honor, and prestige intermingle. The monastic, even penitential, character of the pugilistic "program of life" turns the individual into his own arena of challenge and invites him to discover himself, better yet to produce himself. And membership in the gym stands as the tangible sign of acceptance in a virile fraternity that allows the boxer to tear himself away from the anonymity of the mass and thereby attract the admiration and approval of the local society.

To perceive these different facets of the gym and detect the protections and profits it affords to those who place themselves under its aegis, it is both necessary and sufficient to follow the unknown footsoldiers of the manly art in the accomplishment of their daily chores and to submit oneself along with them to the rigorous regimen, at once corporeal and mental, that defines their state and stamps their identity. That is what I did during three years at the Woodlawn Boys Club, a gym in the black ghetto of Chicago where I was initiated into the fundamentals of the craft and where, having developed close friendships with the trainers and boxers of the place, I was able to observe *in vivo* the social genesis and unfolding of prizefighting careers.

A reflection on an experience of apprenticeship in progress, this first part of the book pursues a triple objective. The first is to contribute precise and detailed ethnographic data, produced by means of direct observation and intensive participation, on a social universe that is all the more unknown for being the object of widely disseminated representations. On the basis of this documentary corpus, I will then uncover some of the principles that organize the complex of specific activities that is boxing such as it is practiced nowadays within the black American ghetto, highlighting in particular the social regulation of violence that the training gym effects through the bifid relation, made of

2. Émile Durkheim, *L'Éducation morale* (Paris: Presses Universitaires de France, 1963, orig. 1902–3), translation: *Moral Education: A Study in the Theory and Application of the Sociology of Education* (New York: Free Press of Glencoe, 1961).

intermingled affinity and antagonism, that links the street and the ring. Finally, I will sketch an analysis of an initiation to a practice of which *the body is at once the seat, the instrument, and the target.* This is to say that my intent is neither to condemn nor to defend this sport reputed as the most "barbaric" of them all, so often celebrated and castigated, scorned and revered,[3] but rather to suggest what its specific logic, and especially that of its inculcation, can teach us about the logic of any practice.[4]

To anticipate the first lessons of this initiation, I propose that the fabrication of what one may call the *pugilistic habitus,* that is, the specific set of bodily and mental schemata that define the competent boxer, is founded on a twofold antinomy. The first stems from the fact that boxing is an activity that seems situated at the borderline between nature and culture, a sort of empirically realized limiting case of practice, yet one that requires an exceptionally complex, quasi-rational management of the body and of time, whose transmission is effected in a purely practical mode, without recourse to the mediation of a theory, on the basis of a largely implicit and barely codified pedagogy. Whence the second contradiction, at least apparent: boxing is an individual sport, no doubt among the most individual of all athletic contests in that it physically puts in play—and in danger—the body of the solitary fighter, whose adequate apprenticeship is quintessentially collective, especially because it

3. One quotation among a thousand others: "It is not by happenstance that boxing is the sport that has inspired the greatest number of talented film directors and novelists. In our civilization, it is an archaism, one of the last barbarisms permitted, the last mirror authorized to still reflect our dark side" (Guy Lagorce, "Mort dans l'après-midi" *L'Express Magazine,* 17 March 1989, on the death in the ring of Ivorian boxer David Thio). For an ode to the Manly art, see George Peters, *Pleins feux sur les rings* (Paris: La Table Ronde, 1970), esp. 199–220. One finds a recapitulation of this dialectic between the fascinated cult and the horrified condemnation of prizefighting in the United States in Jeffrey Sammons's thorough historical study *Beyond the Ring: The Role of Boxing in American Society* (Urbana and Chicago: University of Illinois Press, 1988).

4. According to Pierre Bourdieu, "sport is, with dance, one of the sites in which is posed with maximum acuity the problem of the relations between theory and practice, and also between language and the body. . . . The teaching of a bodily practice [encloses] a set of theoretical questions of the greatest importance, inasmuch as the social sciences endeavor to theorize conducts that are produced, for the vast majority of them, beneath the level of consciousness" ("Programme for a Sociology of Sport," in *In Other Words,* chap. 2, Cambridge: Polity Press, 1990 [1987], 166, my translation).

presupposes a belief in the game that, as with all "language games" according to Ludwig Wittgenstein, is born and persists only in and through the group that it defines in turn through a circular process. In other words, the dispositions that make up the accomplished pugilist are, like any "technique of the body" for Marcel Mauss, the "work of individual and *collective practical reason.*"[5]

Finally, to become a boxer is to appropriate through progressive impregnation a set of corporeal mechanisms and mental schemata so intimately imbricated that they erase the distinction between the physical and the spiritual, between what pertains to athletic abilities and what belongs to moral capacities and will. The boxer is a *live gearing* of the body and the mind that erases the boundary between reason and passion, explodes the opposition between action and representation, and in so doing transcends *in actu* the antinomy between the individual and the collective that underlies accepted theories of social action. Here again I concur with Marcel Mauss when he speaks of "the physio-psychosociological assemblages of series of acts . . . more or less habitual or more or less ancient in the life of the individual and in the history of the society" that are "assembled by and for social authority."[6]

An Island of Order and Virtue

One cannot understand the relatively closed world of boxing outside of the human and ecological context in which it is anchored and the social possibles of which this context is the bearer. Indeed it is in its *double relation of symbiosis and opposition* to the neighborhood and to the grim realities of the ghetto that the gym defines itself. Much like joining a gang or becoming involved in street crime, two germane careers from which it offers a potential escape route,[7] membership in the gym acquires its full social meaning only in regard of the structure of life chances offered—or

5. Marcel Mauss, "Les techniques du corps," in *Sociologie et anthropologie* (Paris: Presses Universitaires de France, 1950, orig. 1936), 368–369, trans. "Body Techniques," in *Sociology and Psychology: Essays* (London: Routledge and Kegan Paul, 1979), 101, my translation and emphasis.
6. Ibid., 383, trans. 120, my translation.
7. Martín Sánchez-Jankowski, *Islands in the Street: Gangs in Urban American Society* (Berkeley: University of California Press, 1991); Mercer Sullivan, *"Getting Paid": Youth, Crime, and Work in the Inner City* (Ithaca: Cornell University Press, 1989); and Philippe Bourgois, *In Search of Respect: Selling Crack in El Barrio* (Cambridge: Cambridge University Press, 1995).

denied—by the local system of instruments of social reproduction and mobility, namely, the public schools, the deskilled labor market, and the activities and networks that make up the predatory economy of the street. It is therefore indispensable, before venturing inside the gym, to sketch in rough strokes the portrait of the neighborhood of Woodlawn and its recent historical evolution. This African-American community is far from being the most dispossessed of Chicago's South Side ghetto: of the 77 "Community Areas" that compose the city, it ranks only 13th on the poverty scale. Nonetheless it offers the gripping spectacle of an urban and social fabric in agony after nearly a half-century of continual deterioration and increased racial and economic segregation.[8]

On the morrow of the Second World War, Woodlawn was a stable and prosperous white neighborhood, a satellite of Hyde Park (the stronghold of the University of Chicago) which borders it to the north, and boasted a dense business district and an active real estate market. The intersection of 63rd Street and Cottage Grove Avenue was one of the liveliest in the city and throngs streamed through the countless stores, restaurants, movie houses, and jazz clubs that lined these two thoroughfares. Thirty years later, the neighborhood had mutated into a vast enclave of poverty and despair emblematic of the decline of Chicago's "Black Metropolis"[9] in which the most marginalized fractions of its population are concentrated. Between 1950 and 1980, the number of neighborhood residents fell from 81,000 to 36,000 as the racial makeup of the population went from 38 to 96 percent black. (During that time, the number of whites dropped from 50,000 to fewer than a thousand.) The swelling influx of African-American migrants from rural southern states triggered a massive exodus of whites, soon followed by the outmigration of the black middle class, which fled the core of the ghetto to found its own peripheral

8. In 25 of these 27 areas, nearly all of them African American and Latino, over one fifth of the population lives under the official "poverty line." For comparison, see the succinct sociography of the accelerating deterioration of the neighborhoods that compose Chicago's black ghetto in Loïc Wacquant and William Julius Wilson, "The Cost of Racial and Class Exclusion in the Inner City," *Annals of the American Academy of Political and Social Science* 501 (January 1989): p 8–25.

9. To invoke the title of the master-book by St. Clair Drake and Horace R. Cayton, *Black Metropolis: A Study of Negro Life in a Northern City* (Chicago: University of Chicago Press, 1994, orig. 1945).

neighborhoods (which turned out to be just as segregated).[10] This demographic upheaval, amplified and aggravated by the city's policy of "urban renewal" in the 1950s—locally known as "Negro removal"—and by the "gang wars" of the 1960s, provoked a crisis of local institutions that combined with record levels of unemployment and school elimination to complete Woodlawn's transformation into an economic desert and a social purgatory.

A few empirical indicators give a measure of the socioeconomic hardship and vulnerability visited upon the residents of Woodlawn.[11] According to the 1980 census, one-third of the families lived below the official federal poverty line and the average annual household income of $10,500 amounted to barely half the citywide figure. The percentage of households recorded as female-headed had reached 60 percent (compared to 34 percent ten years earlier), the official unemployment rate was 20 percent (twice the city average after tripling over a decade), and fewer than one household in eight owned its home. Only 34 percent of adult women and 44 percent of adult men held a job; 61 percent of households had to rely in part or whole on support from public aid. Among the workforce, the single largest occupational category was that of clerical, at 31 percent, with service work, security personnel, and private household coming in second at 22 percent. Fewer than 8 percent of adults possessed a higher education degree and more than half had not even completed their secondary studies, even though no exam is required to graduate. The neighborhood no longer has a single high school or movie theater, library, or job training and placement facility. Despite the close proximity of one of the world's most reputed centers of medical innovation, the University of Chicago Hospital, infant mortality in Woodlawn is estimated at about 3 percent and *rising,* a figure almost three times the national average and exceeding that of many Third World countries.

---

10. Arnold R. Hirsch, *Making the Second Ghetto: Race and Housing in Chicago, 1940–1960* (Cambridge: Cambridge University Press, 1983).
11. The data that follow are drawn from Chicago Fact Book Consortium, *Local Community Fact Book: Chicago Metropolitan Area* (Chicago: Chicago Review Press, 1984) 114–116. For an extended analysis of the transformation of Chicago's black ghetto over the past half-century, see Loïc Wacquant, "The New Urban Color Line: The State and Fate of the Ghetto in Postfordist America," in *Social Theory and the Politics of Identity,* ed. Craig J. Calhoun (Cambridge: Blackwell, 1994), 231–276.

The entrance of the woodlawn Boys Club on 63rd Street

A liquor store across the street from the gym

Urban desolation, a stone's throw from the prosperous white neighborhood of Hyde Park

Like other inner-city public establishments in Chicago, local schools "are hostage to poverty and crime."[12] Chronic shortages of supplies, overcrowded and insalubrious facilities, and underqualified and demoralized teachers have combined to reduce them to custodial institutions that are content with warehousing students until their eventual discharge—most ghetto establishments do not even offer college preparatory courses. No wonder many youth find the illegal economy of the street more attractive than school when the latter leads to unemployment or, at best, to $4-an-hour jobs without benefits. Aside from the University of Chicago, there is no large employer within a four-mile radius.

As with other African-American ghettos, "the predominant institutions [of Woodlawn] are churches and liquor stores,"[13] although most of the thirty-some religious institutions still operative at the end of the 1960s have long since closed their doors. The lack of any new construction in decades (70 percent of buildings predate World War II) and the spectacular erosion of the housing stock from 29,600 units in 1950 to 15,700 in 1980 (due mostly to an epidemic of criminal "insurance" fires in the turbulent period of the black uprisings of 1966–70) in a neighborhood located near the shores of Lake Michigan within a dozen miles of the heart of the country's third largest metropolis says better than any statistic the marginal position occupied by this community in the life of Chicago.

The gym of the Woodlawn Boys and Girls Club is located on 63rd Street, one of the most devastated thoroughfares of the neighborhood, in the midst of a landscape of urban desolation that reporters from the *Chicago Tribune,* the city's main daily, described as follows:

[W]alk under the "L" [elevated train] along 63rd Street in Woodlawn, down what used to be, after State Street, the second-busiest shopping street in Chicago. It's as much a ghost town as a Wild West set: boards cover doors and windows, but the grime and decay only half cover the names of businesses that once thrived there—an A & P, Hi-Lo, a Walgreens, the Kimbark Theater, the Empire Warehouse, the Pershing Hotel, the Southeast Chicago Bank.[14]

12. Chicago *Tribune, An American Millstone: An Examination of the Nation's Permanent Underclass* (Chicago: Contemporary Books, 1986), 149.
13. Melvin L. Oliver, "The Urban Black Community as Network: Toward a Social Network Perspective," *Sociological Quarterly* 29, 4 (December 1988): 623–645.
14. Chicago *Tribune, American Millstone,* 170.

Indeed, the section of the street where the gym stands has been reduced to a corridor of crumbling or burned-out stores, vacant lots strewn with debris and broken glass, and boarded-up buildings left to rot in the shadow of the elevated train line. The few commercial establishments that have survived (a busy "Currency Exchange," several liquor stores, a children's clothing outlet, a drugstore that doubles as a beauty salon, a secondhand furniture and appliance shop, a grocery, and a family restaurant that each employs a handful of workers at best) are huddled behind wrought-iron bars waiting for hypothetical customers. The Woodlawn Boys Club is flanked, on one side, by the former Kimbark Theater, closed down in 1973, of which only the facade, boarded up with rotten plywood, and the weather-beaten marquee remain and, on the other, by a bumpy vacant lot in the middle of which stands a children's playground and a sheet-metal shed surrounded by a fence where jobless men from the neighborhood come to share a "taste" on sunny days. Immediately in back of the club stands a large abandoned red brick building whose broken windows are obstructed by rusty bars and whose metal doors are closed by heavy locks. Garbage and flying papers accumulate in the recess formed by this rear courtyard onto which opens the boxers' entrance to the gym.

In this cutthroat neighborhood, where handguns and other weapons are commonplace and "everyone"—according to DeeDee, the club's head trainer—is walking around with a can of Mace in their pocket for self-defense, purse-snatchings, muggings, battery, homicides, and lesser crimes of all kinds are part of the everyday routine and create a climate of pervasive fear, if not terror, that undermines interpersonal relationships and distorts all the activities of daily life. Thus neighborhood residents barricade themselves behind armored doors and barred windows, refrain from going out after dark, and if at all possible avoid public places and public transportation for fear of criminal violence. Several stations on the local Chicago Transit Authority (CTA) train line have been closed to entry, and CTA buses are trailed by special police cars along their entire route. Extortion by members of the El Rukn gang (formerly known as the Disciples), which controls drug trafficking, racketeering, and prostitution in this part of the South Side, is not the least source of insecurity—although there exists an unofficial pact of mutual noninterference between the Boys Club and the leadership of El Rukn, owing to the personal ties DeeDee maintains with those of their leaders who were once his students at the gym. A fourteen-year-old

Pandemic unemployment dooms half the men to idleness

Under the elevated train line, a storefront
church and a youth club lie in ruins

club member who lived not far from the gym had these words to encapsulate the mood of the neighborhood: "This project where I stay here ain't too bad. The one over there is somethin' else. I mean *they all bad,* you know, but *this one's badder: it's 'Murdertown' over there."*

The club shelters itself from this hostile environment in the manner of a fortress: all entrances are protected by metal bars and solidly padlocked; the windows of the day-care and Headstart center are latticed with iron; the heavy metal door that opens onto the rear of the gym has two enormous bolts that can be opened or shut only with the help of a hammer; and an electronic alarm system is set by the last person leaving the building. Two baseball bats are at hand near the entrances, one behind the counter of the day-care office, the other behind DeeDee's desk, in case it proves necessary to repel the intrusion of unwanted visitors *manu militari.*

As I'm wrapping my hands, Eugene O'Bannon (a former boxer, a mailman by occupation, who comes by regularly in his work uniform to chew the fat with DeeDee) takes a can of Mace out of his jacket pocket and holds it out to me. "Here, it's for your wife, give it to her from me, we wouldn't want anything to happen to her. . . . You point it at the dude's face and you press here." I ask him what effect it has. "It burn your eyes and face horribly, you can't see a thang for about ten minutes." DeeDee immediately takes his can out of his jacket too, adding, "I got it on me at all times. In d'gym, on d'streets, when I go get my groceries on 67th, *always* carry it on me." Everyone recounts times when he had to use his canister. I thank O'Bannon and ask if he too always carries one on him. "Usually yeah, but *right now, I don't:* I'm naked now since I gave you mine. Gon'to hurry up and get home, I can't walk around naked like this." Laughter. [Field notes, 13 December 1988]

The conversation returns to the situation of the city's black neighborhoods. DeeDee and O'Bannon outdo each other with comments on the surrounding devastation and on the insecurity that infects the vicinity. The old coach notes that under no circumstances would he take the Cottage Grove Avenue bus [which links Woodlawn to the downtown Loop by crossing the length of the South Side ghetto] and that he never goes into nearby Washington Park after dark without his pistol. He himself dwells south of

Woodlawn, at the edge of South Shore, and he castigates his neighborhood in merciless terms: "It's full-a drugs everywhere, you can buy dope on d'street from jus' about any guy you see. Young punks who bother you, gettin' in your face. Ain't got no schoolin', no jobs, runnin' d'streets—what they gonna do? Me, I don' care but that ain't my neighborhood, it's too much punks and low-lifes. It ain't my class a-neighborhood." The building where he lives is a well-known selling spot for crack, cocaine, and PCP. [Field notes, 13 August 1988]

Today Tony called the gym from the hospital. Two members of a rival gang shot him on the street not far from here, on the other side of Cottage Grove. Luckily he saw them coming and took off running, but a bullet pierced his calf. He hobbled behind an abandoned building, pulled out his own gun from his gym bag, and opened fire on his two attackers, forcing them to retreat. He says he'd better get out of the hospital real quick because they're probably out looking to get him now. I ask DeeDee if they shot him in the leg as a warning. "Shiiit, Louie! They don' shoot to injure no leg, they shoot to kill you. If Tony don' have his gun with him and pull it, they'dave track him down an' kill him, yeah: he be dead now." [Field notes, 27 September 1990]

So much to say that the young men in the neighborhood are, very early on, accustomed to a range of predatory behaviors entailing the most varied and unpredictable forms of physical and street violence, before which the strictly controlled violence of boxing cannot but pale in comparison, as DeeDee noted one day in May 1989: "Useta be you hadda be tough to survive in these streets. But now it's just plain crazy to live here. Gotta be nuts, with all d'dope an' guns goin' around, and the people goin' crazy out on d'street. Guys don' even live to be thirty years old. [He shakes his head in disbelief.] It's true, tha's the average age, you don' often get past that in this neighborhood here, jus' look at d'numbers: if dope don' kill you, some guy is gonna blow you off or, if you lucky, you gonna win' up in prison. Then maybe there you got a chance of makin' it past thirty. You're in a tough spot here, yep. You better know how t'defend yourself. If you're lookin' for trouble, you're in the right neighborhood."

Violent crime is indeed so commonplace that nearly all members of the gym have personally witnessed killings and have been either shot at or stabbed themselves.[15] Most also grew up having to fight on the street, sometimes on a daily basis, to keep their lunch money, their coats, their reputation, or simply to be able to walk around their neighborhood. Butch recalls a typical scene from his adolescence: "Right in that square block area it was definitely rough, it was *dog-eat-dog*. I had to be a mean dog. A lotta concentrated people, young guys wan'ed to take yer money and beat ya up an' you jus' had to fight or move out the neighbo'hood. I couldn't move, so I had to start fightin'." Many gym members were thus "pretrained" on the street in the art of self-defense, if not by personal taste then by necessity. In point of fact, a good number of them are former "street fighters" reconverted to boxing. "I used to fight a lot when I was younger *anyway,*" recounts Lorenzo, "so my father figure like, you know, 'If you gonna fight, well why don't you take it to a gym where you gonna learn, you know, a little more basics to it, maybe make some money, go further and do somethin'... insteada jus' bein' on the streets you know, an' fightin' for nothin'.'"

By contrast to this hostile and uncertain environment, and despite its severe dearth of resources, the Boys and Girls Club constitutes an island of stability and order where social relations forbidden on the outside become possible again. The gym offers a relatively self-enclosed site for a *protected sociability* where one can find a respite from the pressures of the street and the ghetto, a world into which external events rarely penetrate and onto which they have little impact. (The war against Iraq went virtually unnoticed, and the soap-operatic Clarence Thomas–Anita Hill hearings elicited little reaction or interest from anyone). This collective closure, which borders on "claustrophilia," is what makes life in the gym possible and goes a long way toward explaining its attraction.[16] Mike is nineteen years old and comes to the gym every afternoon as soon as his high school classes are over. "You can go there

15. The extreme concentration of violent crime in the ghetto and its devastating effects on young urban blacks over the past decades are described and analyzed by Jewelle Taylor Gibbs et al., eds., *Young, Black, and Male in America: An Endangered Species* (Dover, Mass.: Auburn House, 1988); Darnell F. Hawkins, ed., *Ethnicity, Race, and Crime: Perspectives across Time and Place* (Albany: State University of New York Press, 1995); and Joan McCord, ed., *Violence and Childhood in the Inner City* (Cambridge: Cambridge University Press, 1997).
16. This suffocating climate of the gym is well rendered in Leonard Gardner's novel *Fat City* (New York: Farrar, Strauss and Giroux, 1969) and in the film by John Huston of the same name, which takes place in the small boxing gyms of the city of Stockton, in California's Central Valley. The feeling of confinement is reinforced

and you feel good about yourself. Like I said, you feel *protected, secure.* You in there, aw, you're alright—it's like a second fam'ly. You know you can go there for support. . . . If you feelin' down, somebody be there to pump you up. I say, take your frustration out on the bags. Gettin' up in there and sparring, you might have felt down when you got there, then, make you feel a whole lot better." Bernard, an older member of the club, whose pro career was recently brought to a premature close by a hand injury after a dozen fights, explains what keeps bringing him to the gym as often as his job as a radiology technician will allow: "I jus' like watchin' the guys train an' do somethin' positive with theyself, burn energy in a way where it's not gonna git them in trouble and they're lettin' them *gangs* and *drugs* and *jail* go all aroun' them, 'cause they in the gym doin' somethin' with theyselves, so tha's real good to see that."

Indeed, it is common to hear a boxer exclaim that "all the time in the gym is that much less time spent out on the street." "It keeps me off the street." "I rather be here than gettin' in trouble on the streets." Many professionals willingly confess that they would most likely have turned to a life of crime if not for the discovery of boxing. And many past and present stars of the ring, among them Sonny Liston, Floyd Patterson, and Mike Tyson, first learned the Sweet science while sojourning in correctional facilities. The former world light-heavyweight champion Mustafa Muhammad admits: "If I hadn't started boxing, I would have been a bank robber. There were times, that's what I wanted to do. I didn't want to sell drugs. I wanted to be the best, so I wanted to rob banks." Pinklon Thomas, the 1985 WBC heavyweight title holder, chimes in: "Boxing brought me out of a hole and made me a worthwhile person. Without it, I'd be selling heroin, dead, or in jail."[17] Likewise, several participants in the 1989 Golden Gloves do not hesitate to mention this motivation in the biographical capsules that accompany their pictures in the official tournament program: "Vaughn Bean, 16, 5'11", 178 lbs. Representing the Valentine Boys Club, he has been boxing for one year. A freshman at Calumet High School, his brother brought him to boxing to keep him out of trouble." "Gabriel Villafranca, 18 years old, 5'9", 140 lbs, represents

by the absence of physical opening to the outside: the Woodlawn gym has not a single window (as is the case of several other gyms of which we have detailed descriptions, such as Gleason's or Rosario's).

17. Cited in Thomas Hauser, *The Black Lights: Inside the World of Professional Boxing* (New York: McGraw-Hill, 1986), 113 and 186.

the Harrison Park Club. He has been boxing for three years and has a record of eight wins and three losses. A senior at Juarez High School, he started boxing to stay out of trouble." During a junior (under age sixteen) tournament at the International Amphitheater, DeeDee confirms to me that the mothers of the young pugs, who generally follow the debuts of their offspring with anguish laced with admiration, concur in crediting boxing with this protective virtue: "No, they don't discourage them. They rather know that their kid is in d'ring than doin' nuthin' out in the streets and gettin' in trouble. They know it's better for them for their sons to be in d'gym." Members of the Woodlawn Boys Club fully agree.

LOUIE: Where would you be today if you hadn't found boxing?

CURTIS: Uh, prob'ly in jail, dead or on the streets turnin' up a bottle.

LOUIE: Really?

CURTIS: Yeah. 'Cause it was that peer pressure I was goin' through at d'age of sixteen an' fifteen, hangin' out with the wron' guys an' tryin' ta *blend in* an' you know, not bein' what they woul' call a *punk*, a *poot-butt*,[18] you know, not lettin' guys bully you on d'street an' stuff. You know, it's peer pressure that every teenager go through at that age, see what I'm sayin'? [chuckling] You wanna be *a'cepted* by the group o'people that you surroun' yourself in comin' through the neighborhood an' the community.

LORENZO: I figure if it weren't for the gym I might be doin' somethin' that I wouldn' wanna do, you know so it's, it's good, the gym help me a lot.

LOUIE: Like?

LORENZO: Like you know, prob'ly *killin'somebody,* you know, stickup, you know drugs—*anythin'.* [pointing towards the sky with both hands for emphasis] You can't never tell! You never know what the world holds.

LOUIE: The gym has taken you away from that?

18. A "poot-butt," a subcategory of the "lame," is somebody who is socially inexperienced, too young (literally or emotionally) "to take care of business," though he "may blunder or bully ahead as if he knew what to do or how to act," of whom one says that "he's tryin' to be so old, don't know shit! Still wet up under d'lip. . . . Momma didn't teach 'im enough. Let 'im out on d'streets too young"; cited in Edith Folb, *Runnin' Down Some Lines: The Language and Culture of Black Teenagers* (Cambridge, Mass.: Harvard University Press, 1980), 39.

LORENZO: Yeah, the gym takes my mind off a lotta things, you know, especially outside a—when you have problems too, you know, you come to the gym workout, it seem like it jus' *blanks out the mind,* like all you know, you're in the gym work out on the bags.

The closure of the gym onto itself represents one of its major virtues for its members and orients the entire policy of its coach. It is expressed, among other things, by the fact that the highlights of public life, municipal and national, pass without having any repercussion whatsoever within the club. Thus, during the entire presidential campaign, not a single mention is made of the contest between George Bush and Michael Dukakis, with the exception of this disillusioned remark by Gene O'Bannon on Election Day itself: "Me, I ain't gonna choose between a plate of horseshit and a plate of dogshit." Likewise, the downfall of the city's black mayor, Eugene Sawyer, to the benefit of the son of the former white mayor, Richard Daley (who ruled Chicago with an iron first under a racist patrimonial regime for half a century) elicits only a few cursory comments on the fact that politics is "rotten."[19]

11 November 1988. I shake everybody's hands, amid loud "How you doin' today? Hey, what's up?" DeeDee is wearing gray pants and his inimitable blue "Moonglow Lounge" jacket (a ghetto tavern, hangout and stronghold of Flukie Stokes, the long-time leader of the gang that rules the South Side) plastered with boxing patches, his long spider-like hands wrapped around a cigarette, his lower lip hanging, his eyes dull. He tells me that everything's fine, "ain't nuthin' goin' on, just like usual." Did he go vote? "Sure, I done it this mornin'," he mutters in a dreary voice. It doesn't seem to excite him any more than that. I ask him what he thinks of the presidential campaign and who, between Bush and Dukakis, he thinks is going to win. "I don' give a damn, Louie. I don' give a damn 'bout what happen outside these walls. It don't matter to me. What matter to me is what happen in here, *between these four walls here.* I don' give a damn about the rest." And he puts an end to our conversation with a disgruntled wave of his hand toward the outside.

19. One does not find within the club the passion that the (white) American working class has for public and private scandals and abuses by politicians, as described by David Halle in *America's Working Man* (Chicago: University of Chicago Press, 1984), chap. 9.

The Woodlawn Boys and Girls Club, which runs the boxing gym and the adjacent day-care center, is part of a network of thirteen clubs maintained in Chicago by the United Way, a national charitable organization with branches in all the major U.S. cities, most of them situated in dispossessed black and Latino neighborhoods. Founded in 1938, the Woodlawn club merged in 1978 with its larger counterpart of Yancee, a couple of miles west in the bordering black neighborhood of Washington Park. According to the informational brochure (entitled "A Year of Personal Victories"), these clubs count more than fifteen hundred participants a year between them, 70 percent of whom are boys between 6 and 18 years old, nearly all of them of African-American parentage. The activities offered—early learning exercises for schoolchildren, cultural outings, sports—are 90-percent financed by gifts from businesses whose heads sit on the club's board of directors. In 1987, the Woodlawn-Yancee Unit received nearly fifty thousand dollars from these firms.

The full title of the organization—Woodlawn-Yancee Unit, Boys and Girls Club of Chicago: "The Club That Beats the Street"—tells its mission well: it defines itself in opposition to "the street" and to the social and economic marginality of which it is the vector. Its proclaimed goal is to provide a structured setting capable of lifting young people living in the ghetto out of urban exclusion and its gloomy cortege of crime, gangs, drugs, and poverty:[20] "An investment in the youth of today is an investment in the Chicago of tomorrow. It is today's youth who represent the leadership, the force and the vision of our city. But too many potential leaders of tomorrow learn, too early, that the street is the scene of a struggle for survival and that the only choice available to them is a life

---

20. For a description of the process of marginalization of black youth in the ghetto, see Douglas G. Glasgow, The Black Underclass: Poverty, Unemployment and Entrapment of Ghetto Youth (New York: Vintage Books, 1980); Terry Williams and William Kornblum, Growing Up Poor (Lexington, Mass.: Lexington Books, 1985); John M. Hagedorn, People and Folks: Gangs, Crime, and the Underclass in a Rust Belt City (Chicago: Lakeview Press, 1988); and William Julius Wilson, When Work Disappears (New York: Knopf, 1996). One will also find a set of personal portraits of men confined to the ghetto in the acclaimed Newsweek series republished by Sylvester Monroe and Peter Goldman under the celebratory title Brothers: Black and Poor—A True Story of Courage and Survival (New York: Morrow, 1988), as well as in the narrative drawn from the radio documentary made by two preteenagers from the South Side, LeAlan Jones and Lloyd Newman, Our America: Life and Death on the South Side of Chicago (New York: Washington Square Press, 1997).

without a future. The programs of the Woodlawn-Yancee unit have been created to overcome these social, economic, and academic barriers. Thanks to constructive learning, we ensure the development of the skills that are the basis of self-esteem and that open the doors to success. Offering the young people of today a better tomorrow is our responsibility. Let's 'beat the streets' together!'"

The gym runs on the most bare-bone of budgets, as most of the Club's funds are allotted to the operation of the day-care center. The Boys and Girls Club covers only the utility bills and upkeep of the building. The supervision of the boxers is based entirely on volunteer work, with head coach DeeDee receiving no remuneration whatsoever. Worn-out or damaged equipment must be replaced by the gym itself, which explains the state of advanced wear of the bags and gloves, as well as the chronic shortage of certain implements (the club consumes speed bags at a rate that far exceeds supply and regularly finds itself without one; likewise for the double-end bag used to work on the jab and on timing).

Every year, at the beginning of winter, the Woodlawn gym organizes a "gala" evening for which admission is charged ($25 per person, including members), during which amateur boxers from the area perform before an audience of local notables and celebrities, relatives and friends, so as to raise the funds necessary to pay for the repair and replacement of equipment. If a bag gets torn or deflated, one alternative solution consists of asking the regulars to contribute, each according to his own modest means, to a collective kitty that will serve to purchase another one. But DeeDee is not much fond of this method for as he puts it, "Nobody give nuthin' and we end up back to square one, right away." In point of fact, outside of paying for the pictures made on demand by the house photographer, Jimmy Kitchen, it is exceptional to see any money circulate in the club.

▌ A temple of the pugilistic cult

The boxing gym of the Woodlawn Boys Club occupies the back of an old brick building dating from the interwar decades that had to be altered to accommodate sporting activities: makeshift showers and a locker room were added; the narrow storage room recently repainted a humming-bird blue, where boxers change their clothes, is equipped with a simple wooden table covered by an exercise mat.[21] The same building houses a day-care center financed by the United Way with the help of the city's social services where every afternoon children (all of them black) from the nearby elementary school devote themselves to early learning exercises in two large rooms plastered with multicolored educational posters exhorting them to racial pride—thus this series of banners devoted to the great black figures of world history, science, and literature. In the entry hallway, a wooden rack offers a panoply of brochures aimed at the youth in the club and their families: "Children First: CURE, Chicago United to Reform Schools"; "How to Find A Job: Ten Tips"; "HELP-AIDS in the Black Community"; "Become a Mechanic Thanks to the Truman Course in Auto Technology." The day-care center and the boxing gym coexist but live separate lives; only the periodic intrusion into the gym of a flock of kids, swiftly repelled by DeeDee, and the daily shuttling of food to and from the little kitchen adjacent to the shower room serve as reminders of their joint occupation of the building. The entrance for the boxers, which is located at the back of the building so as not to disturb the children, is cluttered with building materials and tools covered by a thick blue tarp.

The gym itself is rather crumbly: bare water pipes and electrical wires run in the open along the walls, from which the peeling yellow paint is coming off in sheets; the baseboards are broken or missing in many spots; the doors are off their hinges; and it is not unusual for pieces of plaster to come falling down in front of the mirrors. But the room is clean and well maintained and, by contrast with the advanced state of decay of the surrounding neighborhood, the gym does not at all give the impression of being run down.

The part of the gym where boxing proper takes place, which sports wooden flooring on top of the linoleum, measures about twelve by

---

21. The room does not have its own heating system. In the summertime, when the temperature often exceeds 90 degrees, it is weakly air-conditioned, barely enough to keep the heat from becoming intolerable. During the periods of hard freezes of the winter (the thermometer frequently drops to below zero in January and February), the pipes that bring hot air from the furnace located four buildings away sometimes freeze and burst, leaving the gym with no heating at all. The head coach DeeDee then takes refuge in the kitchen, where he spends the day sitting in front of the wide-open door of the oven, all fires blazing. If the gym is really too cold, someone turns the two showers on full blast, scalding hot, in order to drown the main room in a lukewarm steam which brings the temperature up to a bearable level.

ten yards. It is delimited, on one side, by the massive body of the blue-matted ring which cuts off the hallway leading into the day-care center and, on the opposite side, by the back-room "office" (which houses the coach's desk, a long coat rack, two cabinets for training gear, a large round trash can, and an ancient metal scale), from where DeeDee observes the boxers at work through a long rectangular window, and by a small cube of a room that serves as second locker room. Two big punching bags hanging from long metal chains take up the center of the exercise area: the "soft bag," a long, overstuffed black leather bolster, and the "hard bag," an enormous red sausage filled with sand, hard as cement, wrapped tightly with duct tape and patched in several spots. Against the east wall, two mirrors—one about five feet wide and slanted against the wall on the floor, the other narrower and bolted to the wall— and a bag hung horizontally, snug against the wall, for rehearsing uppercuts. A speed bag, suspended from a sort of wooden turret that can be raised or lowered by turning a metal handle, serves for working on one's timing and hand-eye coordination. In the corner lie an iron pole for limbering up, a row of rarely used dumbbells, and a fire extinguisher.

The rest of the equipment consists of jumpropes, gloves, cups, and headgear for sparring, each stored in their respective cabinet or piled up on the table in DeeDee's office, as well as a red double-end bag, attached to the floor and ceiling by rubber straps, on which a boxer hones his jab. A table covered with a gummy exercise mat reinforced by silver duct tape and crossed by a strap is used for situps. Near the smaller mirror, a bucket collects the water from a leaky drainpipe; another one collects the boxers' spit through a funnel and plastic tube running alongside one of the ring posts.

The other walls are lined with narrow metal cabinets secured with big padlocks, their doors adorned with boxing photos and posters. One of them, near the kitchen door, proudly displays a dazzling red and blue sticker trumpeting "Say No to Drugs!" In the opposite corner, three large wooden frames sport collages made up of dozens of photographs discarded by Jimmy Kitchen, the club's self-proclaimed photographer. *"Life in the Big City 1986"* is a patchwork of boxing images (before, during, and after the fights, training scenes, coaches surrounded by their students, an evening's winners brandishing their trophies), snapshots of card girls showing off their curves between rounds, political meetings (the late mayor Harold Washington, laughing his heart out; a contemplative Jesse Jackson), religious ceremonies (weddings, baptisms), evenings out dancing (musicians in action, couples arm in arm, partygoers all smiles), and the city. This montage condenses and expresses the mutual imbrication of all these aspects of African-American culture in Chicago.[22]

The back-room wall behind DeeDee's armchair is itself a sort of work of popular art, made up of out-of-date promotional calendars, black pinup girl pictures from the sixties, small multicolored boxing pennants, and faded posters hawking big-time fights (Gerry Cooney versus Larry Holmes) on which telephone messages have been scribbled; a *Newsweek* cover shows Muhammad Ali grimacing in pain on his corner stool during his farewell fight ("Ali: One Last Hurrah") among photocopies of covers of *Ring Magazine,* views of Chicago at night, and advertisements for luxury cars, not to forget portraits of DeeDee and assorted fighters from the club, boxing stickers, two American flags, yellowed old official notices sent by the state Boxing Commission, a diploma in first aid and phlebotomy awarded by a local private school, and the club's license scotch-taped above DeeDee's seat—all of this set against the background of a green curtain representing a gigantic dollar bill (in total no fewer than sixty-five images and photos).

Likewise the walls of the gym are dotted with posters of boxers, billboards of local fights, and covers of trade magazines (such as *Ring, Knockout, KO,* and *Ringworld*) scotch-taped just about everywhere.[23] Prominently displayed above the big mirror is a black-and-white photograph of a young, bare-chested colossus, all muscles flexed, a menacing gaze on his face, inscribed with this injunction: *"Select the things that go into your mind!"* Hanging over it is a big red, blue, and yellow poster announcing the Tyson-Spinks duel and a color portrait of the ex-star of the club, Alfonzo Ratliff, flaunting his WBC world light-heavyweight championship belt (which he has since lost). The mirror is flanked by two posters for local

22. The close interdependence of the worlds of entertainment, politics, sports, and religion in the African-American community is superbly documented by Charles Keil in *Urban Blues* (Chicago: University of Chicago Press, 1966).
23. This decoration is typical of American boxing gyms. Thomas Hauser notes that "almost always there is a poster of Ali"; *Black Lights,* 68.

cards, yellow and beige; to the left a photo of Tyson in action; to the right another snapshot of Tyson in fight gear, caught laughing on the phone, and covers of *Knockout* magazine showing the fearsome features of Leon Spinks, Marvin Hagler, and Tony Lalonde. Occupying a prominent position to the right of the "office" door are two large monochrome portraits of Martin Luther King and Harold Washington (the first black mayor of Chicago, recently deceased). A cartoon of a boxer endowed with a tiny body and a gigantic head, accompanied by a caption with a double meaning, inciting each to both modesty and excellence—*"Don't let your head get big in the ring"* can be read as meaning either "Don't let yourself get punched in the head in the ring" or "Don't get too full of yourself in the ring"— and yet another poster of Mike Tyson making a terrifying scowl brighten the kitchen wall.

In both layout and adornment, the gym constitutes something of a temple of the pugilistic cult by the presence on its walls of the major fighters, past and present, to whom the budding boxers from ghetto gyms devote a selective but tenacious adoration. Indeed, the champions demonstrate *in vivo* the highest virtues of the profession (courage, strength, skill, tenacity, intelligence, ferocity) and incarnate the various forms of pugilistic excellence. They may moreover intervene directly into the life of the most modest apprentice pug, as attested by the photograph of Mike Tyson flanked by DeeDee and Curtis (who, for the occasion, is wearing a blue cap emblazoned with "WAR" in enormous red letters) prominently displayed on the main wall of the back room, which reflects a speck of the symbolic capital of the star from the ghetto of Brooklyn on them.

There are no fewer than five different pictures of Tyson on the wall where the mirrors and the speed bag are hung, plus two on the opposite wall and three on the north wall. The second most honored champion is Sugar Ray Leonard, who appears on five posters, just ahead of Muhammad Ali. However, it is less the number of images than their *placement* that gives this sort of spontaneous profane iconography its full power and meaning. It is noteworthy that each cluster of posters includes one or several photos of champions in the heat of action, generally placed *above* the announcements for regional fights. This visual "syntagm," this physical proximity, suggests an association, a quasi-genealogical link between the local pugs, who fight for negligible purses on regional cards, and the superchampions who divide up among themselves the fabulous purses of the prestigious events televised from Las Vegas and Atlantic City. The idea is thereby given, concretely, of a great pugilistic "chain of being": that there would exist a continuity from the anonymous footsoldier of the most modest club to the global star trained under state-of-the-art computer and medical surveillance and whose very name suffices to unleash torrents of dollars and to make the most fearless opponents tremble (as the Tyson myth would have it). All boxers would partake of one and the same essence: providence and individual determination will decide which of the little will become big, assuming they have the requisite talent and courage.

This seemingly innocuous mural iconography, which juxtaposes a Michael Spinks being demolished by Tyson ("At what price glory?" asks the article accompanying the picture) with a local advertisement for a second-rate fight between second-rank fighters (Craig "Gator" Bodzianowski against Manning "Motor City Madman" Gallaway), upholds the belief in an ideal by definition inaccessible to virtually all boxers and contributes to maintaining the illusion of a continuous and gradual "ladder of mobility," leading step by step from the base to the summit of the pugilistic pyramid—when everything that transpires of the social and economic organization of professional boxing indicates rather that there is discontinuity, that the networks that manage the business of bruising are less like "ladders" than strongly segmented networks, access to which is tightly controlled by those who possess the specific social capital.[24]

The posters and mural decorations of the gym play a significant role in the establishment of hierarchies within the club. There is an ongoing traffic in posters (they are given, exchanged, searched for, and put up on the wall by the interested parties) through which everyone tries to affirm or increase his value on the pugilistic market by displaying and circulating the signs of his participation in this or that card, as this note of 15 November 1988 indicates:

24. Cf. Hauser, Black Lights, 146–171 and 179–183; Sammons, Beyond the Ring, 235–245; Brunt, Mean Business, pp. 101–138; Sam Toperoff, Sugar Ray Leonard and Other Noble Warriors (New York: McGraw-Hill, 1986); and Andy Ercole and Ed Okonowicz, Tiberi: The Uncrowned Champion (Wilmington: Jared Co., 1992).

While I'm drying off with a towel, I ask DeeDee if the out-of-date posters for local fights piled up in the big cardboard box near the jump-rope cabinet are to be thrown away and if I can take a few. Charles (an assistant trainer) tells me right away: "Yeah, you can take 'em all if you want to, we gonna throw 'em out anyway." DeeDee cuts him off, retorting vigorously: "What you talkin' about? I ain't gonna throw 'em away! You crazy? Let me take a look in that box an' I'll get out four or five old ones for you, Louie, but you can't take just any of 'em. Not d'ones with the pictures of guys from the gym, guys from here. 'Cause I wanna keep those and put 'em on the wall. . . . Guys like to have their picture on the wall. . . . They like seein' posters with their picture on 'em. Tha's the first thing they show their buddies when they come in for the first time. [pointing to a poster] They go straight over to the poster with their name an' picture on it and they call their buddy over and tell 'im: 'Check-it-out, man, tha's *me* in that picture, right there'. Tha's very important to 'em. It's like . . . you remember Duane? He thought he was a big-time fighter, so he thought his picture already be out here somewhere. First time he show up, he's walkin' 'round the gym, he's lookin' all over [grinning at the remembrance], ain't got one single picture of him on the walls. He couldn' believe his eyes, man! He was so furious he brought one in to me *the very next day."*

A protective shield against the temptations and dangers of the street, the gym is not simply the site of a rigorous training of the body; it is also the locus and support of what Georg Simmel calls "sociability" (*Geselligkeit*), forms of social interaction devoid of significant purpose or endowed with socially anodine contents, processes of pure sociation that are their own ends.[25] This is because of the unspoken code according to which members do not carry into the club their outside statuses, problems, and obligations, be they work, family, or love. Everything takes place as if a tacit pact of nonaggression governed interpersonal relations and ruled out any topic of conversation liable to threaten this "playful form of association," hamper the smooth functioning of daily individual exchanges, and thereby endanger the specific masculine subculture that the gym

25. Georg Simmel, "The Sociology of Sociability," *American Journal of Sociology* 55, 3 (1949): 254–261.

perpetuates.[26] Politics is rarely touched on; issues of "race," such as discrimination in hiring or police brutality, are occasionally broached but are unlikely to lead to much elaboration or disagreement given the ethnic homogeneity of the gym's membership. Crime and "hustling" are a common topic of conversation, just as they are a banal component of daily life. Only sporting events are automatically given center stage. But the closer to combat the sport is and the more it requires virile qualities, the more likely it is to be talked about. The gridiron battles of the Chicago Bears are often commented upon, especially on the day after the game, in terms of the toughness and physical courage displayed by this or that player. By contrast, it takes an exploit by Michael Jordan, the super-star of the Chicago Bulls, for the performance of the latter in the NBA championship to be mentioned. It is of course boxing contests, local and national, regularly televised from Atlantic City, Las Vegas, and Reno by cable sports channels like ESPN, SportsChannel, and Sportsvision, or specially broadcast via pay-per-view by TVKO and Showtime, that are the main fodder for chatter and whose results and implications are most abundantly debated. The brunt of "shoptalk" revolves around the maintenance of the body, the perennial problem of "making the weight" and assorted technical subtleties of the game;[27] advice and tips are continually traded; sparring sessions are avidly dissected; information on past tournaments and upcoming cards is sought.

In the course of these endlessly revived conversations head coach DeeDee and the older gym members display a nearly encyclopedic knowledge of the names, places, and events that make up pugilistic folklore. The outstanding fights of history, especially regional, are frequently evoked, as are the successes and setbacks of boxers on the rise or the decline. Through a deliberate reversal of the official hierarchy of values, the great televised bouts (such as Leonard versus Hagler or Holyfield versus Foreman) are less prized than local clashes, and the strings of names

---

26. The boxing gym is comparable in this respect to pool halls, which, along with bars, constitute one of the last refuges of the male bachelor subculture, as shown by Ned Polsky, *Hustlers, Beats and Others* (Chicago: University of Chicago Press, [1967] 1985), 20–30.

27. The techniques and dilemmas of the management of bodily capital are analyzed below (*infra*, pp. 127–149) and in Loïc Wacquant, "Pugs at Work: Bodily Capital and Bodily Labor among Professional Boxers," *Body and Society* 1, 1 (March 1995): 65–94.

mentioned in gym gossip include many more obscure fighters than stars favored by the media or known to the general public. Conversations insensibly shift back and forth between boxing and stories of street fights, shady traffics, "hustles," and street tricks and crime, of which everyone has an extended personal repertory. Under this angle, DeeDee's "office"—the back room heavily adorned with old boxing posters and pictures, from which he supervises the training area through a large rectangular window—functions in the manner of a stage on which each can offer proof of his excellence in the manipulation of the cultural capital proper to the group, namely pugilistic information and knowledge of the street and its demimonde.

Conversations at the club are highly ritualized. The sequencing of the locutors, the import of their speech, the location they hold in the confined space of the back room (one rarely chats on the gym floor itself when training is in progress),[28] all map out a complex and finely hierarchized structure. A strict pecking order governs who occupies what chair as well as who talks when: it is the trainers and the old-timers who have precedence (in descending order of authority: head coach DeeDee; Ed Woods, a manager-cornerman and head of a similar gym in St. Louis; Charles Martin, another coach and a close friend of DeeDee; old Page, an instructor at a nearby city Park District gym; and the mailman O'Bannon); next come the boxers, in rough order of caliber and seniority (Curtis, Butch, Smithie, Lorenzo, Ashante, Rico, and so forth), followed by the occasional visitors. The high swivel armchair from which DeeDee monitors the moves of the athletes on the ring and floor is strictly reserved for the master of the premises. The official explanation is that DeeDee does not want anyone else to sit in

---

28. This note from 27 June 1989 is typical on this count: "I'm starting to warm up while watching Lorenzo and Big Earl spar from the foot of the ring post when Billy comes over to shake hands. He looks distinctively pale and worried, and for good reason: 'I'm fightin' tomorrow, it's my first fight. You think it's gonna be okay?—Sure, you prepared yourself well, you're in shape. This is a good gym, you're going to see that you're a notch above the others.—You think so? I'm really nervous. I'm starting to get the runs, ya know.' Billy's confession is abruptly interrupted by trainer Eddie, who chides him: 'What you think you doin', gabbin' over there? What you think this is, *a social club?* You ain't in your living room, now get to work, Billy! Skip rope or do some situps, but don't stand 'round like that doin' nuthing, com'on!' Billy swallows his anguish and sheepishly gets back to work."

it on grounds that they would stain it with their sweat. But the prohibition applies also to those who come dressed in civilian clothes and do not train—only Curtis, the club's up-and-coming star, allows himself to transgress from time to time, and even that happens more often than not when the old coach is not present. The hygienic excuse cannot hide the social reason behind this taboo: the armchair materializes DeeDee's place and function in the gym. An observation post, it is the seat of his authority, from which he can embrace in a single glance, supervise, and thus control all the phases of training and the tiniest gestures of each and every one.

One should not underestimate the importance of these seemingly mundane conversations, for they are an essential ingredient in the "hidden curriculum" of the gym: they convey in oral and osmotic fashion to the apprentice boxers the folk knowledge of the occupation. In the form of more or less apocryphal stories, gym gossip, fight anecdotes, and other street tales, these conversation impregnate them with the values and categories of judgment in currency in the pugilistic universe, the core of which are those same ones that anchor the culture of the ghetto: a mix of peer-group solidarity and defiant individualism, physical toughness and courage ("heart"), an uncompromising sense of masculine honor, and an expressive stress on personal performance and style.[29]

■ The promises of prizefighting

10 June 1989. As I'm starting my third round on the heavy bag, Curtis suddenly comes out of the locker room in his underwear (that's when you realize he's smallish, but what a knot of muscles!) and calls over to Reggie and Luke—the one bare-chested in red trunks, the other wearing long shorts and a blue jersey—who started their workout late and are gossiping while shadowboxing lackadaisically in front of the mirror. In a stentorian voice that I didn't know he had, he vigorously admonishes them for their behavior before drawing for them this picture of the rewards of the boxer, all

29. See Roger D. Abrahams, *Positively Black* (Englewood Cliffs, N.J.: Prentice-Hall, 1970); Sánchez-Jankowski, *Islands in the Street;* and Folb, *Runnin' Down Some Lines.*

that they will be able to do and get when they are champions, while glancing over at Anthony, who's sitting with his legs stretched on the table alongside the ring, to bear witness for him.

"Instead of doin' nuthin', bein' nuthin' and turnin' bad on the streets, you can *be somebody.* With boxing, you can become somebody, you can be proud of yo'self and make your momma proud of you, man. If you train hard an' you work hard, you train hard in d'gym and you do yo' homework, man, be serious, you can be a big-time fighter an' win big fights. You gonna do the (Golden) Gloves and win 'em and bring home a trophy so big, yo' mutha an' grandmutha won't believe their eyes, a trophy so big they gonna cry just thinkin' that you're the one who won it.

"If you train hard, man, you can go places, the Olympic team, an' them promoters, they gonna take you in their gym, man, you won't believe d'gyms they got, an' they'll take you to their training camps where they give you sweatpants and sweatshirts for free, man, and they gonna give you clothes to wear, feed you, feed you that good food three times a day for free.

"You'll get a chance to go to places like you never dreamed in your life that you go there, you go to France or England, and Europe for big fights—ask Anthony! (Anthony nods somberly in agreement.) But you gotta work hard. *No pain, no gain.* It ain't gonna come to you by magic. You gotta work hard, train hard, *e-ve-ry day:* run, shadow box, hit the bags, you gotta be serious about your work, man. Then all of that can become yours."

Stunned—and, to say the least, enticed—by this tirade unleashed by a half-naked and inspired Curtis, Reggie and Luke put their heads down and get back to working with renewed seriousness and ardor.

"The Boys Who Beat the Street"

It is well known that the overwhelming majority of boxers come from popular milieus, and especially from those sectors of the working class recently fed by immigration. Thus, in Chicago, the predominance first of the Irish, then of central European Jews, Italians, and African

Americans, and lately of Latinos closely mirrors the succession of these groups at the bottom of the class ladder.[30] The upsurge of Chicano fighters (and the strong presence of Puerto Ricans) over the past decade, which even a casual survey of the program of the great annual tournament of the Chicago Golden Gloves immediately reveals, is the direct translation of the massive influx of Mexican immigrants into the lowest regions of the social space of the Midwest. Thus, during the finals of the 1989 edition of that joust, clearly dominated by boxers of Mexican and Puerto Rican extraction, DeeDee points out to me that "if you want to know who's at d'bottom of society, all you gotta to do is look at who's boxin'. Yep, Mexicans, these days, they have it rougher than blacks." A similar process of "ethnic succession" can be observed in the other major boxing markets of the country, the New York–New Jersey area, Michigan, Florida, and southern California. By way of local confirmation, when they first sign up at the gym, each member of the Woodlawn Boys Club must fill out an information sheet that includes his marital status, his level of education, his occupation and those of his parents, and mention whether he was raised in a family without a mother or father as well as the economic standing of his family: of the five precoded income categories on the questionnaire, the highest begins at $12,500 a year, which is *half* the average household income for the city of Chicago.

It is necessary to stress, however, that, contrary to a widespread image, backed by the native myth of the "hungry fighter" and periodically validated anew by selective media attention to the more exotic figures of the occupation, such as former heavyweight champion

---

30. S. K. Weinberg and Henri Arond, "The Occupational Culture of the Boxer," *American Journal of Sociology* 57, 5 (March 1952): 460–469 (for statistics on the period 1900 to 1950); T. J. Jenkins, "Changes in Ethnic and Racial Representation among Professional Boxers: A Study in Ethnic Succession," M.A. thesis, University of Chicago, 1955; Nathan Hare, "A Study of the Black Fighter," *Black Scholar* 3 (1971): 2–9; John Sugden, "The Exploitation of Disadvantage: The Occupational Subculture of the Boxer," in *Sport, Leisure, and Social Relations,* eds. John Horne, David Jay, and Andrew Tomlinson (London: Routledge and Kegan Paul, 1987), 187–209; and Sammons, *Beyond the Ring,* chapters 2–6. On the trajectory of American Jews in boxing in the first half of the twentieth century, see Stephen A. Reiss, "A Fighting Chance: The Jewish-American Boxing Experience, 1890–1940," *American Jewish History* 74 (1985): 233–254, and, for the broader context, Benjamin G. Rader, *American Sports: From the Age of Folk Games to the Age of Spectators* (Englewood Cliffs, N.J.: Prentice-Hall, 1983).

Mike Tyson,[31] boxers are generally not recruited from among the most disenfranchised fractions of the ghetto subproletariat but rather issue from those *segments of its working class that are struggling at the threshold of stable socioeconomic integration.* This (self-)selection, which tends de facto to exclude the most excluded, operates not via the constraint of a penury of monetary means but through the *mediation of the moral and corporeal dispositions* that are within reach of these two fractions of the African-American population. In point of fact, there is no direct economic barrier to participation to speak of: yearly dues to enroll at the Woodlawn Boys Club come to ten dollars; the mandatory license from the Illinois Amateur Boxing Federation costs an additional twelve dollars per annum, and all the equipment necessary for training is lent gratis by the club—only the handwraps and the mouthpiece have to be purchased in one of the few sporting-goods stores that carry them, for a total outlay of less than ten dollars.[32] Youngsters issued

31. It would be difficult to overstate the influence of the Tyson phenomenon on boxing in the black ghetto in the late 1980s. The veritable media tidal wave that accompanied his rise (out of the ghetto of Brooklyn and out of prison where, as a teenager, he was initiated into boxing), his conjugal and financial troubles with the African-American actress Robin Givens (featured in several prime-time television specials), his economic ties to the white New York real estate billionaire Donald Trump, his acquaintances in the artistic milieu (via the agency of Spike Lee), and his personal and legal conflicts with his former entourage made him a legendary character who not only fed a continual flood of rumors, stories, and conversations but who was furthermore capable, by the sole virtue of his symbolic value, of stimulating vocations en masse (as did Joe Louis and Muhammad Ali, who were, in their days, the inspirations of thousands of apprentice boxers). The phenomenon has since gone through a spectacular reversal following Tyson's stunning defeat at the hands of James "Buster" Douglas in February 1990, then his sentencing to six years of prison for rape, and the series of bizarre incidents that followed. See Peter Niels Heller, *Bad Intentions: The Mike Tyson Story* (New York: Da Capo Press, 1995), and, on the multiple meanings of Tyson's trajectory as a living emblem of rough masculinity, the stimulating article by Tony Jefferson, "Muscle, 'Hard Men' and 'Iron' Mike Tyson: Reflections on Desire, Anxiety and the Embodiment of Masculinity," *Body and Society* 4, 1 (March 1998): 77–98.

32. The boxing gyms of the city's Park District are even less costly since they levy no dues; one other professional gym in Chicago requires monthly payments of $5 for amateurs and $20 for professionals but allows many waivers. In other cities, some gyms post notably higher dues: for example, $55 per quarter at the Somerville Boxing Club in a working-class suburb of Boston, where I boxed from 1991 to 1993, and $50 a month at a gym in the Tenderloin, a disreputable area in downtown San Francisco.

from the most disadvantaged families are eliminated because they lack the habits and inclinations demanded by pugilistic practice: to become a boxer requires a regularity of life, a sense of discipline, a physical and mental asceticism that cannot take root in social and economic conditions marked by chronic instability and temporal disorganization. Below a certain threshold of objective personal and family constancy, one is highly unlikely to acquire the corporeal and moral dispositions that are indispensable if one is to successfully endure the learning of this sport.[33]

Preliminary analysis of the profile of the 27 professional boxers (all but two of them African-American, ages ranging from 20 to 37) active in the summer and fall of 1991 in Chicago's three main gyms confirms that prizefighters do, on the whole, stand above the lower tier of the male ghetto population. One third of them grew up in a family receiving public aid and 22 percent were currently jobless, the remainder being either employed or drawing a "weekly salary" from their manager. Thirteen of them (or 48 percent) had attended a community college (if only for a brief period and with little if any educational and economic gain to show for it); one had earned an associate degree and another a bachelor of science.[34] Only three (or 11 percent) had failed to graduate from high school or obtain a GED, and about half held a current checking account. For comparison, of men ages 18 to 45 living in Chicago's South Side and West Side ghettos, 36 percent have grown up in a household receiving welfare, 44 percent do not hold a job, half have not completed their high school education, and only 18 percent have a current checking account.[35] The educational,

---

33. Or else lack of internal government must be compensated by truly exceptional aggressivity, physical prowess, and ring "toughness." Such fighters, however, tend to "burn out" prematurely and rarely fulfill their potential, pugilistic as well as economic. The ring prodigy and three-time world champion Wilfredo Benitez, the son of a Puerto Rican sugar cane cutter, is an exemplary case in point: though he turned "pro" at age fourteen and was world champion by his seventeenth birthday, his irregularity in training and notorious lack of eating discipline quickly cut his career short.

34. Though they are purported to offer a bridge to four-year campuses, community colleges (or junior colleges) function as remedial courses for high school education and deliver degrees that are largely devoid of value on the labor market. Stephen Brint and Jerry Karabel, "Les 'community colleges' américains et la politique de l'inégalité," *Actes de la recherche en sciences sociales* 86–87 (September 1987): 69–84.

35. Wacquant and Wilson, "The Cost of Racial and Class Exclusion in the Inner City," 17, 19, 22.

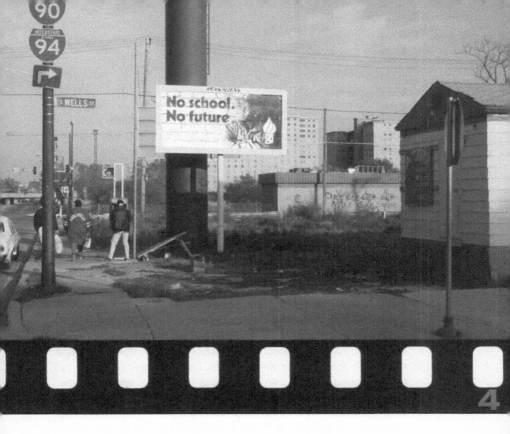

employment, and economic status of professional boxers is thus quite a bit higher than that of the average ghetto resident. Most distinctive about their background is that none of their fathers received a high school degree and nearly all held typical blue-collar working-class jobs (with the exception of the son of a wealthy white entrepreneur from the suburbs). And partial evidence culled from biographies and native accounts suggests that the social recruitment of fighters tends to rise slightly, rather than descend, as one climbs up the pugilistic ladder. "Most of my boys," says veteran trainer and founder of the world-renowned Kronk gym in Detroit, Emanuel Steward, "contrary to what people think, are not that poor. They come from good areas around the country."[36]

By and large, then, professional boxers do not belong to that disorganized and desocialized "dangerous class" the fear of which fed the

36. Cited in David Halpern, "Distance and Embrace," in *Reading the Fights,* eds. Joyce Carol Oates and David Halpern (New York: Prentice-Hall, 1988), 279.

recent pseudoscientific discourse on the consolidation of a black "under-class" supposedly cut off from "mainstream society."[37] Everything tends to indicate instead that most of them differ from other ghetto youths by virtue of their stronger social integration relative to their low cultural and economic status, and that they come from traditional working-class backgrounds and are attempting to maintain or recapture this valorized status by entering a profession that they perceive as a skilled manual trade, highly regarded by their immediate entourage, which furthermore offers the prospect— however illusory—of big financial earnings. The great majority of adults at the Woodlawn Boys Club are employed (if only part-time) as a security guard, gas station attendant, bricklayer, janitor, stockman, fireman, messenger, sports instructor for the city's Park District, copy shop clerk, bagger at Jewel's food store, counselor at a youth detention center, and steel mill worker. To be sure, these pro-letarian attachments are in most cases tenuous, for these jobs are as a rule insecure and low paying, and they do not obviate the chronic need for "hustling" in the street economy to make ends meet at the end of the month.[38] And a contingent of professional fighters does come from the lower fractions of the working class, namely, large female-headed families raised on public aid in stigmatized public housing projects for most of their youth and plagued with endemic and quasi-permanent job-lessness. But they are not the majority; nor are they the more successful competitors in the pugilistic field in the medium to long run.

Furthermore, if their mediocre income and early educational disaffec-tion do not differentiate them clearly from the mass of ghetto residents of their age category, prizefighters come more often from intact families and are much more likely to be married fathers living with their children. And they have the privilege of belonging to a formal organization—the boxing gym—whereas the overwhelming majority of the black residents of the city's poorest neighborhoods belong to none, with the partial ex-ception of their few remaining middle-class members.[39] However, con-jugal and familial integration wields its influence in a subtly contradictory manner: a necessary condition for practicing the sport regularly, it must be sufficiently strong to enable the acquisition of the dispositions and

---

37. For a methodical critique of this bogus concept and its social usages, see Loïc Wacquant, "L'*underclass*' urbaine dans l'imaginaire social et scientifique américain," in *L'Exclusion: l'état des savoirs* (Paris: La Découverte, 1996), 248–262.

38. Betty Lou Valentine, *Hustling and Other Hard Work: Life Styles in the Ghetto* (New York: Free Press, 1978).

39. Wacquant and Wilson, "The Cost of Racial and Class Exclusion in the Inner City," 24.

motivations necessary for prizefighting but at the same time not so strong as to allow work and household life to compete too intensely with investment in boxing.

"No, Ashante, he don't come ev'ry day, you know that, Louie," explains DeeDee. "It's only them young guys in high school who come regularly ev'ry afternoon. Tha's what's wrong with them grownups: they're married, they got a family, kids, they can't be in d'gym ev'ry day. Rents are high, same with food, an' you gotta go out make some money for all that. They gotta have some job on the side, they gotta find themselves a job that give 'em the money they need for their wife and kids. An' when you got a chance to bring some money home, you gotta go, you ain't gonna come to work out. Tha's Ashante's problem right there. Ashante, he got two kids. He gets jive jobs here an' there. He missed the last event, where he was on the card, cause he had an opportunity to work three-four days in a row and make himself a lil' money. It's a warehouse, when they lookin' for overtime, they call him up [to work as a stockman on a spot basis]. He ain't no regular employee, but they call him often, yep, soon as they need somebody. He can make more workin' that jive job than he can gettin' in d'ring. [A preliminary fight guarantees a purse of about $150 to $300 to each of the contestants.] And he don't have to get beat up. So he gotta take it." [Field notes, 13 January 1989]

The conversation turns to Mark—a new guy who has been working as an attendant in a photocopy shop since he left high school without finishing three years ago. He arrived really late but DeeDee let him start his workout anyway. He boxes with fervor, leaning over the sandbag, machine-gunning it with short hooks, which earns him praise from DeeDee. "This dude's good. He move well. *He's a natural.* Look at his moves. He's strong. Good hands. Tha's cause he used to fight in d'streets. He's comin' along quick. But he got stiff legs, he don't know how to bend his legs. An' then he got a job, which mean he can only come in late like this. He's gotta train more than that but he don' have the time. It's a real pity, a real pity, yep, 'cause he could make a good boxer. If only I had had'im earlier, when he was younger . . ." "How old is he?" "He's twenty-two. He was tellin' me hisself how he wish he coulda gone to d'gym when he was fifteen–sixteen years old. But there was no gym where he lived, so he didn' do nuthin'. He hung 'round an' spent his time fightin' in his neighborhood. He weighs 127 pounds, he's not big but he's stocky, tha's why. He played football on his high-school team. He can lose some more weight, but it's a shame that he don't have d'time to train more . . . Unfortunately, with guys like him, tha's often the case." [Field notes, 22 March 1989]

DeeDee articulates here in passing one of the factors that differentiate "street fighters" who eventually fall into petty or serious delinquency from those who exercise their skill in the ring and participate, however irregularly, in the wage-labor economy: the same dispositions can lead to one or the other career depending on the space of activities on offer, here deeply rooted gangs that rule a housing project, there a gym that "stays busy" in a comparatively quiet neighborhood.

The enrollment of the Woodlawn Boys Club fluctuates markedly and irregularly from one month to the next. Anywhere from 100 to 150 boys and men sign up over the course of a year, but most of them stay for no more than a few weeks as they soon find out that the workout is too demanding for their taste—an attrition rate in excess of 90 percent is commonplace for a boxing gym.[40] Attendance is at its highest in winter, just before the Golden Gloves (whose preliminaries take place in early February every year), and in the late spring. A nucleus composed of a score of "regulars," including an inner circle of eight older members who recently turned professional after rising through the amateur ranks together, forms the backbone of this shifting membership. The motivations of participants vary according to their status. Most of the regulars compete officially in the amateur and professional divisions; for them the gym is the locus of an intensive preparation for competition. The others come to the club to get or to keep in shape, sometimes with the explicit design of seducing members of the opposite sex (as does Steve, a massive, twenty-nine-year-old black Puerto Rican who is there "to lose weight, for the chicks. I wanna lose this belly, you know, for the women: that's what they want, man, they're the ones who decide"), to stay in touch with boxing friends (this is the case of several retired "pros" who spend more time talking in the back room than working out on the bags), or to learn techniques of self-defense.[41] In

---

40. The rate for the Woodlawn Boys Club is comparable to that of the East Harlem gym described by Plummer, *Buttercups and Strong Boys*, 57, in which the annual turnover hovers around 80 percent.

41. I explain to the director of the day-care center adjoining the gym, who is inquiring as to why I got into this "sport for brutes," that I come here mostly to get in shape.

addition to the fighters and trainers, many former pugilists in their old age drop by the gym to chat with DeeDee, spending countless hours in the windowless office reminiscing about the olden days, "when fighters were fighters." For the veteran Woodlawn coach, only competitive boxing really counts. And although he attentively monitors the progress of those who come to the gym only for the sake of exercise, he does not hide his preference for the real pugilists. When the occasion arises, DeeDee does not hesitate to try and entice the "fitness boxers" to the pleasures of the virile embrace of the ring. The following conversation offers a good characterization of this attitude.

6 December 1988. As I'm returning to the back room, a tall black man in his forties, very elegantly dressed in a light brown suit and a matching dark brown tie, graying, hairline receding at the temples, with a curly, well-trimmed beard, a little on the plump side, looking very much like an upper-level manager in the public transportation sector, cranes his neck across the door to ask to see "Mister Armour." DeeDee replies that he's he and invites him to seat himself on the little red stool in front of his desk. I pretend to read that day's *Chicago Sun-Times* in order to discreetly listen in on their conversation.

"I'd like some information about boxing lessons for adults. Do you give them yourself?"

"Yep, it depends on what you wanna do: you jus' wanna keep in shape or you wanna fight? How old 're you?"

"I'm forty-one. No, it wouldn't be to fight, not at forty-one years old. . . . It's more for stayin' in shape and also for self-defense on the street."

"Okay, but later you might get interested in fightin', you know. It's quite a few guys who're pretty old, forty-nine, fifty, even fifty-three—we

---

She immediately adds, as if it went without saying: "Oh, yes, and then it can't hurt to know a little bit of self-defense in *this* neighborhood. You also got to keep that in mind" (field notes, 8 October 1988). While I am jumping rope to wind down after a sparring session, Oscar, Little Keith's manager, asks me if I want to turn pro (I reassure him, I'm only a dilettante boxer but I would like to go as far as to have a few amateur fights): "'Cuz you box pretty good, you doin' a good job, ya know . . . And then it give ya confidence in the street 'cuz you can defend yo'self better" (field notes, 17 June 1989).

got T-Jay at fifty-three—who come in to keep their selves in shape an' then after three-four months, they wanna do d'Golden Gloves. Of course [in a matter-of-fact tone], they're gonna find themselves squarin' off with these young guys who're gonna cut'em to pieces and bust'em up, but then they lovin' it: they don' care, all they want to do (hissed with an undertow of admiration) is *fight.*"

"At forty-one years old? Isn't that a little old to fight?"

"Yeah, but it depen's, we got young kids as well as adults . . ."

The mustachioed executive retorts: "No thanks. What I'm interested in is self-defense, that's all, to fight in the street if I get attacked." He will never be seen in the gym again.

Within the Woodlawn Boys Club, indigenous perception establishes a distinction first, among "serious" boxers, between youth who are still in high school and adults who are free of academic obligations but subject to the more constraining obligation of work and family. The youngest is 13 years old, the oldest 57, with the median age hovering around 22.[42] All members are men, as the gym is a *quintessentially masculine space* into which the trespassing of the female sex is tolerated only so long as it remains incidental. "Boxing is for men, and is about men, and *is* men. . . . Men who are fighting men to determine their worth, that is, masculinity, exclude women."[43] While there exists no formal obstacle to their participation—some trainers will even verbally deny having any reticence toward female boxing—women are not welcome in the gym because their presence disrupts if not the smooth material operation of the pugilistic universe then its symbolic organization.

42. One can obtain an amateur license at age thirteen, and some tournaments allow the participation of children as young as ten, who are called "subnovices." According to Henri Allouch, "Participation in Boxing among Children and Young Adults," *Pediatrics* 72 (1984): 311–312, 15,000 or more kids from ages ten to fifteen are boxing in North America.

43. Joyce Carol Oates, *On Boxing* (Garden City, N.Y.: Doubleday, 1987), 72. Boxing pundits and commentators sometimes complain about the increasingly constraining regulation of pugilistic violence, which they depict and denounce as a "feminization" of prizefighting apt to pervert it: the reduction from fifteen to twelve rounds for championship bouts, the increased role of physicians, the mandatory 45-day waiting period after suffering a defeat by knockout, and especially the growing latitude given to the referee to stop a fight as soon as one of the protagonists appears unable to defend himself or is at risk of serious injury.

Rodney and two female admirers of the day

Only under special circumstances, such as the imminence of a big-time fight or the morrow of a decisive victory between the ropes, will the girlfriends and wives of boxers have license to attend their man's training session. When they do so, they are expected to remain quietly seated, motionless, on the chairs that line the flanks of the ring; and they typically move carefully along the walls so as to avoid penetrating the actual training "floor," even when the latter is vacant. It goes without saying that they are not to interfere in any manner with the training, except to help extend its effects into the home by taking full charge of household maintenance and the children, cooking the required foods, and providing unfailing emotional and even financial support. If a woman is present at the Woodlawn Boys Club, boxers are not allowed to walk out of the dressing room bare-chested to come weigh themselves on the scale in the back room—as if men's half-naked bodies could be seen "at work" on the public scene of the ring but not "at rest" in the backstage of the workshop. In another professional gym located near Chicago's Little Italy, the head coach resorts to this heavy-handed method to keep women at a distance: he firmly warns his boxers to not bring their "squeeze" to the gym; if they disobey him, he sends them into the ring to spar with a much stronger partner so that they receive a beating in front of their girlfriend and lose face. At the Windy City Gym, on the edge of the West Side ghetto, a separate area, enclosed by a waist-high wall, is officially reserved for "visitors" to sit in; in practice, it serves only to park the female companions of boxers in training. The famed Top Rank Gym in Las Vegas formally bars entrance to women.

Among regular practitioners, the main division separates amateurs from professionals. These two types of boxing form neighboring universes that, though they are tightly interdependent, are very distant from each other at the level of experience. A pugilist may spend years fighting in the amateur ranks yet know next to nothing about the mores and factors that mold the careers of their "pro" colleagues (especially when it comes to their financial aspects, which all conspire to keep in the dark).[44] Moreover, the rules that govern competition in these two divisions are so different that it would scarcely be an exaggeration to consider them two different sports. To put it simply, in amateur boxing the goal is to accumulate points by hitting one's opponent as many times as possible in rapid flurries, and the referee enjoys ample latitude to stop the contest as soon as one of the protagonists appears to be in physical difficulty; among professionals, who do not wear protective headgear and whose gloves are notably smaller and lighter, the main objective is to "hurt" one's opponent by landing heavy blows, and the battle continues until one of the fighters is no longer able to carry on. As the head trainer from Sheridan Park puts it, "professional boxers don't screw around, they'll knock you *outa your mind,* you know. It's a rough game, you turn professional, it's a rough game: (abruptly catching himself) it's *not* a game. Amateur, you have your fun. Professional (whispering by way of warning) they're tryin' to kill you." The vast majority of amateur boxers do not "turn pro," so that those who do constitute a

44. Professional boxers never reveal the amount of their purses, even to their regular sparring partners; all monetary negotiations and transactions among fighters, trainers, managers, and promoters take place *sub rosa.* See Loïc Wacquant, "A Flesh Peddler at Work: Power, Pain and Profit in the Prizefighting Economy," *Theory and Society* 27, 1 (February 1998): 1–42.

highly (self-) selected group. Here again, the transition from one category to the other has a better chance of being successful if the fighter can rely on a family environment and social background endowed with a minimum of stability.

Within each of these categories, the other distinctions current in the gym refer to style and tactics in the ring: "boxer" (or "scientific boxer") against "brawler" or "slugger," "counterpuncher," "banger," "animal," and so on. Beyond those differentiations, the gym culture is ostensibly egalitarian in the sense that all participants are treated alike: whatever their status and their ambitions, they all enjoy the same rights and must acquit themselves of the same duties, particularly that of "working" hard at their craft and displaying a modicum of bravery between the ropes when the time comes. To be sure, those who benefit from the services of a personal trainer are in a position to command added attention, and the professionals go through a more demanding and more structured workout. But DeeDee is as keen to teach a sixteen-year-old novice who might never set foot in the gym again after a week of trial how to throw a left jab as he is on polishing the defensive moves of a ring veteran preparing for a televised bout. Whatever their level of pugilistic competency, all those who "pay their dues" are wholeheartedly accepted as full-fledged members of the club.

As he progresses, each apprentice boxer finds his comfort zone: some are content to stick to the role of "gym fighter," one who trains and "gloves up" more or less frequently to spar and enter an occasional tournament; others decide to venture further in competition and launch themselves onto the amateur circuit; still others crown their amateur careers by "turning pro." The differentiation between the mere dabbler boxer and the full-fledged pugilist is made visible by the expenses each consents to acquire his gear and by the use of a permanent locker. Only competitive fighters train with their own gloves (of which they generally own several worn pairs accumulated over the years), their personal head guard and jumprope, which they keep preciously under lock and key in their individual lockers. The purchase of boxing boots (which cost 35 to 60 dollars) and, even more so, sparring headgear (60 dollars minimum) suffices to signal a long-term commitment to fighting for both the boxer and his entourage. Training outfits also provide a good clue as to the degree of involvement in the sport, although this is easier to manipulate and therefore less reliable. The firm Ringside, which supplies boxing equipment by mail order, sells a wide range of custom-made gear (trunks, tank tops, jerseys, and robes), and anyone can order a sweat-suit cut to a unique pattern or emblazoned with the likeness of a great champion. Moreover, professional boxers never wear their fighting apparel during workouts. It nonetheless remains that the amount of money spent on training gear is usually a faithful measure of a boxer's material and moral investment in the pugilistic field.

In addition to the group of the athletes themselves, there is that of the coaches, advisers, visitors, relatives, friends, and onlookers who come to the gym to "conversate" or to watch the workouts, and whose successive presence continuously renews the ambiance of the place: Kitchen, a former boxer and unemployed metalworker who gets by between side jobs by snapping pictures of boxers during cards, which he then sells to them at exorbitant prices; O'Bannon, our mailman, who brags about his brilliant ring record (35 amateur victories, 33 of them by stoppage of the contest), for which however he has never been able to produce the least sliver of proof; a city employee by the name of T-Jay, a former European amateur champion in the welterweight division (he won that title while serving on an army base in Germany), who comes to monitor in person the workouts of his son, Carlo, who is starting out on an amateur career; Romi, a tiny Filipino who works as a foreman and serves as trainer-cornerman for the former cruiserweight world champion Alfonzo Ratliff; Oscar, a jovial businessman in his fifties who directs a contracting firm that specializes in building rehab (he regularly pitches in alongside his laborers), and who paces up and down the gym for entire afternoons, wearing a tall cowboy hat and a river of thick gold-plated chains and medallions around his neck, observing and advising the fighters for hours on end, despite the fact that he knows next to nothing about the Sweet science; Elijah, the owner of a small chain of laundromats in the ghetto and proud manager of two of the club's fresh recruits who have just turned pro; Charles Martin, a former trainer who occasionally serves as cornerman for the younger members of the gym; and a whole phalanx of old-timers, most of them retirees from the surrounding areas, for whom training sessions at the club are the major source of daily diversion.[45] Periodically, the (white) matchmaker Jack Cowen and his candy-pink suit will make a much-noted appearance; on these days, he holds mysterious confabulations with DeeDee to decide which of the club's boxers will participate in the cards he organizes every

---

45. Boxers who finish up their lives thus, as passive spectators in gyms, are referred to by the revealing term "lifers"; Hauser, *Black Lights,* 135.

month at the Park West, a yuppie nightclub in a prosperous neighborhood on the north side of town. The back room thus harbors at any given time from three to six people deeply immersed in passionate pugilistic discussions or absorbed in commenting on the sparring in progress.

We have seen how the ecology of the ghetto environment and its street culture predispose the youths of Woodlawn to conceive of boxing as a meaningful activity that offers them a stage on which to enact the core values of its masculine ethos. Viewed from that angle, the ghetto and the gym stand in a relation of contiguity and continuity. However, once *inside* the gym, this relation is ruptured and reversed by the Spartan discipline that boxers must obey, which harnesses street qualities to the pursuit of different, more astringently structured and distant goals. Thus the first thing that trainers always stress is what one is *not* supposed to do in the gym. Eddie, the coach-in-second at Woodlawn, offers the following enumeration of the prohibitions of the gym: "Cursin'. Smokin'. Loud talkin'. Disrespect for the women, disrespect for the coaches, disrespect for each other. No animosity, no braggin'." To which one could add a host of lesser and often implicit rules that converge to *pacify* the conduct of the gym's members.

Without having to display his severity, DeeDee sees to it that an iron discipline reigns in the Woodlawn gym as regards both behavior and training routines: it is forbidden to bring food or beverages into the club, to drink or talk during workouts, to rest sitting on the edge of a table, to alter the sequence of drills (for instance, to start a session by skipping rope instead of loosening up and shadowboxing) or modify a standard technical figure. There is no using of the equipment in an unconventional fashion, firing punches at objects, or sparring if one is not in full gear for it or, worse yet, faking a fight or tussling outside the ring. (Indeed, such "floor incidents" are so rare that they remain inscribed in the collective memory of the gym, unlike the routine violence of the street.) It is mandatory to wear a jockstrap under one's towel when coming out of the shower room and a dry change of clothes when leaving the gym. Finally, the children from the day-care center or the neighborhood who come in to admire the efforts of their elders must not under any pretext get near the bags. One must even watch closely one's language: DeeDee will not allow the expression "to fight" to be used in lieu of "to box" (or "to spar" for sparring sessions); and neither he nor the club regulars use vulgar language or curse words in their conversations in the gym.

Most clauses of these implicit "internal regulations" of the club are visible only in the deportment and demeanor of the regulars who have gradually internalized them, and they are brought to explicit attention only when violated.[46] Those who do not manage to assimilate this unwritten code of conduct are promptly dismissed by DeeDee or strongly advised to transfer to another gym. All in all, as will become apparent hereafter when we examine the regimen and ethics of training, the gym functions in the manner of a *quasi-total institution* that purports to regiment the whole existence of the fighter—his use of time and space, the management of his body, his state of mind, and his most intimate desires. So much so that pugilists often compare working out in the gym to entering the military.

BUTCH: In the gym, you learn discipline, self-control. You learn tha' you s'pose to go to bed early, git up early, do your road work, take care of yerself, eat the right foods. Uh, yer body is a *machine,* it's s'pose to be well-tuned. You learn to have some control so far as rippin' an' runnin' the streets, social life. It jus' gives you kin' of like an *army, soldier mentality,* an' [chuckling] tha's real good for folks.

CURTIS: The average guy that trains in this gym, kid or man, he *matures,* see, 85 percent, 85 percent more than if he was out on d'street. 'Cause it discipline him to try to be a young man, to try to have sportsmanship, ring generalship, you know, uh, I don' know . . . [stumbles] It's more like, I coul' sit up here an' give you a line of things, you know, but [you can] break it down to: it works *like bein' in the military,* it show you how to be a *gentleman* and all, and learn *respect.*

The *boxing gym thus defines itself in and through a relation of symbiotic opposition to the ghetto* that surrounds and enfolds it: at the same time that it recruits from among its youth and draws on its masculine culture of physical toughness, individual honor, and bodily performance, it stands opposed to the street as order is to disorder, as the individual and collective regulation of passions is to their private and public anarchy, as the constructive—at least from the standpoint of the social life and sense of self of the fighter—and controlled violence of a strictly policed and clearly circumscribed agonistic exchange is to the violence,

---

46. Most of the other gyms I have observed in Chicago and visited in other cities broadcast their rules in the form of a standardized list posted on the entrance door or on a wall, or yet hung from the ceiling for all to see. It appears that the more unstable and socially disparate the membership of a boxing club, the more explicit and conspicuous its regulations.

seemingly devoid of rhyme or reason, of the unpredictable and un-bounded confrontations symbolized by the rampant crime and drug trafficking that infest the neighborhood.

The law of the gym

Trainer Mickey Rosario welcomes a new recruit to his boxing gym in East Harlem, Manhattan's main Puerto Rican neighborhood:[47]

"Okay, first thing you got to know is the rules. We don't allow no cursing here. We don't allow no fighting, except in the ring. I ain't here to waste your time and you ain't here to waste mine. I don't smoke and I don't drink and I don't chase womens. Sure, I like pretty girls. But I'm just looking. I got nice furnitures up at my house. I can take my wife out and have a dinner somewhere. I work. I work in a hospital and if I can't work in a hospital, I work as a mechanic. I got license number two and three. I can drive whatever kind of truck. I can work in drugstores. You understand?"

The kid clearly did not.

"What I'm saying, I'm sacrificing my wife and kids and myself for you, you sure as hell going to sacrifice yourself for you. Rules is rules, no argument. You understand?"

"Yes," said the kid. He'd been drawn in, as if on a string, to stand in front of the trainer's desk.

"If you right you wrong, if you disagree with me. Understand?"

"Yes."

"I say six rounds of rope, I don't mean four. I say 'jump,' I want you to jump."

"Yes."

"And you don't come down till I tell you. If I tell you."

"Yes."

"Ain't but one boss here."

47. The following dialogue is excerpted from Plummer, *Buttercups and Strong Boys*, 56–57.

"Yes."

"And you looking at him."

"Yes."

"Understand?"

"Yes."

"Still want in?"

"Yes."

"Sure?"

"Yes."

"Okay, I need your I.D. papers. I need four pictures. I need fifteen bucks for the ABF card. I need another twenty-five dues for the year. . . . What you doing with youself nowadays? School? Working?"

"Well, I'm kind of between things just . . ."

"You a bum."

The kid jerked back as if he'd been struck. He stared at the trainer in disbelief. Then quickly looked about him to see who else has heard the taunt, his eyes lighting on my eyes, using them as blocks and sprinting off. After a while he spoke.

"Yes, I'm a bum. But I don't want to be one no more."

"You going to hate me," said Mickey, finally softening. "That come first. Later, you going to love me."

A Scientifically Savage Practice

If the hallmark of practice is, as Pierre Bourdieu contends, that it follows "a logic that is performed directly in bodily gymnastics" without the intervention of discursive consciousness and reflective explication,[48] that

---

48. Pierre Bourdieu, *The Logic of Practice* (Stanford: Stanford University Press, 1990), 89.

is, by excluding the contemplative and de-temporalizing posture of the theoretical gaze, then few practices may be said to be more "practical" than boxing. For the rules of the pugilistic art boil down to bodily moves that can be fully apprehended only in action and place it at the very edge of that which can be intellectually grasped and communicated. Moreover, boxing consists of a series of strategic exchanges in which one pays for one's hermeneutical mistakes immediately, the force and frequency of the blows taken (or the "punishment" received, in pugilistic parlance) providing an instantaneous assessment of the performance: action and its evaluation are fused and reflexive return is by definition excluded from the activity. This means that one cannot construct a science of this "social art," that is, of a "pure practice without theory," as Emile Durkheim defines it,[49] without undergoing a practical initiation into it, in real time and space. To understand the universe of boxing requires one to immerse oneself in it firsthand, to learn it and experience its constitutive moments from the inside. Native understanding of the object is here the necessary condition of an adequate knowledge of the object.[50]

The "culture" of the boxer is not made up of a finite sum of discrete information, of notions that can be transmitted by words and normative models that would exist independently of their application. Rather, it is formed of a diffuse complex of postures and (physical and mental) gestures that, being continually (re)produced in and through the very functioning of the gym, exist in a sense only in action, and in the traces that this action leaves within (and upon) bodies. This explains the tragedy of the impossible reconversion of the prizefighter at the end of his career: the specific capital he possesses is entirely embodied and, once it has been used, devoid of value in any other domain. Pugilism is an ensemble of techniques in Marcel Mauss's sense, that is, of *acts* traditionally thought to be effective,[51] practical knowledge composed of

49. Émile Durkheim, *Education and Sociology* (New York: Free Press, [1922] 1956), 78.
50. It is no doubt for this reason that the most sociologically perspicacious studies remain, some thirty years after their publication, the two short articles previously cited by Nathan Hare (a young professional fighter who went from the ring to earning a doctorate in sociology at the University of Chicago) and by the pair of S. K. Weinberg (a sociologist and amateur boxer) and Henri Arond (a trainer).
51. "I call technique an act that is traditional and efficacious," writes Marcel Mauss, "Les techniques du corps," 371 (translation, 104), before going on to emphasize that the body is "the first and most natural technical object, and at the same time technical means, of man."

schemata that are thoroughly immanent to practice. It follows that the inculcation of the dispositions that make the boxer comes down to a process of *Bildung* of the body, a particular (re)socialization of physiology in which "the function of pedagogical work is to replace the savage body. . . . with a body 'habituated,' that is, temporally structured"[52] and kinetically remodeled according to the specific demands of the field.

The training of the prizefighter is an intensive and exacting discipline—all the more so when the club is of high caliber and the head coach demanding while seeming to ask nothing—that aims at transmitting, in a practical manner, by way of *direct embodiment* a practical mastery of the fundamental (corporeal, visual, and mental) schemata of boxing. The most striking character of the workout is its repetitive, denuded, ascetic quality: its different phases are infinitely repeated day after day, week after week, with only barely perceptible variations. Many aspiring boxers turn out to be unable to tolerate the "monastic devotion, . . . [the] absolute subordination of the self"[53] that this training demands and give up after a few weeks or else vegetate in the gym until DeeDee invites them to pursue their careers elsewhere.

"The first two qualities a good trainer needs. . . . are punctuality and reliability, for him and his fighters."[54] The gym is open every day except Sunday, during the hours when DeeDee is there, meaning one to seven (with minor seasonal variations). The athletes come when they want to or when they can; most train between four and six in the afternoon and invariably occupy the same time slot, during which they repeat the same exercises to the saturation point. The imperative of regularity is such that a reputed boxer only has to stop training for a prolonged period for the most outlandish rumors to immediately spread. Thus, in February 1989, when Curtis temporarily stopped coming to the gym, the word was going around that his career was over: he was "fooling around" with neighborhood girls and had "caught AIDS."

Among the most frequent misrepresentation of the Sweet science is the idea that the training of professional boxers consists essentially of endlessly punching each other silly. In fact, pugilists spend only a small fraction of their total time of preparation facing an opponent—or a partner: the importance of the distinction will become clearer later—in the ring. Much of the workout consists not of "ringwork" but of "floorwork"

52. Pierre Bourdieu, *Esquisse d'une théorie de la pratique. Précédée de trois études d'ethnologie kabyle* (Geneva: Droz, 1972), 196.
53. Oates, *On Boxing,* 28–29.
54. Star trainer-manager Gil Clancy, cited in Hauser, *Black Lights,* 43.

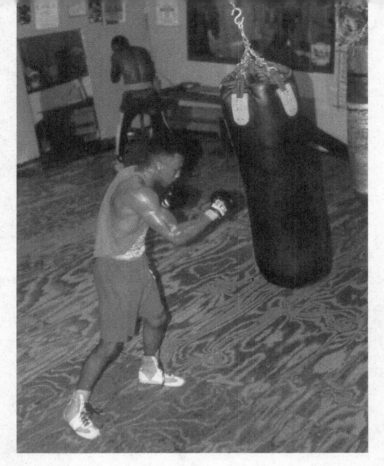

"Floorwork": Tony beats the heavy bag while Anthony shadowboxes in front of the mirror

and "tablework." The members of the Woodlawn Boys Club train in the gym on average four to five times a week, sometimes more. The typical menu of a session, which lasts for forty-five to ninety minutes, consists always of the same ingredients, which each boxer calibrates to his taste and needs: in order, "shadowboxing" in front of a mirror and in the ring, working the hard bags and on the speed bag, jumping rope, and abdominal exercises. The frequency and duration of the workouts fluctuate notably over time and from one boxer to another. As an example, here is Pete's typical session, which would apply to most pugilists "in training" for a fight. He gets to the gym just before 5 p.m., takes his clothes out of his locker, and changes quickly into a boxing T-shirt in honor of

"Ringwork":
Lorenzo working on
the pads with his
trainer Eddie

▷ 11A

"Tablework": Curtis
doing sit-ups
with the help of
his cousin

Smithie and Anthony
jumping rope at the
end of their workout

"Leonard-Hearns: The War II," white high-top shoes, and tight black shorts. After wrapping his hands and chatting with DeeDee and colleagues in the back room, it is time to get to work. He begins with three rounds of shadowboxing in front of the small mirror, throwing combinations (jab, jab, right, left hook), moving forward and back across from his reflection—and sometimes using weights (short metal cylinders) held in each hand to increase muscular traction. Then he climbs into the ring for three rounds of simulated boxing, during which he practices his slips, polishes his feints and pivots, and moves swiftly about and along the ropes, battling an imaginary opponent. Pete climbs back out of the ring to take his favorite pair of "bag gloves" from the office, then starts three rounds on the soft bag: he fires intense series of jabs, followed by straight punches with both hands, short uppercuts and hooks, and works on punching his way out of simulated clinches—the full repertoire of the pugilist. In the last round, Pete fills the gym with the sound of little guttural cries as he "unloads" and lets his fists fly. Taking just enough time to rinse his face off with the communal water bottle sitting near the ring, he then goes for one last round of slugging on the uppercut bag hanging against the wall near the ring. Next come two rounds on the speed bag to hone his hand speed and hand-eye coordination. Pete closes his workout with three rounds of rope skipping at fast speed and sets of varied stomach exercises (designated by the generic term "tablework") and pushups (classic ones, with his feet propped up on a chair, leaning on his closed fists, or clapping his hands each time he comes up off the floor).

Onto this basic pattern, which varies little, are grafted other exercises, like work on the jab bag or double-end bag (a contraption formed of one or two small punching balls tied to the floor and ceiling by rubber ropes), stretching and windmill movements with a heavy metal bar, as well as drills expressly conceived to reinforce one's defensive muscular armature: once a week, Pete patiently lets Eddie hammer at his stomach with a medicine ball; every other workout, he spends long minutes doing neck lifts, sitting on a chair, with a weighted helmet on his head. Working the pads, where Pete fires punches at padded mitts held out by his trainer, supplies a bridge between the imaginary fighting of shadowboxing and hitting the bag, on the one hand, and the actual sparring in the ring, on the other. Exercises inside the gym are preceded and supported by a demanding regimen of "roadwork" outside: boxers from Woodlawn run an average of three to five miles a day, six days a week, in winter as in summer.

■ **Working the pads**

2 March 1989. I'm ready: wearing blue sweat pants with black bermuda shorts over them and a red sweatshirt and gloves, I bounce up and down in place waiting for Eddie, who's slipping on his pads with care; he thrusts his fingers through their sleeves to the ends, and O'Bannon helps him slip on the second pad and tighten the buckle. DeeDee woofs: *"Time, work!"* Eddie plants himself in front of me and raises his right hand up above his shoulder: "Jab!" I lunge forward and smash my left fist into the leather mitt he's holding out to me. *Snap, snap, snap,* I got juice, I feel great and my punches are landing right on target—you know right away if you're hitting the bull's-eye because the pad makes a snapping sound instead of a muffled one. My fist shoots out from my guard at the second he calls for it. The moment I hit his hand, Eddie gives a sharp little downward poke of his wrist to counter the force of my jab. "Double up on yo' jab, that's it . . . Step in, move in with your jab."

I'm throwing furious punches into the pad that he's now holding out on the right and on the left in turn. Their snapping fills me with joy and whips up my energy. I'm already streaming with sweat. "One-two, jab an' right hand com-bi-na-tion, com'on, one-two." I can't get both fists to snap sharply, so we go back to simple jabs. It's killing. Eddie moves around on the gym floor in small steps, circling about me. I try to keep in motion at all times and stay on him. "Now throw a right to d'body, that's it." *Snap-snap!* It's starting to really snap again! Tch-tch, snap-snap! Eddie changes the exercise: "Now, throw a jab to d'head [holding his pad up in the air], jab to d'body [with the pad halfway down]. Then double up on yo' jab to d'body. Yeah tha's good, *keep it up!"* I keep marching forward and punching in synch, my breathing has taken on the rhythm of the blows. Eddie, still planted in front of me (he's so round everywhere, he looks like a miniature sumo wrestler), is holding out both leather mitts to me at once: "Now, gimme a jab, left-right-left an' finish up with a right cross, 'kay?" I take little steps forward, jab, snap-snap-snap, pivoting on my back foot and stretching out as far as I can to hit my target cleanly with the last right. "Keep goin', keep goin', keep yo' left shoulder lined up when you throw the right." *"Time out!"* Whew, already I can't take any more: my lungs are burning and my arms weigh a hundred tons. I take deep breaths during the rest period to try and get my second wind. I've only got thirty seconds. I concentrate to gather up all my energy. I may do two rounds at this pace, but never three.

"Time in!" Eddie holds out the pads, turned down toward the floor, to work on short uppercuts. It's a more difficult movement, which comes less "naturally" (if it can be said that anything comes naturally to me in the ring). The punch is thrown upward from underneath, with the hand perpendicular to the elbow. You have to really turn your fist clockwise toward the inside as it comes up, but I always feel like I'm missing my target even when I hit it. I lean forward a little more to get under Eddie's invisible guard. "Com'on, you can do it, right, left, keep movin', move yo' feet." Right uppercut, left uppercut. Thumping. "That's good, keep yo' left hand up after d'jab, *keep goin'!"* Eddie roars, as he backs around the heavy bag to force me to combine punches and footwork. I fire a right uppercut, a left uppercut, a jab to loosen up my arm, then a double uppercut, right and left, really bending my knees with a pelvic thrust forward—this is killing me! I can't feel my right wrist or my shoulders anymore. I'm gasping for oxygen while dispensing uppercuts nonstop like a robot. When they make the right sound against the mitt, it motivates me to hit harder the next time. But I really can't take any longer and I have to let my guard drop so I can catch my breath.

We move on to a new drill: "Now you throw a one-two, duck to slip my right an' counter with another one-two from d'other side." At first I don't quite understand the maneuver, but after two or three tries I find the rhythm: left jab to the right pad, right cross to the same pad, immediately followed by a left hook on the other pad by pivoting the arm bent in a half-circle and then another right hook; Eddie responds by throwing a wide hook at me, which I elude by bending my upper body just enough, then retort with two short hooks. If he counters from the right, I slip and counterattack right-left, and vice versa. It's super but even more exhausting than the other combinations. Snap, snap-snap, snap-snap, slip, snap-snap!

I tend to lose my balance when I pivot. DeeDee's voice thunders from the back room: "Stay on your feet, keep your right leg back an' turn your foot inside." I chase Eddie between the hanging bags. He stops for a second to readjust the pads. I keep moving around him, pretending to parry and block imaginary punches. We start back up. "Com'on, man, you're gettin' there! Yeah, *that's it, punch,* that's good, Louie, pump yo' jab!" He barks out his encouragement more and more loudly. I can no longer see anything other than the black slabs he's holding out to me and that I have to hit at all costs, and his pudgy blue chest slipping away. My lungs are about to explode; I don't have any legs or strength left. I follow him, jabbing in a fog of fatigue, sweat, and excitement. My fists are quickly growing too heavy, my arms numb. I'm exhausted but I keep boxing like a punching machine. Snap-snap, bang, bang-bang. I'm losing my energy at lightning speed and my punches aren't snapping any more. Eddie's stentorian voice lifts me up: "Com'on, one mo', one mo', keep it up, Louie!"

In a half-coma, I keep hitting and breathing in synch, throwing a punch with every gulp of air I expel. I have the sensation of being mounted on a machinery of which I'm both the engine and a piece. Eddie yaps his encouragements. I find extra sources of energy and march forward, punch, bring my fists back, aim, hit. I draw on my last reserves to close out this series. "Keep goin', *you're cookin', you're cookin' in d'kitchen!* Com'on, Louie! You're cookin' in d'kitchen! *Mind over matter!* Com'on, you can do it, 's all in yo' head, you're cookin'!" One more push, snap-snap, bang, boom-boom. *"Time out!"* Finally it's over! I am at the edge of asphyxiation, tetanized with exhaustion, totally drained in six minutes. I feel like I'm going to vomit up my lungs and pass out.

Prizefighters have often been compared to artists, but a more apposite analogy would look to the world of the factory or the artisan's workshop. For the Sweet science resembles in manifold aspects a skilled, if repetitive, manual craft.[55] Professional boxers themselves consider training as work ("It's a job I gotta do," "I got to do my homework," "It's like havin'

---

55. As Gerald Early perceptively puts it in his "Three Notes Toward a Cultural Definition of Boxing": "The one word that comes to mind more than any other watching the fighters work in the gym is 'proletariat.' These men are honestly, and in a most ghastly way, *toiling,* and what is most striking is how much more grotesque this work is than, say, the nightmare of an assembly line. And proletariat is such an appropriate word for fighters whom we also call stiffs and bums." "Three Notes toward a Cultural Definition of Boxing," in *Reading the Fights,* ed. Oates and Halpern, 33.

a second job") and their body as a tool. Knowing that their performance in the ring depends directly on their preparation in the gym, they train with obstinacy so as to be at the peak of their physical form and technical mastery when the time comes to face off in the squared circle and thereby curb their anxiety: "You win your fight in the gym" says a boxing adage well known to the regulars. The preparation can be so intense and grueling that the bout will seem easy by contrast; indeed many boxers deem that training is the hardest facet of their trade. George Plimpton's description of champion Joe Frazier's training could be borrowed to depict many anonymous club fighters: "He is a joyful masochist in the gym, flogging himself without respite in pursuit of the toughness that will make him oblivious of his opponent's aggression. . . . 'I work so hard in camp, punish myself, and then when I get to the real thing it's that much more easy for me. When the bell rings, I'm ready. I'm turned on.'"[56]

But the sacrifices demanded of the boxer do not end at the doors to the gym. The monastic devotion required by the preparation for a bout extends deep into his social life and permeates every realm of his private existence. To reach his optimal fight weight, every boxer must abide by a strict diet (avoid all sugar, starchy and fried foods, eat fish, white meats and steamed vegetables, drink water or tea). He must keep regular hours and inflict on himself an early curfew to give his body time to recover from the day's exertion. And, as soon as he first enters the gym, he is taught that he must forsake all sexual contact for weeks before his fight for fear of losing his vital bodily fluids and sapping his physical strength and his mental resolve.[57] More so than the training, these rules of abstinence make the life of the professional fighter difficult, if not downright burdensome. Thus, for Jake, a lightweight from the nearby town of Gary, on the Indiana border, who had come to Woodlawn one afternoon to "glove up," the most painful sacrifice demanded by his preparation for a fight is not clocking in to train every day, but

> layin' off the junk-food-the-hamburger-the-french-fries, *no sex* you know. I like drinkin' beer, no beer, you know no light beer, you know, *dedication* when you gotta really dig deep down inside of you and go for what you want—you gotta say like "well no women this month," you know, an' no hamburgers. [Quickly, his voice rising to a feverish

56. George Plimpton, "Three with Moore," in Oates and Halpern, *Reading the Fights,* 150–170; quot. 173.
57. Wacquant, "Pugs at Work," 75–82, for an extended analysis.

pitch as if revolted at the mere thought] You know what it's like to eat no junk food for a whole month, no cokes or ice cream or chocolate cookies? *It be hell* wouldn't it!?

The extreme repetitiousness and monotony of training does not preclude finding a host of small pleasures in it, without which it would be hard to persevere in the trade.[58] There is first the virile friendship of the club, expressed through glances and smiles, snatches of conversation, jokes and encouragements muttered during "timeouts," or affectionate taps on the back and hand (boxers ritually salute one another by hitting each other's gloved fists first from above and then from below).[59] As I learned from boxing regularly with Ashante, a very special carnal fraternity ties habitual sparring partners to one another, based on the risk that each takes with the other and in turn imposes on the other.

Next comes the joy of feeling one's body blossom, loosen, and gradually get "tuned" to the specific discipline. Besides the oft-vivid sentiment of corporeal wholeness and "flow" it provides,[60] training becomes its own reward when it leads one to master a difficult gesture that offers the sensation of decupling one's power, or when it enables one to score a victory over oneself (as when you overcome the anxiety of sparring with a rough partner). Finally, boxers relish the fact that they "share membership in the same small guild," renowned for its physical toughness and bravery; they enjoy knowing that "they are different from other people. They are fighters."[61] This satisfaction is no less real for being discreet,

58. For similar observations about the training of competitive swimmers in California, see Daniel F. Chambliss, "The Mundanity of Excellence: An Ethnographic Report on Stratification and Olympic Swimmers," *Sociological Theory* 7, 1 (spring 1989): 70–86.
59. It should be emphasized here that the forms of respect current in the gym are exclusively masculine ones, which affirm not only the solidarity and hierarchy among the boxers but also, and in a manner that is all the more effective as it is more hidden from consciousness, the superiority of men ("real" men, that is) over women, a term that is physically absent but symbolically omnipresent in negative in the gym as in the entire pugilistic universe.
60. Boxers talk about "a natural high" and compare the sensorial experience of intensive training (or fighting) to having sex or to an orgasm. For an instructive parallel analysis with the sentiment of "flow" among mountain climbers, see R. G. Mitchell, *Mountain Experience: The Psychology and Sociology of Adventure* (Chicago: University of Chicago Press, 1983), 153–169.
61. George Bennett and Pete Hamill, *Fighters* (New York: Dolphin Books, 1978), 23; also Sammons, *Beyond the Ring*, 237; Weinberg and Arond, "Occupational Culture of the Boxer," 463; Hare, "Study of the Black Fighter," 7–8.

and the "regulars" of the gym express it by proudly wearing boxing patches, T-shirts, and jackets bearing the insignia of the trade. Added to all this is the emotional attachment to one's gym, which boxers readily compare to a "home" or a "second mother," terms that clearly speak of the protective and nurturing functions it possesses in their eyes.

The surface simplicity of the boxer's gestures and moves could not be more deceiving: far from being "natural" and self-evident, the basic punches (left jab and hook, right cross, straight right hand and uppercut) are difficult to execute properly and presuppose a thorough "physical rehabilitation," a genuine remolding of one's kinetic coordination, and even a psychic conversion. It is one thing to visualize and to understand them in thought, quite another to realize them and, even more so, to combine them in the heat of action. "For a punch to be really thrown effectively, it is unimaginable the number of conditions that have to be met."[62] For instance, throwing a jab to keep your adversary at a distance or to set him up for an attack requires, among other simultaneous conditions, properly placing your feet, hips, shoulders, and arms; you must "pump" your left arm out toward your adversary at the opportune time (aiming at the head or upper body) while taking a step forward, with knees slightly bent and chin tucked into the hollow of the shoulder; you must line up your hand and front shoulder, tighten and turn your wrist clockwise forty-five degrees at the moment of impact—but no sooner—and transfer your body weight to the front leg, all the while holding your right hand close to your cheek so as to block or parry your opponent's counter.

Theoretical mastery is of little help so long as the move is not inscribed within one's bodily schema; and it is only after it has been assimilated by the body in and through endless physical drills repeated *ad nauseam* that it becomes in turn fully intelligible to the intellect. There is indeed *a comprehension of the body* that goes beyond—and comes prior to—full visual and mental cognizance. Only the permanent carnal experimentation that is training, as a coherent complexus of "incorporating practices,"[63] can enable one to acquire this practical mastery of the practical rules of pugilism, which precisely satisfies the

---

62. "Avancer, reculer, riposter," interview with French national trainer Aldo Consentino, *Libération,* 11–12 February 1989: 31.
63. Paul Connerton, *How Societies Remember* (Cambridge: Cambridge University Press, 1989), chapter 2.

condition of dispensing with the need to constitute them as such in consciousness.

To provide an adequate account of the almost imperceptible process whereby one becomes involved and invested in the game (more so than one would sometimes wish), the long climb that takes the novice from initial horror or indifference, mingled with bodily shame and embarrassment, to curiosity and thence to pugilistic interest, and even to the carnal pleasure of boxing and the irrepressible desire to "get it on" in the ring (the erotic connotation of the folk expression is not innocent), one would need to quote *in extenso* the field notes taken daily after each workout over the months. Their very mundanity and redundancy would make it possible to grasp concretely the maddeningly slow drift that occurs, from week to week, in the mastery of the moves; in the understanding—most often retrospective and purely gestural—of pugilistic technique; and the modification that transpires in one's relationship to one's body and one's perception of the gym and the activities of which it is the support. The assimilation of pugilism is the fruit of a *labor of mutual involvement* (*intéressement*) of the body and mind, a labor that, produced by the infinite repetition of the same moves, proceeds through a discontinuous series of infinitesimal motions, difficult to discern individually but the accumulation of which over time produces appreciable progress, without one ever being able to separate them out, date them, or measure them precisely.

What is most likely to elude the outside observer[64] is the *extreme sensuousness of the pugilistic initiation.* One would need to call up all the tools of visual sociology or even those of a truly sensual sociology that remains to be invented to convey the process whereby the boxer becomes organismically "invested" by and bound to the game as he progressively makes it his—boxers commonly use metaphors of blood and drugs to explain this particular relation akin to a *mutual possession.* For it is with all of one's senses that one gradually converts to the world of prizefighting and its stakes. To give this proposition its full force, one would need to be able to capture and convey at once the odors (the

64. And even more so the reader, who can enter into the pugilistic universe only through the mediation of the word. Now, the mere passage to a scriptural medium of communication irrevocably transforms the experience to be conveyed. What Willener writes about music is very apposite to boxing here: "One of the hurdles to any sociology of music remains that *one does not know how to talk about it.* For one must translate a musical sense in a nonmusical language." Alfred Willener, "Le concerto de trompette de Haydn," *Actes de la recherche en sciences sociales* 75 (November 1988): 54–63; quot. 61, emphasis mine.

heady smell of liniment sniffed full force, the sweat hanging in the air, the stink of the situp table, the leathery scent of the gloves); the cadenced "thump" of punches against the bags and the clanking of the chains they hang from, each bag having its own sound, each drill its tonality, each boxer his own manner of accenting the machine gun–like rattle of the speed bag; the light "tap-tap" or frantic galloping of feet on the wooden floor while skipping rope, or the muffled squeak they let out as they move gingerly on the canvas of the ring; the rhythmic puffing, hissing, sniffing, blowing, and groaning characteristic of each athlete; and especially the collective layout and synchronization of the bodies in the space of the gym, whose mere sight suffices to wield lasting pedagogical effects; not to forget the temperature, whose variation and intensity are not the least relevant properties of the room. The combination of all these elements produces a sort of *sensuous intoxication* that is key to the education of the apprentice boxer.

Initiation

15 October 1988. I enter the gym from the back. DeeDee's sitting in the office, along with big Butch and three youngsters. I greet everyone and shake hands. (We always do: it's a daily routine and a much-valued mark of respect.) Right away DeeDee asks me: "Louie, you got yo' mouthpiece wichyou?" "Yeah, I got it, *why*?" The old coach nods slowly with his chin, a gleam in his eye. I realize that today is my baptism by fire: I'm going to do my first tryout in the ring! I feel a twinge of apprehension simultaneously with the satisfaction of having finally come to this rite of passage. I hadn't expected it and I'm worried about not being in very good shape; what's more, I still have a tenacious pain in my right wrist. But I just can't back out now. Besides, I'm eager to get it on; after all, I've been waiting for this moment for weeks—is it not strange to get all excited at the prospect of getting smacked in the noggin? . . .

I scope the place out to see who's going to give me my first thrashing in the ring. Will it be Butch? Just then Olivier walks in through the back door. DeeDee tells him that he's going to spar too and so he should get ready: "I wanna see your nose bleed. You're a doc so you can treat yo'self. I just wanna see your nose bleed a lil', hu-hu." Black humor. The Doc and I try to comfort each other by laughing loudly as we put on our gear . . . It is indeed Butch who's going to break us in. He's warming up on the floor, ripping through the air with ferocious punches in his sleeveless blue jersey. At the thought of discovering him across from me between the ropes I suddenly find him even more muscular than usual, a veritable colossus even: Butch is almost a head taller than I; his torso and arms are like rolling balls of ebony glistening under the gym's pallid ceiling lights. . . . Is it really reasonable to climb into the ring with such an athlete? He asks me to lace up his sparring gloves for him. I take advantage of the opportunity to remind him that it's the first time I'll be boxing for real, just so there are no misunderstandings (my good old pal Butch, there's a nice Butch . . .). He complains that his last fight at the Park West was cancelled because his opponent didn't "make the weight" prescribed for the bout. As for him, Butch has no trouble getting under the bar: he just has to pay attention to what he eats and run like a hare. That's all good and fine, but he still outweighs me by a good twenty pounds (it would be less intimidating if he were an eighty-pound shrimp).

I ask DeeDee to wrap my hands; better have him do it this time, when it counts. I get going with a round of shadowboxing in front of the mirror. There are six of us today, including Reese, Boyd and Tony, and each is warming up in his own corner, getting ready for the sparring. I do one round on the speed bag to loosen my right wrist, but as I start in on another set in front of the mirror (jab-right moving forward, pivot and left hook, jab and a step back), DeeDee shouts to me: "Louie, what d'hell you doin'? Don't wear yourself out like that or you won't have no energy left for sparrin'. You're gonna get knocked flat on yo' ass right away." "He's gonna knock me on my ass anyway." The old coach calls me into the back room to put on my cup—this thick leather breeches that protects the groin and pelvis resembles a rigid harness; you put your legs through it then lace it up and tie it behind your waist. I have trouble squeezing my ass into it. DeeDee then hands me a small head guard that looks more like a net shopping bag than the real heaume that Butch is wearing—a massive half-cylinder that covers his entire face, with two cross-slits that show only the eyes, nose, mouth, and chin. I sink my head into the head gear and buckle it up; too tight and . . . backwards! I turn it around, rebuckle it, and DeeDee adjusts it. "Is that tight enough? Where's your mouthpiece?" I hook my white plastic mouthpiece onto my upper teeth, which makes me feel like an animal being readied for the slaughterhouse.

DeeDee instructs me to slather my face with grease. I dip two fingers into the jar and start nervously spreading the Vaseline on my temples, my cheekbones, my brow. I put on way too much, which gets a laugh out of DeeDee: *"Not so much! Just on your nose and above your eyes, do it in front of d'mirror."* I remove the excess Vaseline and spread it carefully along the ridge of my eyebrows and then my nose—I better not get it broken during training! Does that ever happen, I ask? Sure does, says DeeDee . . . From the metal cabinet in the corner, the old coach digs out a pair of big red gloves into which he makes me slip my wrapped hands—enormous, overpadded red mittens, twice as long as my hands (competition gloves are much thinner and lighter). He has me make a fist inside the glove, then laces it up for me, carefully going underneath my wrist before closing the glove up with the help of a big piece of silver-grey duct tape, which he skillfully sticks over the laces. While he's gloving me up, DeeDee follows the two young guys moving around in the ring out of the corner of his eye. The tall one is named Rico; he's a superb athlete, stout and long-limbed, with a magnificent musculature and a technique that makes him look like a pro. I'm nonplussed to learn that he's only fourteen years old. "Yep, he's young but he got a long way to go too. He's gotta work harder'n that. But he's a good kid." Between rounds, a tyke who's knee-high to a grasshopper shadowboxes in the ring, then comes over to have DeeDee put a pair of miniature gloves on him: he's nine years old and already fights in tournaments.

Back in front of the mirror, I feel like I'm hallucinating when I see myself for the first time outfitted in the gear of the complete boxer. Is that really me, decked out in this black leather belt girdling my hips halfway up my belly, with my spindly legs sticking out below in purple sweatpants? My gigantic red gloves make me feel as if I had artificial limbs; the leather helmet squeezes my head and collapses my field of vision; the mouthpiece sticking through my lips gives me the features of a Cro-Magnon. A total metamorphosis! I am at once stunned, impressed, and incredulous. [. . .]

No more time to anguish: Olivier is stepping out of the ring, doubled over from exhaustion, it's my turn. I quickly climb the little step-stool and slip through the ropes—just like in the movies. And, all of a sudden, finding myself alone in the ring, which seems at once immense and minuscule, I come to the brutal realization that I'm the one squaring off with Butch and that he's going to clean my clock. I'm tense and at the same time furiously eager to see what it's going to be like. Submerged in a hyperacute awareness of my own body, of its fragility, in the carnal sensation of my *corporeal integrity* and of the risk at which I'm putting it. At the same time, the leather shell into which I've been strapped gives me the unreal sensation that this same body has escaped from me—as if I had mutated into a sort of human tank. The cup is sawing at my abdominal muscles and slowing down my movements. The head guard is gripping my skull. Instead of hands, I have two large appendages like soft hammers at the ends of remote-controlled arms that respond to my commands only imperfectly. I sneak a peek over at Butch, who's hopping in place, puffing heavily, with an inscrutable look on his face. Olivier survived, there's no reason it should be any different with me. But what if I took a hard punch and stupidly got myself injured? What if he knocked the jibbies out of me? Come on, this is just some unpleasant drill you got to go through, like going to the dentist.

DeeDee's hoarse voice resounds; *"Time!"* and we're off on a three-minute journey into the unknown! I crouch and walk toward Butch, who does the same. We touch gloves in the center of the ring. An exchange of friendly jabs. Feint, approach, back up, feint, we're checking each other out. I attempt a jab-right combination, only to immediately collect Butch's big yellow glove smack in the chops. First hit absorbed without too much damage. Phew! It comes fast! I move forward hesitantly and jab. Butch slips; another jab, another slip. I march resolutely onto him, but he slides away, avoids me with a simple twist of his upper body, pivots, and disappears from my field of vision. So begins a race-chase that will last a good half of the round. I follow him step for step, jab-jab-jab; he parries my fists with ease, sends me back a straight right that I counter with my right glove, another that I block . . . with my nose. I try to get in closer and, like the conscientious student that I am, repeat the moves that I've executed a thousand times in front of the mirror. I attempt a straight left followed by a right, like I do on the bag, only to get pasted with three juicy jabs. It feels like I've got hot coals up my nose. I beat a hasty retreat, chased by Butch, who now seems truly gigantic to me. His reach is too long and he moves too fast: I've hardly thrown my jab before his head is no longer there and he's punching my ticket with his left at will. *Ouch!* I always see his big yellow fist coming too late. *Pow!* Another right in the puss! I react with a few reckless jabs and finally land a left to his chest, yippee! But nine-tenths of my punches catch nothing but air or else curl up and die in his gloves. Butch stands me up with a mean right that snaps my head back. Afraid he's really rung my chimes, he interrupts the action: "You okay?" I signal him to keep going and readjust my head guard as best I can. I strain to advance on him, trying to execute my moves properly, aim, hit, pivot, but it's all in vain: I'm incapable of putting my combinations together while taking into account his movements and anticipations. *"Time out!"* Whew! Catch your breath, quick.

I go back to my corner, sucking in great gulps of air. Inexplicably, I am already completely wasted. Sparring looks easy from the outside, but once you're in the ring, it's not the same thing. Your perimeter of vision shrinks and gets saturated in the extreme: I'd be frankly incapable of saying what's happening outside a circle of about two yards around me. You've got to move constantly and sensory tension is at its peak, which is why I'm already drenched in sweat from head to toe. The perception of your opponent is warped: Butch's gloves seem to have become so enormous that they fill up the entire ring; and when by chance I manage to get close enough to him, I can't discern any place to hit him between his belt and his big yellow paws. My own body also seems different to me and doesn't obey me as promptly as I would wish. The punches don't really hurt (because we're not banging away) but they are irritating: it's vexing to "eat" several jabs in a row and you have the unpleasant sensation of your mug swelling up. The fists arrive at lightning speed and at surprising angles, whereas from the outside everything looks slow and predictable. Above all, the guy across from you is moving and slipping, which constantly changes the equation you're trying to solve. I wonder what Butch is thinking. Impossible to guess, since the face of a boxer surrounded by a head guard and deformed by a mouthpiece doesn't reveal very much—even the mean look he sports is artificially created by the mouthpiece, which makes the handsomest athlete look prognathous.

I've barely caught my breath when DeeDee bellows *"Time!"* again from the back room. The second round already? Damn, I didn't see that one-minute rest period go by! We resume our dance in the center of the ring. My apprehension has left me and I resolve to put pressure on Butch. But he sees that I'm getting bolder and he too kicks it into higher gear—just enough to keep me constantly off balance. I attempt a wide left hook, which earns me a sharp reprimand from DeeDee: "What're you doin'? Stop that right now, Louie, I don't know what you be doin' up in there." A second later, I collect a cement-truck right full in the face that makes me meditate on my mistake. Things are speeding up, yet these three minutes are truly in-ter-mi-na-ble. I feel like my gloves are too heavy, too bulky, they hamper me. I'm having trouble seeing behind my guard and following my opponent's movements. I'm always one beat behind, if not two: by the time I've made out that Butch is throwing a jab, it's already landed in my kisser. How to describe the sensation when his fist swoops down on me? I see a yellow saucer that all of a sudden grows bigger and bigger at breakneck speed, completely blocking my field of vision and *pow!* A stinging, some stars, and the screen clears again. The yellow saucer has pulled away, the light returns. But before I can attempt the slightest reaction, the flying saucer swooshes back to crash into my face again.

I'm getting a first-class ass-whipping. Butch is landing every punch he throws—fortunately he's not hitting hard, otherwise I would have been knocked down and out eons ago. I feel like I'm bleeding and wipe my nostrils with my fist: sure enough, there are traces of blood on my glove but they're dry, so it's not mine. Whew! I try my best to close in on Butch and get him in a clinch. But it's impossible to find a spot to hit: everywhere I run into his big yellow gloves and his arms knotted up with bulging muscles. He, on the other hand, is tossing me around as he likes. I step back and then lunge at him fearlessly—the hell with the jabs in the mug: I've got to get my licks in, too, after all. I manage to land several soft jabs and suddenly, divine surprise, I hit the bull's-eye, a straight right dead center in Butch's mullin. Instinctively, I almost say "Sorry!" out loud to Butch—but it's impossible with my mouthpiece in. Jeez, I definitely don't have a boxer's mentality! I feel vaguely guilty about having bopped him right in the schnoz, since I don't have any intention of hurting him. But mainly I fear his retaliation. And in fact things start moving faster, blows are coming in from every direction now. Butch is circling around me like a buzzard and landing every punch. I feel my fists flailing haphazardly while he lards me with stinging jabs. Suddenly

I again feel an irrepressible urge to flee and I even turn all the way around, my back to my partner, to protect myself from the blows raining down on me. *"Time out!"* The voice of deliverance!

DeeDee has no sooner hooted the end of the round that I've slipped through the ropes. I've had enough: I am de-ple-ted! I jump out of the ring to collapse into the waiting arms of Eddie, who's chortling with delight. "You still alive? You *survived?* How many rounds?" "Two, this is the first time I've ever sparred." "No kiddin'? First time? You're a *big-time boxer* now." He's gurgling with pleasure as he unlaces my gloves and helps me extirpate my hands, which are burning hot and moist. It's superexhausting, I truly don't understand how the pros can last ten and twelve rounds, while heaving truckloads of cinderblocks at each other to boot. Butch steps down out of the ring, I slap his gloves as a sign of thanks. Olivier tells me that my face is all red. My brow and nose are flaming, but when I look in the mirror I'm pleasantly surprised to discover that my face isn't as swollen as it feels. Gasping for breath and streaming with sweat, I make my way to DeeDee's office, where the old trainer is discreetly jubilating behind his little goatee. That's good, Louie, jump a lil' rope now." . . .

I close out the session with three rounds of jumping rope and two hundred situps. Afterward Olivier and I go tell DeeDee how pleased we are. "You did awright, botha you. You'll get in there again." "I sure hope so!" It's a lot more fun than working out endlessly on the heavy bag or in front of the mirror. We take leave of everyone with great ceremony, then once again go thank Butch, who's changing back into his civilian clothes in the little locker room. Warm handshakes. "I'm the one to thank *you* guys, that's a good start. You're gon' learn, learn how to hit and learn how to be mean. It's all about learnin'." We leave the gym proud as peacocks and go celebrate by devouring a giant-sized stuffed pizza on 57th Street.

The Social Logic of Sparring

If the typical professional boxer spends the bulk of his time outside the ring, endlessly rehearsing his moves in front of a mirror or on an assortment of bags so as to hone his technique, increase his power, and sharpen his speed and coordination, and even outside the gym eating up miles and miles of daily "roadwork," the climax and yardstick of training remains the sparring. The point of sparring—one also says "putting on the gloves" and "moving around"—is to approximate the conditions of the fight, with the difference that the boxers wear protective headgear and heavily padded gloves and that, as we will see, the brutality of the confrontation is greatly attenuated. Without regular practice in the ring against an opponent, the rest of the preparation would make little sense, for the peculiar mix of skills and qualities required by fighting cannot be assembled but between the ropes. Many a boxer who "looks a million dollars on the floor" turns out to be inept and helpless once faced with an adversary. As DeeDee explains:

> Hittin' bags is one damn thing—runnin', hittin' bags, shadow boxin's one thin', an' sparrin' is a hun'red percent different. 'Cause it's diff'rent use of muscles, so *you have to spar to git in shape to spar.* Yeah, I don't give a damn who you are, 'less you're a helluva damn good fighter that's *relax'* . . . . You gotta be relax', cool, the breathin's different an' everythin'. That's what it's all about. That's from experience.
>
> Louie: So you can't instruct a boxer on how to relax or breathe on the floor?
>
> DeeDee: *Hell no!* No, [shaking his head] uh-uh, you can't tell. You can talk about it, but it don't work.

Sparring, which has its own tempo (unless he is about to fight, a boxer should "put on the gloves" lightly or at distant intervals so as to minimize the wear and tear on his body),[65] is both a reward and a challenge. First, it represents the tangible payoff for a long week of hard and dull labor— it is on Saturday that most of the amateur boxers of the Woodlawn Boys Club tangle between the ropes. The gym's trainers pay close attention

---

65. Here again, one must note pronounced variations among gyms and individuals: some boxers prefer to spar on a regular basis, even when they do not have a fight coming up, either to be ready in case of a last-minute opportunity or because they are particularly fond of "putting the gloves on." Other clubs in Chicago, run by less attentive (or less competent) trainers, give their members more latitude. The municipal gym of Fuller Park, for example, is notorious for its laxity in this matter: according to several boxers who trained there before joining the Woodlawn Boys Club as well as my own observations, sparring sessions involving partners of very unequal grade in which one beats the other to a pulp, without holding back, without even any supervision, are a common occurence.

to the physical condition of their charges and do not hesitate to bar from sparring those who are in their eyes culpable of having neglected their preparation. "Little Anthony ain't puttin' no gloves on today, DeeDee," Eddie brays, one hot afternoon in mid-August. "He don't do no runnin', he got no gas, no stamina. It's a waste-a time to get him up in there. It's a disgrace."

Next, sparring is a redoubtable and perpetually renewed test of strength, cunning and courage, if only because the possibility of serious injury can never be completely eliminated, in spite of all precautions. Two boxers got their noses broken while sparring in the year after I joined the gym. In July 1989, I suffered the same fate as a result of two particularly rough sessions three days apart, the one with Smithie, a light heavyweight who bloodied my face (to DeeDee's guilty dismay, as he had briefly stepped out to fetch a cup of soup at Daley's), the other with Anthony "Ice" Ivory, a middleweight whose crisp and sharp jab I could not find a way to avoid. Some boxers become "punchy" (i.e., develop the medical syndrome of the "punch-drunk fighter," *dementia pugilistica,* sometimes confused with Parkinson's disease) not so much from beatings suffered during official bouts as from the cumulative effect of the blows absorbed in the gym during sparring. Cuts to the face are rare, owing to the protective headgear worn for that purpose (and not to cushion the shock of the blows), but black eyes, bruised cheekbones and swollen lips, bloody noses, and battered hands and ribs are the habitual lot of those who put on the gloves on a regular basis. Not to mention that every time a boxer steps into the ring, be it to "shake out" with a novice, he puts a fraction of his symbolic capital at stake: the slightest failing or slip-up, such as a knockdown or a sloppy performance, brings immediate embarrassment to the fighter, as well as to his gym-mates who hasten to assist his "corrective face-work" so as to restabilize the fuzzy and labile status order of the gym.[66] Boxers have at their disposal a variety of socially validated excuses for this purpose, ranging from minor health hassles ("I been battling the flu, man, it's killing me") to imaginary injuries (a damaged knuckle, a sore shoulder) to the alibi most readily called upon, especially by trainers, a breach of the sacrosanct code of sexual abstinence during the phase of training nearing a fight.[67]

---

66. Erving Goffman, *Interaction Ritual: Essays on Face-to-Face Behavior* (New York: Pantheon Books, 1967), 19–22.
67. Loïc Wacquant, "The Prizefighter's Three Bodies," *Ethnos* 63, 3 (November 1998): esp. 342–345.

Curtis throwing a jab at
Ashante during a sparring session

Although it occupies only a small fraction of the boxer's time in quantitative terms, sparring warrants a close analysis because it demonstrates the *highly codified nature of pugilistic violence*. Moreover, being situated midway between "shadowboxing" and the actual fighting of a competitive bout, sparring allows us to discern more clearly, as if through a magnifying glass, the subtle and apparently contradictory mix of instinct and rationality, emotion and calculation, individual abandon and group control that gives the work of fabrication of the pugilist its distinctive touch and stamps all training exercises, down to the most banal.

1. Choosing a Partner

Everything in sparring hinges on the choice of partner, and for this reason it must absolutely be approved by DeeDee. The matching of opponents has to be adjusted in a manner such that both boxers benefit from the exercise and the risk of physical injury is kept below an acceptable level. Considerations of honor reinforce these technical reasons: ideally, one does not spar with an opponent who is too superior for fear of "getting a good ass-whuppin'," or one so feeble that he cannot defend himself (for fear of being accused of taking advantage of a weakling).[68] However, vagaries in attendance and divergences in the training and fighting schedules of club members can make it difficult to find a steady partner who fits the threefold rubric of weight, skill, and style. So it is good policy to strive to maintain amicable relations in the gym with the one(s) you have, spare their feelings by respecting a degree of balance in the encounters (a boxer who gets "whipped" repeatedly in front of his mates will refuse to go on boxing with the fighter who inflicts such humiliation on him), and to always be ready and willing to "give back" a sparring session to someone who bailed you out on another occasion. In sum, sparring partners are part of the specific social capital of pugilists. This is why asking a boxer to "glove up" with you is always a delicate matter: it means interfering in the network of reciprocal obligations that ties him to his current and past partners; it is better not to ask if you surmise that the answer will be negative.

In the absence of adequate sparring partners, one turns to boxers of lesser caliber to make do, or even to beginners as a last resort. Nonetheless, one must always *maintain a measure of equilibrium,* even if it requires deliberately handicapping one of the protagonists. In the case of an overly uneven matchup, the more experienced fighter tacitly commits himself to "holding back" his punches and to working on his speed, footwork, and defensive moves while the weaker boxer

---

68. The personality and coaching philosophy of the head trainer is decisive because it determines the main parameters for the social management of ring violence. In more impersonal, even anomic, gyms (such as many "park district" facilities) devoid of a clear authority structure and formal membership, the rules that govern sparring are much looser and less strictly enforced. I witnessed numerous sparring incidents in these gyms that would be unthinkable at Woodlawn. In one of them, a hulky black teenager walked in off the street into a predominantly white gym and, though he had never "smelled a glove" before, dared a veteran white fighter to slug with him. The coach validated the challenge and let the boastful youth step into the ring in his civilian clothing, whereupon the professional boxer proceeded to dismantle him in less than a minute of merciless punching, eliciting general laughter. In another gym, I observed a welterweight sparring with no head guard on with a heavyweight who himself did not wear handwraps under his gloves and unsuccessfully tried to "take his head off" for four rounds. In some gyms, spectators bet small sums of money on the outcome of sparring sessions, thereby increasing the incentive for excessive violence.

concentrates on offense and hard punching.[69] When one of the fighters is a novice, it is essential to select an "initiator" who has a perfect command of his punches and emotions. If DeeDee waited almost eight weeks before letting me enter into the "lion's den," it is not only because I needed to improve my conditioning and gain a handle on the basics of the craft but also because he had to find me an appropriate partner. "Gotta be somebody who can control hisself. I don' want just any guy to get up there withyou and knock the hell outa you, Louie. He gotta know how to control hisself." Certain boxers have a style or a mentality that makes it difficult to "move around" with them in the ring because they do not know how to adapt to their partner.

> As I was talking ring tactics with Curtis, DeeDee thought that I wanted to spar with him. He calls me off the floor and warns me sternly: *"No way* you gonna spar with Curtis, you got me, Louie? Not even to play around in the ring!" . . . "Why?" [Irritated at my feigned ignorance: he's repeated this prohibition to me a hundred times] "'Cause he don't have an ounce of sense in the ring, that's why. He ain't got no sense, you know that damn well, Louie. He would knock you out cold as a milk shake." [Field notes, 6 March 1989]

> Sitting in the back room, we're watching Mark work out on the heavy bag. He's made tremendous strides and his movements are technically very good; his combinations flow, he looks like a real pro. I ask if I can "move around" with him. DeeDee responds in the negative: "He hit too damn hard. He's too strong. Look at his body, his legs. He only weigh 125 pounds but he ain't got no legs, look how thin they are. Tha's why he's so light with the strong upper body he got. He's stronger than all them other guys in this gym. Real strong." [Field notes, 17 April 1989]

Much as one does not spar with just anyone, one does not spar just any old way either. The brutality of the exchanges between the ropes is a function of the balance of forces between partners (the more uneven

---

69. If a far superior boxer, either in weight or ability, fails to restrain himself and inflicts a beating on his sparring partner, he is sure to be vehemently reprimanded by DeeDee. The light heavyweight Smithie thus was sharply berated for continuing to box me after having busted my nose and covered me with blood during the particularly rough sparring session mentioned earlier (all the more so since he had already knocked out my friend Olivier the week before).

this balance, the more limited the brutality) and of the goals of the particular sparring session, that is, its coordinates in the twofold temporal axis of training and competition. As the date of the fight draws nearer, sparring sessions become more frequent and last longer (up to eight or ten rounds a day during the final week, with a letup in the final two or three days to make sure that you "don't leave your fight in the gym"), the confrontation more intense, and inexperienced boxers are temporarily kept away from the ring. On the eve of an important bout, sparring can become almost as brutal as the fight itself. While gearing up for his much-awaited confrontation with Gerry Cooney, the latest "Great White Hope," heavyweight world champion Larry Holmes offered a bounty of ten thousand dollars to the sparring partner who would send him to the canvas, as a way of enticing them to slug away without compunction.[70] Yet, as with every well-run training camp, those sparring partners had been carefully selected to give Holmes a clear advantage so as to preserve his strength and bolster his confidence for the fight.

2. A Controlled Violence

During a session, the level of violence fluctuates in cycles according to a dialectic of challenge and response, within moving limits set by the sense of equity that founds the original agreement between sparring partners— which is neither a norm nor a contract but what Erving Goffman calls a "working consensus."[71] If one of the fighters picks up his pace and "gets off," the other automatically reacts by immediately hardening his response; there follows a sudden burst of agression that can escalate to the point where the two partners are hitting each other full force, before they step back and jointly agree (often by a nod or a touch of the gloves) to resume their pugilistic dialogue a notch or two lower.[72] The task of the coach is to monitor this "fistic conversation" to see that the less accomplished fighter is not being silenced, in which case he will instruct his opponent to diminish pressure accordingly ("Circle and jab, 'Shante, I told you not to load up! And you keep that damn left hand up, Louie!"), or

70. Hauser, *Black Lights,* 199.
71. Erving Goffman, *The Presentation of Self in Everyday Life* (New York: Anchor/ Doubleday, 1959), 65.
72. One would need to analyze here, from a perspective inspired by Goffman, the "interaction rituals" specific to sparring that serve to reaffirm periodically the measured and playful character of the violence it enacts, to solemnize the mutual respect between fighters, and to trace the shifting boundaries of their revels.

that the two partners do not let the intensity of their exchanges drop too far below that of a fight, which would defeat the very purpose of the exercise ("What you be doin' up there, *makin' love?* Start workin' off that jab, I wanna see some nice right hands and counters off the block").

I return to the back room and ask DeeDee, who is finishing a precooked noodle soup in a plastic cup, comfortably seated in his armchair: "DeeDee, Saturday, if I can, I'd like to put on the gloves. Maybe I can move 'round with Ashante?" "I dunno, Louie, I dunno 'cause them guys are gettin' ready for that card next week [at the Park West], so they don't need to be playin' around right now: they need to be hittin', and hittin' hard." And he punches the palm of his left hand with his clenched right fist. [Field notes, 1 December 1988]

Standing in the office, DeeDee, Eddie, and I are watching Hutchinson, a sort of human control tower (at more than 6'8" and nearly 280 pounds, he fights in the super heavyweight division), spar with Butch. Butch himself is a fine specimen, but he looks like an overexcited dragonfly next to the giant's placid and impregnable body. Hutchinson moves around slowly and holds his guard up high, with his fists extended far in front of him. Butch has a terrible time getting to him, so long is Hutchinson's reach. It looks like he's going to smash himself to pieces against him. DeeDee warned Hutchinson to hold his punches, given the height and weight difference between him and his partner of the moment. "I told 'im not to hit hard. If he starts hittin', I'm d'one who's gonna come out of here and beat him with a baseball bat. He's too big. He better watch out!" All of this said in a lively and vigilant tone. At the end of the three rounds. Butch comes out fairly well worked over (and yet his partner seemed to have just grazed him): his lips are swollen, his face reddish, and he's out of breath. But not a word of complaint. [Field notes, 11 November 1988]

The principle of reciprocity that tacitly governs the level of violence in the ring dictates that the stronger boxer not profit from his superiority, but also that the weaker fighter not take undue advantage of his partner's willful restraint, as I discovered at the end of a vigorous sparring session with Ashante. On 29 June 1989, I am dumbfounded to learn that Ashante complained to DeeDee that I hit too hard and that he is forced to respond by firing back solid shots right in the mug. "He told me he cain't have fun witchyou no more, you hit too hard. You made enough progress now, he gotta be careful not to let you land your punches or you can hurt him. If you hit him clean, you can knock him down. He was complainin', you don't back off and you don't never stop throwin' punches when he's backed up against the ropes, you keep on throwin' hard punches. You nailed him with a right, if you'd follow up with another one, you woulda've sent him to the canvas. See, when you started out, he could play witchyou without worryin' but now you're gettin' stronger, he gotta watch out." I am so surprised that I make him repeat and confirm that Ashante was actually talking about me. "Yeah, he wanted me to tell you to hold your punches 'cos you could hurt him now. . . . You know how to punch now. Tha's why he gotta rock you with a good one from time-t'time. It ain't that he wanta hurt you, but he gotta show you *he mean business* and he gotta pay you back to make you control yourself a lil' better."

The coach obviously plays a major role in the regulation of this mutually consented violence. If the boxers from Woodlawn measure their punches with such attention, it is because DeeDee, out of respect for his art, will not tolerate all-out "slugging." But it is also because each phase of sparring calls for an appropriate level of intensity that is useless (and dangerous) to exceed and below which one must not fall, lest the benefits of the exercise vanish. This optimal level cannot be determined before stepping into the ring; it varies according to the partners and the circumstances (fatigue, motivation, time left before the fight, etc.). It is up to the boxers to set it by jointly feeling their way—in the literal as well as figurative sense—to it with the assistance of DeeDee. Ever attentive to what is transpiring in the ring, the latter is swift to give a good dressing-down to a pugilist who allows himself an immoderate use of his punching power or to exhort another to display more aggressiveness. If need be, Deedee does not hesitate to order the sparring partner of a nonchalant boxer to pick up the pace, as when he shouts from his armchair to Little John, who is battling with Curtis: "John, damn it, make 'im keep his left up when he jabs, stick him with a good right since he don't wanta box an' keepin' his hands on his knees like a fool. Ah! I wish I could get up in that ring."

Thus what has every chance of looking like a spree of gratuitous and unchecked brutality in the eyes of a neophyte is in fact a regular and finely codified tapestry of exchanges that, though they are violent, are nonetheless constantly controlled, and whose weaving together supposes a practical and continual collaboration between the two opponents in the construction and maintenance of a dynamic conflictual equilibrium. Properly educated boxers relish this ever-renewed duel that is sparring, but they know that this clash is, at every moment, bounded by "noncontractual clauses" and that it is quite distinct from a fight, even though it approximates it, in that it entails an element of "antagonistic cooperation"[73] that is expressly banned from a bout. Curtis expresses this distinction thus:

> I don't dislike anythin' [about sparring]. I like it all, 'cause ya learn at the same time. In a gym you not tryin' to win a fight, you in here *learnin'*. It's all about *learnin'*. Practicin' on doin' what you wanna do when d'upcomin' fight come, ya know. . . . I cain't hurt my opponent—[smiling coyly] I mean my sparrin' *partners*. They helpin' me out, just like I'm helpin' *them* out. They not gonna get in there and try and hurt me. . . . Here and again, now an' then, ya know, ya have your little flashy stuff, where he might hit you hard, you might get caught with a nice punch and you gonna try and retaliate and come back with somethin'.

Many boxers need a long phase of adjustment before they bend to these tacit norms of cooperation which seem to contradict the public principle and ethos of unlimited competition. As in the case of bicycle racing,[74] this "cooperative informal order" is particularly problematic for novices, who, because they mistake the facade for the building, are incapable of calibrating their aggressiveness and rest convinced that they must go all out to prove themselves, as DeeDee indicates in this note from 23 November 1989: "This new kid, he think he can beat up e-ve-ry-body: [in an exaggeratedly belligerent tone] 'I can whup dis guy, I can kick his ass! I'm bettah than 'im, lemme get in d'ring!' an' he just wanna fight with e-ve-ry-body. We gonna have problems with him. I don' know what to do 'cos I cain't let him spar with that kinda attitude, uh-uh." They will have to be taught *in actu* how to "read" the discreet cues whereby their partners enjoin them either to back off and to soft-pedal and when, on the contrary, to increase pressure so as to make them work harder.

---

73. I borrow this notion from William Graham Sumner, *Folkways* (Boston: Ginn, [1906] 1940).
74. Edward Albert, "Riding a Line: Competition and Cooperation in the Sport of Bicycle Riding," *Sociology of Sport Journal* 8 (1991): 341–361.

3. Sparring as Perceptual, Emotional, and Physical Labor

As a hybrid figure between training—which it extends and accelerates—and fighting—to which it is a prelude and a sketch—sparring completes the thorough re-education of the body and mind during which is forged what Foucault calls a "multi-sensorial structure"[75] quite specific to boxing that can be articulated or discerned only in action. Ring experience decuples the boxer's capacity for perception and concentration; it forces him to curb his emotions; and it refashions and hardens his body in preparation for the clashes of competition. In the first place, sparring is an education of the senses and notably of the visual faculties; the permanent state of emergency that defines it effects a progressive reorganization of perceptual habits and abilities.

To realize this, one need only track the transformation that occurs in the structure and scope of one's visual field as one climbs the hierarchy of sparring. During the very first sessions, my vision is obstructed in part by my own gloves, saturated by the stimuli that are rushing at me from all sides with neither order nor meaning. The advice DeeDee shouts at me and the sensation of being armored in my cup and headgear, not to mention the muffled but omnipresent anguish about being hit, all contribute to exacerbating this feeling of confusion. I experience then the utmost difficulty in fixing my gaze on my opponent and seeing his fists coming at me, especially as I am uneducated about the clues that are supposed to help me anticipate them. From session to session, my field of vision clears up, expands, and gets reorganized: I manage to shut out external calls on my attention and to better discern the movements of my antagonist, as if my visual faculties were growing as my body gets used to sparring. And, above all, I gradually acquire the specific "eye" that enables me to guess at my opponent's attacks by reading the first signs of them in his eyes, the orientation of his shoulders, or the position of his hands and elbows.

▎ *Slugging it out with Ashante*

> 3 June 1989. I warm up by moving around in front of the mirror. My body has gotten used to being in boxer's gear and I no longer have that feeling of being shelled in bothersome trappings. I climb the

---

75. Michel Foucault, *The Birth of the Clinic: An Archaeology of Medical Perception* (New York: Pantheon Books, 1973), 165, my translation (this expression is wrongly rendered as "multi-sensorial perception").

little ring stool and slip through the ropes. . . . Sparring has become routine now. I bounce up and down across from Ashante. He's wearing a pair of tight black-and-green shorts, a black wrestling singlet, and his own superpadded yellow headguard. He's glistening with sweat after the four rounds he's just done with Rodney. . . . We have a few seconds to observe each other and I still surprise myself by wondering what in the world I'm doing in this ring facing this stocky, nasty little guy who may become welterweight champion of Illinois at the end of the month!

"Time!" Let's get busy! We touch gloves. I move on Ashante right away and badger him with quick jabs, which he parries. He stops me in my tracks to tell me, "If you're comin' at me, keep yo' han's up or I'monna deck you." Thanks for the advice, which I take into account by swiftly raising my guard. I resume my march forward. I'm determined to hit harder than usual, even if this means that Ashante's also going to hit harder—and that's exactly what happens. We test each other out. I try to find my distance. A few jabs and a few rights, blocked on both sides. I land a jab to the body, then jump on him with a left-right-left hook combination. *Boom!* In the mug! Ashante backs up and immediately counters. Instead of withdrawing, I stand fast and try to parry his punches. He hits me with a straight left flush on my mouth. I get him in a clinch and catch him out thanks to my favorite trick: a feint with the jab and a wide right cross to the face just as he moves to his left to slip away from my left. *Pow!* My fist pings right into his cheek. He nods "okay" to me. He seems surprised that I'm boxing so energetically and picks up the pace.

Ashante's walking onto me, mouth deformed by his mouthpiece, eyes bulging with concentration. I back up and jab to try to protect myself. He fakes a straight left and throws a sharp right directly to my side: I reel under the blow and beat a hasty retreat. (We smile for a second, both thinking about what he did to my ribs last week.) I chase him down into a corner, jab, right, jab, and catch him with a nice right uppercut when he leans over to avoid my jab. Nonetheless he's blocking most of my hard punches very effectively: I see the opening just fine, but in the time it takes for my fist to get there, he's closed up the passage or moved away by rotating his torso. (Ashante anticipates where my fists are about to go so well that it's almost like we're dancing a ballet together.) He suddenly kicks into higher gear and drills my head with short straight punches that I scarcely see coming. The left side of my chin stings like hell. I stagger under the blows and decide (actually, I don't decide anything, it's just a formula, I do it, that's all! Everything moves much too fast, you react instinctively) to march onto him, but he stops me dead in my tracks with several hard jabs to the body. *"Time out!"* DeeDee's voice resounds.

We separate, I return to my corner and catch my breath. I'm not too tired, but it's only the first round. Big Earl advises me, "Keep him away with your jab: jab, jab, don't let him get under your guard. Like [Sugar Ray] Leonard. Want some water?" He climbs onto the table, directs the straw of the water bottle toward my mouth and shoots me a stream of warmish water, which I swallow (something a real boxer never does). Come on, let's get it on some more.

"Time in!" Second round, both of us go on the attack from the get-go, without even touching gloves in a display of friendliness. Ashante is boxing faster. I struggle to keep up with his cadence, but I react better and protect myself more effectively than the previous times. He starts to punch for real: three hooks to the sides cut though my guard like butter and knock the wind out of me. *Whew!* That hurts. I counter with a few jabs but he dodges them by moving his head just enough for my fist not to reach him. Ashante traps me several times against the ropes and lards me with pointed and heavy hooks. One of his attacks even makes me lose my head and I let my defenses down for a second. Luckily, he spares me and interrupts the hailstorm of punches, satisfied with letting me know that I'm wide open. I then launch an awkward attack, as I no longer have good control over my coordination. Ashante greets me with a right-left-right combination flush in the face which reddens my nose; I feel my bottom lip start to swell. I respond wildly, but still manage to sting him in the snout with a right followed up with a short left hook right on target. He always tries to duck down to his right and I catch him with two hooks straight in his headguard. *Yahoo!* Which makes him react immediately. He cuts the ring off, marching straight onto me, not even bobbing and weaving, to show me that he's going to throw punches and couldn't care less about my counters. He fakes me with both hands in turn until I leave myself open and *boom!* A wide left hook sends my head snapping back. I stagger under the punch but wave to him, "Okay, it's all right." We find ourselves face to face again, both a bit surprised at so much viciousness. Jabs from

me, blocked by his fists, versus jabs from him, blocked by my nose.
I'm better able to see his punches coming but I still don't move fast
enough. He lands another punch on my face, a right that makes my
headgear turn sideways. DeeDee growls: "Move yo' head, Louie!"
I'm trying! Things are really heating up now. Ashante machine-guns
my torso, then knocks the wind out of me with a mean right uppercut
to my side (I'll remember that one for awhile). I get him in a clinch
again. He shoots me some short punches to the ribs and even to
the back, as if we were in a real fight (I think this is the first time he's
done that). *"Time out!"*

We shake each other's fists briefly, to reaffirm the controlled nature
of the exchange. "Tha's good, Louie, you're doin' good, you're
punching hard today, keep it up." "Yeah, the only problem is I'm not
sure I can hold out for another round at this pace." I'm really worn
out, both by Ashante's punches and by the tempo of the session,
which is much too brisk for me. I catch my breath as best I can,
leaning on the ropes.

"Time in! Work!" The third round goes just as fast and I absorb a
bushel of punches. . . . The level of aggression rises little by little, but
in a reciprocal and graduated manner—meaning that, near the end,
when I don't have enough energy left to simply keep my guard up
properly and respond even feebly to his punches, Ashante pretends
to be boxing me but is only hitting me superficially, whereas if he
kept on punching as hard as he was at the beginning of the round,
he would send me rolling to the canvas. . . . I get him in a clinch again
but don't have the strength to return his punches. Shoot, it should
be over with by now! This round's so damn long! I keep whining to
myself in my head: "Time out! Time out!" Come on, DeeDee! Fuck,
what's the matter, has he forgotten us or what? We must have been
boxing for a good five minutes! *"Time out!"* Oooofff!

Ashante falls onto me and holds me in his arms, patting the back of
my neck with his glove. Wow! It feels so great to duke it out among
buddies! He laughs and seems delighted. "How're you, how you
feelin'?" . . . I go take off my gear in the office. For the first time,
DeeDee compliments me: "You're gettin' better up in there, you
looked sharp today, Louie. But you gotta get out of his way when
he's throwin' his right. Block it or move yo' head more. You're still
takin' too many punches." He forbids me to sit down on the table.

My breathing gradually calms down. . . . When I come back from the locker room, the old coach yells at me for all to hear, with a knowing look toward Kitchen: "But we didn' see your nose bleed, Louie? Did it really bleed?" . . .

I'm so exhausted from this sparring session that I'm incapable of copying all my notes until the next day. My chin hurts and my entire face is sore (as if it were swollen on the inside), my bottom lip is puffed up, and I have a superb reddish bruise under my left eye. But it was especially the blows to the body that wore me down. The uppercuts to the ribs have left me with a large mark that will veer imperceptibly from red to black to yellowish over the course of the next dozen days. Tonight, as I type these lines, I'm dead tired, my hands are numb, my forehead and nose bone are on fire (as if my entire face were throbbing in the manner of a ventricle) and I've got aching spots across my chest that stab me at the slightest movement. Just the craft getting pounded in.

But sparring is not only a physical exercise; it is also the means and support of a particularly intense form of "emotion work."[76] Because "few lapses of self-control are punished as immediately and severely as loss of temper during a boxing bout,"[77] it is vital that one dominate at all times the impulses of one's affect. In the squared circle, one must be capable of managing one's emotions and know, according to the circumstances, how to contain or repress them or, on the contrary, how to stir and swell them; how to muzzle certain feelings (of anger, restiveness, frustration) so as to resist the blows, provocations, and verbal abuse dished out by one's opponent, as well as the "rough tactics" he may resort to (hitting below the belt or with his elbows, head-butting, rubbing his gloves into your eyes or over a facial cut in order to open it further, etc.); and how to call forth and amplify others (of aggressiveness or "controlled fury," for instance) at will while not letting them get out of hand.[78] In gloving

76. On the notion of "emotion work," see Arlie Hochschild, "Emotion Work, Feeling Rules, and Social Structure," *American Journal of Sociology* 85, 3 (November 1979): 551–575.
77. Konrad Lorenz, *On Aggression* (New York: Harcourt, Brace and World, 1966), 281.
78. One could show that this "sentimental education" is not limited to the sole pugilist: it encompasses all the specialized agents of the pugilistic field (trainers, managers, referees, judges, promoters, etc.) and even extends to the spectators.

"Fat" Joe and Smithie at work in the ring

up at the gym, boxers learn to become "businesslike" in the ring, to channel their mental and affective energies toward "getting the job done" in the most effective and least painful manner.

A boxer must exercise not only a constant inner surveillance over his feelings but also continual "expressive control" over their external "signaling"[79] so as not to let his opponent know if and when punches hurt him, and which one. Legendary trainer-manager Cus D'Amato, the "discoverer" of Mike Tyson, sums up the matter thus: "The fighter has

---

79. Erving Goffman, *Presentation of Self in Everyday Life,* 59–60.

mastered his emotions to the extent that he can conceal and control them. Fear is an asset to a fighter. It makes him move faster, be quicker and more alert. Heroes and cowards feel exactly the same fear. Heroes react to it differently."[80] This difference has nothing innate about it; it is an acquired ability, collectively produced by prolonged submission of the body to the discipline of sparring. Butch explains:

> BUTCH: You have to stay in control, because yer emotions will burn up all yer oxygen, so you have to stay calm and relaxed though you know this guy's tryin' to knock yer head off. You have to stay calm and relaxed. So you have to deal with the situation.

> LOUIE: Was it hard learning to control emotions, like to not get mad or frustrated if a guy is slippery and you can't hit him with clean shots?

> BUTCH: It was hard for me. It took me years-an'-years-an'-years to get that and *juuus'* when I was gettin' it under control real goo', then thin's, hum, started movin' for me. It works, well, I guess when it was time, it worked itself into place.

> LOUIE: Is that something that DeeDee taught you?

> BUTCH: He kept tellin' me to stay calm, relax. Jus' breathe, take it easy—but [his pace picks up] I found it hard to stay calm and relax when this guy's tryin' to kill ya over in the next corner, but eventually it sunk in and I understood what he was sayin'.

Indeed, the deep imbrication among gesture, conscious experience, and physiological processes—to recall Gerth and Mills's distinction between the three constituent elements of emotion[81]—is such that a change in any one triggers an instantaneous modification of the other two. Failure to tame the sensory experience of punches flying at you amputates your ability to act and by the same token alters your corporeal state. Conversely, to be at the height of physical fitness allows you to be mentally ready and therefore to better master the feelings triggered by the flow of blows.

---

80. Cited by Brunt, *Mean Business,* 55.
81. Hans Gerth and C. Wright Mills, *Character and Social Structure* (New York: Harcourt, Brace and World, 1953).

Finally, the strictly physical aspect of sparring should not be neglected on account of being self-evident: one must not forget that "[b]oxing is more about getting hit than it is about hitting"; it is "primarily about being, and not giving, hurt."[82] The idiolect of boxing is replete with terms referring to the ability to take a punch and glorifying the capacity to endure pain. Now, beyond one's congenital endowment such as an "iron chin" or the mysterious and revered quality called "heart" (which also holds a central place in the masculine street culture of the ghetto), there is only one way to harden yourself to pain and to get your body used to taking blows, and that is to get hit regularly. For, contrary to a widespread popular notion, boxers have no personal predilection for pain and hardly enjoy getting pummeled. A young Italian-American welterweight from the Windy City Gym who recently turned pro gets indignant when I mention the lay stereotype of the "sadomasochistic" fighter:[83] *"Nah, we're human man! We're human,* you know, we're jus' like anybody else, our feelings are jus' as much as your feelin's, we— you can't put us outside, you know, (vehemently) *we're no different than you:* we're in the same world, we're the same world, the same flesh, same blood, same everything."* What boxers have done is to elevate their threshold of tolerance for pain by submitting to it in graduated and regular fashion.

This learning of indifference to physical suffering is inseparable from the acquisition of the form of sang-froid specific to pugilism. The adequate socialization of the boxer presupposes an endurance to punches, the basis of which is the ability to tame the initial reflex of self-preservation that would undo the coordination of movements and give the opponent a decisive advantage. More so than the actual force of the latter's punches, it is this gradual acquisition of "resistance to excitement

---

82. Oates, *On Boxing,* 25 and 60.
83. This stereotype can be found in numerous scholarly works, such as Allen Guttmann's historical thesis on the evolution of sports, *From Ritual to Record: The Nature of Modern Sports* (New York: Columbia University Press, 1979: see 160), as well as nonscholarly works, such as the encyclopedia of academic and journalistic clichés about prizefighting compiled from newspaper and sports magazine articles by André Rauch, *Boxe, violence du XXe siècle* (Paris: Aubier, 1992). I detail other problems with Rauch's tome in the French edition of this book, *Corps et âme* (Marseilles: Agone, 2d expanded ed. 2002), pp. 276–277.

[*résistance à l'émoi*]," as Mauss says,[84] which one is hard pressed to as-cribe either to the realm of will or to the physiological order, that exhausts the novice during his first sparring sessions as well as inexperienced fighters during their bouts. This is because, in addition to the hyperacute attention demanded by the duel in the ring, one must fight at every mo-ment one's first reflex, which is to shell up on oneself, and forbid one's body to disobey by turning away from one's opponent, coming undone, or running away from his flying fists in a mad dash for safety.

> 23 March 1989. I bump into Ashante slipping on his gloves in front of the situp table. He jokingly calls out to me: "Hey Louie, how you feelin'? Your ribs awright?" [This is in reference to the ribs of mine he roughed up during our last sparring session and that prevented me from training for several days.] "They're okay, you didn't break them, just bruised." He smiles, shaking my hands affectionately between his gloved fists. "I knew I didn' break 'em. But you gotta start doin' some serious situps and get in shape for real, Louie. Gotta do them situps to protect yo' body. See, I worked your body 'cuz I didn' want to hit you in d'face too much, 'cuz you *not used to takin' too many shots to d'head yet*. That's why I hit you more to d'body. What happen is, yo' body got tired 'cuz you're not used to takin' shots to d'body either. I know I hit you pretty hard, but you was goin' at it pretty hard too, y'know."

To learn how to box is to imperceptibly modify one's bodily schema, one's relation to one's body and to the uses one usually puts it to, so as to internalize a set of dispositions that are inseparably mental and phys-ical and that, in the long run, turn the body into a virtual punching ma-chine, but *an intelligent and creative machine capable of self-regulation* while innovating within a fixed and relatively restricted panoply of moves as an instantaneous function of the actions of the opponent in time. The mutual imbrication of corporeal dispositions and mental dispositions reaches such a degree that even willpower, morale, deter-mination, concentration, and the control of one's emotions change into so many reflexes inscribed within the organism. In the accomplished boxer, the mental becomes part of the physical and vice versa; body

84. Marcel Mauss, "Les techniques du corps," 385, transl. 123.

and mind function in total symbiosis. This is what is expressed in the scornful comments that DeeDee makes to boxers who argue that they are not "mentally ready" for a fight. After Curtis's loss in his first nationally televised fight in Atlantic City, the old trainer is fuming: "He don't lose 'cos he's not 'mentally ready.' That don' mean nuthin', mentally ready. If you're a fighter, you're ready. I was just tellin' Butch: mentally ready, tha's bullshit! If you're a fighter, you get up in d'ring an' [hissing for emphasis] you *fight,* there's no bein' mentally ready or not ready. It's not mental, ain't nuthin' mental bout it. If you're not a fighter, you don't get up in there, you don't fight. If you're a fighter, you're ready and you fight— tha's all. All d'rest is just *bullshit for the birds.*" [Field notes, 17 April 1989]

It is this close imbrication of the physical and the mental that enables experienced boxers to continue to defend themselves and eventually rebound after skirting being knocked out. In such moments of quasi unconsciousness, their body continues to box on its own, as it were, until they regain their senses, sometimes after a lapse of several minutes. "I went into a clinch with my head down and my partner's head came up and butted me over the left eye, cutting and dazing me badly. Then he stepped back and swung his right against my jaw with every bit of his power. It landed flush and stiffened me where I stood. Without going down or staggering, *I lost all consciousness, but instinctively proceeded* to knock him out. Another sparring partner entered the ring. We boxed three rounds. I have no recollection of this."[85] In the famous "Thrilla in Manila," one of the most brutal battles in the history of the Manly art, both Joe Frazier and Muhammad Ali fought much of the bout in a state bordering on unconsciousness. Several years later after the third contest between the two great corrivals of the decade, "Smokin'" Joe recalled how, by the sixth round, "I couldn't think anymore. All I know is the fight is there. The heat (nearly 104 degrees), the humidity (of the Filipino summer). . . . That particular fight, like, I just couldn't think, I was there, I had a job to do. I just wanted to get the job done."[86] He would continue to march onto Ali, drunk with punches and blinded by the swelling around his eyes, until his trainer, fearing that he was going to get himself killed in the ring, threw in the towel at the bell calling for the fifteenth and final round.

85. Former world heavyweight champion Gene Tunney, as cited in Sammons, *Beyond the Ring,* 246, emphasis mine.
86. *The Thrilla in Manila,* videotape of the Ali-Frazier heavyweight title fight (New York: NBC Sports Venture, 1990).

Boxers and trainers seem on first cut to hold a contradictory view of the "mental" aspect of their activity. On the one hand, they assert that boxing is a "thinking man's game" that they frequently liken to chess. On the other, they insist that there is no ratiocinating once you set foot in the squared circle. "Ain't no place for thinkin' in the ring: it's all reflex! When it's time to think, it's time to quit," DeeDee admonishes. And yet Woodlawn's old head coach fully agrees with Ray Arcel, the dean of American trainers, still on duty at a solid ninety-two years after having groomed eighteen world champions, when he maintains that "boxing is brain over brawn. I don't care how much ability you've got as a fighter. If you can't think, you're just another bum in the park."[87] The riddle solves itself as soon as one realizes that a boxer's ability to cogitate and reason in the ring has become a faculty of his undivided organism—what John Dewey would call his "body-mind complex."[88]

Pugilistic excellence can thus be defined by the fact that the body of the fighter computes and judges for him, instantaneously, without the mediation—and the costly delay that it would cause—of abstract thinking, prior representation, and strategic calculation. As Sugar Ray Robinson concisely puts it: "You don't think. It's all instinct. If you stop to think, you're gone." An opinion confirmed by trainer Mickey Rosario: "You can't think. . . . out there [in the ring]. You got to be an animal."[89] And one must add: a *cultivated* instinct, a *socialized* animal. It is the trained body that is the *spontaneous strategist;* it knows, understands, judges, and reacts all at once. If it were otherwise, it would be impossible to survive between the ropes. And one readily recognizes novices, during amateur fights, by their rigid and mechanical moves, their slowed-down, "telegraphed" combinations, whose stiffness and academicism betray the intervention of conscious thought into the coordination of gestures and movements.

Thus the strategy of the boxer, as product of the encounter of the pugilistic habitus with the very field that produced it, erases the scholastic distinction between the intentional and the habitual, the rational and the emotional, the corporeal and the mental. It pertains to an embodied practical reason that, being lodged in the depths of the

87. Cited in David Anderson, *In the Corner: Great Boxing Trainers Talk about Their Art* (New York: Morrow, 1991), 121.
88. John Dewey, *Experience and Nature* (Chicago: Open Court, 1929), 277.
89. Sugar Ray Robinson is cited in Hauser, *Black Lights,* 29, and Mickey Rosario in Plummer, *Buttercups and Strong Boys,* 43.

socialized organism, escapes the logic of individual choice.[90] Indeed, one could characterize the strategy of the boxer in the ring by what Hugh Brody says of the Athabascan Eskimo hunters of the Canadian Northwest:

> To make a good, wise, sensitive hunting choice is to accept the interconnection of all possible factors, and avoids the mistake of seeking rationally to focus on any one consideration that is held as primary. What is more, *the decision is taken in the doing;* there is no step or pause between theory and practice. As a consequence, the decision—like the action from which it is inseparable—is always alterable (and therefore may not properly even be termed a decision).[91]

Confrontation in the ring calls for synoptic judgments, stamped by responsiveness and flexibility, made in and for the moment, informed by an embodied pugilistic sensitivity, which are the very antithesis of the systematically planned and measured decisions of "calculating reason." This is what Joyce Carol Oates recognizes well when she writes: " 'Free' will, 'sanity,' 'rationality'—our characteristic modes of consciousness—are irrelevant, if not detrimental, to boxing in its most extraordinary moments."[92] Once in the ring, it is the body that learns and understands, sorts and stores information, finds the correct answer in its repertory of possible actions and reactions, and in the end becomes the veritable "subject" (insofar as there would be one) of pugilistic practice.

Successfully learning to box thus requires the combination of *quasi-antinomic dispositions*: impulses and drives rooted deep within the "biologic individual" dear to George Herbert Mead[93] that may be

90. One glimpses here in passing all that the strand of sociology inspired by game theory could gain by taking as paradigm a very "corporeal" game such as boxing rather than an eminently "intellectual" one like chess or military strategy.
91. Hugh Brody, *Maps and Dreams* (New York: Pantheon Books, 1982), 37, emphasis mine.
92. Oates, *On Boxing,* 108.
93. George H. Mead, "The Biologic Individual," addendum to *Mind, Self, and Society from the Standpoint of a Social Behaviorist,* ed. C. W. Morris (Chicago: University of Chicago Press, 1934), 347–353.

characterized as "savage," at the borderline of the cultural, wedded to the ability to channel them at every moment, to regulate, transform, and tap them according to a plan that is objectively rational even as it remains beyond the reach of the explicit calculus of individual consciousness. This contradiction, inherent in the pugilistic habitus, explains that the belief in the innate character of the boxer's ability can peacefully coexist with an unrelenting and rigid ethic of work and striving. The native myth of the gift of the boxer is an illusion founded in reality: what fighters take for a natural capacity ("You gotta have in it you") is in effect this peculiar nature resulting from the protracted process of inculcation of the pugilistic habitus, a process that often begins in early childhood, either within the gym itself—where one routinely sees children brought in by members of the club trying their hand at boxing—or in the antechamber to the gym that is the ghetto street.

One could quote entire pages of field notes in support of the notion according to which "You're born a boxer." One will make do with one excerpt (from 1 October 1988) in which DeeDee insists at length on the innate qualities of the fighter, which training can only nurture and bring out: "If you got it in you, nuthin's gonna stop it from comin' out. It's gonna come out one way or d'other. Now if you don' have it in you, it ain't no use. You got tonsa guys, they can train all their lives, they work out and they box here, they do their sparrin', but they ain't never gonna make it. I tell 'em. I don't keep em here. You got tonsa guys in Chicago whom I told it's time for them to go, 'Ain't no use comin' to d'gym 'cos you never gon' make it.'" Eddie adds: "Me, my son, he gonna box if he want to. But I ain't gonna push him t'fight. It's gotta come from within his self. 'Cuz you gotta have it in you, you can't cheat with that. So I ain't gonna push him." The expression "a natural," which comes up frequently in the vernacular of boxing gyms, denotes this *cultivated nature* whose social genesis has become literally invisible to those who perceive it through the mental categories that are its product.

An Implicit and Collective Pedagogy

To an essentially corporeal and little-codified practice, whose logic can be grasped only in and through action, corresponds an implicit, practical, and collective mode of inculcation. The transmission of pugilism is effected in a gestural, visual, and mimetic manner, at the cost of a regulated manipulation of the body that somatizes the knowledge collectively held and exhibited by the members of the club at each level in the tacit hierarchy that runs through it. In this respect, the Manly art offers the *paradox of an ultraindividual sport whose apprenticeship is quintessentially collective.* And, paraphrasing Émile Durkheim, one can go so far as to assert that the gym is to boxing what the church is to religion: the "moral community," the "solidary system of beliefs and practices" that makes it possible and constitutes it as such. Which is to say, in passing, that the private forms of pugilistic practice that the new entrepreneurs in body management, always on the lookout for exotic exercises with which to renew a chronically overcrowded fitness market, tried to popularize for a time have nothing in common with boxing but the name.[94]

One readily understands, for all the reasons noted in the foregoing, that it is not possible to learn how to box "on paper." So it comes as no surprise that the head coach of the Woodlawn Boys Club expresses overt hostility toward manuals, diagrams, writings, and other bookish methods of teaching, as the following fieldnote attests:

As I'm drying myself off with a towel, I let slip: "Hey DeeDee, you know what I found in the library on campus the other day? A book called *The Complete Workout of the Boxer,* which shows all the basic movements and exercises of boxing. Is it worth reading it to learn the fundamentals?"

DeeDee screws up his face in disgust: *"You don' learn to box from books. You learn to box in d'gym."*

"But it could help you to see the different punches and to understand them better, no?"

---

94. Here I am thinking for example of the book by Peter Depasquale, *The Boxer's Workout: Fitness for the Civilized Man* (Garden City, N.Y.: Doubleday, 1988), 5, which invites dynamic executives to discover the joys of boxing . . . at home, by hitting a bag alone in their garage: "This book is dedicated to the growing legion of white-collar men, from accountants to actors and stockbrokers, doctors and businessmen, who make a boxer's workout an important part of their professional success." None of the boxers from Woodlawn has a punching bag at home. For DeeDee, training at home is nonsensical, even though most of the specific exercises can in fact be done "in a broom closet."

"No, it ain't helpful. You don't learn how to box readin' no books. I know them books, they got a buncha pictures an' diagrams in'em that show you how to place your feet an' your arms, the angle your arm is supposed to move at an' all that, but it's all standin' still! You don't get no sense of *movement*. Boxin's movement, it's the movement that count." I persist: "So you can't learn anything about boxing in books then?"

"No, you cain't."

"But why not?"

In a tone irritated by my insistence, as if all of this went so much without saying that it was useless for him to repeat himself: *"You just can't! Period.* You can't. In a book, everything's standin' still. They don' show you what's happenin' in d'ring. Tha's not boxin' all that stuff, Louie. You can't, that's all."

"But for a beginner like me, it couldn't hurt to understand things mentally before I come to the gym."

"Of course *it hurt, 'specially* if you're a beginner. Them books, they gonna mess you up complet'ly. You never gonna be a boxer if you learn in a book."

This opinion is confirmed by Eddie, DeeDee's "disciple." When I ask him how you become a boxing coach, he explains to me that there's a little technical exam to take at the Boxing Commission, but that what's really essential is to "drag your ass 'round in d'good gyms like this one and lil' by lil' you startin' to get it. It's not somethin' you can learn in a book." [Field notes, 30 May 1989 and 11 November 1988]

What the old trainer DeeDee objects to about the written text is its effect of totalization and detemporalization. The virulence of his reaction reveals practically the antinomy that exists between the abstract time of theory (that is, of contemplation) and the time of action, which is constitutive of it. To consider boxing from the sovereign point of view of an observer standing outside the game, to uproot it from its proper time and tempo, is to impose on it an alteration that destroys it as such. For, like music, pugilism is a practice "entirely immanent to duration. . . . not only because it is played out in time, but also because it plays strategically with time and especially with tempo."[95] If textbook instructions and the diagrams of academic methods have something unreal in DeeDee's eyes, it is because the most beautiful uppercut is devoid of value if it is unleashed at the wrong moment; the most technically perfect hook fired as a blank move is null and void if it is not integrated into the tempo of the exchange and suited to the style of the boxer.

In contrast to other more codified combat sports such as judo or aikido,[96] where the master breaks down and demonstrates holds at leisure, with a concern for detail and analysis that can go so far as to turn into theoretical study, and where progress is marked by visible signs and official titles (such as belts and *dan* degrees), initiation into boxing is an *initiation without explicit norms,* without clearly defined stages. It is effected collectively, by imitation, by emulation, and by diffuse and reciprocal encouragement, the trainer's role being to coordinate and stimulate routine activity, which turns out to be a much "more powerful source of socialization than intentional pedagogy."[97]

In point of fact, DeeDee's teaching "method" is not a deliberate pedagogy, fully thought out and organized according to an overall design. I never heard him spell out the whys and wherefores of the basic gestures, or describe in synoptic fashion how they fit together, or break down the different stages of the expected progression. The pieces of advice he distills, parsimoniously and intermittently, are so many summary descriptions of the movement to be executed that are thoroughly pleonastic with reality and consist, in most cases, of abbreviated and negative remarks: "Don't drop your left hand when you bringin' back the jab"; "Don't draw your fist back behin' your head"; "Keep your right leg under you at all times." Because the moves of the boxer are of such simplicity and obvious transparency to him, DeeDee sticks to the notion that they require no exegesis at all: "It's easier than counting one-two-three";

95. Bourdieu, *Logic of Practice,* 81, my translation.
96. See Jean-Pierre Clément, "La Force, la souplesse et l'harmonie. Étude comparée de trois sports de combat: lutte, judo, aïkido," in *Sports et société. Approche socioculturelle des pratiques,* ed. Christian Pociello (Paris: Vigot, 1987), 285–301.
97. Jean Lave, *Cognition in Practice: Mind, Mathematics and Culture in Everyday Life* (Cambridge: Cambridge University Press, 1988), 14 and passim. Lave shows that even in the case of arithmetic, an intellectual form of knowledge if there ever was one, it is not possible to separate the body, the self, the activity-support of apprenticeship, and the social and physical setting within which it is utilized.

"There ain't nuthin' to explain, what you want me t'explain?"; "We'll see later, just box." When one does not grasp his indications straight away, he contents himself with reiterating them, adding gestures to the words if need be, without concealing his annoyance, or else he gets angry and asks one of his acolytes to take over for him. If a boxer proves unable to correctly execute a blank move on the floor, sparring offers a pedagogical procedure of last resort. Having run out of advice and patience, DeeDee grudgingly resigns himself to calling on the reflex of self-defense to tame a rebellious gesture.

"What did I tell you, Louie? Where you supposed to put your right hand, uh, where? Yeah, right up there, against your right cheek, to protect yourself from the left hook, not down there. You gonna get your head busted, Louie. You don't keep it where it's supposed to be. I'm gonna tell Ashante to show you where you gotta keep that damn right hand. Next time [you spar with him], *I'm gonna tell him to teach you with his left hook* if you don't wanna listen."

"That's the best way to learn, right?"

"No, it ain't the best way. *It's the hard way.* I rather you learn it on your own when I tell you, not by gettin' your face beat up." [Field notes, 17 May 1989]

When he corrects a boxer, DeeDee does it in the most public fashion there is: most of the time, his reprimand is shouted in a loud voice from the back room and heard by everyone. Given the deplorable acoustics of the building, one can never know with total certainty who it is addressed to. In doubt, everyone tends to take it into account for himself and redoubles his attention and application. Similarly, when DeeDee is posted in his armchair behind the office window, from which he takes in the entire exercise area in a single glance, it is difficult to say exactly who he is observing. Here again, one is better off assuming that you are the one he is watching and box the best you can so as not to risk drawing his wrath. Finally, the fact that one can go for days, even weeks, without receiving the slightest evaluation from him, positive or negative, makes one anxious to know whether one is making progress or not, if what one is doing is good or not. This uncertainty gives one the feeling of groping one's way forward blindly, and it forces the apprentice boxer to be conscientious and apply himself in every session and at every drill.[98] Every one of DeeDee's interventions and the very manner in which he deploys them act as a mechanism of *permanent collective correction*. One might even speculate that the rarer DeeDee's visible interventions, the more durable and ramifying their effect.

What might pass for a lack of interest on the coach's part or a deficiency in his supervision is in fact the very essence of his teaching method. Guided by his pugilistic sense, the fruit of experience accumulated over decades of practice, DeeDee strives to fine-tune, in an empirical manner, by successive adjustments, the combination of repeated reprimands, silent attention, ostensible indifference, and exhortations best suited to making the practical schemata enter into the corporeal schema of the apprentice pugilist. Everything occurs as if his instructions had no function other than to facilitate and reinforce the proper effect of the manipulation of the body by rendering it more vigorous, more industrious, and more intense, and by instilling in the boxer the belief that a causal link does indeed exist between the efforts demanded of him and the results counted upon, in spite of the repetitive and disjointed character of the advice he receives.

▌ *The conductor*

DeeDee ("DD" or "DeDe," a nickname he owes to his brother, who mocked his stutter thus when he was a child) was born Herman Armour in 1920 in Georgia, where his grandparents were sharecroppers on land owned by a white society family from Atlanta. In 1922, like millions of southern blacks, his parents fled Dixie to rally in Chicago in search of a less oppressive racial climate and less laborious living conditions.[99] His father found work as a city street sweeper, a job with steady pay that was well regarded in the black community at the time, but it was the illegal brewing and selling of liquor to whites during Prohibition that allowed the family to make ends meet. The patriarch made a little money before being killed

---

98. It was during these periods that I discovered that, much like a researcher in the academic field, there is nothing worse for a boxer in the gym than indifference. And it was with relief that I welcomed the reprimands with which DeeDee put an end to it.
99. Loïc Wacquant, "De la 'terre promise' au ghetto. La grande migration noire américaine, 1916–1930," *Actes de la recherche en sciences sociales* 99 (September 1993): 43–51.

by members of a rival gang of bootleggers. "He wasn't pushing his broom much, see, he was pushing his moonshine wagon instead of his broom." DeeDee was seven years old.

During the Great Depression and until the war, DeeDee lived with his mother and six brothers and sisters in a little house with an adjoining kitchen garden and a henhouse at the edge of the South Side ghetto. "Nobody had work in those days, *nobody.* Not d'white folks, not d'black folks. Everybody was desperately lookin' for work, lookin' for money. You had to survive hustlin' in those days. Only the war pulled us out of that mess. They did it on purpose to get out of the depression, that I know for sure. All of a sudden, all them factories were lookin' for labor. You got work everywhere! People were earnin' lotsa money. Scrap metal was selling for crazy prices: guys who had a pile of old metal in their backyards, they became millionaires overnight, when they were gatherin' up all the metal they could to make airplanes an' bombs. Junkyards became gold mines."[100]

A notorious scrapper from the age of six, DeeDee got initiated into boxing at school as a teenager, at a time when "everybody dreamed of only one thing, to be Joe Louis," the first great black champion of the modern era.[101] After a brief and rather unglorious career in the ring (he fought forty amateur matches and a single "pro" fight against one of the fighters he was training, who out of courtesy allowed him to claw out a draw), he stepped to the other side of the ropes for good. For although he had arthritis in his hands and knees,

---

100. For an intimist portrait of the South Side at midcentury, read the classic work by St. Clair Drake and Horace Cayton, *Black Metropolis,* and Richard Wright, *Twelve Million Black Voices: A Folk History of the Negro in the United States,* with photographs by Edwin Rosskam (New York: Viking Press, 1941; new ed. New York: Thunder's Mouth Press, 1988).
101. The "Brown Bomber," whose rise coincided with the second "Golden Age" of prizefighting in America, was then a national hero, for having symbolically crushed Nazism in the person of German champion Max Schmeling in June 1938, but also and especially a living legend for the African-American community, to which he gave ethnic pride and self-confidence by destroying, in the ring, the myth of the congenital inferiority of blacks. Chris Mead, *Champion: Joe Louis, Black Hero in White America* (New York: Scribner's, 1985); Sammons, *Beyond the Ring,* 96–129.

DeeDee gives "time" from the back room

young Herman unquestionably had the eye and touch required to teach the Sweet science, whose infinitely varied figures he had discovered in the teeming gyms of the South Side and in the movies he would devour for hours on end. "You had them movie machines in the taverns, where you put in a nickel an' you could watch a little snippet of a boxing film through a viewer. I spent hours an' hours watching 'em and tha's how I learned." Following in the footsteps of Joe Louis's trainer, Jack Blackburn, who briefly took him under his wing before he died, DeeDee soon made a regional and then a national reputation for himself. Between 1978 and 1985 he took a dozen boxers into the top ten of the international rankings; two of his charges won a world title: Roberto Cruz as a welterweight and Alfonzo Ratliff in the cruiserweight division. He has always exercised his talents in Chicago, except for six years spent in Japan and the Philippines training some of the best Asian fighters, and a brief sojourn in Los Angeles instigated by a big West Coast promoter. Considered by his peers one of the best coaches in the history of American boxing, DeeDee was elected to the Boxing Hall of Fame in Louisville, Kentucky, in 1987. But he did not have the means to pay for the trip, and so he missed the induction ceremony that was supposed to mark the apotheosis of his career.

Nowadays DeeDee scrapes by on the $364 he receives every month from Supplemental Security Income (a federal program of aid to senior citizens without resources who suffer from disability). He owns no possessions and does not receive any retirement benefits, having only worked as a wage earner for a total of two and a half years. "I had all kindsa jobs, in restaurants, hotels, cook, waiter, handyman for hire, and I lived off the street. You do what you gotta do to survive on d'street, Louie, see what I mean?" Among the trades he plied, if only briefly, alongside his primary activity as a boxing trainer: manual laborer, metal worker, window washer, bouncer, taxi driver, street vendor, exterminator of cockroaches and other insects and rodents that infest the ghetto's hovels, housepainter, and bodyguard in a brothel.[102] He does not complain: "I know guys who slaved away for twenty, thirty years and who get, what? not even five hundred bucks worth-a retirement? I get that much and I didn' even

102. This "double activity" is typical: with the exception of boxing instructors employed by the city's Park District, all the trainers in Chicago have a second job outside their gym.

work." Every week DeeDee sets aside a dollar or two to buy a few lottery tickets in a nearby liquor store. He improves his usual fare by levying from time to time a "private tax" on the few boxers in the club who have the means to give him "a lil' somethin' on the side, five or ten dollars." On occasion, the director of the day-care center next door gives him leftover food from the children's tea parties. When there are fights in town, Curtis's manager sometimes brings him bags of fruits and vegetables from his ranch.

The collective ascesis of which DeeDee is the conductor at the gym matches his own Spartan personal life: up at dawn, early to bed, a diet based on boiled vegetables, fresh fish, and lean meat (chicken and turkey), never any soda pop or sweets, rarely a drop of alcohol (except for the Armagnac I bring him every time I return from a trip to France), and a visit to the doctor every six months (paid for by Medicaid, on account of his circulation problems and the arthritis in his wrists that prevents him from driving). DeeDee shares a tiny apartment on 67th Street that he rents with an adopted niece, a single mother who takes classes in a small, private beauty school to get a hairdresser-manicurist diploma and who helps with the housework in exchange for her lodging. This diploma is the ultimate for her and she talks about it as an exceptional achievement, which she attributes in good measure to DeeDee's unshakable moral support. When she was thinking of quitting school, he threatened her: "If you don't finish school, I'monna give you the whuppin' of your life, a whuppin' you'll remember 'til the day they put you in the ground."

For his part, DeeDee has no activities outside of boxing and he spends most of his days at the gym, even when almost no one comes in on the brutally cold days of winter. His time is divided between supervising the workouts and endless phone conversations and discussions with the gym's habitual visitors. His schedule is unchanging: just before noon, he takes the bus near his house, stops by Daley's (the family restaurant on the corner of Cottage Grove and 63rd Street) to drink a bowl of soup, then opens the gym. A little after seven, having wrapped up the day's training, he closes the heavy grate that protects the storefront of the Boys Club and catches a ride home with one of his boxers—this is how I became his regular driver. In the evening, he looks after his great-nephew

Will while watching the boxing matches broadcast on the sports networks that he gets thanks to an illegal cable hookup one of his nephews set up for twenty dollars. He never goes to the movies, does not like to eat out, no longer frequents nightclubs (where he loved to display his recognized talents as a dancer in years past), and he detests taking walks. The fight cards in which his boxers participate are his only outings.

DeeDee has been in charge of the Woodlawn boxing club since it opened in 1977, but he refuses to consider himself to be "working" there. First, because he is not remunerated for it—"They don't pay me a dime, it's all volunteer. Every year, they palm off another nice lil' plaque to thank me for keepin' it goin' and tha's it. But you cain't eat no plaque"—and, next, because he cannot conceive of being anywhere else or doing anything else: "See, Louie, I don't work here. It's not a job. I hang around d'gym, tha's all. I hung around in other gyms before, at Fuller Park, at Johnny Coulon's place, over on the West Side. If I wasn't here, I probably be down at Fuller Park. Gotta find me a gym where I can hang 'round, pass the time. . . . Gotta be in a gym, watch them guys work, be involved with boxin' in some kinna way, 'cos tha's how it is when you got it in your blood. I couldn't get on without boxin'." The rest of DeeDee's time is taken up in preparation for the fights of the boxers he trains and to whom he offers his services as "cornerman" for a small fee that the latter insist on giving him (around 10 percent of their modest purses or a couple of twenty-dollar bills for an evening). As much on principle as for lack of financial means, DeeDee never attends a local card if he cannot get in free: he finds the idea of paying to see a bout utterly absurd. Besides, his notoriety in the area is such that it is unusual for him not to have complimentary tickets.

Like most coaches, especially those from the "ole school," DeeDee maintains complex and ambiguous relationships with his charges, for whom he is at once trainer, mentor, watchdog, life adviser, and personal confidant, and who pay him a filial piety that far surpasses their professional admiration.[103] It used to be this way

---

103. One finds a profusion of precise notations on these relationships of intermingled authority and affection between trainers and their boxers in Ronald K. Fried's *Corner Men*.

in the old days with Alfonzo, for whom DeeDee went so far as to cook at the gym every afternoon to make sure he was eating right. These days it is this way with Curtis, whom he treats with a mix of feigned lack of interest and rough affection that sometimes turn into authoritarianism, and with whom he has developed a quasi-paternal relationship over the years. In front of Curtis, DeeDee pretends to be indifferent to his behavior outside the gym, when in reality he worries about it constantly: proof, he is in daily phone contact with Sherry, Curtis's wife, to find out if the latter is following his instructions in those areas of life presumed to affect his performance in the ring: food, family relations, and sexual habits. DeeDee acts as buffer between Curtis and his manager; he helps him handle his tumultuous relations with the woman directing the day-care center that occupies the front part of the Woodlawn Boys Club building, for which Curtis works as janitor; he attentively follows the course of his financial troubles, his housing problems, and his wranglings with the welfare office. In short, DeeDee is intimately involved in every facet of Curtis's private life, and Curtis for his part considers the old coach a second father and greatly valorizes his wisdom: "DeeDee an' me, we have a relationship, we talk, we always jokin' with each other, but we have serious conversations too—I believe everything he tells me, 'cuz, after all, (lowering his voice to stress his respect) *it's not for nothing that he's managed to live seventy years,* uh? You know he wasn't seventy years old when he was born, so he knows *so much more* than me. I couldn' even catch up with him. But him and me gotta have a lil' argument from time t'time, just to make his day. That way, when I leave the gym, he can smile and shake his head an' stuff . . ."

Thus, on the morning of the fight in which Curtis would win the title of Illinois state champion, DeeDee is complaining—half-serious, half-ironic, and clearly proud—that Curtis treats him like a child, preventing him from drinking and smoking, when he should have the right to indulge in those little pleasures at his age: "If he see me smokin', he comes over an' yells at me: 'Drop dat cigarette, DeeDee, put it out right now!' and he start yellin' at me like I'm a lil' kid. (Grumbling) Hey! I'm sixty-nine damn years old, if you can't let yourself have a little fun at sixty-nine, then I don't know when . . . If he see me with a glass a-wine or liquor, he gets mad at me and chews me out, he tell me to put it down. Same as with the cigarette.

Com'on! I ain't his father and he ain't my son, damn it! I take care a-him, sure, but he's not my son, no, to tell me what I should and shouldn' be doin'." We laugh and tease him by pointing out that after all, he's lucky that Curtis pays so much attention to him and that he'll only live longer for it. [Field notes, 25 November 1988]

But pugilistic pedagogy does not aim solely at transmitting a technique; it also has for function to constitute, in a practical way, the objectively rational expectations liable to facilitate the apprentice boxer's climb through the fistic hierarchy. To find and keep one's place in the pugilistic universe, one must indeed know and always take account of one's physical and moral limits, not let one's aspirations "take off" unrealistically, not seek to rise higher and faster than is reasonable, on pain of squandering one's energy, risking getting demolished by far superior opponents, and exposing oneself to losing face. This is why the trainer's instructions to his boxers frequently take the form of incitements to modesty, invitations to repeat the same gestures without shirking and without trying to overstep their capacities, to respect the seemingly stationary pace that he impresses on their apprenticeship.

Through his remarks, his criticism, and his encouragement but also his prolonged silences or his attentive presence, DeeDee lifts up those who, from lack of confidence or shyness, stoop below their worth ("You know how to box as well as d'rest of them now, Louie: if I put in you in there with Jeff, you're gonna give 'im a good ass whuppin'") and takes down those who, elated by their progress in the gym or by their success in the ring, start to bluster, thinking that they have "made it" and try to box beyond their capacities. Pugilistic pedagogy is thus inseparably a pedagogy of humility and honor whose goal is to inculcate in each the *sense of limits* (which is also a sense of the group and of one's place in the group), as these two fragments from my diary attest.

22 October 1988. At the "gala" night organized every year to replenish the club's coffers, Little John (twenty-four years old, a messenger and security guard in a feared housing project of the South Side) is fighting for the first time. He is overanxious and blundering, and he hits very hard and without rhyme or reason. . . . I see DeeDee fulminating in his office. All of a sudden, he bursts out into the main room, glaring, and vociferates in the direction of the ring: "What you think you tryin' to do, John, uh? Cut out this bullshit and just box.

You tryin' to look like a boxer and you look like nuthin'!" He turns on his heels with a disgusted look and returns to the back room to wrap Rico's hands.

22 March 1989. Curtis has left for a spell in the South Carolina countryside to rest at his manager's farm in order to get ready for his first big fight in Atlantic City next month—a chance for him to break into the international rankings very shortly. I ask DeeDee if he's gone by plane or by bus. "I be damned, Louie, he took the bus! Who is he to think he'd fly over, uh?" Killer Keith is surprised: "It's not gonna be too exhausting for him to be on the bus that long, DeeDee? 'Cuz it take what—fifteen, eighteen hours on the bus?" "Takes nineteen hours to get to South Carolina by Greyhound [a low-price bus company] It don't bother me. *Who does he think he is, Curtis? He's nobody, he's nuthin'.* I told 'im. All that time on the bus, that'll give him some time to think an' get somethin' into his head."

This propaedeutic in modesty applies particularly to novices who are always tempted, out of a desire to do well mingled with ignorance or out of admiration for their more advanced colleagues, to skip stages and try out drills that require more technical skill than they have. Here is DeeDee's reaction when, on 10 January 1989, I succumbed to that temptation by trying to punch the double-end bag in the same way as Tony, a professional pugilist with six years of experience in the amateurs.

While I'm putting my clothes back on, DeeDee comes out and gives me a piece of his mind: "You was a total disgrace on that bag, Louie, really horrible, awful to watch." I didn't hear what he said and I have the misfortune of asking him to repeat his remark. He doesn't mind at all: "You was a real disgrace, jumpin' around that bag swinging your arms. What you think you're doin' on that bag, it's for workin' your jab and here all you're doin' is swing your body in every direction without keepin' your hands up, awful! What is that? I couldn't even look it was so awful."

This really pisses me off. I could sense that I didn't know how to box properly on that bag, but still! "Next time, I'll come earlier and you can show me how to use that bag."

"Ain't nuthin' to it, Louie, *I got nuthin' to show you, what d'you want me to show you?* You just got to work on your jab, you stand close to the bag and work on your jab, your timin', tha's all."

On that note, he walks out of the office with us and goes into his stance in front of the bag, which he starts to pat lightly, while explaining: "Just stay near the bag, jab, jab, let it slip, one-two, jab, one-two, jab, like on the speed bag. If it come back at you, you block it with your right hand." He teases the double-end bag with short lefts, in cadence with its swinging, very lightly, his legs slightly bent, his torso leaning forward—he is very graceful. I apply myself, trying to throw several little jabs in cadence, slowly, like he did; it's obviously easier than what I was attempting to do earlier.

"Here you go, tha's all you gotta do. *Nobody's askin' you to do more'n that.* If the bag swings all the way back at you, you block it like this" [with the palm of the right hand open, near his face].

"Okay, I'll try to do better next time, DeeDee."

He's already disappeared into the kitchen.

If DeeDee can allow himself such an economy of words and gestures, it is because *the gist of pugilistic knowledge is transmitted outside of his explicit intervention,* through a "silent and practical communication, from body to body,"[104] which is not a dialogue between the sole teacher and his pupil but rather a conversation of multiple voices open to all the regular participants in the workout. The teaching of boxing at the Woodlawn Boys Club is a collective teaching in three respects: it is effected in a coordinated manner, within the group created by the synchronization of drills; it makes each participant a potential visual model, positive or negative, for all the others; and, finally, the most seasoned pugilists serve as so many assistants who relay, reinforce, and if need be substitute for the trainer's seeming (in)action. In this way, whether he knows it or not, each boxer collaborates in the education of all the others.

At the heart of the apparatus of pugilistic apprenticeship stands the common rhythm that envelops all of the gym's activities and saturates them with its specific temporality. Like a human stopwatch, DeeDee sings out the gym's peculiar tempo all day long, alternately yelling *"Time in!"* to indicate the start of a round of exercise and *"Time out!"* to mark its end. At the sound of the *"Time in!"* all the boxers get to work as a single man. Each three-minute block of time thus delineated is followed

104. Bourdieu, "Programme for a Sociology of Sport," 166.

by a thirty-second rest period (one minute if sparring is simultaneously in progress), during which a precarious calm sets in, before a new *"Time in!"* sets the merry-go-round spinning again. Not a moment of dead time or free time. No matter what hour they begin their workout or what drill they are doing, the pugilists are always working in concert, because respect for this tempo is an imperative that brooks no exception and that imposes itself, by itself, on everyone—it is unthinkable to be working out of sync, and an inattentive boxer who misses the start of a round or confuses it with the rest signal is promptly called back to order by DeeDee or by one of his peers ("DeeDee said *'Time in!'* Get t'work, man").

Gym time is a time filled, a time constrained that brands the body and fashions it according to its rhythm. Drills paced in this manner gradually habituate the organism to alternating intense effort with fast recuperation according to the tempo specific to the game, to the point where the body becomes *inhabited* by that necessity.[105] Over time, it adjusts the boxer's "biological clock" so that his body can, on its own, chant the succession of rounds. (I realized that my own body had become capable of counting in three-minute segments one frigid winter day when DeeDee had left the gym early and I trained by myself with a stopwatch).

Once it is realized that the temporalization of pugilistic practice forms the very plinth of its teaching, one understands why control over the collective tempo of training assumes a particular importance. Barring unusual circumstances, only DeeDee, his second Charles Martin, and the student trainer Eddie are authorized to give the *"Time!"* signal, and no one is allowed to use DeeDee's stopwatch without his express permission. That stopwatch is to the old coach of Woodlawn what the *skeptron* was to the kings of medieval courts, according to Émile Benveniste[106]— the symbol and the instrument of the authority that he wields over the collective thus delineated. To take it away from him would be tantamount to questioning that authority, to depriving DeeDee of the sole emblem of his function in the gym (other than the navy blue polo shirt with "Staff, Chicago Boys and Girls Club" emblazoned on it that he always wears).

---

105. A boxing match consists of three rounds for amateurs and four, six, eight, or ten rounds for professionals, according to their level (twelve for a world title fight). Each round lasts three minutes, with a one-minute rest period between rounds.
106. Émile Benveniste, *Indo-European Language and Society* (Coral Gables, Fl.: University of Miami Press, 1973, orig. 1969).

Stopwatch in hand, DeeDee supervises
the sparring from his desk

This is probably why the Woodlawn gym, unlike most others, never got
an electric timer that automatically signals the rounds.[107] Besides, after
a lifetime spent in boxing gyms, the stopwatch has become a sort of
supplementary organ for DeeDee, like an extension of his body. Even
his phone conversations are interrupted by the rhythmic refrain of the
"Time in!" and *"Time out!"* and he sometimes finds himself, at the end
of a long day spent at the club, still mechanically reeling off the rounds
even after the last boxer there has finished his workout.

107. The gyms described by Hauser (*Black Lights*) and Plummer (*Buttercups and
Strong Boys*) are equipped with automatic clocks that signal the beginning and
end of the rounds with two distinct bells. The three other "pro" gyms in Chicago all
operate with an electric bell.

The mere synchronization of movements in time and the physical proximity of the pugilists in space are such that one is *seeing* bodies in action at every moment—including your own when you are shadowboxing in front of the mirror. This continuous visual and auditory reinforcement generates a state of "collective effervescence" quite reminiscent of the frenetic excitement of the great aboriginal totemic ceremonies of colonial Australia,[108] which has the effect of facilitating the assimilation of gestures by prodding participants to drop their inhibitions, to "let go" of their bodies, and to whip up their energy. The fact that one is always *being seen* at every moment by all the others also forces you to apply yourself, for fear of appearing ridiculous, as can be glimpsed in this description dated 26 September 1988.

> Today there's a crowd of people, I've never seen so many boxers in the gym: fifteen when we started out and thirty-five when we finished, a total zoo! It's impressive to see everyone get busy with so much ardor. DeeDee yells out his *"Time! Work!"* in a firm voice, particularly stressing the *"work!"* On the contrary, his voice drops and dies out when he yells *"Time out!"* I say hello to everyone. . . . Guys follow one after another without interruption into the ring for rounds of vigorous sparring. A veritable swarm of boxers invades the back room in waves, putting their gear on, coating their faces with Vaseline, slipping on their gloves, fastening them with tape, bouncing nervously in place, or taking off their headguard and cup before going back out in front of the mirror to resume their workout. . . .

> I'm wasted, but it does me a world of good to work like this in unison in such a maelstrom of punches, exhalations, slips across the ring, jumping, and efforts of all kinds, in this atmosphere of joyous physical high. After a moment, it is *as if you were in an altered state, carried forth by the collective cadence of the drills and by the noise* that grows deafening (especially when Smithie is on the sand bag and Ratliff on the speed bag: you'd think you're hearing a combination of bazooka and machine-gun fire). Intoxicated by moving and shaking at the same time as everyone else, you let yourself get swept along. *"Time in, work!"* Three minutes, all out.

108. Émile Durkheim, *The Elementary Forms of Religious Life,* trans. Karen Fields (New York: Free Press, 1995, orig. 1912), esp. pp. 218–228.

"Time out!" Everyone comes to a stop at the same time. The guys take advantage of the opportunity to exchange a few words, often brief wisecracks, because above all you have to catch your breath and a thirty-second respite doesn't leave you time for conversation. Or else they drink in silence from the water bottle sitting on the table near the ring, then spit the water back out into the bucket. *"Time, work-work-work!"* And here we go, all over again!

The temporal coordination of the drills is such that every boxer has at all times before his eyes a complete gamut of models from whom to draw inspiration. Pugilistic knowledge is thus transmitted by mimeticism or countermimeticism, by watching how others do things, scrutinizing their moves, spying on their responses to DeeDee's instructions, copying their routine, by imitating them more or less consciously—in other words, outside of the explicit intervention of the coach. Over the course of workouts, one learns, in the tacit mode documented by Michael Polanyi,[109] to spot potential models by finding one's location in the subtle hierarchy, at once fuzzy and precise, and imperceptible to the non-initiated, that structures the space of the gym.

If actual practice is here the necessary passage (*methodos*) toward understanding the "social art" that is pugilism, it is because it alone allows one to engage the mutual solicitation between a body and a field that question and provoke each other. It is only from the moment that the habitus of the apprentice boxer is able to "recognize" the stimuli and invitations of the gym that the apprenticeship truly sets in. Every gesture, every posture of the pugilist's body possesses an infinite number of specific properties that are minute and invisible to those who do not have the appropriate categories of perception and appreciation, and that DeeDee's advice struggles to convey.[110] There is an "eye of the boxer" that cannot be acquired without a minimum of actual practice of the sport and that in turn renders that practice meaningful and comprehensible.

109. Michael Polanyi, *The Tacit Dimension* (Garden City, N.Y.: Doubleday, 1967).
110. Howard Becker's remarks on photography are quite apposite here: just as one must know how to decipher a snapshot according to a specific code in order to bring out all the sociological information it contains, so the beginning pugilist cannot derive all the potential benefit of the "visual advice" he gets from his peers until he knows how to decipher all the messages being emitted around him. Howard Becker, "Photography and Sociology," in *Doing Things Together* (Evanston, Ill.: Northwestern University Press, 1986), 223–271.

Training teaches the movements—that is the most obvious part—
but it also inculcates in a practical manner the schemata that allow one
to better differentiate, distinguish, evaluate, and eventually reproduce
these movements. It sets into motion a *dialectic of corporeal mastery
and visual mastery:* to understand what you have to do, you watch the
others box, but you do not truly see what they are doing unless you have
already understood a little with your eyes, that is to say, with your body.
Every new gesture thus apprehended-comprehended becomes in turn
the support, the materials, the tool that makes possible the discovery
and thence the assimilation of the next.

▌ *A visual and mimetic apprenticeship*

I slip on my red training gloves and climb into the ring. I'm all alone
at first and it's a little intimidating to shadowbox in front of all the
old-timers and the matchmaker Jack Cowen, who are watching me
from the foot of the ring. I concentrate on throwing my jab well, on
doubling up on it, on following it up with left hooks while keeping my
feet firmly on the mat and turning my torso correctly. In the second
round, Smithie (in a blue tank top and shorts, his hands wrapped
in red, a white bandana around his forehead) climbs into the ring,
and I can observe him up close and imitate his moves. He's like
a boxing machine: bent forward slightly from the waist, his hands
set out like a fan in front of his face, his gestures are short, precise,
restrained, and so well coordinated they seem almost mechanical.
He is streaming with sweat and his face looks serious to the point of
sullenness; every gesture rips a Homeric grimace from him. I follow
him like a living model: when he doubles up his jab, I double mine
up; when he bends his legs to deliver a series of short uppercuts by
slipping under the guard of his imaginary opponent, I do likewise.
It's terrific, it forces me to really apply myself. And now Cliff also slips
through the ropes and joins us. I love his short, low jab and I try to
imitate it. I follow him closely and box like he does (or at least I try
to). *"Time out!"* We catch our breath.

Rodney climbs into the ring, so I decide to hang on and keep going.
In a hoarse voice, DeeDee shouts out an energetic *"Time-work!"*
I'm having a whale of a time in the ring, stimulated to be amid
Smithie, Cliff, and Rodney. For three minutes, our four bodies enact
a spontaneous, noisy ballet: hissing, huffing, sweating, gnashing,
snorting, clawing the air with our fists, we fence without respite. This
multiplies my energy and I stay two rounds longer than planned.

KODAK 5076   28*

▷ 27A   28

Eddie (back to the camera) keeps an eye on Lorenzo
and Little Keith (warming up shadowboxing on the
floor and in front of the mirror before sparring),
Jimmy and Steve (working in the ring), and
"Boxhead" John on the speed bag

I feel like I'm getting my punches off better and I concentrate on landing cleanly on my imaginary target with every one of them. Rodney pretends to spar at a distance with Smithie; they thrash around, miming lively attacks, slips, and counterattacks. I outdo myself, putting together advances of jabs followed by vigorous rights and snappy uppercuts, before backing up, still throwing series of hooks and straights and blocking the punches of my "mental opponent." Whew! I can't take it any more. I get down out of the ring, liquefied but as if transported by the presence of my buddies. [Field notes, 30 May 1989]

I wrap my hands and come over to post myself between Mark and Curtis in front of the small mirror for three rounds. It's exhilarating to be shadowboxing next to the Illinois state champion! I watch Curtis like a hawk out of the corner of my eye and try to reproduce all of his gestures: hooks and short jabs; nervous, fast, sharp movements with a "give" of the shoulder; nimble and precise footwork. I imitate him as best I can, and in the enthusiasm of the moment I frankly feel like a real boxer. To my left, Smithie is showing Ashante a slip that Ashante apparently doesn't have in his repertoire—which goes to show that you always have something to learn. [Field notes, 24 June 1989]

Finally, the teaching of boxing is a collective enterprise in the sense that the trainer is assisted in his functions by all the members of the club. First, by the most experienced professional boxers, who collaborate informally but actively in the instruction of beginners, as well as by the other trainers or old-timers who come spend an afternoon in the gym from time to time. (Their involvement is welcome as long as it is directed to the amateur boxers; in the case of professionals, only the trainer to whom the boxer is linked by contract is allowed to supervise his workout, along with DeeDee.) Once he has demonstrated his earnestness through his assiduity, abnegation, and courage in the ring, each newcomer is taken under the group's wing; his progress then becomes a matter of a diffuse collective responsibility. In the course of my initiation, I received advice from the main habitués of the club, who one by one took it upon themselves to correct and encourage me, this one rectifying the position of my back leg, that one the angle of my uppercut, while yet another indicated to me how to block my opponent's punches by relying on my elbows and initiated me into the secrets of slipping. Ashante, Smithie, Big Earl, Anthony, and Eddie each taught me a facet of the craft, either

Reggie shows an attentive recruit
how to throw the uppercut

on his own or in tandem with DeeDee, by relaying or complementing his instructions. After a year of regular training, DeeDee asked me in turn to show the rudiments of footwork and the use of the speed bag to a fresh recruit who, like me, had come from the University of Chicago.

Each member of the club passes on to those below him in the objective and subjective hierarchy of the gym the knowledge that he has received from those situated above him. Boxers of equivalent strength also share their experience, teaching each other techniques and tricks. Even bad boxers have the virtue of serving as negative models for the others: in the manner of crimes against the "pugilistic collective conscience," they function as so many living reminders of the practical norm to be attained and respected. This type of organization is not specific to the Woodlawn gym. The gym run by Mickey Rosario in East Harlem operates according to the same collective and graduated scheme, which Plummer characterizes with the following analogy: "The gym operates as a family, with the older or more veteran kids looking after their smaller, less seasoned or able siblings. Skills are handed down like clothes in a large family. Each kid is but the custodian of the know-how some bigger kid has entrusted to him and is obliged, in turn, to pass it along to the next youngster in line."[111] Here, for example, is how DeeDee and Anthony joined to teach me how to block an opponent's jab one fine day in May 1989.

I start off with five rounds in front of the mirror. I try to move my head properly, right and left, between punches. From the back room, DeeDee tells me to bring my right fist back toward the inside at the same time to catch my opponent's fist. "Make a cup, make a cup with yo' hand to catch his glove, Louie. . . . Keep your elbow close to your side, your elbow shouldn't move, only your hand moves. . . . Keep your right up and turn it like a cup, your head goes to the right." I don't understand very well what he's yelling to me and I step into the back room. DeeDee shows me how to make my wrist pivot while opening my palm to the inside and curving my fingers so as to form a cradle in which to hem my opponent's jab. "It's easy, it's like A, B, C. You turn just your wrist outward, curve your fingers an' catch his glove, but your elbow don't move. It's easy, Louie, ain't nuthin' to it, watch." Yeah, it's easy when you know how to do it.

I apply myself to rehearsing the gesture that DeeDee is showing me but without really managing to do it. My elbow keeps lifting up in spite of my efforts. "Don't move yo' elbow, Louie, what did I tell you? You see d'guy across from you, you tell him: 'You wanna throw your jab, man? Okay, go ahead!' You block it with your right hand and then, *wham!* Hook to the body, like that." [He does this little demonstration for me sitting in his chair.] "It's not easy, DeeDee." "Yeah it's easy, damn it, it's like A, B, C, I'm tellin' you."

111. Plummer, *Buttercups and Strong Boys,* 67 (the past tense is changed to present).

Shoot, *every time you think you've mastered a move, you realize that in fact that's not the case at all and that it's a lot more complicated.* I thought I knew how to slip with my head and block jabs, but I was dead wrong. It's not so much the head that moves as it is the hand that seizes the opponent's oncoming fist to interrupt its trajectory; as for the head, it only swivels on its axis behind the protective cradle of the fist. Anthony interrupts me during the next round to show me how to catch his fist. It's embarrassing to have to have this movement, seemingly so simple, explained to me again, but in fact it's not as simple as that: the wrist pivots, the hand forms a cradle, elbow immobile, then the weight of the body is shifted left to counter with a jab or a left hook. Anthony mimes a jab that he has me catch with my right hand, then he guides my other arm to execute the counter with the left. My left fist slips too low and hits my other hand. He shows me again, once, twice. From his chair, DeeDee also continues to give me advice. I think that I'm starting to grasp the mechanics better, but it's hard to go from mental comprehension to physical realization.

I start up my round again after Anthony leaves me. Instead of trying immediately to redo alone the movements he showed me, I first throw some jab-straight combinations to get rid of my nervousness. DeeDee is walking around the room, from one guy to another, when he's not on the phone. Passing near me, he corrects my footwork. "Your knees should always be bent ten percent. You don't turn your damn right foot, you just lift it up." So much attention honors and intimidates me at the same time. But it's still super, I'm having a ball. [Field notes, 17 May 1989]

This particular form of collective "learning by doing" presupposes certain definite conditions. First, a condition of numbers: in my experience, there must be neither too many nor too few boxers involved. Beyond a score of fighters, you tend to get lost in the crowd and it becomes difficult to attract DeeDee's attention or the advice of peers. At the opposite end, if there are fewer than four or five, the "collective effervescence" effect is nullified and one disposes of too few models in action, or the models are too remote to spur you on—when that happens at the end of the day, and with the onset of fatigue, DeeDee sometimes even briefly loses interest in the training, to the point of forgetting to give the *"Time!"* The second condition is that the volume of pugilistic capital collectively held by the members of the club (including in objectified forms, as one must not forget to count among the gym's pedagogical tools all the equipment, special clothing, furniture, posters and advertisements, certificates, trophies, photos, etc.) must pass a minimal threshold. Relatedly, the distribution of competencies must be sufficiently continuous so that no one finds himself too far from his immediate neighbors in the specific hierarchy (this applies equally to sparring, where a boxer who does not have adequate partners on hand in the gym may be forced to bring some in from the outside, sometimes for pay). The third necessary condition is a stable nucleus of professional boxers (whom a good many gyms have great difficulty holding onto) which gives mutual teaching its continuity in time by counteracting the ebb and flow of the novices.

One must therefore guard against the mistake of focusing on the trainer for, comparable in this respect to the king in the court society dissected by Norbert Elias,[112] it is only through and thanks to the complete network of relations constituting the space of (physical, auditory, and visual) exchanges of the Woodlawn Boys Club gym that DeeDee exercises his proper efficacy. Within this spatiotemporal setup, he operates in the manner of an *implicit orchestra conductor*, walking around among his pupils and correcting their gestures by little touches, now out loud with comments of a general order that because they are aimed at no one in particular receive the immediate attention of everyone, now with specific remarks ("Keep your guard higher," "Turn your wrist to the inside when you're makin' contact," "Throw a right to the head instead a let-tin' your arm hang there") that each boxer diligently applies to himself, even when they are addressed to others, or, finally, by his attentive presence which suffices more often than not to produce a spontaneous self-correction of the movements by the pugilists who can feel themselves under DeeDee's gaze. This silent and negative pedagogy, which leaves very little room for words or visible actions, seeks above all to ensure that everyone respects the communal tempo and remains in his proper place in the collective enterprise. At any given moment, a *mutual correction by the group* is taking place, which propagates and multiplies the effects of the slightest actions on the part of the coach.

Doxic adhesion to this traditional mode of transmission expresses and perpetuates a pugilistic "sense of honor" based on respect for the

---

112. Norbert Elias, *The Court Society,* trans. Edmund Jephcott (New York: Pantheon Books, 1983, orig. 1969).

heritage received and on the notion, accepted by all as tacit condition for admission into the specific universe, that everyone must pay with his person, not take shortcuts, not cheat his body and his sport by innovating heterodox methods. The refusal to rationalize training and to systematically explicate the apprenticeship is anchored in *ethical dispositions* whose internalization is the hidden face of the learning of gestural technique: an ethic of individual work, mutual respect, physical courage, and humility nourished by the "belief in the sanctity of rules existing since time immemorial," as Max Weber says.[113] This refusal is not due simply to the very real penury of the club's material means. Witness the unused equipment such as the rowing machine, the dumbbells, and the inclined situp board sleeping in a dusty corner of the back room. The way the gym uses video is symptomatic of this deliberate rejection of advanced technological means and of the "scholarly" relation to boxing they require and foster: when DeeDee borrows the VCR of the neighboring day-care center to watch tapes of fights of members of the club, it is only out of a desire for entertainment, to liven up the training routine, *never with a pedagogical intention*. Granted, the boxers might watch the same fight several times, and everyone enjoys commenting on its highlights; but it would never occur to anyone to rewind the tape and view the same passage several times in a row or in slow motion, or to break up the action sequences into distinct visual segments for the purpose of analyzing them.

Here is another symptom of this refusal of rationalization, under which one might also place the fact that the exercises and dietary regimes followed by the boxers are the object of no methodical calculation or planning:[114] the total disinterest of members of the Boys Club in their future opponents once the contract for a fight has been approved. This indifference, which is manifested by the professional boxers ("It don't matter who he is, I don't give a damn, I gotta fight my fight") and the trainers alike (once the contract has been inked, they hardly bother

113. Max Weber, *Economy and Society: An Outline of Interpretive Sociology*, ed. Guenther Roth and Claus Wittich, 3 vols. (New York: Bedminster Press, 1968), 2:301.
114. None of the trainers or boxers at Woodlawn keeps a written record in which he notes the composition of his training sessions, his food intake, the length and distance of his roadwork, or even his weight, as is recommended for example by a textbook in boxing training such as Jean-Claude Bouttier and Jean Letessier, *Boxe. La technique, l'entrainement, la tactique* (Paris: Robert Laffont, 1978), 97.

to inform themselves ahead of time about their charge's opponent so as to get to know his style, his preferred strategy, his strengths and his weaknesses),[115] would seem at first glance to contradict the continually reaffirmed ethos of optimal and meticulous preparation that suffuses the atmosphere of the gym. This rejection of modern observation and training techniques is no doubt linked to the relative indivision of the functions of support and inculcation in the pugilistic space. Whereas other sports have given birth to complex bureaucracies composed of a multitude of ultraspecialized functions, boxing continues to operate with the old-fashioned triad of the trainer, the cornerman, and the manager, and sometimes the same person assumes all three roles. More profoundly, it is an ethical principle, another relation to the body and to the craft that is affirmed in this way—perhaps even another era of boxing that is surviving into our own.[116]

It is clear that it would be perfectly pointless to try to distinguish, within the knowledge that an apprentice boxer acquires, between what pertains to DeeDee's deliberate interventions and what comes from the influence of the apprentice's peers or from his personal efforts and his individual "talent."[117] For the spring of this *self-regulated pedagogical machinery* constituted by the gym resides neither in the mechanical imitation of certain gestures nor in the sum of the exercises indefatigably

---

115. As is done in more rationalized and bureaucratized sports such as basketball or American football, where the coaches are seconded by a myriad specialized assistants who watch game films of the opposing teams, collect acres of detailed statistics on each of their players and his tendencies, go "spy" on them during their practices, and so on. On the historical process of the rationalization of sports, with a focus on the United States, see Gutman, *From Ritual to Record,* esp. chap. 2.
116. If the opponent of one of his boxers promises to pose particular problems (due to the fact that he is left-handed and boxes as a "southpaw," for example), Eddie sometimes uses the VCR to watch his fights ahead of time if such tapes exist, and he might even (but this is exceptional) travel over to observe him in the ring. This tends to confirm the hypothesis of the rise of a new, more "modern" mode of preparation within the Woodlawn Boys Club. What we know about the preparation of champions through autobiographies and specialized magazines does not enable us to settle the question of the rationalization of pugilistic training one way or the other: the same who adopt the most advanced scientific, dietetic, and medical techniques are quick to return to the venerable methods established by tradition after a defeat (but not vice versa).
117. If one can even give analytic meaning to the folk notion of "talent" after Daniel Chambliss's radical critique of it. Chambliss, "The Mundanity of Excellence," 78–81.

repeated by all, and still less in the *"savoir-pouvoir"* of such agent (in this case, the coach) situated at the nerve center of the edifice. Rather, it resides in the indivisible system of material and symbolic relations that obtain among the different participants, and particularly in the arrangement of their bodies in the physical space of the gym and in its specific time. In a word, it is the "little milieu" of the entire gym "as sheaf of physical and moral forces"[118] that manufactures the boxer.

Managing Bodily Capital

There are few practices for which the French expression *"payer de sa personne"* (which literally means "paying with one's person") takes on a more powerful meaning than for boxing. More than in any other sport, the successful pursuit of a career, especially in the professional ranks, presupposes a rigorous management of the body, a meticulous maintenance of each one of its parts (most notably the hands but also the face),[119] an attention of every moment, in and out of the ring, to its proper functioning and protection. In other words, it requires an extraordinarily efficient relation to the specific capital constituted of one's physical resources, at the edge of rational management. This is because the pugilist's body is at once the *tool* of his work—an offensive weapon and defensive shield—and the *target* of his opponent. Nonetheless, this relation is neither the product of a deliberately maximizing attitude guided by individual decisions made in full knowledge of the facts nor the mechanical effect of external constraints acting onto the body without mediation (in the manner of *"dressage"* according to Foucault),[120] but rather the expression of a *pugilistic practical sense,* a sense of corporeal thrift acquired gradually through long-term contact with other athletes and with coaches, workout after workout and fight after fight, which remains as such inaccessible to conscious and deliberate mastery, in spite of the conjugated efforts of the boxers, trainers, and managers most

118. Durkheim, *Elementary Forms of Religious Life,* 447, my translation.
119. These are the two parts of the pugilist's body exposed to the most severe damage: fractures of the hands (metacarpal, thumb, joints), of the nose and jaw, cutaneous cuts, detached retinas, chronic cerebral lesions that can lead to *dementia pugilistica,* repeated hematomas of the ear followed by detachment of the scapha. G. R. McLatchie, "Injuries in Combat Sports," in *Sports Fitness and Sports Injuries,* ed. Tim Reilly (London: Faber and Faber, 1981), 168–174.
120. Michel Foucault, *Discipline and Punish: The Birth of the Prison* (New York: Vintage Books, 1979; orig. 1975), 170–194.

inclined to the rationalization of their trade.[121] For the knowledge that boxers acquire of the functioning of their bodies, the practical apprehension they have of the limits that must not be exceeded, of the strengths and weaknesses of their anatomy (a low center of gravity or great hand speed, an overly slender neck or brittle hands), the conduct and tactics they adopt in the ring, their conditioning program, and the rules of life they follow pertain not to systematic observation and reflective calculation of the optimal path to follow but, rather, from a sort of "concrete science"[122] of their own bodies, of their somatic potentialities and shortcomings, drawn from daily training and "the often grisly experience of hitting and being hit repeatedly."[123]

There exist many techniques for preserving and making one's *bodily capital* fructify. From the manner of wrapping their hands (and the type of protective bandages used) to the way they breathe during a workout, to all kinds of defensive tricks, to the use of creams, unguents, and elixirs expressly concocted, to special exercises and culinary regimens, the Woodlawn boxers resort to a wide gamut of devices designed to husband and replenish their reserves of energy and protect their strategic organs. Some imitate former champion Jack Dempsey, famed for dipping his hands in brine in order to toughen the skin on his knuckles. Others coat their chest and arms before training with Albolene, an oil that "warms up the body and relaxes the muscles" (according to its directions for use) or spray a vitamin E solution on the ridge of their fists after working out.[124] One slips a dry sponge under his handwraps, so as to cushion the impact of the repeated shocks against the heavy bag, while another, whose bones are fragile relative to his punching power, gets regularly checked out by a hand therapist. Professionals who have the means to hire the services of a paid trainer, such as Ed "Smithie" Smith or former world champion Alfonzo Ratliff, end each workout with a long rubdown under his expert hands. And I could reproduce here nearly

---

121. Recall that "practical sense. . . . orients 'choices' which, though they are not deliberate, are no less systematic, and which, without being ordered and organized in relation to an end, are nonetheless charged with a retrospective finality"; Bourdieu, *Logic of Practice*, 66, my translation.
122. I borrow this expression from Claude Lévi-Strauss, *The Savage Mind* (Chicago: University of Chicago Press, 1966), especially chap. 1, "The Science of the Concrete."
123. Sammons, *Beyond the Ring*, 236.
124. William Plummer reports similar practices in a gym in New York's East Harlem (*Buttercups and Strong Boys*, 62).

Ashante, in his vinyl "sweatsuit," unwrapping
his hands after his workout

word for word the description that Weinberg and Arond offer of the gyms in Chicago in the early 1950s, so closely does it apply to what I observed at the Woodlawn Boys Club:

The boxer comes to consider his body, especially his hands, as his stock-in-trade. Boxers have varied formulas for preventing their hands from excess swelling, from excessive pain, or from being broken. This does not mean a hypochondriachal interest, because they emphasize virility and learn to slough off and to disdain punishment. But fighters continually seek nostrums and exercises for improving their bodies. One practiced Yogi [sic], another became a physical cultist, a third went on periodic fasts; others seek out lotions, vitamins, and other means of improving their endurance, alertness, and punching power.[125]

125. Weinberg and Arond, "Occupational Culture of the Boxer," 462.

This is one of the main paradoxes of boxing: one must *make use of one's body without using it up,* but the management adapted to that objective does not obey a methodical and considered plan, if only because of the precarious living conditions of those who practice it. The pugilist thus navigates "visually" between two equally dangerous reefs—all the more dangerous because they are invisible, mobile over time, and to a great extent subjective: on the one hand, an excess of preparation that squanders resources in vain and needlessly shortens a career; on the other, a lack of discipline and training that increases the risk of serious injury and compromises the chances of success in the ring by leaving part of one's fighting capacities unexploited.

The couple formed by Butch and Curtis offer an ideal-typical realization of this opposition. On the one side, Butch is pugilistic frugality incarnate: he trains and boxes with sobriety and economy; he knows how to deny himself for very long periods of time any deviation from the dietary, sexual, emotional, or professional rules of the craft. Everything in his punctilious conditioning expresses an acute sense of equilibrium and the long term. But Butch's asceticism, which, in its rigor, borders on abstinence with respect to anything that could injure his preparation, sometimes turns into anxiety and then pushes him to train too hard, to consume his forces to the point of consummating them. Curtis, on the other side, embodies a deficit in rationality that manifests itself in sometimes irregular training and in fluctuating moral and physical hygiene. Outside of the gym first, where he does not always prove able to deprive himself of the little pleasures of life (carbonated drinks, sweets, fatty foods), and where his sexual temperance knows highs and lows. In the gym next, where he will sometimes go through long stretches without training (especially after a bout), in contrast to Butch who "clocks in" at the club with the regularity of a metronome. Unlike his older gym-mate, Curtis makes tumultuous, unbridled, almost "crazy" use of his body—that is to say, deviant according to the canons of a rational boxing—as when he walks up to his opponent, nay his sparring partner, with his guard down so as to offer his uncovered face as a provocation, daring the other to risk an attack. In so doing, he uses up his body for nothing, gratuitously exposing himself to injury and to DeeDee's ill-contained ire.

These differences in disposition between the two boxers are redoubled by their respective constitution and character: Butch is easygoing, placid, and always even-tempered; Curtis's moods are constantly changing and unpredictable, his emotions brusque and edgy, worn on his sleeves, and his energy level as erratic as a fever chart. Whereas Butch's training schedule is rarely perturbed by health troubles, Curtis gets sick frequently (DeeDee likes to say that "Curtis, he gets a cold every other day"), to the point that his manager insists on sending him to spend the middle of winter on his farm in South Carolina so he will not have to sacrifice precious weeks of preparation to a tenacious flu. This contrast of personalities is closely correlated with and reinforced by the gap in social condition between the two club-mates: Butch is a proletarian, a member of the blue-collar aristocracy, endowed with a solid job and income; Curtis is a subproletarian, shorn of all social and economic security, subjected to the cycles of employment in unskilled and unstable labor.[126] And the two diverge even in their economic expectations as regards their trade: Butch recognizes that his chances of making money are minimal; Curtis daydreams of a lightning-quick rise that would miraculously catapult him to the very top of the social ladder.

■ Curtis:"In one night, I can make a million dollars"

At 130 pounds and five feet seven inches, Curtis Strong campaigns in the super lightweight category. He is twenty-seven years old and has been boxing as a professional for three years. He came to the Manly art late, after having made a name for himself as a "tough cookie" in his neighborhood. "Since I was short, I always had a whole buncha guys givin' me grief, so I really had to learn how to fight. When I was a kid, I fought *before* school, *during* school and *after* school. Had to defend myself." On the strength of an amateur record of 37 wins for 6 losses, Curtis turned pro in 1986, after taking the title in his division at the Chicago Golden Gloves, the city's most prestigious amateur tournament. Since then, he has confirmed all the hopes pinned on him by the club by winning eight consecutive fights before conquering the Illinois championship in a tough battle, outscoring a Mexican fighter feared for his experience and his punch. (Headlining the card that night was the legendary Roberto

---

126. We find here a classic opposition, established by Bourdieu in the case of the Algerian working class, between two types of social position and between the two systems of expectations and dispositions that correspond to them. Pierre Bourdieu, *Algeria 1960,* trans. Richard Nice (Cambridge: Cambridge University Press, [1977] 1979).

"Manos de Piedra" Duran who, at the ripe age of thirty-seven, took his fourth world title in his 97th pro victory.)

Curtis's manager, Jeb Garney, a rich white dog breeder who owns several farms and stables in Illinois and South Carolina and who sits on the board of directors of the Woodlawn Boys Club, harbors great ambitions for him: "Curtis doesn't know how good he is. If you watch films of the truly great boxers, like Johnny Bratton, Sugar Ray Robinson, Sandy Saddler, or Henry Armstrong, you see that he's got some of the punches and some of the moves of the great ones. He's got it in him. He's young and inexperienced, he sure got a lot to learn, but I feel like he can become a great fighter." However, Curtis is passably lacking in personal discipline and does not always impose on himself the hygiene of life that his career demands. To allow him to train under good conditions and to be able to watch over him better, the Boys Club came up with a quarter-time job as janitor for him. After his daily workout, Curtis waits for closing time to clean the gym, mop the locker room, vacuum the carpet in the entry hall, empty the trashcans, and set the tables in the day-care center back in place.

A catlike and impulsive boxer, gifted with great arm speed and an acute sense of counterpunching, his exceptionally aggressive behavior in the ring, at the edge of losing self-control and breaking the rules, has rightfully earned him the reputation of being a "badass" between the ropes. This nasty athletic persona is in perfect accord with his style, which is to submit his opponent to relentless pressure by marching straight at him and punching from all angles without respite. Yet it is from his Christian faith that Curtis draws his inspiration in the squared circle: he always wears a crucifix on a chain, which he keeps in his boot during fights and never fails to kiss ceremoniously before and after every bout. He never climbs into the ring without first having prayed amid his five brothers and his minister cousin. When I ask him if he "celebrated" after his surprise victory over the state champion at the International Amphitheater, Woodlawn's star boxer answers soberly: "I don't celebrate, I thank God. I dedicated my fight to God. I don't do anything other than what he tell me to do. I'm only executin' his plans for me, in the ring, outside the ring, an' then I thank him, tha's all." Curtis's ambition is that of many young boxers on their way up, who think

A victorious Curtis posing with his brothers, who
brandish his freshly conquerred belt of Illinois
state champion

"the sky's the limit": to win a world title, or, better yet, to unify the three major titles in his weight class and pocket purses numbering in the millions of dollars along the way.

Curtis issues from a subproletarian family at the border of complete destitution (nine children, an absent father, a mother who works sporadically as a barmaid and survives mainly on measly welfare payments), whose reputation is well established in the street. DeeDee tells that "all his brothers are street fighters. They all know how t'fight. But none of 'em come to d'gym, he's the only one. He got a older brother who's shorter than him but even meaner, *really* mean. (With regret in his voice.) It's a damn shame he don't come to d'gym. He's tough, real tough, he's a natural. But he ain't got too much upstairs, he don't get too tired for usin' his mind. Kinda like Curtis."

Long an avid skirt chaser and the father of a two-year-old boy and a one-year-old girl, Curtis resigned himself to marrying their mother when she threatened to leave him after four years of a rocky life together. When a gym-mate reminds him that "DeeDee say that there's only one thing worse than junk food (for a boxer), that's women," Curtis acquiesces: "Yeah, tha's why I got married. All them fights I lost, that was when I was messin' around with chicks. Afterwards, my wife she told me, if we don't get married, she's gonna leave me, it's over with. It make me think, 'cuz I love her an' stuff, you know, so I said to myself, I don't wanna lose her, no I don't, and then, all this messin' around messes up my boxin'. So I married her."

Owing to the feebleness and irregularity of his income (his job at the Boys Club earns him less than $100 a week after taxes and includes no benefits or medical coverage), it is often hard to make ends meet at the end of the month and the food stamps that the family receives are a vital complement—Curtis sometimes sells me some to generate cash when his finances have run completely dry. His wife, who, like him, dropped out of high school, is taking an evening typing class in the somewhat unrealistic hope of one day becoming secretary to the clerk of the municipal court. In the meantime, she has been working as a waitress in a takeout restaurant owned by a Thai family in an ill-reputed section of the black neighborhood of South Shore, south of Woodlawn.

"See, what's really great, Louie, is that we both got our own career, it's not like one of us has to carry the other on his back. My wife, she has her career, she work hard at it, an' I got my career here, I can concentrate on my career, win for my career. . . . All I gotta do is fight hard an' God will help me win the big fight tha's gonna earn me a lotta money, win the world title and a great pile of dough. I'm gonna become a big man an' stuff." He laughs and throws a series of mock punches to my belly. I laugh with him, but the scene is rather pathetic, he holding his broom and dustpan, painting a picture that is as attractive as it is improbable and rejoicing over "careers" that are so far nonexistent, while I, a young graduate of elite universities, come slumming to this boxing gym to get away from the horror and boredom of academic routine and its privileges. [Field note, 11 October 1988]

Butch:"I can't quit now"

At six feet two inches and 175 pounds of muscle, twenty-nine-year-old Wayne Hankins boxed for seven years among the amateurs before "turning pro" in 1985. Better known at the gym by the nickname "Butch," he is one of the rare members of the club who can boast having a stable and coveted job: he is a firefighter for the City of Chicago, a very well-paid public job (about $3,000 a month) dutifully protected by the powerful civil service union (which affords him unemployment and health coverage as well as paid vacations). On fight nights, "The Fighting Fireman"—Butch's nom de guerre—struts onto the squared circle draped in a magnificent, flaming red robe emblazoned with the municipal firefighters' union seal and logo. And, at each of his appearances, a faithful legion of colleagues from work come to cheer him on noisily from the stands. Married and the father of a large family ("At home I've got four kids, my father, a dog, a cat, seven birds, and a giant aquarium"), Butch supplements his work as a fireman with that, much less prestigious and certainly less remunerative, of bagger at one of the outlets of the Jewel supermarket chain in order to improve the daily standard of living of his household. On weekends, he also occasionally cuts hair and trims moustaches on the barber chair he has installed in his basement garage.

Butch is reputed and admired for his implacable self-discipline, both during training and outside the gym, and for his fierce will to

26

Butch, forever placid, honing his skills on the speed bag

succeed, but also for his equanimity, his sang-froid and total self-control, which are perfectly adapted to his strategy as a "boxer-puncher." Between the ropes, he is the archetype of the economical fighter: every blow is accounted for, every slip planned, every move adjusted to the millimeter so as to minimize his expenditure of energy and to maximize that of his opponent. Does the objective rationalization of life imposed on him by his job as a firefighter (which suffers neither delays nor approximations in matters of schedules and readiness) underpin this pugilistic style, or, conversely, did a general predisposition toward economy and frugal efficiency propel him into both this stable manual profession and into the ring? It is hard to decide. In any case, there is a striking affinity between the regularity and predictability of the daily practices required by his occupational attachment—which extends that of his father, a former construction worker—and the manner in which Butch engages his body in the gym and in the ring.

In 1983, Butch won the Chicago Golden Gloves and nourished the hope of taking the national amateur middleweight title, which would have earned him a spot on the U.S. Olympic team. But, after being seriously weakened by a training injury (lips cut and tongue shredded by an uppercut thrown by his partner after the bell, which required fifteen stitches in his mouth), he was beaten by a hair in the finals, having heroically gotten through four preliminary bouts. With a quaver of admiration in his voice, DeeDee recalls how Butch refused to quit, even though he practically could not eat and was growing visibly thinner as the date of the national tournament drew near. "I told him: 'You cain't fight in that shape, it's no use, we're done, you gotta give up the fight.' He replied, 'No way, DeeDee, I've worked too hard, I've suffered too much to get here, I can't quit now.' And he went."

After that bitter disappointment, Butch stopped boxing for three years. He preferred the security of the firefighter's job he was offered at the time to the very uncertain prospects of a career as a prizefighter. It was at this time that he got married and founded a family. But the demon of the ring soon won out and Butch found his way back to the gym with an exponentially greater will to win. His passion for boxing does not prevent him from remaining lucid and realistic: he wonders about his sporting future and does not envision quitting his job to bet everything in the ring; his success between the ropes will determine how far he goes. For the moment, he has set himself the objective of becoming "the best in Chicago" and he counts his earnings expectancy in the tens of thousands of dollars at best. His entire family supports him in this pugilistic "second career" which has taken off in a whiz (five straight wins, four of them by kayo, for one draw): his wife and father, who were definitely reticent when he started out, come to all his fights and shower him with encouragement every minute, at home as well as at the boxing cards, where they number among his most demonstrative supporters.

One of the obsessions of the practioners of the Manly art is keeping themselves, if not at their optimal weight, at least in the vicinity of their official weight.[127] The old sliding-weight metal scale that sits throne-like in the back room is there to remind everyone of this requirement. Pugilistic folklore abounds with stories of boxers forced to perform fantastic—and often medically dangerous—athletic feats at the last minute in order to lose superfluous pounds before the fateful weigh-in.[128] The members of the Woodlawn Boys Club resort to draconian diets or interminable jogging sessions to rid themselves of impermissible pounds before a fight; others train wearing several layers of clothing or plastic wrappings, or with their chests squeezed by a latex girdle that is supposed to help

127. It is always possible to fight in the next weight class up if you happen to put on weight. But that constitutes a considerable handicap, for purely physical reasons of weight (and height) differences between divisions, with which tactical differences are associated. It is a rare pugilist who can go up a division and "bring his punch with him," as the saying goes.
128. On the local and regional levels, amateur as well as professional, differences in weight are rarely decisive, and it is unusual for a manager to decide to pull his fighter out of a bout at the last minute on grounds that his opponent is slightly over the official weight, as he is allowed to do by the contract agreed to in advance. However, the higher one goes in the hierarchy of the Sweet science, the finer weight management becomes, particularly in the intermediate classes, from lightweight to middleweight. A difference of a single pound can suffice to decide the outcome of a close clash, as for example with the first meeting between Thomas "The Motor City Hitman" Hearns and Sugar Ray Leonard in 1981: the specialists readily explain Hearns's defeat by technical knockout in the fourteenth round by the fact that he had for no reason conceded a full pound to his opponent by stepping onto the scale below the maximum authorized for his weight class.

them slim down. One summer on the eve of a bout, Cliff lost more than eight pounds by running the entire afternoon under a blazing sun dressed in sweaters, a thick wool cap, and two pairs of pants. One fine June evening, I found the locker room closed and so steamed up one would think it was a Turkish bath. Tony was there, shadowboxing and jogging in place next to the shower running full blast and scalding hot, bundled into a heavy track suit, his head and torso enveloped in a clear plastic hooded jacket: "Gotta lose nine pounds, Louie, *pfff-pfff,* tha's why I'm in here, *pfff-pfff.* The weigh-in's tomorrow mornin', *pfff-pfff,* I'monna make it, only two more to go."

DeeDee exercises a punctilious surveillance of every moment over the physical state of his charges so as to make sure that they are not straying too far from their "fight weight," either downward, which would signal dangerous overtraining (or the possibility of a malignant ailment),[129] or upward, which is by far the more frequent case. And to lead them back to the straight and narrow path of frugality, he resorts now to humor, now to affection, now to raw authority or sarcasm, as one can see in this field note dated 25 August 1990.

Ashante put on the gloves with Mark, then with Reese, three rounds each. He has a little bit more "gas" this time but he still seems heavy and is dragging himself around the ring. DeeDee is worried: "Ashante ain't doin' well at all. He cain't get rid of those extra pounds and he don't have no speed no more. Reese hit'im with everything he threw today, he was just standin' right in fronta him." It's true that Ashante lacks vivacity and side-to-side movement, he who usually has no trouble making the young amateurs who "move around" with him miss. When he arrived earlier, DeeDee was quick to ask him the supremely humiliating question: "What's *that belly there?*" (when Ashante is in jeans and T-shirt, it's easy to see that he's overweight). Ashante responded with an embarrassed smile, pretending not to

129. This was the tragic case of Big Earl, a truculent heavyweight who enjoyed "moving around" with lighter amateurs to make them work on their offensive technique (I loved to pummel his massive belly in the clinches). DeeDee had worried out loud several times about Big Earl's sudden weight loss, which seemed to him to be disproportionate to the effort expended in the gym, both in its amplitude and its rapidity. Indeed, Big Earl would die in the hospital several weeks later of a virulent strain of leukemia caused by the handling of toxic products at his job as a technician in a copy shop. The old coach had unfortunately seen correctly when he figured that Big Earl was gravely ill.

understand that DeeDee was talking to him: "What belly, where?" "There, right in front of you, *right under your eyes.*" Ashante didn't squawk and scrammed looking really pissed.

A good trainer needs not make his boxers step on the scale to know whether they are over the limit: he can "read" their weight from their physical appearance, the way they carry themselves, even the mere bounce of their step. One day in August of 1990, Lorenzo shows up at the gym again after several days of unexpected absence and a stormy spat with Eddie, his trainer. Eddied looks him up and down, and snaps in a negative and falsely inquisitive tone: "How much you weighin', a hundred-'n'-fifty?" Lorenzo does not let himself get rattled; he inspects himself from head to toe in the mirror and mentally weighs himself: "I'm a lil' over my weight (of 139 pounds), 'round one forty-five, I think." "You look like you're at least one-fifty when you walkin'." "No, I'm sure I'm 'round forty-five." End of the argument—but not the end of the problem.

One of the major functions of the pair formed by the trainer and the manager is to modulate and adjust the trajectory of their charge over time so as to optimize the "return on pugilistic investment" of the trio, that is, the ratio between the corporeal capital stacked and the dividends procured by fights in the form of money, ring experience, notoriety, and usable contacts with influential agents in the field such as promoters. This management is effected in three relatively independent orders that one must strive to make coincide: the temporality of the boxer's individual career, the trajectory of potential opponents, and the "economic time" of promoters. The ideal is to bring one's boxer to his peak (be it local) at the moment when the opportunity comes to fight, for a meaningful purse, a renowned boxer who is himself at the cusp of a phase of decline, and who thus still bears an accumulated symbolic capital (ranking, titles, and fame) that is well above his current pugilistic capacities.[130] But the higher one climbs in the hierarchy of the

---

130. The fight for the WBC super-welterweight world title held in February of 1989 between René Jacquot and Donald "The Cobra" Curry is a good example of successful management on the part of the French boxer and his entourage. Uplifted by the event, Jacquot caught Curry at the moment when the latter still enjoyed enormous prestige but was in fact already greatly diminished (he had just suffered two stinging defeats, then won his world championship belt back). And what was supposed to be a mere "warmup fight" with a view toward the "second coming of The Cobra," the "live execution" of an obscure and scruffy opponent, turned into an upset, giving the Frenchman the unhoped-for chance to "enter into the legend" of prizefighting. Astolfo Cagnacci, *René Jacquot l'artisan du ring* (Paris: Denoël, 1989), 13.

boxing field, the more control over time slips away from the fighters to fall into the hands of specialized economic agents, notably promoters and executives in charge of sports programming for the networks that broadcast the big-media bouts. As Thomas Hauser aptly notes, "time [is] the enemy" of boxers, and not only because they get old and wear themselves out.[131]

This management of duration begins among the amateurs, some of whom—left to their own devices or poorly advised—burn themselves out in pursuit of an ephemeral regional or national glory with uncertain economic repercussions so that, when they join the ranks of the "pros," they have already seriously amputated their bodily capital and can hardly hope for a long and fruitful career. According to DeeDee, that was the case of Kenneth "The Candy Man" Gould, a recent U.S. Olympic medalist in Seoul, whom he believes expended himself too much in the amateurs by competing in over three hundred matches: "He already had too many fights. He ain't got enough pep left in him. I dunno, we'll see. I told him to turn pro, it's gotta be years ago." Why did he not do it? Saddled with a manager who was inexperienced or poorly connected within networks of influence, Gould was adamant about fighting in the Seoul Olympics in Korea (where the Frenchman Laurent Boudouani beat him in the semifinals). The future of twenty-two-year-old Kelcie Banks, another young hopeful from Chicago (a Woodlawn Boys Club alumnus and amateur world champion), also defeated in the preliminaries for the last Olympics, appears even more compromised: he has over six hundred amateur fights to his record, as many as three a week in worthless little tournaments: "Tha's a lot of punches and a lotta wear and tear on a young body . . . too much wear and tear," DeeDee grumbles when we evoke his case. A few months later, his prophecy seems to be coming true: "Kelcie ain't doin' nuthin', he's not gonna do nuthin': he's washed up, done. Think about it, nobody wanta sign some guy who's already washed up. He went to that training camp in Texas (where new professional recruits are picked up by the big national promoters), it didn't work out. Nobody signed him. If he'da won in the Olympics, he wouldave gotten a thirty- or forty-thousand-dollar bonus up front. But he got beat and he didn't get a damn thing out of it. He's too beat up now, nobody's gonna put money on a guy who's already washed up" (notes from 7 February and 3 June 1989).

131. Hauser, *Black Lights,* 166.

Of a boxer at the end of his career, it is said that "he's done his time" and "his time has passed," that he is "washed up" or "shot" or, worse yet, that he has fallen to the rank of "dead meat": his bodily capital is too devalued for him to hope to beat younger fighters, who are more vigorous and less damaged. At best, he can aspire to be hired by promoters and matchmakers as a foil or "opponent" for up-and-coming boxers, the overexploitation of his bodily capital allowing the latter to beef up their records at the cost of a lesser expenditure of theirs, as these field notes indicate:

> While DeeDee is gloving me up, I ask him a few questions about Hightower—with my mouthpiece in, I'm chewing on my words so much you would think I'm speaking a foreign tongue, but that doesn't seem to keep DeeDee from understanding me. Hightower is a former pro from the club who decided to return to the ring at age thirty-one; he is bent on sparring with Butch. DeeDee doesn't like that very much, because he boxes rather brutally without much self-control, no doubt in order to restore his worth on the pugilistic stock market: "He think he can fight again but he's finished. He's finished, but the man keep dreamin', he still got that dream [of glory]. He think he can hold his own an' fight some more, but he's too used up. *It's too late.* Back then, he was a good fighter, but now he's way too beat up." [Field notes, 17 December 1988]

The imperative to hoard corporeal energy also applies in the short term of a workout. Proof is the insistence with which DeeDee forbids us from working on the bag before climbing into the ring to spar: "Slow down, take it easy, Louie, save your strength for sparring. . . . I told you to leave that bag alone, damn it!" [Field notes, 17 December 1988]

This same need to let the body rest justifies the periodic rest phases, especially on the morrow of a rough fight. DeeDee generally grants his boxers a long week off duty after a match—two if the bout was particularly tough physically. After I reluctantly had to interrupt my training for two weeks during the Christmas holidays, the old coach consoles me: "You need to get outa d'gym from time to time, it gives you a breather, it's good for you. Then when you get back to it, you got more juice. But you can't stop too long either. Otherwise you get outa shape, you lose your speed, your timing is off." [Field notes, 5 January 1989]

The regulation of violence in the ring is an integral part of the general setup aimed at preserving the pugilist's body. In the following excerpt from my notebook dated 28 August 1989, DeeDee reminds Eddie of this management rule after a sparring incident.

In the second round, Rodney got his bell rung by Ashante, who explains: "I saw right away that I hurt him, I was ready to hold him up, DeeDee, in case he fall down. I knew we shoulda stopped." But the two club-mates kept on going at it, even though Rodney was barely able to stay on his feet. DeeDee calls over to Eddie, with a stern look in his eye and a sharp tone of reproach in his voice: "When your guy's hurt like that sparrin', you take him outa d'ring. You don't let him take a beating or try to pull through by hisself. *You make him come outa d'ring.* Tha's *your job* to take him out at that point, you understand?" Eddie, sheepish, in a low voice: "Okay, DeeDee, okay. I didn't know. Next time I know, I'll take him out right away."

The practical mastery of time is a central dimension of a successful apprenticeship of the craft of prizefighting. "It takes time," "Take your time," "Keep on workin', it comes with time," "Don't rush yourself" are expressions that come up constantly on the gym floor, whatever the stature of the boxer, and that contribute to making every boxer learn to spread out his physical and emotional investment over the specific duration of the field. It is also this corporeal investment over time, the slow process of incorporation of pugilistic technique and of somatization of its basic principles, that marks the boundary between recreational practitioners and regular boxers and prohibits an immediate passage from one category to the other. Assistant trainer Eddie reminds a visitor who is awkwardly trying to hit the speed bag with this deliberately exaggerated sarcasm: "Oo-ooh, no! You better stop right there: it takes *years of work* to learn how to hit that bag." A former boxer who has kept himself in good physical shape needs at least three months of intensive conditioning to get back in shape to fight. It takes a minimum of two to three years for an amateur to achieve a reasonable mastery of the basic panoply of the pugilist, and three more years before turning into an accomplished professional. Boxing "teaches patience and discipline and stick-to-itiveness," it is "anti-immediate-gratification."[132] The following three field notes bear witness to this, among a hundred others that could be cited here.

132. Plummer, *Buttercups and Strong Boys*, 123.

19 November 1988, Eddie comes over to encourage me while
I'm jumping rope: "I was watchin' you work the heavy bag, Louie,
you've really improved, your coordination has improved." "Thanks,
but I need to do more sparring now." "Don't rush things, it'll come
in time, keep on workin' and you'll get there. It's a matter of time."
On December 17 of the same year, Butch, lying down on the table
catching his breath between two sets of situps, slips to me that I'm
making progress but that I still get hit too much: "You gotta protect
yourself better. You'll learn. It don't come in one day. It takes time."
On 4 March 1989, Butch again: "When you start to feel your jab,
when you feel that you can keep your opponent at bay with your jab,
everything else's gonna come together by itself. You just gotta work
at it, it come slowly. How long you been trainin'?" "'Bout six months."
"Tssss, that's nothin'. You need time, you gotta keep workin'."

To persist with patience, to bide your time without recess or respite,
to measure out your effort, to spread your expectations over time and
smooth over your emotions accordingly: so many critical qualities in a
boxing apprenticeship. If the fighter does not possess them, his coach
can compensate by imposing them upon him from the outside, for instance by depriving him of sparring for a preset period if he is too impatient or by moving up his bouts so as to quicken the pace of his routine.
Aside from the advice of peers and the directives of the coach, it is the
body that, of itself, regulates in the final analysis the speed and the
slope of progression. A sudden or repeated excess of training provokes
injuries that, even when they are minor, quickly prove sufficiently both-
ersome to force one to slow down the tempo: tenacious little sores on
the knuckles or too many broken blood vessels between the fingers limit
work on the sandbag; a tender knee prevents you from jumping rope;
a rib bruised in a brutal sparring session forbids you from doing situps.
More than serious injuries, the accumulation of minor nicks and physical
annoyances serves as a natural regulator of the workload, as attested
by this passage from my journal dated 6 October 1988.

Yesterday, Wednesday, I woke up with my right wrist swollen and
very painful: I overdid it on the heavy bag Tuesday, banging it like a
brute, and now I'm paying for it! It is still weakened today and I can't
turn it or pick up anything heavy with that hand. So I won't be able to
work the bag, to my great regret. I'm going to the gym anyway. . . .

DeeDee, who gave me plenty of warning, but in vain, advises me to make do with a little shadowboxing so as to take it easy on my wrist. Training is atrociously burdensome: my right hand hurts like hell and I can't jump rope. I do a set on the speed bag with one hand. And shooting pains in my left arm very quickly start giving me trouble as well; it is numb, as if dead, to the point where I feel like quitting after only two rounds in front of the mirror.

The physical exhaustion that results from excessive exercising diminishes your vivacity and tonicity in the ring, increasing the chances of injury and of a protracted interruption, and thereby lack of training. A forced stoppage can in turn push you to resume working out too quickly, leading to yet another excess, and so on. To box over the long run, one must learn, through gradual rationing, to adjust one's effort so as to enter into a virtuous cycle in which training in the gym and clashes in the ring feed and reinforce each other and wherein their respective temporalities come into synergy.

Four figures in the management of bodily capital

The following four excerpts from my notebooks illustrate the various ways in which boxers encounter the problem of managing their body, preserving its integrity and energy, as much in the gym and in the ring as in daily life.

After Butch's draw at the Park West

(8 May 1989) The first hitch in Butch's professional record: after five straight wins, including four by way of kayo before the third round and only one going the distance, he was kept in check yesterday on the Park West card. Was his opponent too strong? DeeDee asks ironically: "What you talkin' about? Butch was lucky to get outa there with a draw. He didn't have nuthin' left from the second round on. No gas. The guy didn't know how to *spell fight* but Butch couldn't knock him down. He tried but he didn't have no pep. Too much sparrin'. I told him not to spar so much, damn it, and he found a way to spar eight rounds the Saturday before! So, he had no more juice for the fight and he's gotta chase the guy around the whole time for nuthin'. . . .

It ain't the wear and tear of the fights: it's from too much trainin'. Butch is a worrier, he's the nervous type, an' he train too damn hard,

he train too much. He's always afraid that he's not gonna be ready.
I've yelled at him, really yelled at him, because of that. [Vehemently.]
I told him not to spar so much. I told him not to work on the bag after
the sparrin'. All he need to do is loosen up, work on his jabs, tha's all.
But he don't wanna listen to my advice. *Fine!* He's gonna learn the
hard way who's right. And this time, he got lucky, he came out with
a draw, but he couldave easily lost, 'cos he was exhausted already
in the second round. After all, tha's none of my business. Guys who
don't wanna listen, okay, too bad for them! He wanted to spar, fine. I
knew he be worn out, burned out. Some guys, they think they're jus'
smarter, they think they already know it all." The old coach throws a
chagrined look at the ceiling.

After Curtis's tough fight in Harvey

(7 December 1988) It's DeeDee's turn to come out of the makeshift
Woodlawn locker room, followed closely by Curtis, who's jumped
into his jeans and wool sweater. They go sit down at the far end
of the hall, away from everything, to draw the lessons of the fight.
With a hard look on his face, DeeDee leans toward Curtis and
admonishes him with gusto. He's hopping mad that Curtis let himself
get hit so much by his opponent without slipping and protecting
himself better. The fact that the latter was clearly overweight (a
good 137 pounds instead of the 130 required by rule, as opposed to
132 for Curtis, who keeps repeating, "That guy was a pit bull, man,
every time they givin' me a pit bull") is no excuse for Curtis letting
himself get manhandled the way he did. He absorbed way too many
blows and emerged very wearied, his face swollen, a nasty cut on
his right cheekbone, and a deep gash on his left eye that will likely
require stitches. The general consensus is that Curtis should have
"finished" his opponent in the second round, when he sent him to the
canvas with a jolting combination. And, in any case, he should have
fought more intelligently by keeping at a distance instead of giving
in to his rival's provocations and getting drawn into brutal infighting.
O'Bannon confides to me later: "Curtis ain't gonna go too far if he
lets hisself get beat up by guys like that, if he don't know how to
economize hisself better than that. It's a long road. Guys like that,
he's got to dispatch them quickly."

Boxers themselves are quick to ascribe the sudden downfall of one
of their own to a shortfall in the corporeal discipline and hygiene that

every pugilist must impose on himself outside the ring. Any infraction of the worldly ascesis that defines the Spartan regimen of the ideal boxer is promptly interpreted as the direct cause of his failings in the ring.

Alfonzo's physical and pugilistic decline

(19 November 1988) Curtis is miming punches, ripping through the air with his fists with a sonorous *"Wham! Wham!"* Butch is watching him attentively. It takes me a few minutes to understand that they're talking about last Thursday's fight, in which Alfonzo Ratliff lost his national title and, according to them, took a tremendous beating (he bit the dust twice in the fourth round before getting kayoed in the fifth).

Curtis: "The man was landin' every punch, every punch landed to the body or the head, not in his gloves. Alfonzo, he was just holdin' his arms like this [he puts his guard up, his head tucked into his forearms] and he wasn't doin' nuthin'." Curtis and Butch make no secret of their disapproval of the fact that Alfonzo was bragging so much before the fight. "He be hollerin', 'I'monna knock him cold, he's not gonna last five rounds with me,' you don't say stuff like that before the fight, man! And then he's the one who gets knocked out cold." The match was broadcast on a Chicago cable channel, which makes it all the more damaging to Alfonzo's reputation. Curtis and Butch agree that Alfonzo has come to the end of the road. "He's goin' downhill, for sure. He be better off hangin' em up. He's finished, man, he's finished. He ain't never gonna fight for the title, man."

I ask why Alfonzo got beaten so decisively: was his opponent that much better than him, or didn't Phonzo prepare himself properly for the fight? Butch: "See, the man is thirty-three years old now, Louie. When you get to that age, you gotta stay in shape. Don't mess with alcohol, don't mess with drugs, and don't mess with them women." Sitting on his stool, he mimes copulation with an unmistakable thrust of his hips. "Takes a toll on you. If you don't stay away from that, at thirty-three, man, you're finished, washed up. Check me out, I don't mess around with any of that stuff an' I stay in shape. But Alfonzo, he messes around with all three, especially d'women." Another suggestive movement of the hips. "He's too old for that kinda stuff now, man. He did his time. He should give it up, hang it up for good."

The scandal of the smoking boxer

(28 July 1989) Ashante is chatting with Luke, who's just finished his workout, over the deafening noise Smithie is making nearby banging away on the speed bag. He's telling the story of a guy named Ray, who was "the best heavyweight in the city. Man, that guy was the real deal, he had a helluva punch. But then, he didn't take care of his-self, he wasn't serious about it. He do whatever he wanta do and he didn't train hard—everybody knew it. But the day I saw him, with my own eyes, smokin' a cigarette just after his fight, man, I knew he'd never be good again."

Luke remains silent for about ten seconds, without reacting. Then, suddenly, as if he realized the enormity of the thing with a lag, he stares at Ashante with an air of incredulity. And in the tone of a priest who's just heard a curse word uttered in his sacristy, he exclaims, rolling scandalized eyes: *"He was smokin'* after a fight?!! He was smokin' *in the dressing room* after the fight?" [As if this were an inconceivable monstrosity.] "No, not in the dressing room, in the audience. I saw him sittin' in the audience after the fight, puffing away with one of his buddies. *Right away, I knew it was over for him,* man."

The specific wisdom of the coach consists in knowing how to stimulate and calibrate the efforts of his charges, both in relation to their bodies and to the multiple enmeshed temporalities of the institution, and to ensure the harmonious functioning of the complex collective machinery that transmits knowledge and spurs the investments of the boxers (in the twofold sense of economics and psychoanalysis). By orchestrating the multiple actions that, through their mutual imbrication, define the gym as a mobile configuration of interdependent agents, DeeDee contributes to the production and solidification of pugilistic belief. Contrary to what Weinberg and Arond suggest,[133] this moral function does not come into play only during times of crisis, when disillusionment suddenly threatens, but ongoingly in the everyday routine of the gym. Critical situations, such as the morrow of defeats, which often provoke a practical questioning of the pugilistic *illusio* and in which the trainer overtly fills the roles of confidant, supporter, and proselytizer, obscure the anodyne work of maintenance and the continuous production of belief that takes place on a daily basis, invisibly and

133. Weinberg and Arond, "Occupational Culture of the Boxer," 462.

unconsciously, through the mediation of the very organization of the gym and its activities.

At the end of this initiatic march—temporarily interrupted by the work required by sociological objectivation—boxing reveals itself to be a sort of "savage science," an eminently social and quasi-scientific practice, even as it might seem to involve only those individuals who risk their bodies in the ring in a singular confrontation that appears rough and unbridled. And the pugilist emerges as the product of a collective organization which, while not thought out and willed as such by anyone, is nonetheless objectively coordinated through the reciprocal adjustment of the embodied expectations and demands of the occupants of the various positions within the space of the gym. These elements of an anthropology of boxing as "biologico-sociological phenomenon"[134] set into relief the central place of practical reason in this limiting case of practice that is pugilism and invite us to move beyond the traditional distinctions between body and mind, instinct and idea, the individual and the institution,[135] by showing how the two terms of these perennial antinomies are constituted together and mutually support one another, specify and reinforce themselves but also weaken each other in the same movement.

134. According to the formulation of Mauss, "Techniques du corps," 384, trans. 121.
135. For those who would doubt the possibility of generalizing this interpretation of pugilistic practice, one can recommend reading the studies by Jean Lave on the learning of calculus (*Cognition in Practice*); Jack Katz on the moral and sensual logic of criminal careers, *Seductions of Crime* (New York: Basic Books, 1989); David Sudnow on improvisation among jazz pianists, *Ways of the Hand: The Organization of Improvised Conduct* (Cambridge, Mass.: Harvard University Press, 1978); Joan Cassell on the craft of surgery, *Expected Miracles: Surgeons at Work* (Philadelphia: Temple University Press, 1991); and Joseph Alter on the social, moral, and symbolic organization of traditional Indian wrestling (*Bharatiya kushti*) in Benares, India, *The Wrestler's Body: Identity and Ideology in Northern India* (Berkeley: University of California Press, 1992), to take but five deliberately diverse and dispersed universes among others. And recall, with Max Weber, that "in the great majority of cases actual action goes on in a state of inarticulate half-consciousness or actual unconsciousness [*Unbewußtheit*] of its subjective meaning. The actor is more likely to 'be aware' of it in a vague sense than he is to 'know' what he is doing or be explicitly self-conscious about it. In most cases his action is governed by impulse or habit. Only occasionally and, in the uniform action of large numbers, often only in the case of a few individuals, is the subjective meaning of the action, whether rational or irrational, brought clearly into consciousness. The ideal type of meaningful action where the meaning is fully conscious and explicit is a marginal case." *Economy and Society*, 1:21–22.

Fight Night at Studio 104

Monday, 30 July 1990. Nervous wakeup at 8:30, the weather is cloudy. Let's hope it doesn't rain. A month's worth of intensive preparation down the drain, that would really take the cake! The weigh-in is scheduled for 11 a.m. at the Illinois State Building in the heart of downtown, a stone's throw from the Chicago River. I drive by to pick up DeeDee at his house as planned at 9:20 so we can head back to our base camp at the gym together. He's in a very good mood: his catfish stew was succulent and the weather report says it's going to clear up.

As we enter the Boys Club, we come upon Curtis sitting in the back room with the door closed, leaning over the desk, bare-chested in his blue jeans overalls, a thoughtful frown on his face. In front of him is a pile of bills, a fifty, a little stack of tens and twenties, then a fistful of ones, carefully placed next to a small pile of multicolored tickets. This is the money from the seats he's sold for tonight's card, sixty-one in all—he's got nine left out of the quota allotted to him by Jack Cowen, the matchmaker.[1] (For small local fights, it isn't uncommon for boxers to be paid,

---

1. A matchmaker is the middleman between promoters and managers who recruits and pairs up the boxers so as to "fill" the card for an evening of boxing. One can find an analysis of this craft, and of the economic and financial organization of professional boxing in the United States in Loïc Wacquant, "A Fleshpeddler at Work: Power, Pain, and Profit in the Prizefighting Economy," *Theory and Society* 27, 1 (February 1998): 1–42.

aside from a very modest fixed "purse" ranging from $150 for a four-round match to between $400 and $1,000 for an eight- to ten-rounder, with a percentage of the revenue from tickets they fob off on their family, friends, and gym-mates, with the typical price of a ticket ranging from fifteen to twenty dollars).

DeeDee asks him point-blank: "Is the money right?" "Yes," Curtis snorts, then adds, with regret in his voice: "I'd sure like to keep that dough." The gaze of the old coach stops at the antique iron scale towering next to his desk: "Tha's what it say?" "Yeah, one-thirty-two and a half." That's the right weight since Curtis must fight at 133 pounds. For once, he won't have to shed extra pounds on the morning of his fight . . . He disappears into the locker room. The toilet flushes. "It's always d'same story," DeeDee grouses. "The day of d'fight, his bowels don't wanna work."

Curtis counts his loot again one last time and patiently organizes the pile of banknotes. Usually you stack them the other way round, DeeDee remarks, with the small bills on top and not on the bottom. Curtis's only response is to ceremoniously hand him the money as well as the remaining tickets. The old coach briskly slips it all into his chest pocket (he's wearing his best white cotton shirt and a matching white ball cap). Curtis advises him to put it in the back pocket of his pants instead, where it would be less visible and thus less risky: you never know who you might meet up with on the street. "No, I put'em in front here, ain't nobody gonna bother *me.*" Then he's the one who grumbles: "Shiiit, I could keep that money an' use it, sure could." Grinning, Curtis throws out: "How about I knock you out, DeeDee, and take the money, an' then we tell Jack somebody done robbed you on the street, what you say?" "Yeah, but Jack'd tell you to go talk to d'gangster."

"You Scared I Might Mess Up 'Cause You Done Messed Up"

DeeDee is fulminating about Papa Page, an old-timer from the gym and boxing trainer employed by the city who is nearing retirement. Page called DeeDee at the crack of dawn yet again this morning to subject him to one of his usual endless monologues on the well-worn theme of "what shoulda been." To hear Page tell it, DeeDee missed the boat: he should be rich today, given all the success his fighters had in the ring over the years. At the least, the State Boxing Commission should have dug up a cushy little job for him. "He be tellin' me: (imitating Page's whining voice) 'You shouldn't be dat way. There's certain ways to do things, DeeDee, you can do things. Like, you could get the Commission to give you a job at nine thousand a year.'" Curtis, surprised: "Nine thousand a year, that ain't nuthin'!" "Yep, but at least I'd have my little thing (health insurance). . . . He be sayin' how I shoulda made money and 'now we're through, we ain't gonna make it'. An' I tell him: 'You're thru, I'm not. I'm sick, I can't work, period. I got this health problem. Now, *if I'd hadda been healthy,* I'd hadda been gone long ago. I'dda've stayed outa Chicago. I'dda've left Chicago for Philly and *I be in Philly right now.*"[2] Not a whiff of nostalgia in DeeDee's voice.

Curtis is worried about the seven tickets he gave to Lorenzo, who should have given him the money he made from selling them this morning. He tries three times to reach him on the phone, and he will later try again twice more from downtown. DeeDee remarks, in an annoyed tone, that Anthony has gone to train at Fuller Park again—the other gym located in the heart of the black ghetto of the South Side—which he disapproves of, because the way the young middleweight trains there does not suit him. "Anthony, he ain't the fighter he used to be." Why not? "On account of listenin' to this damn Ford (his manager, an African-American owner of a small family cleaning business who is totally ignorant in boxing matters). Ford want him to stand in there an' fight. But that ain't Anthony's style: he ain't no inside fighter, he don't have the build for it. He useta be a runnin' and duckin' ass, he slip and counter, slip and run an', *wham!* hit you good. Now he wait, standin' still, his feet on the mat, and he get bullied by guys stronger'n him." (Ford is pressing Anthony to change his style to be more aggressive and "take the fight" to his opponent, in spite of his slender build and his

2. On the strength of a long tradition and the many clubs scattered in the city's northern ghetto, Philadelphia is one of the crucibles of U.S. boxing. Its fighters are reputed and feared throughout the country for being especially tough and ferocious—in the mold of "Smokin'" Joe Frazier, Muhammad Ali's archrival of the 1970s. The disability DeeDee is referring to is severe osteoarthritis in his knees and wrists, from which he has suffered since his teenage years and which allows him to benefit from a small disability pension as well as Medicaid coverage (without which he would soon be reduced to indigence by the astronomical cost of health care).

predilection for counterpunching, because promoters always prefer to put even a mediocre offensive boxer on the card rather than a talented defensive one, especially for televised bouts aimed at an audience ignorant about boxing and thus incapable of judging the technical and tactical virtuosity of the fighters.)

The other drawback to training in rival gyms in the city is that the supply of potential opponents for local fights dries up. "If you spar in the other gyms and you give beatin's to guys your size, when the time come to face them on a card, they're not going to take the fight. Maybe then good ol' *Mister* Ford will learn his lesson . . . You don't do that with opponents.[3] Why they gonna get in d'ring witchyou for a fight if you've given them a good ass-whuppin' in their own gym, huh, tell me why? Tha's what happen with Butch (with irony bordering on glee): Mister Hankins asked Bama—you know 'Alabama,' Louie—to spar with him here in d'gym, 'cause he figure that sooner or later he's gonna have to fight him. Man, I shoulda told Butch to make 'im believe, to pretend like Bama was givin' him a whuppin'. Instead, Butch got it in his head to pound him, and he did give him a poundin'. After that, don't hold your breath: Bama's never gonna take a fight against Butch. For what?"

It's 10:20, time to go. We hop into Curtis's Jeep Comanche, whose electronic remote door opener still doesn't work (he complains about it loudly, but it's just for show since he doesn't have the money to get it fixed.) Curtis settles himself into his seat and announces proudly that he hasn't "touched any pussy" for days and days. And even if someone offered him five girls, right there and then, that he could have all to himself in his bed, he'd turn them away because his fight comes first. We've no sooner started out that he turns on some soul music, syrupy as can be, on the radio—DeeDee detests rap with a passion—and we're soon tooling along Lake Shore Drive. The conversation returns to old Page's recriminations and what he perceives as the foibles of DeeDee's career.

> DeeDee: He talkin' about "Man, you turnin' old, you shoulda been in d'money"—I say "Man, don't worry about *my life!*" Sayin' I *shoulda been* there. An "with all them good people you knew, man, crazier'n'hell about you DeeDee" . . .

3. In pugilistic parlance, the term "opponent" designates an adversary of inferior quality whom one fights precisely because he offers every chance of an easy victory. The operative lay typology of boxers is discussed below, pp. 193–195, 204–205, 319–20 and 346–347.

CURTIS: You's'posed to be rich, DeeDee, you know that don'tcha? You know that don't you, but you just hate *to think 'bout it, don'tcha?*

DEEDEE [dismissive]: *Noooo,* I'm not s'posed to be *rich:* if I was s'posed to 've been rich I *be* rich.

CURTIS [very fast, as if to say "I know exactly what you're thinking deep inside"]: You s'posed to bein' rich but-you-know-you-messed-up that's why you always b'gettin' on my back so *I won't mess up.* [forcefully] *You scared I might mess up* 'cause you know *you* done messed up.

DEEDEE [on the defensive]: Y'see if I'da had my family, then it be a dif'rent story.

CURTIS [smiling at my tape recorder, which is rolling]: He got his tape recorder on, DeeDee.

DEEDEE: I wouldn't give a damn.

CURTIS [mirthful; I'm laughing with him]: He wanna listen to our conversation, on our way to the weigh-in . . .

DEEDEE: I know it, I know it. When they get a whuppin' on his ass one day, I'm gonna stand up and look! [All three of us laugh.] I told ya, if you don't—you jus' got a hard head. . . .

DEEDEE: Yeah, old Page, boy he tell me 'bout what I *should have,* what I shoulda been doin', where, what, where *I should be.* I said "I'm just where I'm s'posed to be—right at [inaudible]. Ya man, you an' "you haven't did right, an' t'get Ratliff off that dope an' shit man an' if you'd had did, you never handled 'im right."

CURTIS: If Ratliff woulda handled hisself right, how you gonna try an' keep up with a grown man?

DEEDEE: Man you know what I say: [with an annoyed tone] "You know you sound like *a idiot?"*

A flame-red Alfa Romeo passes us with a roar. Sitting up in his seat, Curtis takes off after it and brays with admiration at the gleaming machine.

DEEDEE [turning around toward me in the back seat]: Who makes that, Louie?

LOUIE: Italian.

DEEDEE: Italian, hmm. Probably costs a nice buck, uh?

LOUIE: Yeah. 'Specially in the States.

DEEDEE [raising his voice]: I wonder what the Mercedes Benz—I'm sayin' I had a buddy who had five Mercedes Benz [when he was working for a big Japanese promoter in the Philippines]. . . .

And he and Curtis launch into one of those endless ritualized arguments that the two pals are accustomed to having about the respective advantages of different brands of cars. . . . Curtis maneuvers in close to the Alfa Romeo at the stoplight and honks at it frenetically. DeeDee rolls down his window to hail the driver.

DEEDEE [shouting over the noise of the motors]: What's the price? What do they cost? [The driver answers.] Oh, that's nice.

We take off again and zoom past the municipal stadium of Soldier's Field, on the lakefront.

CURTIS: Thirty-five? I think a lil' more than that. This car's [his Jeep Comanche] thirty-two ha-ha! That's a Cadillac.

LOUIE: My car cost three hundred dollars, ah?

We commiserate about Alfonzo Ratliff's career, which didn't deliver all that it promised. The former cruiserweight from Woodlawn won the WBC title in 1985, but he never earned large purses and after that brief moment of glory it was all downhill and defeat. In 1986, diminished by drugs, he was destroyed in two rounds in Las Vegas by a young heavyweight on a meteoric rise to the top by the name of Mike Tyson. There is a tinge of nostalgia in DeeDee's voice and in his eyes: "When he was at the top of his game, Phonzo was somethin' else." Alfonzo served six years behind bars for robbery in a hard labor camp down South where he developed his already colossal musculature and steeled his determination. Back in Chicago after doing his time, he signed up at the Boys Club. But five months later, DeeDee kicked him out of the gym after he trashed the locker room in a fit of rage because he kept getting beat up in sparring sessions. The Woodlawn giant made amends and the old coach took him under his wing. From that moment on, Alfonzo became indestructible in the ring. He fought like a man possessed: "Soon as he came out his corner, he'd start throwin' punches, before the other guy was even in range."

What does DeeDee think of Riddick Bowe, the new darling of New York City, predicted by many to be the world heavyweight titleholder before long? "I haven't seen him in a long time. He's stopped doin' drugs. He's a project boy. Tough. Maybe he decided that he's goin' to be serious 'bout it this time. He strong, like a lotta them project boys. But they're all heathens,[4] every one of'em. You got some guys, see, who find a way outa d'projects, but you got other guys, they cain't get out: too many heathens all concentrated in d'same place, so many of'em you ain't got nuthin' but heathens. And they'll never get out 'cos they don't know nuthin' else, they don't know how to behave any different." The conversation drifts to the fight between Michael Carbajal and the IBF champion Muangshai Kittikasen from Thailand, broadcast on television. Curtis is curious to know how much was the purse that Carbajal got, fifteen or twenty thousand dollars? DeeDee: "You kiddin'?" Thirty thousand? "Shit, you on network television, prime time, on Sunday afternoon, whatchyou think? He must have gotten at least six figures, a hundred or a hundred-fifty thousand." Another world, but one that nonetheless seems so close, so close you could grab it with your fists . . .

All along the eight miles to downtown, Curtis keeps spitting into a paper bag that he holds in his left hand, so as to lose a maximum of water and thus bring his weight down a little bit more, as much habit as precaution. The eternal dilemma of the mastery of the body.[5] During the whole trip, he and DeeDee scrutinize the women on the street, intensely and with an abundance of salty commentary. It is as if it were de rigueur, the morning of a fight, to give a public expression—public because innocuous—to one's heretofore muzzled sexual appetites. They each take turns making circumstantial evaluations of the shapes and putative amorous talents of female passersby. Same drill after the weigh-in when we come back out of the Illinois State Building. Curtis catches sight of two girls kissing each other goodbye flush on the lips and immediately alerts his trainer. "That don't mean nuthing, my friend! I know lotsa women who kiss each other like that." Curtis retorts with an excited leer: "I should ask her to kiss *me* like that, just to see." From the Jeep, DeeDee shouts to a matronly black lady behind the wheel of a

4. In the local vernacular, the term "heathen" designates a loutish individual, lacking in both education and manners, who behaves in violation of accepted norms of civility. It was commonly used at the Woodlawn gym, where it could be invoked either as an accusation or in an affectionate registry—as we will see later, between Curtis and DeeDee.

5. On this ethic of corporeal mastery to which the boxer must submit and the privations it implies in matters alimentary, in social and familial life, and in sexual commerce, see Loïc Wacquant, "Sacrifice," in *Body Language,* ed. Gerald Early (Saint Paul, Minn.: Graywolf Press, 1998), 47–59.

little pickup truck with a Pisces sticker, *"I'm a Pisces too!"* He doggedly insists that another equally plump woman on the sidewalk was giving him the eye. The two accomplices titter and shoot each other challenging looks as we walk behind a tall black woman with elephantine buttocks. "You couldn't do nuthin' with her, DeeDee, she'd crush you first." "Sure I could. *I* always can . . ."

Weigh-in at the Illinois State Building

We are way early and park in the ramped garage on Randolph Street, then walk to the Illinois State Building. Straight to the ninth floor in the glass elevator that overlooks the mall. Curtis is surprisingly relaxed, which is a welcome change from his previous fights (usually, the anticipation of a match makes him irascible, even aggressive, and it's best to let him stew in his corner). We run into the cutman Laury Myers, sitting with old Herman Mill in the waiting room outside the Office of Professional Regulation, the body charged with supervising the professions, including that of boxing, for the state.[6]

Mill is a puny, grizzled old-timer who has over 200 amateur bouts and 150 professional fights (for only fourteen losses) on his record; he mixed it up with legendary featherweight champ Willy Pep in the forties—that's how far back he goes. In those days, he divided his life between prizefighting and tap dancing: one night he would dance and the next he would perform in the ring. He fought that way several times a week, up to three or four evenings in a row, in dance halls, movie theaters, and sports arenas, knocking about from one town to the next on the train. No time for training: dancing kept him in shape for boxing and vice versa. He had learned to dance at the age of three, and to box at six, from his musician father, who formed a violin-banjo duo with his

---

6. There exists no national organization in the United States entrusted with administering professional boxing. Each state is free to regulate (or not) the profession according to its own principles and rules. Forty-four of the fifty members of the Union have a "commission" charged with pugilistic affairs. The vast majority of them are offices devoid of both authority and means: placed under the aegis of the Office of Veterans' Affairs or Consumer Protection, as of the early 1990s many did not even have telephones and fax machines to verify the identity and record of the fighters they were licensing. This helps explain why boxers are by far the least protected professional athletes in the country and why irregularities, cheating, and embezzlement are quite routine in this sport, as was proved by a senatorial inquiry commission. See United States Senate, *Hearings on Corruption in Professional Boxing before the Permanent Committee on Governmental Affairs, One Hundred Second Congress, August 11–12, 1992* (Washington, D.C.: Government Printing Office, 1993).

brother. "I ain't never stopped! Jus' died down, ha-ha, jus' died down." Mill rambles on badly and tells me the same story several times—how he once clashed with a boxer who was fifty pounds heavier than him in a bar in Minnesota, in ten-below weather, after the boiler in the joint had gone out—then finishes his story by sketching out a few brisk tap-dance steps. DeeDee and the others don't even pretend to listen to him: they've heard these stories dozens of times.

Laury is sprawled in his armchair, looking morose. He has come, as he does to all the weigh-ins, to offer his services as a "cutman" to whoever will want them. Always ready to get to work, and with heart. I give him the picture I took of him at Smithie's fight in Atlantic City last month, and suddenly he's tickled pink. He calls Curtis over on the sly and proudly shows him his horrid gunsmith necklace, studded with faux diamonds, from which hangs a heavy gold pendant that screams "CUTMAN" in big letters and another of the same make that spells out "MACHO." And he proposes to let the boxer from Woodlawn have the gleaming "MACHO" for a friendly price: "I know you like gold, Curtis, and I want to sell it, so I thought I'd show it to you first. (In a confidential tone.) Come on, I'll let you have it for only seventy-five bucks, just between us." Curtis examines the baroque object with interest, turns it over and over in his palm before handing it back to its owner with a regretful frown: "It's nice, for sure, but I don't have d'money right now."

■ *"Boxing is my life, my woman, my love"*

For three long decades, Laury has been slaving away fifty hours a week as a salesman in the same furniture store in a working-class neighborhood, for a salary that barely covers his meager needs. Fifty-six and divorced, he lives alone, without any contact with the three daughters and thirteen sons he has fathered with five different women. Issued of a Jewish family that came from Italy, Laury's grandfather was a tailor and his father a professional boxer turned worker in the Chicago slaughterhouses (immortalized by Upton Sinclair in *The Jungle*) until they closed in 1951.[7] When he was

---

7. For a vivid portrait of life and labor in and around Chicago's slaughterhourses during this period, see Thomas J. Jablonsky, *Pride in the Jungle: Community and Everyday Life in Back of the Yards, Chicago* (Baltimore: Johns Hopkins University Press, 1993), and Rick Halpern, *Down on the Killing Floor: Black and White Workers in Chicago's Packinghouses, 1904–1954* (Urbana: University of Illinois Press, 1997).

very little, his father took him along to the fight cards being held at that time all over the city. Out of filial devotion, Laury followed his father's footsteps into the ring and fought as a pro at the tender age of seventeen, with a determination equaled only by his ineptitude: lumpish and uncoordinated, he suffered thirty-five defeats in thirty-seven fights, seventeen of them by stoppage: "My mother used to say, I would come home with—she made me a robe and trunks—she'd say, 'Did you fight tonight?' I said, 'Well, yeah, mom, why?' She said, "Cause your clothes are so clean'. [In a sad little voice.] And that was interesting. We never talked about *my embarrassment*. My father, he felt very bad, to see that I just couldn't do it . . . I wish he was alive today to see my accomplishments and my work as a professional cutman. That would give him great strength."

Laury came away from this painful experiment between the ropes with a fascinated admiration for the pugilists he rubs elbows with, be they merely preliminary fighters: "Most people don't know too much about boxers. But they're human beings, too. I feel a man getting in the ring to fight is a *special person*. Treat him as such. And if his accomplishments are good and he does well, compensate him for it." At the end of the seventies, Laury briefly tried his luck as a manager, with no more success ("I got out after five or six months, I was losing money . . . and other things: the two boxers I had, they both drove me crazy, because I wasn't well equipped to be a manager and deal with the personalities"). Then, from having attended so many weighins and hanging around in the company of cornermen so much, he wound up learning the rudiments of the craft and now finds employ as a cutman. This new role allows him to enter at last into the magic circle: "There's nothing more that I like more than boxing. *It's my life. It's my woman. It's my love,* it's my everything. I have such great admiration, and you meet a lot of nice people. But the main thing is, you never heard stories about me that I'm not professional: anybody you talk to, they'd say I was professional. I pride myself on that."

The cutman's task is to make sure that his boxer is not handicapped by a wound to the face suffered in the course of the bout. For this, he has about forty seconds within the one-minute rest period between rounds to close a cut, stop a nosebleed, or tame a bruise that threatens to obstruct the fighter's vision by bulging up. His instruments are rudimentary: cotton swabs, an icepack, an "enswell"

Cutman Laury Myers in his hotel room in Atlantic City

(a small handheld steel paddle used to control swelling), vials of coagulants (avotine, adrenaline diluted to 1:1000 strength), Vaseline, and the precise application of pressure on the wounds.

To find work, Laury goes to all the weigh-ins in the region, inquires about upcoming cards, offers his services in gyms. "With my love of boxing and my knowledge of what I do, I work with anybody: I'd work with King Kong if he needed a cornerman." He often officiates for a token remuneration, ten dollars slipped into his hand, in order to make himself known and recognized ("So that your professionalism is out there for people to see"). What matters above all is to stay active. Ever since the big quarterly magazine *Ringside* published a laudatory portrait of him (he bought forty copies of the issue at his neighborhood newsstand), Laury has nurtured the hope of being called soon for a big televised fight, for which cutmen make as much as two percent of the boxer's purse.

The mustachioed cornerman reads the boxing magazines religiously every month ("Every magazine that comes out, I've gotten. I read them and learn and retain names and so forth."); he avidly watches all the fights he can, on television and on video; and he attends all the cards in Greater Chicago. "On TV, I'm very critical of a lot of 'corners.' You have to keep your head, you can't lose your head. You got to know what you're doing. If you get nervous or excited, you project that to the fighter so all of a sudden your fighter is all excited and nervous. But if you talk to him calmly and you give him good advice, he goes out there and executes what you told him. Simple as that. Sweet Jesus! You got to be a *pro-fe-ssio-nal.*" In his experience, a good third of fights involve a facial cut requiring the intervention of the cutman, and about one in twenty see a more serious injury. Laury's point of pride: in the thirteen years he has been in practice, none of the boxers he has handled has lost a fight due to injury.

"What I like most? This is going to sound corny: doin' my job. Every fight's exciting and thrilling to me, whether it's a small fight, a big-time fight, or a less-experienced fight. Any time I can get in the corner, or the squared circle, that's my job, it's my pleasure. Being with anybody that's well recognized or not, any fight is exciting to me. I can work a fight every day in the week. I love it so much. It's my livelihood. It's my life. I think of nothing but boxing and the beautiful ring card girls."

Just a few yards from them, seated discreetly at the other end of the couch, is a little white guy, stoutly built, with blond hair cropped short and a craggy face composed of twisted features, wearing a gray T-shirt and a faded green sweatsuit. I guess that this is Hannah, Curtis's opponent. He's come alone to the weigh-in—the only cornerman listed on the program for the card is his own father, which sends a chill up my spine. DeeDee is getting impatient and decides to kill time by going to get a coffee. "Where you goin'?" whines Curtis. "Wait till I weigh in, man, then we gonna go for coffee and lunch together." But the old coach is too hungry. So Curtis disappears into the bathroom one more time.

At eleven on the dot, the officials make their entrance and the weigh-in room, a large air-conditioned rectangle carpeted in gray, gradually fills up: the matchmaker Jack Cowen, who put together tonight's show, and Doc Bynum, the physician mandated by the commission to certify the health bill of the fighters; three secretaries, two bleached blondes and a spick-and-span redhead, who expedite the paperwork (licenses for the boxers and cornermen, medical certificates, waivers in case of injury, financial guarantees for the purses, etc.); the referee Sean Curtin; the commissioner with his graying moustache; the old coaches from the area, chirping among themselves, and the usual regulars on the morning of a fight card. I chat for awhile with Sean Curtin, who knows me from having refereed the night of my fight at the Golden Gloves. When I express my surprise that "Jazzy" James Flowers has become state champion in the light heavyweight division, with his pathetic record of four wins and two losses, Curtin sighs. "What d'you want, there are so few guys . . . He didn't have any competition, that's why." The dearth of fighters is so severe that soon it will be enough to turn pro to be automatically elevated to the rank of state champion! Curtin nods his assent with an aggrieved look that twists up his Irish mug: "You got very few guys who get into boxing these days, very few. [Huffing and looking vexed.] It's unbelievable how much it's declined! Parents don't want their sons to do it. Hmm, wheeew . . . [He huffs again, to show how discouraged he is.] And so you got less activity, fewer fights, no publicity either. In my day, when I was a boxer, every time I fought, there was an announcement in the *Chicago Tribune* (the major daily of the metropolis) for anyone who fought. The *Tribune* was the sponsor of the Golden Gloves. All the guys who fought in the Golden Gloves, your name was in the paper. They published your picture. I boxed in the finals for the Golden Gloves title and my picture was on *the front page* of the Sunday papers. You had a ton of publicity and when you're young, gettin' your name out in the paper, it gives you a thrill, you like it. They don't do that any more—nowadays, people on the street, nobody knows who the Golden Gloves champ is."

Meanwhile Jack Cowen is pressing on with the commission secretary to make sure she will indeed send the official results of the fights to all the interested parties, the promoters, trainers, and commissions of neighboring states—"The last show at the Park West, for some reason, Leon Sushay, he's the only one who didn't get his copy. Can you mail him another one today please?" Then he informs DeeDee that Jim Strickland, a pharmacist and trainer-manager on the side, has agreed to act as second in Curtis's corner tonight, since Ed Woods, his usual cutman, won't be there (he couldn't get off work in time to drive all the way from Indianapolis, where he recently moved). So Jack has asked that Strickland be added to the list of people authorized to get into Studio 104 without paying tonight.

Curtis comes up to Cowen and sheepishly breaks the news that Lorenzo is still holding the seven tickets that he was supposed to unload for him; as a result Curtis doesn't have the money that he was expected to deliver to him this morning. Jack replies with a sneering little laugh: *"Call the police!"* Somewhat relieved, Curtis returns to sit down at the back of the room while DeeDee hands Cowen the money corresponding to the sale of the tickets assigned to his protégé. The matchmaker counts the bills meticulously, lining them up on the table, away from the corner of the room where the weigh-in itself is proceeding unceremoniously. He quickly tallies up his accounts on a piece of paper by multiplying the number of bills by their face value, total . . . Surprise! Three hundred dollars are missing, the equivalent of fifteen tickets. Panic strikes. DeeDee grimaces. Jack counts again, quickly: there are indeed three hundred dollars missing. Yet Curtis was sure that all the money was there. DeeDee's face suddenly lights up, the mystery is solved: those are the tickets entrusted to Jeb Garney, Curtis's manager. Jack breathes a sigh of relief. "All right, then, we're all set." He peels off five hundred dollars in cash and hands the wad to DeeDee: "Here's five hundred for Curtis, let's get that settled. We'll see later on for the commission, when everything has come in."[8] What to do with the nine remaining tickets Curtis still has? Jack enjoins DeeDee to keep them,

8. Handing over the fighter's purse in advance, to his trainer and in sight of everyone, is triply unusual: as a rule, payments in the pugilistic universe are made only after the performance, behind closed doors, and between the promoter and the boxer's manager, for those who have one. We can detect in this an indication that this card was put together quickly, in close collaboration between Jack Cowen and the Woodlawn Boys Club, so as to keep Curtis busy with an eye to a more profitable bout soon down the road in Atlantic City—on two separate occasions the month before, he had nearly been called up as an adversary for a world-ranked boxer on a show televised from a local casino.

you never know, maybe he'll find a way to unload them between now and tonight . . . We are informed that Jeb Garney won't be coming to the weigh-in; he sent word for DeeDee and Curtis to meet him at 2 p.m. sharp at Daley's, the family restaurant next to the gym, for the traditional prefight meal. All indications are that there's not much riding on this card; it's a routine fight for the Woodlawn Boys Club star.

DeeDee and Curtis have thus sold $1,200 worth of tickets, which is a pretty good lump. Jack scribbled on a scrap of paper the number of seats allotted to each boxer for sale "on commission": Curtis Strong 70, Keith Rush 20, Windy City 150 (a rival gym on the West Side, which has two members on the card tonight), and two other names that I don't recognize, for 50 and 20 tickets, respectively. This totals 310 tickets to be unloaded by the boxers and their entourage, for a guaranteed take of $6,200—which must cover roughly half the cost of the event. Assuming that all the boxers on the card make their quota of ticket sales, which would be surprising.[9]

Someone comes over to alert Cowen that the guy who was supposed to go pick up the two boxers from Milwaukee arriving at the Greyhound bus station in ten minutes can't make it: his car has broken down.[10] Jack grudgingly decides to dispatch Kitchen, a jovial chronic drunk and habitué of the gyms and fight cards, where he offers his services as amateur photographer. In a falsely formal and overtly patronizing tone, Cowen hails Kitchen, who is hanging around as usual, waiting for a chance to earn a few bucks.

JACK: Okay, I'm gonna send Kitchen—I don't see any other solution. I'm gonna give him some money and put him in a cab, *sober!* . . . [He goes over to Kitchen, who is rambling about, looking dazed, and clasps him with authority by the shoulder.] Miiiiister Kitchen, come here! You are now about to *earn your keep,* uh-uh . . .

9. In point of fact, I will learn later that the total sales for this card came up to a paltry 178 tickets (of which 104 were tickets sold by Curtis and his entourage) and that Curtis's manager had had to pay his opponent out of his own pocket in order to ensure that his fighter would headline the event and thereby "get him some work."
10. The Greyhound bus lines, which link the main cities of the country, are the cheapest means of long-distance transportation for the poor in America. They are frequented mostly by families from the black, Latino, and immigrant (sub)proletariat who do not own functioning automobiles and do not have the financial means to travel by plane.

KITCHEN [humbly]: Somebody call me?

JACK [condescending]: Me. You've been drinking today?

KITCHEN [shakes his head vigorously]: Oh, no.

JACK: You're in shape?

KITCHEN [deferential]: Yessir.

JACK: Okay here's ten dollars. You will go catch a cab to the Greyhound bus station and you will find someone by the name of Dixon there.

He shoulda come in about five minutes ago.

KITCHEN: Okay. What's his name?

JACK: Sherman Dixon, lil' stocky kid. Lil' stocky black kid, round-faced kid. Another kid named Zeb something or other, they'll be— he's a light heavyweight, they should be standin' together.

Kitchen doesn't know where the new Greyhound station is since it has moved from its location in the Loop, and Cowen has to scrawl out the address for him, in his unsightly lefthanded handwriting, on a scrap of paper—you can hardly rely on taxi drivers since they're more often than not recent immigrants who don't know the city. Then he describes the physique of the two pugs from Milwaukee, down to the smallest details. (Cowen briefly tries to convince me to go in Kitchen's stead, but no way: I don't want to miss the weigh-in.)

A young mustachioed Puerto Rican comes up to Cowen (I will learn later that this is Ishmael, a middleweight from Aurora who is debuting in the pros), pleading with the matchmaker to put him on the card. He's dragged himself here from his distant suburb in the hope that Anthony would be here too and that Jack would add the two of them to the night's bill. But Anthony himself had been considered only as a possible last-minute replacement. Ishmael puts on a devastated look. "Man, I trained hard, I was lookin' for that fight. I know Anthony, we spar together: it's a *challenge, man!* I want a challenge. I'm lookin' for the challenge. For me man, to me it's the ultimate challenge, I wish I woulda fought." More than a challenge, what Ishmael needs is cash, and he needs it badly enough to drive forty miles on the faint hope of fighting on a moment's notice. Jack doesn't let the opportunity slip by: he offers the Puerto Rican pug a bout in Cleveland at the end of next month. He assures Avandano, Ishmael's trainer, who is all ears, that this fight is clearly to his advantage: his opponent will be a novice who already has three losses and a draw for only two wins ("The man is sure beatable"). Avandano relays the information to Ishmael with an abundance of nodding. The young slugger looks pretty dejected but ends up accepting this fight "on the road," as a last resort—this is how Cowen moves his merchandise from one market to another so as to fill the cards he gets to set up throughout the Midwest.

A fragile-looking young man, with cream-colored skin and smooth, wavy hair surrounding an angular face, walks up in turn to beg Jack to give him a fight. The matchmaker bluntly brushes him aside with a sarcasm: "You don't even know where the gym is anymore, go on, forget it." In the face of the whining insistence of the supplicant ("Please, just gimme one I'll chance, just one, I'll show you I can fight"), Jack agrees to hire him as a helper, to hand out the gloves and dispatch with other minor chores tonight. I really wonder for what pitiful wages . . . No doubt as pitiful as the audience that has come to the weigh-in: two dozen people at most if you include the Commission employees. DeeDee is fond of recounting how, in the immediate postwar decades, the room would teem with boxers attracted by the prospect of getting hired at the last minute: "You always had fifty-sixty guys waiting, tellin' themselves that maybe some guy wouldn't show up, or twist his ankle, or the doctor wouldn't let him fight on account of a cut that hadn't healed right, an' that way they need a replacement. Yep, the room was packed then, even up 'til the sixties." Not to mention that the boxers of yesteryear were a whole lot tougher. "Shit, *ev'rybody knew how to fight back in them days. I mean, they knew how to fight for real.* Guys today, they wouldn't stand a chance against 'em."

Meanwhile, the weigh-in is following its course. Little Keith, James Flowers, and Danny Nieves have stepped on the scale and sat back down, silent, their faces stony. The secretary of the Commission shouts out in a high-pitched voice: "Are there any fighters that are on the card that haven't checked in with me?" Someone calls out, "Cur-tis Strrrong!" Curtis squeezes his way through the little gathering, takes off his overalls and, without any fanfare, gets up on the machine in his white briefs. Exhalation. One hundred and thirty-three pounds on the nose. Inhalation. No spectacular poses, no unseasonable remarks aimed at his opponent, who's sitting mum in his corner, having weighed in at 129.7 pounds. That's in the range agreed on in advance by the two parties, so everything is rolling right along. The boxers come up one by one to sign their contracts as Cowen calls them—contracts are inked on the morning of the fight, which allows for a last-minute change of personnel on the pro-

Curtis and DeeDee waiting
for the weigh-in to pass,
seated with Cliff and Eddie

24   EL 400 KODAI IIX PROCESSING * F

Jack Cowen and his production assistant
sorting the gloves for the night's fights

gram in case of need, or to modify the weight range of the two fighters if one of them hasn't respected the limit.[11]

Curtis will make $500 for his fight while Little Keith signs a contract for only 200—this is the pay that he told me the other day he thought was "fair": $50 a round, which has been the standard fee for years. Looking over Jeff Hannah's shoulder, I see that he will get a purse of $600. They had to pay him more than his opponent to persuade him to come take a beating up in Chicago. It's getting hard to find adversaries for Curtis since he moved up to ten-round bouts (which are the "headliners"): there aren't many boxers at that level and, what's more, they all make every effort to fight at home and to avoid "serious customers" so as not to risk tarnishing their records.

Curtis and DeeDee go sit at the back of the room with Eddie, who's dozing off in the row behind them. Then Curtis gets up and goes over to introduce himself to Jeff Hannah who's waiting, alone, leaning against the wall, in the opposite corner. Curtis shakes the hand of his opponent for tonight and chats with him for a minute in a friendly tone—from a distance, they look so relaxed you would think they were buddies; Curtis jokingly pats Hannah's chest. (So much for the media myth according to which boxers have to "hate" their rivals in order to fight well, a myth that never fails to aggravate DeeDee because it shows how ignorant the public is about the Sweet science.)

I take advantage of the interlude to give Jack the letter that Ashante's dentist has sent him to demand immediate payment for the care of his jaw, broken during his fight in Cleveland last February, which the Cleveland promoter still hasn't paid. Jack feigns amazement that his good friend Larry still hasn't wiped the slate clean. When DeeDee hears about this, he gets annoyed: "Man, don't bother with that. That ain't nuttin'. You just don't pay it, tha's all." Eddie is sporting a relaxed look, but I know that inside he is tense as a bowstring because Keith, his protégé, is fighting tonight.

11. If there is no possible replacement at the last minute, a boxer can demand that the promoter of the event increase his purse a little in exchange for him fighting an opponent who outweighs him significantly—in which case the bonus is subtracted from the heavier contestant's remuneration. A promoter can freely modify the lineup of fighters up until the last minute without any obligation for reimbursement. Thus it is a common occurrence for one or several boxers whose names are on the posters (often passably misspelled) advertising the card not to appear on the program.

▌ "You can never underestimate any fighter"

Eddie after a card at the International Amphitheater in July of 1990:

LOUIE: Are you nervous when your boxers get into the ring, for example when Lorenzo or Keith gets into the ring?

EDDIE: All of them. *All* of them. It don't make no difference who it is. All of them. It's a gut feelin' I have with all the guys, man. You know, you always have your lil' nervousness—I don't care who they are. I don't care if it's the toughest fighter in the world

LOUIE: When are you nervous, the days before, when you're training coming up for the fight, or just when the fight comes around?

EDDIE: Just when fight time come. Besides that, I'm relaxed. I just want everythin' to go right, tha's all.

LOUIE: And when do you start tightenin' up?

EDDIE: Sometimes at the weigh-in, it depends, sometimes at the fight. 'Cause there's no such thing as a easy fight. Not to me anyway.

'Cause I've seen guys, they brought guys in to lose and they didn't. I seen journeymen knock out top contenders. For example, when Larry Holmes fought Mike Weaver, Mike Weaver had nine losses on his record, he didn't have no impressive record. But he knocked Larry Holmes down three times an' when Larry Holmes knocked him down, he got up. An' Holmes was barely gettin' combinations off [he mimes combinations in slow motion, simulating exhaustion] an' the ref' stopped the fight. 'Cause they was afraid of Weaver hittin' Holmes again and do some serious damage. So that showed you, *you can never underestimate any fighter at any time, not anywhere.* So, that's why I tell guys, I say, even though the guy might seem soft, you have to really still be on your p's and q's 'cause that's part of boxin'.

LOUIE: Because every time you step into the ring, anything can happen . . .

EDDIE: Uh-uh, tha's why I tell 'em, that's what I stress to you all the the time: preparation, pre-pa-ra-tion.

LOUIE: During the fight, when an opponent gets Lorenzo or Keith in trouble, do you get extra tense?

EDDIE: No, well, no, because up in here, I know they prepared for that. It's accordin' to d'way they sparred: they be in difficulty up here, they learned how to deal with it. 'Cause workin' with Curtis, workin' with Lorenzo or Keith, you're gonna catch *somethin'* 'cause that's the way they work. You know, tha's why we don't have too many guys from other gyms come up here and get in there sparrin'. 'Cause they know if they come up here at Woodlawn an' spar, it's gonna be real *hard sparring*. 'Cause that's the way we work.

We head back to Woodlawn, DeeDee, Curtis, Eddie, Little Keith, and me. Last year, Curtis fought the "bum" from Milwaukee that Keith is going to face tonight. In the elevator, Curtis reassures his gym-mate: "He ain't tough. If you put pressure on him, he's gonna crack, you won't have no trouble. I knocked his ass out in the third round, so I dunno if he can go the distance." In any case, the match is only a four-rounder . . .

As we're coming out of the Illinois Center, I draw DeeDee's attention to the art exhibit in the lobby. How would he like to have the sort of bluish, lumpy abstract painting that occupies center stage in the entryway hanging in his living room? "Man, I don't even know what that *thang* is, Louie." By contrast, he knows about women, and so does Curtis. Their contest of salty jokes and lusty eyeballing starts up again as soon as they're back on the street. While the parking garage attendant brings his car down, Curtis nibbles at a chocolate-covered peanut bar and sketches a few boxing steps in the little concrete shed where we're waiting. A thirty-something guy in a black parka comes up who says he recognizes him: "I've seen you on TV, you're a boxer, right?" He shakes Curtis's hand and greets DeeDee with bombast, visibly impressed to be in the presence of practitioners of the Sweet science. In the car, the talk is all about boxing, last night's fights on television and Keith and Curtis's respective opponents for tonight.

An Anxious Afternoon

Back on 63rd Street, we come face to face with a worn old man decked out in an outrageous carnival costume: white spats, red jabot and tailcoat with epaulets, and handcuffs at his belt, topped off with an extravagant hat of shrubbery sporting propellers trimmed with a dozen little American flags. A veritable walking human carnival all by himself! DeeDee and Eddie are surprised that I don't know him—he's a neighborhood character—and they suggest that I go and take his picture, because he's fond of that. I ask the old coach if the guy is a loony: "If I

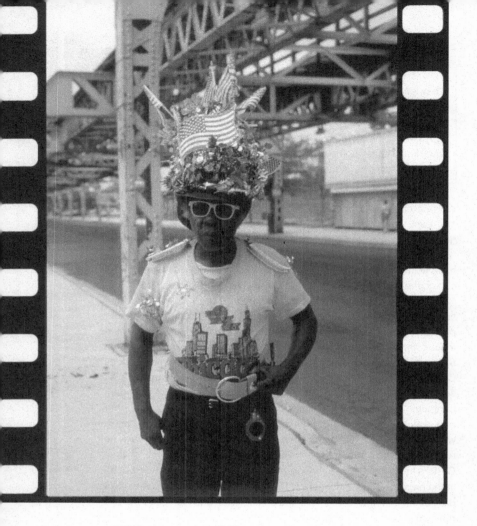

"If I wear a hat like that, Louie, what'd you think?"

wear a hat like that an' I'm walkin' around on d'streets, Louie, what'd you think?" Curtis hurries off to call Lorenzo again to try and find out what became of his tickets. "If you want my advice," Eddie grouses, "if you'd ask me, I'dda told you Lorenzo ain't reliable. Now you know."

Curtis and DeeDee have two solid hours to kill before going to eat at Daley's with Jeb Garney who made an appointment with them at the restaurant. Lunch time is calculated to fall according to the time of the fight, namely five hours before so that the boxer will have digested but still retains the calories from his last meal. DeeDee doesn't want to twiddle his thumbs all that time—he's always in a vile mood as the fights get closer. So we agree to meet up again to leave from the gym together at 5:30. Sherry, Curtis's wife, won't be coming to the event because of her pregnancy, and Curtis won't be bringing along any members of his family either, on DeeDee's express orders. So the three of us will go in his Jeep.

I drive Eddie to his home over on 55th Street. While we're riding down Cottage Grove Avenue, he comments: "It's not too much choice for the youth in this neighbo'hood: *either you get into drugs or the penitentiary.* . . . Did you hear about the blackout on the West Side?" For the past three days, a segment of the city's western ghetto has been without electricity following the breakdown of a power station.

Louie: Yeah, I heard about that.

Eddie: Yeah, well most of d'stores got robbed. Most of 'em was Arab store, storeowners.[12] An' they had such a bad repor' [rapport] with d'neighborhood people they robbed 'em.

Louie: Why is that that uh they have such bad—

Eddie: Well y'know the Arabs they y'know they *disrespect a lot of the black men,* 'cause d'majority of 'em—you know like I told you, you in a urban neighborhood where d'majority of 'em are alcoholics, an' so they come in actin' like fools, so, tha's how they disrespect 'em. It's not too much intelligence between individuals.

Louie: Oh so you think it's more the fault of the blacks in the neighborhood rather than—

Eddie: It's—it's *both fault.*

Louie: —The Arabs an' the blacks?

Eddie: It's both fault. Number one, it's a liquor store on each corner, y'know, so that's that. That has a lotta fault.

Louie: How come there're so many liquor stores in those areas?

12. The majority of the commercial establishments in the black ghetto are held by small shop owners of Middle Eastern (Lebanese, Syrian, Palestinian) or Asian (Korean and Chinese) origin, who employ a family workforce and whose cultural norms regarding face-to-face relations stipulate distance and reserve. Hence the acute tension between them and the residents, who perceive these shopkeepers as intruders who, aside from "pumping" money out of the African-American community without reinvesting there, treat them coldly if not contemptuously. See In-Jin Yoon, *On My Own: Korean Businesses and Race Relations in America* (Chicago: University of Chicago Press, 1997), and Jennifer Lee, "Cultural Brokers: Race-Based Hiring in Inner-City Neighborhoods," *American Behavioral Scientist* 41, 7 (April 1998): 927–937.

EDDIE: Because they know [somberly] when people are *oppressed,* don't work, they gonna sit around an' drink theirself away. Only diff'rence between a liquor store and a crackhouse,[13] a liquor store is legalized. It's *government authorized* tha's why an' then besides that, it's not too much diff'rence. 'Cause you get the same typa people you got hangin' out at d'crackhouse, in front of the crack-house, you got 'em in any liquor store or in front of the liquor store—it's not too much diff'rence. . . .

LOUIE: You must have been to a lotta weigh-ins now?

EDDIE: Yeah, yeah you get used to 'em.

LOUIE: Isn't that a bother to have to go downtown an'—

EDDIE: Not really, no. Tha's the *only time I go downtown.* [chuckles] I'm not a *downtown person.* 'Cause everybody's in a hurry out there, always runnin' around.

Back home, I try to take advantage of the interlude by taking down my notes, but I'm so exhausted from yesterday and nervous about the up-coming fights that I don't get much done. Ashante shows up at the apartment around five. He came to train early today, knowing that the gym would be closing ahead of schedule because of the card. He had a good workout that got him back on track a little—he's had trouble finding his groove since the three-month interruption caused by the nasty frac-ture of his jaw. Yesterday, he went to see the matches at the three-on-three basketball tournament sponsored by Budweiser in Grant Park alongside the shore of Lake Michigan. He tags along with me riding to the Yancee Boys Club on Wabash Avenue to deliver a letter to the Soft Sheen Corporation (a request for funding for the exchange trip that I'm trying to organize between Woodlawn and the boxing club of Vitry-sur-Seine, a working-class suburb of Paris).[14] As we cruise through this neighborhood, which is even more rundown than Woodlawn, Ashante shouts out: "Oh, boy! My alma mater! Good ol' school!" We're in front

---

13. A "crackhouse" is an establishment (often an abandoned building) in which one can purchase and consume on the premises, in "galleries" reserved for that use, cocaine sold in the form of "rocks," as well as other drugs and various sexual services. See Terry Williams, *Crackhouse: Notes from the End of the Line* (Reading, Mass.: Addison-Wesley, 1992), and Philippe Bourgois, *In Search of Respect: Selling Crack in El Barrio* (New York: Cambridge University Press, 1995).
14. For a brief account of this sociological-pugilistic experiment, see "Bienvenue au ghetto," *L'Équipe Magazine* 471 (27 October 1990): 68–71, 75.

of the establishment where he went to school before dropping out in tenth grade, and he's touched, remembering those days, because it's the first time he's been back to this part of the South Side since he was a teenager. The high school is a massive brick building that looks like a garrison, ringed by vacant lots and planted in the shadow of two tall housing projects whose walls are covered with graffiti and ground floor windows are bricked up.

ASHANTE: We used to call it the Woodlawn project . . . It ain't changed, s'cept it's gotten worse, sure is . . . all the people they changed though . . . It ain't the same people. The gangs they change too. Ten years ago, wadden no killin's like now, but see, back then if two gang guys wanna fight, they let 'em two guys fight *one-on-one*. But it's not like that now: if you wanna fight me, I'mma git me a gun an' shoot you, you see what I'm sayin'? Whenever you got a gun, tha's the first thing' you think 'bout—not about *peace treaties* an' let dese two guys fight an' settle their disagreement as real grown men. It's *scary now* because these guys, they don' have—[his pitch rising abruptly in shock] I mean they don' have *no value for life—no value!* Women, baby, kids . . .

LOUIE: It wasn't like that back in your gang?

ASHANTE: No, uh-uh, we didn' shoot nobody, we jus' fistfight mos'ly back then. Now you shoot this guy for nuttin', or you drive-by an' shoot dis guy's three little kids—wadden like that, hell no!

LOUIE: You didn't have drive-by shootings back then?

ASHANTE: [pauses to reflect] We had drive-by shootin's but not like it is now. Not as many as you got now . . .

LOUIE: What about the drug scene. Is it true that it's way out of control?

ASHANTE: Drugs, drugs . . . it's a mess. *Worse!* Shit, drug wadden nothin' like it is now. See, back then, only *certain guys* ha' drug an' now shit! My lil' son [who is five years old] could git any kinda drugs if he wanted some. It's worse, it's worser yeah, it's at a all-time high right now, thanks to the government, the CIA.[15]

15. Ashante is alluding here to the "government conspiracy" theory, carried by rumor and denounced in large segments of the African-American community under the name "The Plan," according to which the federal state would be feeding drugs into black neighborhoods underhandedly so as to undermine the mobilization of their residents and drown their demand for racial equality. Patricia A. Turner, *I Heard*

What has become of the young guys from the neighborhood he hung out with, back in the days? "Mosta them *be on drugs, dead, or in jail.*" There's definitely no escaping that gruesome triptych, since that more or less the answer that all the black boxers have given me when I have asked them this question (but not their white counterparts, for whom a stable blue-collar job is the modal fate). Next we swing by the Coop, where I buy some fruit and film to take pictures of the fights, before returning home.

▌ *The macabre fate of childhood buddies*

LORENZO: Most of 'em are *in jail* or *dead,* you know, some of 'em are still on the streets, doin' good or, most of the ones I really did hang with are currently either in jail—some of 'em might be doin' bad, some of 'em are doin' allright.

LOUIE: You could've been one them who landed in jail?

LORENZO: *I could have,* yeah I could have.

LOUIE: What stopped you?

LORENZO: I don't know, it's jus' me, my mind, I jus' took a different course.

TONY: Well, some of 'em now are like, some of 'em are workin', some of 'em are *drug addicts,* some of 'em are *dope dealers* an' some of 'em are married an' strugglin', but *tryin' t'survive,* which I'm doin' the same thin': strugglin' an' tryin' t'survive.

ANTHONY: They not doin' *nothin'*—uh, some of 'em runnin' from the law, uh, most of 'em *got a good business* but *it's in drugs.* An' probably might, one of 'em might be doin' somethin' *but still* he dealin' drugs *on the side.*

LOUIE: Why are so many guys dealing drugs now?

It Through the Grapevine: Rumor in African-American Culture (Berkeley: University of California Press, 1993). One finds a version of this theory in the life narrative given by a street hustler on the South Side; Loïc Wacquant, "Inside the Zone: The Social Art of the Hustler in the Black American Ghetto," *Theory, Culture, and Society* 15, 2 (May 1998: 1–36 [1992]).

ANTHONY: They want—no, not the quick money, they wants, they want *a dream,* you know: [in a very calm voice] *they want that movie,* that's all that they want, you know, to be in that movie.

CURTIS: My mom told me when I was of age an' stuff, I think aroun' 'bout fourteen or fifteen, she say it's gonna be a time when you gonna see a lotta yo' frien's, some o'them gonna die an' some o' them gonna go to jail. N' *sho' enough* I seen 'em, a lotta 'em, 'bout half o'them—well, not half, that'd be stretchin' it a lil' bit too much, but a lotta my friends has passed away: *gang-bangin'* or a lotta 'em sellin' dope, I have a lotta frien's jus' *sellin',* jus' dealin' dope, [he raises his voice in indignation] *strung out on dope, sellin' cocaine* jus' to do another typa dope, uh—they call it Karachi I think, tha's a downer. [His voice quiets down again and takes on a dejected tone.] N' a lotta my frien's is in jail. Some o'my frien's, I mean, I can count d'friends on my own *one hand that did finish school* and ya know, pursue they career in uh ya know, bus'ness career uh, ya know, tha's jus' tryin' to make somethin' outa theyself. I can count 'em on one hand. But I still see 'em, ya know, and speak to 'em.

Ashante would obviously like to come to the fights tonight, all the more so since Calhoun, the businessman and South Side gangster he's been trying to hook up with for several weeks in the hope that he would become his manager, is sure to be there. He suggests it to me awkwardly: "What y'all doin' tonight? Who's goin' to d'fights? DeeDee got you on that list, right?" (that is, the list of people whom the promoter has authorized to come in free.) I ask him if he'd like to come to Studio 104 with us. "Sure would, but I don't got the money right now." I offer to buy his twenty-dollar ticket for him since I had planned on purchasing mine and I'll end up getting in gratis. "I sure 'preciate, Louie." Before he died prematurely from a heart attack, Charles, his former manager-trainer, always had free tickets and would arrange for Ashante not to have to pay to attend a card. If need be, Charles would go into a wild rage and raise hell at the box office until the promoter caved in.

But Ashante doesn't want to go to Studio 104 in the late afternoon with Curtis, DeeDee, and me: it's too early for his taste. He would rather wait until seven to come with my companion Liz, her friend Fanette, and Olivier (a.k.a. "The Doc"). So we agree that he will take the ticket that was supposed to be for Olivier; Liz has hers and so does Fanette. When the Doc gets to Studio 104, all he'll have to do is send someone to fetch me to buy his ticket from Curtis's supply rather than at the gate, which will increase Curtis's sales and his take. "What? But tha's a joke, Louie," scoffs Ashante. "He ain't gonna get no commission from d'ticket sales. One time, Butch, he sold two hundred tickets for his fight, to his firemen buddies, two hundred, y'hear me. And he got *nuttin'.*"

I propose to Ashante to stay in the apartment and wait for Liz, but after a moment's thought he declines the offer: he's too afraid of being inside alone with Titus, my gentle hundred-pound husky, even if I tie the dog up in the kitchen. (Another time, he confides to me: "I cain't stand bein' in a room with a animal tha's more vicious than me.") I can just open the car for him, which is parked in front of my building, and he'll wait in there. As long as he's going to wait outside, why not sit in the shade, on the grass in front of the building, rather than lock himself in my old Plymouth Valiant, which has neither radio nor air conditioning, in the blaring sun? "Don' be jokin', Louie. I ain't stayin' here, in fronta the door, you know the cops gonna bust me." "For what?" "For what? (rankled.) *For nuthin', damn.* They not gonna lemme sit here waitin'. Man, they don' want no blacks 'round here, Louie, you know that. I told you when I useta go in Hyde Park, every time I be picked up by d'police for just walkin' across the street."[16] I insist but nothing doing: "They gonna arrest me for 'trespassing,' shiiit, you know how it is Louie," says Ashante, exasperated. Finally I take off, leaving him inside the car, in the burning sun, waiting for the girls to get back.

I trek down Ingleside Street to the Boys Club to meet up with DeeDee and the others. The front door is propped open by a piece of wood. Eddie is standing in the doorway, chatting with Anthony and Maurice, his chubby and shy cousin who's into kickboxing. Keith is lying on the situp table at the foot of the ring, head back, eyes closed: he's trying to sleep, as boxers are advised to do before a fight (in order to relax and to conserve energy), but you can read the anxiety on his dozing face. DeeDee returns from the store next door and patiently waits for Curtis

16. My apartment building was located right on the border between the black ghetto of Woodlawn and the prosperous white neighborhood of Hyde Park, the fortified haven of the University of Chicago. The street in front of it was continually patrolled by the city police as well as by the cars of the private police force of the University (the third largest in the Midwest in terms of manpower). Both had the well-deserved reputation of stopping people for questioning based on aggressive racial profiling and for mistreating the black youths from the surrounding areas.

to show up, sitting on the other table in front of the mirror on the wall. Did he call Curtis's house to check whether's he's on his way? "Why d'hell you always be askin' questions, Louie? There's no problem, I ain't worryin' about that."

We talk once again about the blackout that has struck the West Side ghetto as well as part of the posh suburb of Oak Park since Saturday night. A half-dozen grocery stores have been burglarized, but nothing spectacular: "It was nuttin' this time. They didn't have too much lootin'. Not like before. *If they did, it'd be guys all over this neighborhood here sellin' you color TVs for fifty bucks an' stuff.* You'd have guys in this gym right now sellin' their stuff." (Later, Ashante and Eddie will agree that if they dwelled on the West Side, they would go help themselves in the neighborhood stores as soon as night falls: "If I lived in the conditions d'people there live, man, like animals, in real hard-core poverty, man, I mean, I'd be goin' out there every night an' get me two carts fulla merchandise.")

I offer to drive, in case DeeDee wants Curtis to rest until the last minute: "It's all right, this time Curtis can drive. It ain't nothin' but a lil' fifteen-minute drive." Another telltale sign that this is a minor fight, presumed to be no trouble for Curtis; by contrast, when he defended his title as Illinois state champion in Aurora, an hour away from Chicago, DeeDee had insisted that I take the wheel. It's all the more crucial that he win this fight, and in convincing fashion. We chat calmly in the warm semidarkness of the back room, talking about boxing and swapping stories of crime and assorted street tales.

DeeDee always gets organized so as to leave well ahead of time for a card: "I like t'go places early. When I go someplace, I like to be there early, sit down, take my stuff out, relax, then do what I gotta do. I don't like to get there an' rush, nope. I know I gotta be there early to wrap Keith's hands no-how. Strickland ain't gonna be there an' Eddie can't wrap Keith's hands. So I gotta wrap 'im." He doesn't like talkative people—he calls them, derisively, "Morandum runnin' off at the mouth." "One thing I liked about the Philippines (where he lived for five years at the beginning of the seventies) is, if a guy talk too damn much an' run off at the mouth, he's gonna get knocked out, *wham!* Yep, I saw so many strange incidents an' strange ways out there, I said to myself, *'Damn!'*"

Curtis finally arrives, showing off the "Salem" T-shirt that a salesman for the cigarette company offered him so he would wear it tonight. He is also carrying his new ring robes draped over his arms, fresh from a Filipino tailor friend of his. They are sea blue, with "Curtis Strong" embroidered in gold letters on the back. DeeDee cringes: "They shoulda put some gold trims on d'sleeves." It is just after six when the old coach, Anthony, Maurice, and I get going in Curtis's Jeep.

Curtis takes little side streets, pretending several times not to know which way to go, as if he wanted to make the trip longer—as a result, it takes us more than half an hour to complete a trip that normally takes fifteen minutes. He drives on purpose in front of two churches and slows down to silently cross himself. A little beyond South Shore, he points his finger at a big high-rise in the middle of a green residential neighborhood where he lived before he moved to Bennett Avenue and 72nd Street. It was clearly better than his current surroundings, which are replete with drug dealers and border the train tracks, but at six hundred dollars a month he couldn't afford the rent.

Welcome to Studio 104

We zip down the Dan Ryan Expressway until we hit 104th Street, then head east on Torrance Avenue to pull in two blocks down, at the end of the street, at a long, red brick, barnlike building nestled between a junkyard ("Bill's Used Auto Parts"), an industrial brewery, and a vacant lot bordered by abandoned railroad tracks. This is Studio 104 (pronounced "One-o-four"), a tavern and night club located for some thirty years in this declining working-class neighborhood isolated from the rest of the city, at the far end of the South Side.

I discovered this joint last month on the occasion of an outdoor card organized by its owner, the famed Lowhouse, a notorious gangster who, it is rumored, uses the fight nights held in the parking lot of his establishment to launder the monies drawn from the various illegal rackets he runs.[17] In point of fact, DeeDee had warned me to be discreet with my tape recorder because the hoods who turf there could get the idea that I was an undercover cop or an FBI agent. I understood that the Woodlawn coach wasn't kidding when, several days after this card, Jack Cowen came back to the subject during a conversation in the gym. "Louie better be more careful with his tape recorder, with all the dealers

---

17. A well-placed informant whom I had asked if it would be interesting for me to meet Lowhouse had answered abruptly: "That guy is a criminal, he's an ignoramus, you won't get anything out of him. I would not advise you to interview him, you'd be wasting your time. He's crude, suspicious . . . And the guys that hang around his tavern are dangerous. For him, the fights are just a business: he gives money to someone to organize them and that's about it, he doesn't give a damn and doesn't know anything about boxing. Besides, he'd never agree to be interviewed."

who hang out down there. If he walks around with his recorder like that, one of these days we might find a dead body on the other side of those railroad tracks." Here is a description of the place, as recorded in my field notebook following my first visit.

Studio 104 is a place for business, entertainment, and sociability specific to the African-American working class. It exudes a distinctive atmosphere: jovial, quasi-familial and furiously "black." You come to this tavern not only to drink, feast, and dance but also and above all to mingle with friends and "conversate" for hours among regulars.[18] You watch sports championships there, you celebrate birthdays there, you have bachelor parties there, you drown your sorrows and parade your joys there to the rhythm of the music, dance parties, and would-be erotic shows (wet T-shirt competitions, "sexy legs" contests, and assorted striptease gigs). The establishment and the neighborhood and its residents live in osmosis, as testified by the bevy of pickup trucks buzzing around it at the end of the day. On your way out, shy kids are handing out colored flyers announcing Fourth of July picnics thrown by local politicians and cards printed by the district's black representative (recently implicated by one of his secretaries in a murky sexual harassment case).

HEAR YOUR CONGRESSMAN: GUS SAVAGE
10TH ANNUAL REPORT, STATUS OF DEMOCRACY
ON INDEPENDENCE DAY!
(PENDING LEGISLATION) JULY 4TH 1 P.M.,
KICKAPOO WOODS, 146TH AND HALSTED

Clusters of roving young men and burly guys are ambling at the back of the parking lot where the ring has been set up, straight as ramrods, proud to the point of looking a touch threatening in their gaudy sweatsuits and caps with snakeskin visors, their chests heavily loaded with chains and gold medallions. The girls who accompany them—unescorted female spectators are far and few—are hypersexualized, made up and dressed provocatively, often seductive and always fleshly; short skirts, plunging necklines, and glamorous hairdos are a must. (Jeb Garney is

---

18. On the key role played by these establishments in the reproduction of the expressive sociability of the black American community, see the fine book by Michael J. Bell, *The World from Brown's Lounge: An Ethnography of Black Middle-Class Play* (Urbana: University of Illinois Press, 1983).

aroused by it all and loudly bemoans not being twenty years younger). People are happy to be there, to see each other and to be seen, to exchange greetings and full-bellied laughter. Among the crowd are all the regulars at these events, trainers, old-timers, and aficionados of the Sweet science. A good number of the city's pro boxers come to size up possible rivals or simply to be admired, like "Jazzy" James Flowers, who is sauntering among the crowd decked out in his Illinois middleweight championship belt (as well as the stitches he earned along with it).

People mosey back and forth between the parking lot and the bar, knocking back drinks in generous quantities. Beer is flowing freely in spite of the high prices charged for consummables: $1.50 for a plastic cup of Old Style or a hot dog, a dollar for a can of soda, 50 cents for a bag of chips, and 25 cents for a glass of water. The bar alone is worth a visit: it's fifty feet long, with a magnificent gold-framed mirror running along one side, a giant color TV at one end, bathrooms on either side, and eight round tables surrounded by red Naugahyde armchairs in the middle of the room; in a corner stands a mock basketball backboard where customers can shoot hoops for 25 cents. Outside, people follow the fights distractedly, unless they personally know the boxer in action, in which case fanatical excitement erupts: frenetic applause, wild vociferations, yelling and shouting, high-pitched whistling, hooting, and howls of raucous laughter. Whether timid beginners or seasoned professionals, people noisily support the boxers from the area as a matter of local (and racial) patriotism. Kayos are always much appreciated, as is courage in adversity—the quality that practitioners of the Manly art call "heart." But that's about it: this isn't a crowd of connoisseurs, far from it. The vast majority of the spectators at these shows have no knowledge of boxing at all and are therefore incapable of appreciating the fights on a technical and tactical level. Practitioners of the Sweet science, and particularly the trainers, commonly consider them to be "squares" who can be made to swallow anything, much the way jazz musicians view the audiences at the clubs they play.

▮ *"They squares"*

GENE [sixty-nine years old, head trainer at the Fuller Park gym]: The people who come to these shows, they squares. They jus' come in, [in a tone heavy with derision] *they jus' get a kick outa seein' somebody kick somebody's ass,* know what I'm talkin' about? They don't come out—they don't know, well lotta people don't even know what they lookin' at.

LOUIE: Isn't it kinda depressing that you spend so much time perfecting that skill and people can't really appreciate it?

GENE: As long as they payin' the money . . . They don't know the difference, all they doin' is they see somebody gettin' they butt beat, they pay their ticket, [his voice turns into a high-pitched whistle with incredulousness] *some people like dat,* you know peoples are like that!

LOUIE: It doesn't get on your nerves sometimes?

GENE: I been doin' it, seein' it for so long, it goes in *this* ear an' out the other ear, I don't even pay no attention [laughs] . . . Lotta don't understand [the fight] because they *never understand it,* they jus' *talk* about boxing, but they jus' don't, it's nothin' but talk.

The fact that the fights are taking place outdoors adds much to the appeal of the scene. The "card girls" who strut around in the ring between rounds to the great delight of the crowd, two tall, brazen black women turned out in minuscule bikinis that leave nothing to the imagination, are enticing to the point of whoreishness. The private security staff, comprised of three big, easygoing black policemen moonlighting off their job, take care of preventing any incidents and keep gatecrashers to a trickle. But they can't do much about the two dozen Mexicans watching the fights leaning up against the wall of their yellow frame house directly adjoining the parking lot.

We drop DeeDee off at the front door of the club, where Jeb Garney has been champing at the bit, wondering if we haven't gotten lost on the way. (As usual, he's dressed like a bum, in spite of the fact that he's rich in the millions from his racing dog kennels and his ranches). Curtis, who addresses his manager with a deference that is painful to watch— "*Mister Garney,* please close the door, please, thank you sir"—hands him three blue tunics with "Curtis Strong" embroidered on them. Garney also finds that there's a little something missing: "We should have had them put on a gold stripe for each win."

The employees of the restaurant are raising a big blue tarp to cut off the parking lot from the street so that passersby won't have a free view of the ring. They have a terrible time getting it raised on its poles owing to the strong wind that keeps inflating it like a sail every time they lift it up. We run into Kitchen, with his sempiternal camera strapped across his chest. He presses Curtis to let him take pictures of his fight. Curtis recommends that he first check with Jeb Garney since he's the one who holds the purse strings. Kitchen would rather get Curtis's approval so as to put moral pressure later on his manager to buy the maximum number of pictures, but the Woodlawn boxer slips away. An enormous black limousine, sparkling with luxury, is parked in front of the door of the club, its three rows of seats spread out over ten yards behind tinted windows. Curtis whispers to me, a big smile lighting his face, "Pretty soon *it's gonna be my turn to be ridin' in one of those,* Louie, you watch." I just hope that he'll pick me up hitchhiking when that day comes . . .

I glance at the official program for the event and find out that Little Keith, who has achieved four wins in five fights, will be facing an opponent who isn't exactly a titan of the ring, with a record of zero wins for thirteen bouts. As for Jeff Hannah, he's run up 18 wins, 21 losses, and a draw. In other words, he's a solid "journeyman," seasoned but on a downhill slide for a while, who from now on will serve as a stepping-stone for boxers on the rise like Curtis. (This kind of disparity, which might seem shocking at first, is not at all anomalous: it is by pairing them up with notably weaker opponents that a promoter gives local pugilists, especially those to whom he might be linked by an exclusive contract, which is the case between Jack Cowen and Curtis, a decisive advantage, if not a guarantee of victory—a surprise is always possible inside the ropes, as we will soon discover.)[19]

Instead of changing clothes in a van parked on the lot in the midst of which sits the ring, as they did for last month's card, the fighters have a dressing room inside the club at their disposal this time. If you can call it a dressing room, that is: since Curtis is the headliner, the boxers from Woodlawn have been allotted a storeroom behind the ticket window at the entrance to the nightclub. A room ten by thirteen feet, separated from the ticket booth by a blue curtain and encumbered with folded metal tables and chairs, cardboard boxes of Bacardi, piles of mops, cartons filled with various objects (ashtrays, knickknacks, coffee filters, aprons, kitchen utensils), a reel for a garden hose, two dismantled red wooden minibars, two broken popcorn machines, and four big stacks of posters

19. This is how a manager or promoter "builds" a boxer, by "feeding" him inferior opponents until he has a record that will allow him to seek televised bouts for which the purses become sizeable (cf. Loïc Wacquant, "A Flesh Peddler at Work," 6–14).

vaunting Studio 104's weekly festivities: "Sexy Leg Contests," "Happy Hours," and the usual "Ladies' Nights." As we struggle to fit all of us into this cramped space, DeeDee asks the guys who aren't putting on the gloves tonight to make room and leave. We unfold three metal chairs as best we can for Keith, Curtis, and Jeb Garney. As for DeeDee, he sits on a tall barstool (ideal for his knees, which balk at bending) and right away gets busy wrapping Keith's hands, since he will box first. Rolls of gauze, adhesive tape, scissors. Keith's gaze clouds over with apprehension. Meanwhile, the other boxers are changing in the adjoining dance hall next to the main bar, in full sight of the customers who are chatting and drinking away, leaning on one of the three counters.

Curtis whispers to me with an air of mystery, "C'mon, Louie, come with me." He just wants me to go with him to the bathroom, which is pretty scuzzy, with malodorous toilets surrounded by pools of urine. He disappears into one of the stalls, from which he continues to "conversate" with me while defecating with loud noise. "I really needed to take a shit. Ooooh! [sound of a cascade of farts] all that gas! . . . So Louie, *doesn't all this all make you esscited? Dontchya wish you was fightin' pro?"* Yes, it's exciting, no question, but in order to fight with professionals, I would first have to have the requisite skills. It's true that with Curtis on the night's bill, there's electricity in the air. He looks serene, not at all anxious and shifty as he had been these last few days in the gym with his supposed arm injuries.[20] The hardest days are those preceding the bout; then, when the moment to fight approaches, Curtis gets his self-confidence back. He knows that he's going to climb into the ring, where he can express his talent as an "entertainer": once he's in the squared circle, he's in his element, "at the office" or "at home," as pugilists are fond of saying.[21]

20. During the last two weeks leading up to the fight, Curtis complained repeatedly of a mysterious dysfunction in his shoulder that would suddenly make his arm seize up. This was a way of attracting the attention of his trainer (and, indirectly, of his manager) to his disastrous financial situation, a situation that the Studio 104 card would not suffice to resolve.

21. This attraction for the stage is not exclusive to boxers: bodily crafts and a sense of performance occupy an epicentral place in the urban society of black Americans, from music to religion to sports, comedy, and politics. See Loïc Wacquant, "From Charisma to Persona: On Boxing and Social Being," in *The Charisma of Sport and Race* (Berkeley: Doreen B. Townsend Center for the Humanities, Occasional Papers n. 8, 1996), 21–37.

▌"I always wanteda be an entertainer"

It's *very important* to be a performer. One day, I think' I was 'bout thirteen, I wan'ed be *a singer.* Me an' my brothers an' them, they didn' wanna sing. I use to always grab them, you know, from out the kitchen, they be by the f'idgerator, I grab them, [in an excited, giddy voice] 'Come on, I got these steps I wantyall to see 'em.' We go in the bedroom an' be rehearsin' these steps, but they always got *tired,* they tired out fast', they didn'—I guess they jus' didn' really git in to the entertainmen' part like I did: I always wanteda be an entertainer, it played a big part in my life.

Lookin' at television, *Michael Jackson:* you know, [murmuring in awe] seein' him, how he was jus'—how he *blossom like a flower* an' stuff, throughout the crowd, the public y'know. I jus' wan' to be a entertainer when I'm in the ring, I feel like I got to be at my best, you know, t'perform to my best. I know if I'm at my best, an' he [my opponent] at his best, *somebody gotta be winnin', right?* An' the crowd gonna look at the guy that's winnin'. So if I'm in my best, I can git the crowd underdivided [!] attention instead of tellin' them, [in a muffled voice] 'Sit down an' listen! Look at me!' You know, I git up there an' do my thin' an' everybody rootin' for . . . [lowering his voice even more for greater dramatic effect] *Curtis Strong.*

Back in the storeroom that's serving as the dressing room for the evening. Shoptalk. Eddie gives Little Keith his tactical instructions: "We gonna go for a gut check in d'first round, we're gonna go downstairs see what he got. So, right from the start, get on him an' work the body." The two Woodlawn boxers exchange advice when DeeDee and Eddie briefly leave the room.

> KEITH: I'm just worried 'bout that guy hitting hard 'cause he looked kinda heavy this mornin' at the weigh-in.
>
> CURTIS: I cain't tell you nothin' about that 'cuz he didn't hit me much when I fought him.
>
> *He explains that the adversaries that worry him the most are the journeymen. They're seasoned, crafty, and battle hardened owing to their very trajectory of losers:*
>
> CURTIS: You remember that fight you lost—you only lost one fight, right? [Keith nods.] You learn from that fight. Now, guess that man,

that he actually lost all his fights, he *learned* from these fights, y'see what I'm sayin'? It's the *experience,* they get that experience an' stuff. Them are the ones I worry, now I'm worried 'bout these guys steppin' in. If he had a record of—he was undefeated he hadn't fought nobody, see what I'm sayin', tha's how he got undefeated, they just carry 'im along an' stuff, he hasn't really fought a world-class guy. The ones that *lose* all them fights, them are the ones that I worry 'bout . . . Tha's why I take Hannah seriously.

On the program of tonight's card is a pro who's just starting out from Tinley Park, the neighborhood of Craig "Gator" Bodznianowski (a very popular local pug who fights in spite of had his foot amputated after a motorcycle accident and who bought himself a fitness and weightlifting gym in that small white working-class burg with his earnings in the ring). An entire busload of guys from his gym are there to cheer him on. Which leaves Curtis puzzled. "How they get *all those white guys to come out all the way to d'South Side* like that, DeeDee?" DeeDee concedes that the black community doesn't support its own boxers at all, no doubt due to lack of income. In response to which OB (O'Bannon's nickname) maintains that Curtis is the one bringing in most of the crowd tonight: "You're drawin', *you got a name* in Chicago." And then, without further warning, the three of them launch into a verbal joust about the differences between blacks and whites: the mailman starts off by tossing out "But I ain't colored, I never picked no cotton, never owned a mule," and the others instantly follow suit.[22] All the stereotypes about blacks are canvassed, from slavery to the ghetto. "That's what you should be gettin' on your tape, Louie," OB chuckles. To my great chagrin, I didn't catch this chunk of rhetorical bravura on tape and I wouldn't venture to try to transcribe it from memory!

Curtis's brothers come to greet him one by one: Derrick preening as the ultimate male, Lamont playing the part of the shy one, Bernard with his shaved head and spacey demeanor. They are followed by a half-dozen of his buddies who wish him good luck for his fight. Curtis asks

22. On the role of verbal jousts and the importance of the art of speaking well in urban African-American culture and sociability (of which rap is the most recent avatar in the commercial sphere), consult Roger D. Abrahams, *Deep Down in the Jungle: Negro Narrative Folklore from the Streets of Philadelphia* (New York: de Gruyter, 1963), and Thomas Kochman, *Rappin' and Stylin' Out: Communication in Urban Black America* (Urbana: University of Illinois Press, 1972).

OB if he isn't afraid of losing Steve Coakley (a young hopeful from the club that the mailman sponsors) as he earlier lost Cliff, his pet boxer.

OB: I ain't worried. As long as he's in the gym, I got somebody to look out for him [with a pronounced nod toward DeeDee].

CURTIS: But that's what I mean, 'cuz he ain't been in the gym that much . . . You were really taking care of Cliff, too, always askin' him if he need any money and stuff.

OB: Oh, but Cliff, he was my son. The things I did for him, *my God* [rolling his eyes] . . . I went to get him at the gym and drove him back home every night. Found him a job, got his wife a job . . .

The mustachioed mailman goes on to insist that if Curtis succeeds in the ring, "it's because *you got a strong woman behind you,* that's what make the difference." Eddie interrupts them to get Curtis's attention: "Your dad's here at the door, you wanna see him?" Glacial silence—Curtis's father abandoned him when he was little, him and his seven brothers and sisters, and never expressed the slightest interest in him until his career in the ring started to take shape. Curtis darkens suddenly: "No, tell him no, *I don't wanna see nobody till after the fight."* OB avers that Curtis should talk to him, for you don't brush your father aside like that. "And why should I? *You* can see him if you want." DeeDee intercedes in favor of his protégé: "An' he should see 'im for what? What they gonna be doin', uh, lookin' and gapin'? You don' need that now." Curtis swiftly takes refuge behind the authority of his coach: "Tell him DeeDee don't want nobody in d'dressing room right now." Besides, DeeDee is asking all the latest arrivals to clear the premises because we're literally stepping on each other, between Garney, Curtis, Keith, Eddie, Strickland (who has put on his "Curtis Strong" tunic and will officiate as the third cornerman tonight), Anthony, and Maurice. The latter is holed up in the dressing room for fear that the security guards for the night club will find him: he snuck in and doesn't have the money to pay for his ticket; if they throw him out, he'll miss the fights and will have to cool his heels outside until the end of the evening.

Ashante and Liz have just arrived. I ask DeeDee for a ticket from Curtis's quota; it's the last one. I go slip it to the Doc, who's pacing outside the door with Fanette. They haven't missed anything, since the fights, which were scheduled for seven, won't start until eight. Back in the mock dressing room, Ashante is pumping Curtis and Keith up for battle. Curtis catches me scribbling in my field notebook—I decided to take detailed handwritten notes rather than just tape them this time (so as not to risk arousing the suspicions of the bar employees with my recorder). "What you writin'?" We stare at each other intensely, I stay mum. After several seconds of stunned silence, we burst out at the same time with a long laugh. Curtis strikes a blow: "You know what? Some day *you gonna commit suicide,* Louie, 'cuz *you write too much.* What you say, DeeDee? People're gonna be wonderin' (in a worried little voice) 'What happen to Louie?' but we know why, yeah, we know why."

What a strange prophecy! After two years among them, my buddies from the gym are still surprised to see me functioning in my capacity as a sociologist. It's something that is never taken for granted, even if they've gotten accustomed to seeing me walking around with my tape recorder in hand, and now pretend to be irritated by my questions only for show. Eddie leans over me to murmur discreetly: "When you write your book, Louie, ten years from now, I'monna be your technical advisor, okay?"

The young cream-colored guy that Jack didn't want to hire to fight this morning comes around to hand out gloves to us—used pairs, which is against the state regulation that stipulates that brand-new gloves must be used for all official fights. We grope about in his big duffle bag for a pair the right size for Curtis. The tension is imperceptibly, slowly but surely, mounting in the storage-dressing room. We talk less and less loudly. Our gestures are more restrained. We take care not to demand anything of the two boxers who are readying themselves.

O'Bannon is curious to find out more about the upcoming visit to Woodlawn by the French boxers announced in the *Chicago Sun-Times* this past Sunday. I give him the rundown on the organization of the exchange with the municipality of Vitry (a communist-run town in the southeastern industrial ring of Paris), the travel arrangements, the sports meets, and the public debates planned. "An' who's gonna go over there?" Curtis cuts him off: "DeeDee's gonna decide." In fact, that will depend mostly on the amount of money we manage to raise to cover the cost of the airline tickets. And where are the six boxers who will land from Vitry next month going to stay? The plan is for them to sleep at the Yancee Boys Club, on 63rd Street and Wabash Avenue. Anthony is incredulous: *"Whaaat?* At Yancee, right up there by d'projects? Man, it's a rough neighborhood out there, they wanna be careful." Curtis concurs: "Yeah, it sucks, it's right next to the projects. And they ain't brothers either: they not gonna be able to walk down the street like you and me, *'cuz they don't never see white people out on the streets there."* The French boxers have no idea of the universe into which they will find themselves plunged. In any case, there's no question of their going out anywhere on the South Side without a solid escort, otherwise we're sure to bury one or two them there.[23]

During this hourlong wait, Curtis wards off his mounting anxiety by teasing me. When he sees me get out my tape recorder, he slips in slyly, as if in confidence: "Shhhtt! C'mon now, *everybody say some curse words Louie got his tape on,* ha, ha, ha!" DeeDee takes advantage of the opportunity to comment ironically again about the fact that the hoodlums from the area are going to bump me if they ever catch me recording in the tavern. To which I retort: "But before that happens, I'll give them a taste of my mean left hook." DeeDee, in a very dead earnest tone: "An' they'll whup you to death." I counter him with one of his trademark tirades: "Then I'll tell them: 'Careful, I'm DeeDee Armour's main man, you better not touch me: *he controls some killers.'"* The old coach nods without piping a word. All these jokes and banter serve to stave off fear and to curb the tension that is gradually inching up.

▌ *"They full of butterflies"*

A comment by LeRoy Murphy, a boxer from Fuller Park and former holder of the world light heavyweight title:

I know what it takes to get in that ring an' *every time I got in that boxin' ring I was scared,* everytime I climbed in the ring, everytime I put my hands up, I was nervous. Didn't nobody know but me, that be a little thing that you keep inside your own self, an' that's how I was. . . . I was always nervous two, three days before the fight. I get up in the mornin' run, go an' get a workout, light workout, eat breakfast, an' I come back an' I watch cable, I watch videos, like that, I don't go out the room. I'd start eatin' small portions then 'cause I feel nervous, my stomach feel nervous an' I'll try to—usually after the weigh-in I feel better. . . . The afternoon of the fight I never slept, *noooo.* Guys,

---

23. As it turned out, the six young Frenchmen and their three adult trainers wound up sleeping on military cots in the dressing room of the Yancee Boys Club, with the door to the club chained and padlocked shut *from the outside* so as to prevent any of them from risking going out into the neighborhood at night.

> before the fight, they don't sleep, they lay there an' rest but they full of *butterflies*, they be scared, every fighter, even [Muhammad] Ali admitted he was scared when he fought an' I like that: when you're not afraid, somethin' wrong wid' you. Everytime I got in the ring, I was afraid.

Pitiful Preliminaries

The opponents for the Chicago boxers finish getting ready in the barroom which holds the dance floor. They are changing in silence, with slow and deliberate gestures, their clothes and equipment (handwraps, gloves, cups, shorts, and robes) tossed over the back of a chair. Jeff Hannah is sitting absentmindedly on a table, legs dangling; he laces up his boots while chatting in a low voice with his father, head down, as if to better cut himself off from an environment that he senses is hostile. He knows that he is the sacrificial victim being served up to the local hopeful, in front of an audience already rooting for his opponent and judges who won't cut him any slack, and thus that he has every chance of losing his bout. This is the common lot of "opponents" on the circuit: their only chance of winning in their rival's "backyard" is to knock him out. Lots of things must be going on in his head and in his body—where I wouldn't want to be, tonight or tomorrow.

As I'm coming out of the bar, I run into Liz, who kisses me lustily. Eddie grabs me by the shoulder, laughing, like a cop arresting an outlaw: "Come on, Louie, that's enough, stop it, she's gonna make you soft if she keep kissin' you like that, I already warned you 'bout that! You ain't gonna be ready for your next fight."[24] The makeshift spotlights clamped to the metal poles stuck in the four corners of the ring light up. The show is about to begin. Everyone sits where they can—there's no reserved seating or VIP section at ringside for an event of this caliber. For once they skip the national anthem to launch straight into the

---

24. Trainers never miss a chance to remind their charges, even if under cover of a joke, of the commandment of the professional catechism of "sacrifice" which stipulates that the boxer shall strictly limit all erotic contact so as not to risk dulling this instrument for virile battle that is his body; Loïc Wacquant, "The Prizefighter's Three Bodies," *Ethnos* 63, 3 (November 1998): 325–352.

customary introduction of the officials, judges, referees, and timekeeper
by a corpulent, bearded announcer in a black tuxedo jacket:

> Ladies and Gentlemen, *welcome to Studio One-O-Four,* here on
> Chicago's beautiful Southeast Side! The boxing contests on your
> program are sanctioned by, and under the supervision of, the
> Professional Boxing and Wrestling Board of Illinois, the Department
> of Professional Regulation, Mister Gordon Bookman, chairman of the
> Board, Mister Nick Kerasiotis, executive secretary, and Mister Frank Lira,
> supervisor of athletics. This is Rising Star Promotions.[25] Your officials are
> judges Bill Lerch, Gino Rodriguez, and Stanley Berg, timekeeper Joe
> Mauriello, and your referees Tim Adams and Pete Podgorski.

O'Bannon has settled down in the front row with Michonne, behind
the red corner. Liz, Fanette, and the Doc are sitting over in the next
row, with Curtis's family, Anthony, and Ashante. Jack is standing up in
the aisle, keeping an eye on things. Laury Myers isn't around, an indication that he didn't manage to get himself hired for the night. It's Little
Keith who's boxing in the opening bout, as the slanting light heralds
the end of the day. His manager, the dapper Elijah (owner of a chain of
dry cleaners in the ghetto), is teamed up with DeeDee and Eddie in the
corner. His opponent, a short, potbellied black pug from Milwaukee with
very rudimentary skills, is clearly eager for one thing only: to "lie down"
and go home with his "paycheck." Keith has barely enough time to graze
him with a couple of rights to the body before the guy throws himself to
the canvas a first time, then a second, as Keith and the referee look on
in frustration. The referee urges him to fight, but nothing doing: when
the Woodlawn boxer lands a weakish combination, the tub of lard from
Milwaukee crumbles like a pile of rubble and fakes a kayo. The referee
kneels at his side and sharply rebukes him and then, seing that his
remonstrances are to no avail, takes his mouthguard out of his mouth
and sends him back to his corner. This guy is not just a bum but a genuine "diver" and I wonder if he's going to get paid—the judges have the
authority to take away the purse of a boxer who refuses to fight, and the
brotherhood of pugilists severely reproves of those who publicly fail to

25. Rising Star Promotions is merely a local front for Cedric Kushner (via Jack
Cowen), one of four major promoters who then shared the national market, the others
being Don King Promotions, Top Rank, Inc. (Bob Arum's company), and Main Events
(managed by rock concert promoter Shelly Finkel and trainer-manager Lou Duva).

Little Keith
opens the evening
with a four-rounder

uphold its warrior ethos this way. Elijah and Eddie crowd around Keith and raise his arms as a sign of victory, to a combination of whistles and applause from the crowd. It's not very convincing but we're happy for him just the same.

Journeymen, bums, and divers

JACK COWEN: A *journeyman* is a fellow that, in all likelihood, will never be a champion but he's capable of fighting almost anyone and will win on a given day and may lose on a given day. Because they will win once a while and make money. And put up a good fight if they're capable.

I'm not talking about somebody who's just a *diver* and who's gonna go here and get knocked out in the first round and then show up someplace else and get knocked out in the first round again. I'm not talking about those—those are *bums,* that's something that really has no place in boxing although they seem to succeed.

LOUIE: They have no place in boxing and yet there's quite a few of them around . . .

JACK: They . . . I shouldn't say no place because, obviously, there's always a place. You have guys, beginners, starting out, who need poor opponents to go ahead and see what they can do, to get confidence and test themselves: maybe they prove to be no better than the bums themselves after you get them in there—you don't know!

I do a quick count of the audience, which is about 80 percent male and ethnically mixed, with a slight preponderance of whites and Latinos: at most 300 people at the start of the event and about 450 at the end, not including the forty-odd Mexicans crowded against the wall of the house next to the parking lot (after a fruitless attempt, the manager of Studio 104 gave up trying to stretch a tarp in front of the house, to Ashante's great discontent, who insists that they be made to pay even if they're sitting in their own yard). This is about half the number necessary for the promoters to cover expenses.[26] And it's less colorful than last time:

---

26. The resulting deficit is absorbed by the managers who make the initial layout of funds to put together the event so as to keep their boxers active and to enable

the burly toughs who control the various illicit rackets in this part of the South Side didn't turn out in numbers tonight, a weeknight, and the wind blowing in gusts cools things off quite a bit.

The opening bout wasn't a pretty sight, but the second fight is pathetic to the point of becoming comical. It pits two "bums" of the first order against each other: a big flabby white guy from Tinley Park swathed in lard (his lower belly bulges out his trunks so far that you might think he's pregnant) against an older black pug from Milwaukee sporting a powder puff of red hair that gives him a wildly effeminate look. It's all too obvious that the latter never "smelled a glove" before tonight: incapable of putting up his guard correctly, he throws his fists with the backs of his hands in front, as if offering a bouquet of flowers, then flees away on tiptoe with his derriere to his opponent! As his only defense, he does his best to derail his opponent's blows by stretching his wiry arms out in front of him and swings them from left to right with a jerky vacillating movement that makes him look like a sort of human windshield wiper. You would think these are two big numskulls playing at boxing—except that they're both terrified at finding themselves in a ring. Every time the referee calls for them to "break," they lift their fists to the sky in concert, as if performing an incantation, and suspend hostilities with a relief so palpable that it's embarrassing.

The audience is chortling and derisively egging the two fighters on with exaggerated encouragement: "Throw your bomb!" "Come on, champ!" They figure that the white guy from Tinley Park, who is beefier and occasionally manages to land a few halfway decent-looking punches, is going to win (besides, he did win his first two fights whereas his opponent is making his pro debut). But the old pug with the powder-puff hair is getting bolder and his comical tap-tap is growing more accurate, while his rival is tiring visibly. By the third round, the crowd is siding openly with the black "bum," who was clearly served up as "feed" for his opponent, as the saying goes. The sympathy of the audience isn't just racial: the bloke from Milwaukee quite simply doesn't belong in a ring. But when, by sheer accident, he catches his opponent with a sharp right

them to boost their records. At this level of the pugilistic market, the only person who makes any financial hay from the enterprise is the matchmaker, since he invests nothing out-of-pocket and takes a commission as middleman off the top, a share of the boxers' purses (10 percent), and a fixed fee for running the production of the card. Wacquant, "A Flesh Peddler at Work," 23–30.

to the chin, the unexpected intrudes: the big flabby white guy rolls onto his back, tries to get up, staggers around, displays a series of distorted facial expressions that mingle surprise and suffering, then crumples to his knees again, powerless to command his legs. It's a surprise kayo! Consternation in the section where the whites from Tinley Park who came to support their buddy are massed; hilarious jubilation among the rest of the audience. Ashante and Eddie are laughing their heads off, nearly rolling on the ground. And Kitchen is delighted because he managed to slip onto the ring as cornerman for the winner, which will earn him a few bucks.

Gasping with laughter, I call over to Jack Cowen at the end of the aisle: "Ah, I hope you got that one on tape: that was one for the record books, 'Battle of the Superbums'!" Ouch! what did I not say? Looking dismayed and shaking his head in disbelief, Jack is in the midst of a confab with the Tinley Park guys, who are menacingly crowded around him. He's trying to explain to them how the novice from Milwaukee could have beaten their hero, when they had held out the prospect of a victory served up on a silver platter.[27] (Later, when I go apologize for having made such a gaffe, Jack brushes me off: "It doesn't bother me, Louie, it's for you: it's good you don't have go into a back alley with these guys, you might run into trouble.") At that point, Wylie, the *Chicago Sun-Times* reporter to whom I suggested to come watch Curtis fight, turns up. She asks me to introduce her to Jack Cowen because she is bent on having her boyfriend admitted free, and the watchdogs at the ticket window are holding him back at the door of the club. (This is typical of the arrogance of journalists: couldn't she pay for *one* ticket to her first prizefight?) Cowen doesn't want to lose the chance of a possible article in the newspapers and immediately goes over to let him in.

27. This is a concrete illustration of the structural dilemma which every matchmaker finds himself confronted due to the very nature of his activity: when fights go well, people credit the boxers and their entourage and he fades into the woodwork; in the opposite case, it is he who is the target of all the unhappiness and recriminations, such that he becomes everywhere "the most unpopular man in the city," as the famous matchmaker Teddy Brenner notes in his autobiography. Teddy Brenner and Brian Nagler, *Only the Ring Was Square* (Englewood Cliffs, N.J.: Prentice-Hall, 1981), 22.

▌ *"I'm like someone buying and selling stock"*

The only son of a Jewish family that immigrated from Russia in the 1920s, Jack has been immersed in the pugilistic milieu for nearly half a century. When he was little, his father, who owned a chain of dry cleaners, took him to the fight cards held in the Chicago of the Golden Age, when the legendary Jewish fighters were shining their last lights in the ring and the Chicago Stadium vied with the Madison Square Garden for the title of Mecca of the Manly art. This is how he met DeeDee and got to know the main local boxing figures while he was still a kid. "My father was somewhat of a fight fan. He took me to a boxing show when I was about eleven years old and I was *fascinated* with it, and, I implored him to continue taking me to fights, which he did on a fairly regular basis. Once I got old enough to go myself, I went to the fights at every opportunity, which there was quite a few opportunities in those days." Jack put on the gloves briefly at the neighborhood YMCA and competed in a few amateur bouts, but without much success or consequence. No matter: his precocious and intensive exposure to the Sweet science enabled him to develop a deft pugilistic judgment.

After graduating from college. Jack took over the management of the family laundry business and started up another business manufacturing cosmetics. To fill up his spare time, he and a childhood friend got into producing music-hall shows. "It was a sideline for me, the music. It was the kinda thing that we would run maybe six-eight-ten shows a year. We made money, generally speaking. But it was hard and trends in music were changing, it became *tougher and tougher.* (He winces.) The bands were all of a sudden beginning to demand very, very high dollars, where you had to have probably eighty percent capacity in order to break even. And ultimately the places that we were running them got torn down, the picture was changing, the type of music was changing, the moneys were changing. And so we just walked away from that and wanted to do something together. And my buddy's a boxing fan and I suggested boxing and, I said, 'Well, hey! *Let's get us a fighter.'* And we did. And from there I managed fighters, this is back in 1957."

For two decades, Jack would simultaneously run his dry-cleaning business and manage a small stable of fighters. And when the transformations of the pugilistic economy—the drying up of vocations and the disappearance of neighborhood clubs, the deskilling of managers, the contraction of the local market, and the nationalization of commercialization circuits—revealed the pressing need for a middleman capable of compensating for the withering away of traditional networks, Jack was well placed to launch himself into matchmaking. "A lot of the people that have fighters are just *there,* they sit and wait and hope somebody asks their fighter to fight someone. And I was more aggressive and built up numbers and built up acquaintanceships and such, traveling with the fighters continually, and established relationships. Some of the relationships I have with the promoters and other agents, it all goes back fifteen-twenty years, even longer in a couple of cases." After two years of tryout, Jack decided in 1977 to liquidate his dry-cleaning assets and to become a matchmaker fulltime. His subsequent success has earned him a quasi monopoly in supplying fighters for the greater Chicago area today.

Jack Cowen's main activity consists of "filling the card" of the boxing events of the region by recruiting suitable opponents for the star boxer headlining the card and setting up the preliminary matches, called the "undercard." He sometimes takes charge of the material organization of the event: the ring, production, concession stands for drinks and hot dogs, ticketing, and advertising. Jack produces about three hundred fights a year in the Midwest this way, in addition to the matches he negotiates as an agent for the boxers whose services he rents out on the national and international markets. (With his Florida colleague Johnny Boz, Jack exports several dozen mediocre fighters to France and Italy every year, where they serve as stepping-stones for the rising stars and marquee boxers of the Old World.) He also officiates as a representative of Cedric Kushner Promotions, one of the major players in the global pugilistic economy, for which he signs up-and-coming boxers from Illinois. Finally, he is the co-owner of the Chicago Golden Gloves franchise and his wife—who is African American—manages two boxers with his advice.

Concretely, Jack's work day is divided up into endless haggling on the telephone with managers, promoters, and other agents (he makes several dozen calls between six and eleven every morning), making the rounds of the city gyms in the afternoon to keep abreast of the condition and availability of the local pugilists, then a new batch of negotiations by fax and telephone in the evening. He spends six weeks of the year "on the road" to attend cards for which he supplied fighters in neighboring states and abroad: it is vital that he go in person in order to judge *de visu* the quality of the boxers, the venue, the audience, and the trustworthiness of the organizers and other parties involved.

The search for and pairing of boxers takes place according to an iterative and cascading process, each deal leading to the next as a function of the desiderata and needs of the various parties. *"It's like a shopping list:* I'm looking for this and that and something else; by the same token, you call me and maybe I'm looking for something else or we have things that match and (he frowns slightly) the economics of the fight make sense. Like, we're not going to bring a fighter from the island of Tonga for a four-rounder in Gary, Indiana. . . . I'm calling people, people are calling me. It's a *network.* It's a number of people that are agents for fighters in addition to being matchmakers and, or promoters as I am. And they are booking for people in other areas. It's an ongoing thing. You're always talking to people about something. Sometimes you can get through the morning with *nothing in the world* working. And then, two or three phone calls, you've made two or three matches some place and you've picked up a thousand dollars. . . . So that's really what I'm doing: I'm sitting at home, I'm almost like someone *buying or selling stock, if you will.* Or perhaps a bookie taking bets on horses. I have people that have needs, you have people that have needs, and we try to match it up to make sense."

A matchmaker must to take into account three series of constraints in putting together a "card." He must first abide by the bureaucratic rules stipulated by the Boxing Commission of the state concerned (which is hardly onerous, given their extreme laxity). He must then make sure that the fights are economically viable, even profitable, by staying within the budget allotted to him by the promoter who hired him. Last, insofar as possible, he must "pair up" the boxers so as to produce matches that are enjoyable to watch and relatively balanced, while at the same time giving an edge to the boxers to whom he has ties. The requisite qualities for doing all this are a sound sense of organization and good bookkeeping skills, the capacity to cross social and racial lines with ease, and a good "pugilistic eye" to determine with acuity and accuracy the worth, style, and professionalism of the boxers hired. These are

qualities that Jack acquired, respectively, from his experience as
an entrepreneur in the laundry business, from his ethnic origin and
family trajectory, and from his precocious and prolonged contact
with the Manly art. "I was in the dry-cleaning business and in the
cosmetics business, and I took up boxing on the side and it got out
of hand. *You can get into boxing easily but you can't get out.* Once
you're in it, you're in it. [He smiles calmly.] Not a problem, I'm happy.
I like the activity, I like bein' involved in the thing, I get a big kick out
of it, it's still fun after all the years: I'll do it forever."

After the first two fights, I return to the dressing room. With a crisp
"Socks and shoes," DeeDee has ordered Curtis to get into his outfit.
While he slips his socks on, Curtis indicates to his manager that he's
going to need new training shoes." Not boxin' boots, regular gym shoes,
you know, to run an' stuff. 'Cuz these (he points to his tattered tennis
shoes) really hurt my feet, I get blisters." Jeb Garney suggests that he
wrap the soles of his feet with adhesive tape instead. Curtis slips the
crucifix he wears around his neck into his boot (it's his good luck charm)
without saying a word.

DeeDee sets about wrapping his protégé's fists. For the first time
in the two years that I've been following him around, Curtis gives me
permission to take his picture right in his "dressing room" before the
fight—another sign that he's rather relaxed tonight. Eddie comes up to
the old coach and nods discreetly toward Keith while slipping a twenty-
dollar bill in DeeDee's hand, payment for his services for the evening.
"Here y'go, DeeDee." "Awright." As he wraps Curtis's fists, DeeDee
talks boxing with Strickland (whose skin is so light that he could easily
pass for white; but in America there's no question as to where he stands
on the "color line.") Returning to gastronomy, Curtis had picked up
the bad habit of eating a Mars bar and drinking orange juice just before his bouts for a quick sugar fix, despite the strict prohibition by his
trainer. Until the day he vomited it all up at the foot of the ring when
it was time to fight, much to DeeDee's satisfaction. The latter never
ceases to remind his boxers of the rules to be followed in matters of
food and sex, but without ever explaining the reason behind them: it's
up to each boxer to accept the necessary "sacrifice" on faith or suffer the
consequences of failing the professional ethic. "People gotta learn by
they-selves, the hard way, Louie." When an official from the Commission

DeeDee wrapping Curtis's hands in the
storeroom turned dressing room

comes by to verify Curtis's handwraps and initial them before he slips his gloves on,[28] DeeDee announces that "we gonna start Anthony to wrappin' in the gym. I gave him some gauze an' he did good work for me with 'em, the other day. Yep, brother Anthony know how t'wrap pretty good. Maybe brother Louie can learn to wrap too. Smart as he is, he should be able to wrap too." Eddie adds: "You been at Curtis's fights and at three of Ashante's fights now, in the dressing room an' in the corner with us, you seen how we do it." DeeDee and Strickland recollect one of Young Joe Louis's fights, a few years ago, when his cornerman had wrapped his hands improperly and the Chicago boxer had to quit in the fifth round because of unbearable pain in his fists.

I shuttle back and forth between the locker room and the parking lot to follow the preliminary fights while staying close to Curtis. Ashante has seen Calhoun, but the latter says he's "too busy" to talk to him right now; they've agreed to meet up tomorrow at the gym but I seriously doubt that Calhoun will show up. Curtis wants chewing gum and he sends me out to get him some. (In the hours leading up to a fight, the boxer's entourage does its best to satisfy his every whim so as not to annoy him and impair his concentration.) But the bar doesn't sell gum and I can't find anyone in the audience who has any. When I come back to the dressing room with a piece scavenged from a guy from Tinley Park, it's too late: Eddie has already dug some up before me. In my defense, I point out that I don't know as many people as Eddie does. "But you know ev'rybody round here, Louie, and ev'rybody know you!" DeeDee trills, then he adds with regret: "It's too bad those guys from Tinley Park, they cain't spell fight, 'cos they'd get two or three busloads of guys behin' them every time, that's a lotta tickets right there." And a promoter always has a little spot on his bills for a boxer who brings his audience along with him. But it's hard to see how the big white guy from Tinley Park who started off the event this evening could rise above the rank of run-of-the-mill opponent or, at best, journeyman in the ring. Jack has therefore no reason to "protect" him by finding him opponents he can handle.

---

28. This "signature" by the officials guarantees that the handwrapping of the fighter conforms to regulation, that is, that the wraps are of the authorized fabric and length, and that the proper amount of tape has been applied to hold them. There have been cases where boxers hid metal objects inside their gloves and caused grievous (even lethal) damage to their unsuspecting opponents.

■ *"They categorize themselves"*

Jack Cowen on the different kinds of boxers:

Now, you have a fighter turning professional. You have some inkling of what he's going to do based on his amateur record. That's number one, his amateur record. Then, I always try, everybody turning pro, I try to start them out with a couple of wins—confidence-builders if you will. Then at that point you've got to evaluate the fighter. Privately, in my own mind, I've got to evaluate: can this fighter become a good fighter, or is he just another fighter? And I think as fights go on, the fighters put themselves into categories.

They categorize themselves: some become, like a Rodney Wilson, like a Lorenzo Smith, like a Curtis Strong—these are people who want to *achieve in the business,* they want to do something. They're not interested in 'Hey, look, I can pay you three hundred dollars to fight here in Chicago against somebody that I think you'll win. But oh! Wait, I can give fifteen hundred dollars if you can go out to Seattle, Washington, and I don't think you're gonna win and your chances aren't as good.' They'd say 'We'll take the fight in Chicago,' because they're building careers.

You have other fighters, that have skills of varying degrees, and in some cases good skills, but they become a *journeyman.* The idea is, 'Well, hey! I've gotta pay my rent. I'll take the fifteen-hundred fight,' as opposed to the five-hundred-dollar fight. Or I've seen fellows go to Europe *because they wanna go to Europe.* They'd go *fight King Kong* to get a trip to see Paris.

The third fight is a gross mismatch, since it pits Loren Ross, a young black colossus from Tennessee on the rise—he's unbeaten in thirteen fights—against the old ring fox Danny Blake, a plump, fortyish black pug whose fifteen-some defeats in a row indicate that he knows how to take a punch but presents no danger whatsoever to his opponent. (Smithie easily beat him on points last January at Park West, that says it all.) Blake's tactic, governed by his body type and his lack of endurance, is always the same: during the first couple of rounds, he hides his face in his gloves and walks right up to his opponent in a crouch (knees bent and leaning forward), in close in order to compensate for his short stature and lack of reach, and attacks the body. Then for the remainder of the bout he stays put in one spot, barricaded behind his guard, and lets himself get pounded like plaster, but without suffering serious damage—his experience allows him to block and cushion the force of most of the blows with his gloves, shoulders, and elbows. The crowd supports Blake, who passively absorbs a hailstorm of punches that he disrupts from time to time by coming out of his shell to throw a right to the body before quickly shelling up again. A tall dark-haired guy in a black polo shirt next to me shouts: "Jump on 'im, Grandpa!" Ross, who displays an impeccable classic technique utilizing his height and reach to full advantage, has no trouble winning every round by coolly boxing from the outside. But the fight is unsightly and sad. Blake "eats" a dishload of straight punches from both hands; his face gradually turns purple and deformed by a grimace that gives him the look of a blubbering urchin. The entire exercise evokes a workout on a human punching bag rather than a competitive contest.

When I sum up the fight for DeeDee, the old coach comments: "Blake, he been around for a long-long time. Useta be a pretty good fighter, he know how to fight. It happen to d'best of 'em, Louie, when they stay in that ring too long . . ." And he insists that one should never mock a boxer, no matter how mediocre, because it always takes a modicum of courage to put on the gloves. That is why DeeDee never utters the words "bum," "stiff," "trial horse," or "tomato can," by which inept pugilists are commonly designated. "Every guy who climbs into the ring is a *boxer,* Louie, dontchya ever forget that . . . It takes a *helluva man* to be a fighter. See, I give anybody credit that go up in there, whether it's a three-round amateur fighter, win or lose, if he stays in there an' do his best and prepared for it, or a ten- or twelve-round professional fighter: if he's ready, *I'll pat 'im on his back."*

The fourth preliminary match opposes two more duds: Danny Nieves, a stubby and chubby, light-skinned Puerto Rican, and Tony Lins, a tall white guy completely devoid of skills. They shove one another, grab and bounce off each other, smashing into one another's bodies haphazardly. And the worst yet is that Nieves is cavorting in the ring! He waddles around like a duck in his blue trunks, mimicks a few ballet steps, comes out of the breaks by turning his back and walking away from his opponent as if to defy him, fakes being on the verge of a kayo, then gets into an angry rut—in short, he's seeking to regale the audience with his clowning, since he can't do it with his boxing. But the crowd has no taste for his "showboating" and sides with Lins, who is visibly weaker, if that's possible. Every once in a while, Nieves pops him one right in the kisser and you can see the droplets of sweat fly in the glare of the spotlights. At the conclusion of four rounds that resemble professional wrestling more than boxing, the Puerto Rican pug gets the nod, and the two opponents embrace and parade around the ring in each other's arms to the boos of the crowd.

Several months later, I happened to do an interview with Danny Nieves. Danny is twenty-four years old and works as a part-time athletic instructor for the Park District and a bouncer at a nightclub, along with moonlighting as an electrician. He counts four victories, two defeats, and two draws after three years in the pros and explains his attraction for the ring in these terms:

> It feels great, especially when you're in the ring an' people are callin' your name an' stuff, *it's almost like a high.* An' uh, bein' in the ring for me is like bein' like *a actor,* or uh, or like *bein' in the theater:* jus' performin' for your audience an' that's the way I always fought. I always have to show somethin' to my audience, you know, to prove that, you know that I'm a good fighter, an' that's the way I see it, for me bein' in the ring almost come like second nature: I feel comfortable in there—I know a lotta guys that don't, but I do, it's fun.

> [The reaction of the crowd] yeah that's it, that gets you like really charged up, I mean that's it, *that's the only thing that makes it worthwhile.* I mean a lotta people may say the money an' stuff but you see when all these guys are makin' a hundred million dollars an' they makin' all this money, but they miss the limelight. Like Sugar Ray [Leonard], Larry Holmes, and stuff—all these guys an' stuff, they set for life, but you miss that, it's almost like a *high,* that's why you see so many fighters comin' back. . . .

> [After a fight], if you won it it's like a big relief, big satisfaction, uh. If you lost it's a big letdown because you can hear it from your friends, you can hear it from their voices, you know like, you let them down. An' you, me, I feel real bad when I lose, it really gets to me, I feel bad for *like the whole week,* you know. Like I think I'd better get knocked out than lose a fight [on points], I hate losin', I hate goin' up to the middle of the ring an' they raise another guy's hand, I hate, [muttering under his breath] *I hate that with a passion.* . . .

To have fun, it's, *it's thrillin'*: you don't know what's gonna happen in the ring an' *I love it*. I hate bein' bored with the same thing over an' over. An' the boxin' everytime—I could spar with you ten times an' ten times it will be a different fight. So uh, that's the thing I like about boxin': the unexpected always happens. That's like, Buster Douglas an' Tyson: nobody thought that Buster Douglas was gonna beat Tyson, an' it was fifty to nothing that nothing was gonna happen. But Buster Douglas won it. . . . Especially with the heavyweight, you never know when that big punch is gonna land. A guy could land it to you, you could land it to them, an' it's like all over, you know, in a second an' that excitement that goes in, gives you a rush, that excitement, it's like *"Wow!* this is what I want," a little danger . . .

I jot down in my field notebook: this card is really lame, it isn't marked-down merchandise that Cowen is fobbing off on us tonight but real spoiled goods. That's not the way he's going to cultivate any kind of following on the South Side. And this time he doesn't have the excuse of having been swindled by a "meat seller"[29] he doesn't know, like he did for the previous event, since half of the fighters on the program are guys from the Windy City Gym. It's insulting for Curtis to have to perform on such a card, since he has legitimate aspirations to fight in world-class, televised events. Even Wanda, his flighty sister who doesn't know a thing about prizefighting, is screeching: *"I cain't watch that shit!"* The crowd is laughing at the fights more than it applauds them, as they pertain more to circus than to sport—but, precisely, is boxing a sport? Even the announcer, who goes by the beautiful name of Angelo Buscaglio (you couldn't invent that one), is mediocre: he needs to read his text, he stumbles over words, he has no elocution whatsoever. And to top it all off, there are no card girls. At the beginning of the fourth fight, one of the "exotic dancers" from Studio 104 tried her luck: she got up to parade around the ring in her skimpy bikini. But there wasn't any card to

29. This is the term used to refer to the half-dozen gyms and "training camps" scattered around the country that provide, on demand and in industrial quantities, mediocre opponents "who can usually be counted on to lose to the home-town sweethearts. More often than not the 'opponents' need no encouragement to lose. They have been losing for so long that it has become their stock in trade. A few wins and their value decreases; a promoter looking for cannon fodder won't bother taking the risk"; Stephen Brunt, *The Rise and Fall of Shawn O'Sullivan* (Markham, Canada: Penguin Books, 1987), 201–202.

announce which round was coming up, so all she could do was foolishly prance around, indicating "two" with two fingers held up in the shape of a V.

Back in the storeroom. As we're anxiously awaiting the moment for Curtis to climb into the ring, Jeb Garney calls my attention to the big flashy watch on his wrist and its enormous luminous purple dial studded with jewels.

JEB GARNEY: Do you see that, [to the others] do you know what that is? It's real diamonds and the rest is gold.

CURTIS [in a voice that mingles admiration and pleasantry, since he would never dare ask this seriously]: Wow, I like it, you gonna give it to me, Mister Garney?

JEB GARNEY: You don't know what it is, [in a ceremonious tone] it's a *Rolex Presidential,* it's worth five thousand dollars, nothing less.

CURTIS [craning his neck to better admire the device]: I'm serious, Mister Garney, why won'tchya give it to me?

JEB GARNEY: You're kiddin'? No, let me tell you how I got it: [snickering to himself for having pulled our legs] I bought it in *Singapore for twenty-nine ninety-five.* They make these copies there, they look better than the real ones. They're so good, they even got the logo on the back of the watch, look . . .

(I say to myself that it stinks to play a joke like this at Curtis's expense when he's near starving, just as he's about to climb into the ring for five hundred bucks: is this guy braindead or what?)

Little by little, the prefight conversations flicker out and silence falls over the storeroom. Tension creeps up to the point of being almost palpable. Curtis tosses out: "Everyone in there *with me?* All y'all in there with me? So okay then, ev'ryboy get down on your knees an' pray, ha-ha-ha!" We teeter nervously and say nothing.

TKO in the Fourth

It's intermission. The announcer bawls: "After the boxing show this evening, those of you who're holding tickets, you may be entertained inside by the exotic dancers. Tonight we have a tremendous show for you! Don't miss it! And if you don't have a ticket, you can still buy 'em, two for the price of one . . ." And he reminds everyone that the ticket for the fights also gets you two drinks for the price of one at the bar inside.

I come back to the storeroom where Curtis, Garney, DeeDee, and Eddie are discussing the joys and travails of William "The Refrigerator" Perry, a gentle giant and defensive tackle for the Chicago Bears who, after having been idolized, now finds himself vilified for his inability to control his gargantuan appetite—he will be released by his team the following year for being chronically overweight and will then reinvent himself, pitifully, as a tag-team pro wrestler. His money, his tarnished glory, his injuries, his messy divorce and real estate troubles have been the talk of the town. "The Refrigerator" had to stop construction on his $2.5 million house because his agent put him on monthly "salary" in order to force him to put some money aside. DeeDee avers that you have got to be stupid to build a house that expensive, given the cost of the property taxes that come with it. Curtis philosophizes: "See, how all that fame an' money will bring you right back down." But he can't help mentioning with envious admiration the fact that "The Fridge" gave a BMW as a present to his father-in-law . . .

It's time to warm up. Curtis goes out into the hallway and starts bouncing up and down in place, then he loosens up shadowboxing. Eddie puts on his pads and holds them out as targets for him. Jab-jab-right, hooks, uppercuts. The taut punches make a crackling sound under the interrogative gaze of the patrons from the adjacent bar. Sweat glistens at the temples of the Woodlawn boxer and trickles down his chest. A tavern staff comes to warn us that we're on in five minutes. I hit Curtis's closed fist with mine and he returns the ritual prefight salute. Tension. Apprehension. Excitement. DeeDee advises us to leave the dressing room to let Curtis alone, to pray in peace with his brothers. We champ at the bit outside the door. The old coach whispers under his breath to Jeb Garney, "Just peek in there to see if he's done." Yes, the prayer has been said, the time for the "main event" has come. *"Eight rounds of boxing!"* We pass through the bar in single file: Jeb Garney in his blue tunic shoulders his way through with Curtis in tow, bouncing in place, head lowered under his hood, in a white robe; DeeDee and I are behind them, and Strickland brings up the rear. We emerge into the parking lot, greeted by the applause of the crowd. *"Let's Get Busy!,"* Curtis's goodluck song, is buzzing through the loudspeakers.

The Woodlawn boxer climbs up the steps to the ring two at a time and comes up between the ropes. His fans are delirious, especially his

Curtis steps up into the ring

sisters and friends, who are massed behind the opposite side and making an ungodly racket. Curtis slip-steps around the ring, his face taut with concentration, the whole time the fight is being announced. Hannah is warming up shadowboxing in the other corner without looking at him. Then the two fighters face each other in the center of the ring for the referee's final instructions. Curtis comes back to his corner, DeeDee distills him his instructions, Strickland massages his neck and slips in his mouthpiece. *"Ding!"* The match is on. Hannah bolts out of his corner head first, pushes Curtis against the ropes, and before the spectators even have time to sit down—stupefaction!—Curtis takes a sharp right to the jaw that sends him to the canvas, down on one knee. A gust of consternation tinged with incredulity sweeps through the crowd. DeeDee rises to see how his boxer is reacting. Curtis gets back up and starts at first to dance, then plants his feet, snug behind his gloves. Hannah takes to pounding him.

DEEDEE: *Get off, man!*

LOUIE [hollering, like a loud echo, from the foot of the ring]: Get off, Curtis!!!

EDDIE: Get off the rope!

LOUIE [sounding like a madman]: Get off the ropes!!!! *Get off the ropes!!! Get off the ropes!!!*

EDDIE: C'mon now. C'mon Curtis, box him.

LOUIE: Box 'im Curt'!!! Box him!

Bleep! What the hell is he doing? He's staying pat with his back against the ropes and is letting Hanna wallop him at leisure when he's already been thrown to the canvas.

EDDIE [bellowing in his hoarse voice]: Go to work! *Go to work!*

LOUIE [yelling in unison]: *Go to work! Go to work Curtis!!!* Both hands!!

DEEDEE [staid but firm]: Alright now, get goin'.

LOUIE [roaring even more loudly]: Get off the ropes! Alright now, get-off-the-ropes!!!

Fuck it! He's yet again got into his "macho bag," standing still, his guard crossed in front of him, letting his opponent bang away, just to show that he can take his best punches without flinching! He doesn't want to listen to what we're telling him.

Sensing that this is his chance, Hannah lays into Curtis and redoubles his combinations to the body and head. You can't tell whether Curtis is hurt since he's letting his opponent bombard him from close in, satisfied to block his punches without countering them. Finally he comes out of his shell and repels Hannah back to the center of the ring with a series of straights and hooks from both hands. The Indiana pug ties him up and pushes him back against the ropes. DeeDee roars: *"Get off the ropes!"* I shout his instructions again to Curtis who, inexplicably, remains passive and seems to be in trouble. My heart is in my throat: is he hurt? (I'm ready to throw myself into the ring to save him from this rout, even if it means causing a big-time incident.) The answer to my question comes in a flash: Curtis counterattacks with lightning speed and drives Hannah back into the opposite corner. With a flurry of punches to the chest and face, Curtis sends him to the canvas in turn just as the bell sounds the end of the round.

Strickland climbs through the ropes and sets down the corner stool; Curtis comes back to his corner and sits down. "How you feelin'?" DeeDee inquires with a calm that contrasts sharply with the electricity in the air. Curtis reassures us: "I'm awright." Strickland makes the mistake of wanting to rub his wet sponge on Curtis's neck; Curtis brushes him off brusquely: never put any water on him, or else he catches a cold immediately. During the one-minute rest period, DeeDee gives him advice in a steady tone of voice: get out of the clinches, box from the outside, punch first.[30]

Round two. Hannah rushes out of his corner like a bull coming out of its pen and charges at Curtis head down. Again Curtis huddles behind his gloves and lets himself get trapped in the corner—the makeshift lighting attached to the ring post sways and threatens to come tumbling down into the ring! Vigorous exchanges in close, with both boxers trying to "get inside." We yell to him: "Get off the ropes, work with both hands, get your jab out there, box him!" But Curtis wants to do things his own stubborn way. Cowen edges up on my right and squeals in frustration: "I don't know what's the matter with that damn Curtis, but he always

---

30. The instructions given by a trainer to a boxer during a fight are always simple and repetitive in the extreme. They invariably consist of reminding him of the fundamentals (keep your guard up, step in behind your jab, punch in combinations, etc.), and, as the case requires, drawing his charge's attention to a technical defect or a major tactical flaw of his opponent. This is so as to focus the fighter's mental energy without for that interfering with the reflexes patiently put in place during training.

makes an easy fight hard!" In sudden jolts, the Woodlawn boxer goes on the offensive with accelerations that put his opponent in trouble but on which he then fails to follow up. Hannah is experienced and he knows how to break his adversary's rhythm. He even lets his guard down and makes a hideous snarl at Curtis to invite him to hit him. But Curtis doesn't let himself lose his composure.

Third round: DeeDee has implored Curtis to take his time and impose his style of boxing by moving sideways and throwing combinations behind his jab. The match heats up. Beautiful combinations by both fighters. Curtis uses a mix of side-to-side movements, bobbing and weaving to smother or cancel out Hannah's flurries. It is becoming obvious that Curtis is too quick and too powerful for his opponent. The Woodlawn boxer spins around Hannah, draws him in by pretending to open up his guard, only better to slip and counter with sharp straight punches that land right on target. Curtis gets himself out of clinches easily by pivoting to one side and then the other and throwing smooth uppercuts with both hands. He's starting to establish himself as "boss" of the ring.

DeeDee: Step in behin' your jab.

Louie: Use your jab Curtis, behind your jab!

[Fight noises: the squeaking of boots sliding across the mat, the dull thud of punches, the shouts and groans of the crowd.]

Eddie: Keep that left hand workin', work the jab!

Louie [bellowing]: Get outa the corner!

Eddie: Not the middle, not the middle!!

DeeDee: Awright now under there.

Louie: Under!!

DeeDee [insistent]: Step over. [louder, in his hoarsest voice] *Step over!*

Eddie: Yeah, that's it, closer, combination!

Kitchen: *Work! Work!*

DeeDee [irritated]: Come on, man! Get close! With both hands.

Louie [bellowing]: Closer, c'mon, both hands, c'mon!!

A left cross-right uppercut combination sends the Indiana boxer to the canvas for the second time. But Hannah knows how to take a punch

he main event, Strong vs. Hannah
n eight rounds

and he gets up without faltering. Near the end of the round, Curtis throws Hannah into the ropes with a whirlwind of punches punctuated by a short right to the temple. Just as the Indiana pug is falling forward, Curtis picks him up with a left hook flush in the throat. One knee on the ground, Hannah spits up a big, disgusting gob of blood right in front of me. His face twisted in agony, he points at his neck with his glove, gesturing to the referee that he's hurt. But the bell sounds and he's dispatched back to his corner. He collapses onto his stool, his face puffed up, breathing with difficulty.

Confusion. Right then we think that Hannah is going to decline to "come out" of his corner at the bell for the fourth round. But no: he crosses himself and valiantly heads out to the front line again. He knows his goose is cooked and he's going to "go for broke."[31] Curtis responds to this last muddled offensive with a barrage of blows of incredible violence. He dances around his exhausted opponent, who can only retreat behind his gloves and tries desperately to cling to Curtis. It's turning into shooting fish in a barrel. Curtis presses Hannah against the ropes and bulldozes him to the ground. The latter almost rolls out of the ring. It's only a formality now: Hannah is in such bad shape that Curtis is going to "finish him" with the next exchange. But Hannah, doubled over on his knees, calls the referee over and shows him his left hand, as if to indicate that he's injured. (Jack Cowen will confirm to me later that he had indeed serious problems with the ligaments in his shoulder before he even stepped into the ring.)

The referee leans over toward Hannah, then turns to the officials' table to notify them with a hand gesture that the fight is over. Curtis jumps up on the ropes around the ring post and pumps his hands up in the air to the cheers of the crowd. He prances around the ring, bucking with joy, victoriously windmilling his fists through the air. Jubilation in the front rows among the Doc, Liz, Ashante, and Curtis's brothers and sisters. What a relief after getting the bejesus scared out of us in the first round . . . Hannah staggers over to pat Curtis on the shoulder in congratulation: "Good work. You hit hard, man." Curtis hugs him. (I can't help being moved by Hannah and thinking how sad his trip home will be, returning with yet another loss on his record to confirm his status as the perfect "opponent".) While the physician from the commission examines

---

31. In pugilistic jargon, "going for broke" is a last-ditch tactic consisting of using all the strength you have left and taking every possible risk in one final assault aimed at producing a victory by kayo.

the Indiana boxer and we wait for the official decision to be announced, Curtis poses for the evening's amateur photographers, legs bent, left fist out in front, a ferocious scowl twisting his lips. "Ladies and gentlemen, the referee stops the contest at two minutes-ten into the fourth round and your winner, in the blue corner, by technical knockout is *Cuurtiiis Stroooong!* Curtis Strong . . ."[32]

After this anticlimactic epilogue, Curtis is besieged at the foot of the ring by his friends, relatives, and fans, who step onto each other to congratulate him. Jeb Garney wipes his fighter's face and DeeDee urges him to get back inside as quickly as possible so he won't catch cold. But people stop Curtis along the way to hug him and shake his gloves as he walks by, and the crowd is jamming the only door into the nightclub. I suggest that he hold on to my shoulders and I muscle my way through the tide of spectators, clearing a path for him. (I'm damn proud to have the champ in tow.) The crowd is ebbing back into the bar, which fills up with revelers. We tack back and forth all the way to the storeroom-cum-dressing room, followed by a woman photographer who is firing away at Curtis from up close and by Wylie the reporter, who is about to display all her ignorance about the Sweet science with her know-nothing questions.

Curtis is exuberant and chattering like a magpie. He thanks God at every turn, and vigorously defends himself for having been sent to the canvas in the first round, claiming that this was only "a slip." Jeb Garney laughs indulgently: "Okay, yeah, but what was his glove doin' under your chin? You gave us a good scare you know." One of the members of the Boxing Commission, who prides himself on freelancing for the sports pages of a local rag, comes over to interview the Woodlawn boxer with his little tape recorder; I take advantage of the situation and record their conversation on the fly. Curtis explains that he's ready to fight anyone, anywhere, any time, a six-rounder in Atlantic City or a ten-rounder in Aurora against Torres for his title defense, if his manager wants him to: "Whatever, just keep me busy, that's all I ask. I wanna stay active. *If I don't stay active* then you know the-the *'joyment* an' the, the *determination* for it is gone." I help him take off his cup and dry his chest and

---

32. Custom dictates that the ring announcer always expound the winner's name twice according to a codified intonation and rhythm, the first time stretching out the vowels at the top of his voice, the second time briefly and in a deeper voice.

ı

arms with a towel. He's as excited as a kid at Christmas and bouncing up and down in glee. And for good reason: he sold over a thousand dollars worth of tickets, he notched one more victory on his record, and he showed composure and real tactical expertise against a veteran opponent. His manager keeps saying that Jeff Hannah has fought three former world champions—which is true, but that was years ago and he lost all three times.

JEB GARNEY: He got ya, he got ya with a left. It wasn't a terrible punch, but you were off balance. Okay, it added a little bit to the excitement a little while, ah-ah-ah. [Laughing with relief.] It wasn't the prettiest thing I've seen all year . . .

LOUIE: You would have liked other kinds of excitement uh?

JEB GARNEY [laughing all the more]: I do without that! You may have liked that Curtis, but I wasn't havin' any fun outa that deal *at all* there for the first fifteen or twenty seconds. That guy was *really* a *rampaging bull* in there.

CURTIS: You know tha's why I, I just took my time—I knew I was gonna get him *'ventu'ly.*

JEB GARNEY: Oh sure you were. Sure you were.

CURTIS [sure of himself]: I wadden in no hurry to get out there an' just throw a punch an' get caught up with one.

JEB GARNEY: No. That's exactly right.

CURTIS [pleased that his manager has conceded the point]: *Awright.*

JEB GARNEY: You wind up trading with a guy who's givin' everything he has for you know . . .

STRICKLAND [sneaking into the exchange]: That was his strategy.

LOUIE: And he was dead by the fourth round, he couldn't hold out.

JEB GARNEY: Oh I was just sayin' I didn't, I didn't enjoy seeing the first twenty seconds—it didn't bother *him* [Curtis], I said it bothered *me*. [Everyone laughs heartily.]

THE DOC [sticking his head in through the storeroom door]: Alright Curtis, *good luck to you guy!*

CURTIS: Alright, thanks a lot.

KITCHEN: Hey Curtis, when you're dressed, lemme know when you want a picture of you with d'girl here . . . [pointing at a young cutie mincing around near the door].

CURTIS: Allright. [I laugh, and Curtis does too, at Kitchen's persistence in "hustling" for a few bucks.] She got it comin' . . .

I suddenly realize that there are three women in the mock dressing room, which is a first after a fight—you can tell that DeeDee isn't here. Curtis is charmed by their presence and delights in answering their questions with plenty of detail and posing, though they evince amazing naivete. Then he undresses and changes back into civilian clothes (without taking a shower, since there are no facilities for that). As he's pulling up his pants, the girl from the ticket window draws the curtain back and walks through the storeroom without warning. A very embarrassed Curtis exclaims: "Oh-ho! 'Tis is the night for all the pain . . . an' all the joy." Laughter. Eddie comes in, accompanied by Ashante, and the technical and tactical commentary resumes. Both offer their interpretation of Curtis's "slip-knockdown" in the first round and collaborate toward the collective redefinition of an embarrassing incident into a simple accident.

EDDIE: You was cold that's all. Curtis wasn't warmed up when he was . . . Then when he get up he'll be alright. He was just cold that's all. He just in d'freeze.

CURTIS: When he knocked me down [sic] I knew I was in a bind. 'Cause it wadden really no knockdown. But when the referee gave me the eight count that's considered a knockdown.

LOUIE: You, you almost knocked him down the same round, at the end of the first round.

CURTIS: Yeah tha's thanks to God, *all tha's God.*

EDDIE: That sucker started t'walk into that right hand and left hook . . .

CURTIS: He stopped the fight hisself.

KITCHEN: Yeah he did, he had enough.

UNKNOWN VOICE: He had enough.

CURTIS: Hurt his hand.

LOUIE: He hurt his shoulder.

KITCHEN: Oh he did?

EDDIE: But he was feelin' those wild shots too, he got hit with a lotta left hooks, didn' he?

Louie: I'll tell you what, it's the left hook to the throat that finished the fight. 'Cause when he went back to his corner he was gesturing, "No-no, that's it."

Curtis: Yeah he didn't want no more. . . .

[tape cuts]

Louie: Man you hit him with some *bombs!*

Curtis: I could hear you shoutin', tellin' me to stay off the ropes but DeeDee knew what time—tha's why DeeDee didn't say stay off the ropes: he knew the guy was wide—jus' told me to keep my hands tight, don't back straight up like that, to pivot. . . .

Curtis's father is there, hushed, in the backdrop. Curtis pays him no attention. I confess to DeeDee that I was ready to leap into the ring and tackle Hannah to the ground to keep him from kayoing Curtis in the first round. "What? You crazy? You better stay outa the way, Louie, or you don't come to d'fights no more."

"How does it feel when you see your opponent knocked out?"

Smithie: It feel like accomplishin' a goal, uh, you, you have your opponent down. It's a feelin' of accomplishment, you know, you don't—an' you know [his cheerful tone turns somber] you shouldn't feel good about knockin' out somebody, but you feel good about uh, defeatin' your opponent, okay? Now as far as havin' a man put to sleep, uh, what makes you, uh the only good feelin' you get about it is that you glad *it wasn't you,* an' you weathered the storm that you placed yourself in.

Tony: I feel when I see the guy goin' down, I see him goin' down still thinkin' in my min', "he's goin' down." I hope he's okay an' then when they wave the fighter off an' I see him movin' an' he gits up, I say, [breathing as if in relief] "hey, this guy's okay, I didn' hurt him." Then I have more ease on my behalf, because don't feel that I've accomplished things by really damagin' somebody in the ring.

Curtis: You tell yo'self, is this guy alright, you know what I mean? You don't wanna *hurt* nobody, but you wanna win a fight the best way you can. You don't want the judges to stick you up 'cuz they play favoritism to a guy, you know what I mean?

STUDIO 104 PRESENTS

EVERY SATURDAY NITE

Sexy Leg Contest

WIN $200 CASH PRIZE

Admission $5.00-Free w/plugger
8:00 until

**2814 E. 104th St.
2 Blocks East of Torrence
312-768-7109**

*Free Birthday Party, Birthday Cake
& Champagne.*

Make Way for the Exotic Dancers

We come back out into the bar, which is now full of people. Everyone takes turns congratulating Curtis on his victory. He repeats to whomever will listen that his knockdown in the first round was a mere slip and that, in spite of appearances, he was in full control of the fight from beginning to end. He says he's frustrated that Hannah surrendered: he would have preferred to "finish the job" when the latter was on the verge of being kayoed in the fourth round, but well, that part didn't depend on him . . . Seated at a table in the middle of the room, Jeb Garney is savoring a cold beer in the company of his wife and Jack Cowen's spouse. DeeDee is sitting a little farther away, bent over, gabbing with some old-timers. Curtis is making the rounds from one cluster of people to the next, voluble, affable, all smiles.

In the dance room next door, a disk jockey is playing rap fast and loud; from his elevated glass cockpit to the left of the dance floor, he's calling on customers to get up and start dancing, but without much success. Only two couples are flapping around frenetically to the aggressive sound of the music. In the other room, small groups are guzzling drinks at the bar. DeeDee is discreetly knocking back a whisky behind his beret—a genuine Basque *béret,* the one I gave him for Christmas, bought in Montpellier from a hatmaker from Saint-Jean-de-Luz. A baseball game is flashing across the television screen. The house photographer, "George Henderson Productions, Video and Photography," who takes color portraits with a giant, sophisticated Polaroid against a tropical garden backdrop (a carefully drawn curtain in front of which the customers pose) isn't doing much better: at $15 per shot, thumbtacked into a cardboard frame, it's no wonder! He snaps a picture of a portly girl in a blue dress, lying down in a sea of pillows, then one of the trio comprised of Ashante, DeeDee, and a stocky guy I'm not familiar with, an old friend of Charles. He's the one who insisted on being photographed with DeeDee; DeeDee even deigns to smile for the camera, which is rare. The old coach is ensconced on a wicker chair with Ashante and the fat guy flanking him on either side like bodyguards. Meanwhile the crew charged with dismantling the ring has finished its job and the staff from Studio 104 has folded up the chairs, rolled up the awnings, and coiled the ropes.

The bar is now half empty because the show with the exotic dancers has gotten under way in the next room. After the display of masculine bodily capital, manifested by strength and controlled violence, this is the exhibition of its feminine counterpart, in the sexual register. The so-called dancers turn out to be the same girls who were selling tickets at the door and who usually serve as card girls for the fights. Plunged into an orangey semidarkness by the scant lighting (there isn't even a strobe light or a disco ball), a tall and lanky black woman with the physique of a fading model is dancing languidly on the stage in front of about sixty people, mostly men (many of them former or current boxers) slouched against the two bars that run along the opposite wall. She's wearing a silver lamé string with a matching bra, which she nimbly rids herself of before coming over to entice the spectators in the front row with her bare breasts and sagging hindquarters.

As "exotic dancers" go, these are more like pornographic dancers, since the woman doesn't hesitate to straddle a customer's lap to rub her entire body against him, to kneel between his legs to mimic a fellatio, and to climb with her legs astride his shoulders (around which she first delicately draped a towel of dubious cleanliness that she later uses to fan him with), ostentatiously holding his face between her thighs. Her maneuvers are so aggressive that a number of spectators standing at the back are embarrassed and retreat, as if by collective agreement, when the temptress moves in toward them. She no sooner seems to be heading our way that Eddie hightails it, yelping in horror ("I don't want none of that"), and I follow suit. Several guys leave the room because they don't want to be titillated so coarsely or because they're scared of being forcibly dragged up on stage for a mutual striptease. Anthony stands prudently by the door; later, he will loudly express his indignation at the fact that such a spectacle took place in our presence. (It's true he's a Muslim: he was telling me recently that you must "resist temptation, re-sist sin. Why should I look at other women when I have a wife at home?")

We move to the remuneration phase: the men against whom the dancer came up for a rubbing are now urged to slip money into her bra (which she has put back on for this express purpose) or in her g-string, which they do with great diligence. Ashante looks terribly embarrassed by this spectacle, but when the woman swoops in on him by surprise, he stands his ground, stoic. She languorously rubs herself against his chest, then wraps herself around him so that she literally envelops him in her lithe, nearly naked body (she's practically twice his height). Ashante remains gripped in the dancer's tentacle-like arms this way for a good twenty seconds and, when she finally releases him, he tucks a one-dollar bill into her bikini bottom with authority. He's red as a beet and I can't pass up the chance to take a dig at him: "We saw your knees buckle and your face puff up!"—as one says of a boxer who's taking a beating in the ring.

I come back out of the dance room and plot with Eddie to make DeeDee believe that Curtis is on stage doing a striptease with the dancer. "Wow! Look at that, I can't be-lie-ve it! Man, Curtis is getting buck-

The one laughs, the
other drinks: Eddie and
DeeDee at the bar

Eddie, Liz, and
DeeDee posing for
the traditional
postfight picture

Liz, DeeDee, and
Louie celebrating

naked with that chick on stage." DeeDee leaps up from his stool, his glass of whisky in hand. *"What?* Lemme see that! *Where?"* When he realizes that we're pulling his leg, he bursts out laughing with us. "I be damned! *I knock his ass out.* Knock 'im out cold as a milkshake." I ask the old coach why brother Woods (Curtis's comanager and the former director of the Woodlawn Boys Club) isn't here tonight: "Dunno, he was s'posed to come. It don't matter no-how, this was just a lil' warmup fight."

Back in the dance room, the second girl to do a number is even more "exotic" than the first. She straddles the clients, openly imitating copulation with an abundance of facial contortions and simulated expressions of ecstasy. She even lets one of the lucky chosen few grope her breasts and ravenously kiss them. You don't get into artistic delicacy or Baudrillardian simulacrum at Studio 104!

While the show is going on, I catch a scene of sexual provocation between the tall exotic dancer (she's walking around in a skimpy fringed dress that shows her bare buttocks) and Tim Adams, the black referee who officiated Curtis's title fight in Aurora. She clamors that he's afraid of her and that he's not man enough for a woman like her. He retorts vehemently, but with a smile at the corners of his mouth, that he's known harder challenges and that she's the one who's backing off. Since she's so assured of her femininity, why doesn't she follow him into the bathroom where he'll gladly show her a few tricks of his? (This is rather incongruous, given that Tim is accompanied by his current girlfriend.) The dancer tosses the ball back in his court by daring him to unzip his pants right there and then, in front of her and everyone, "to show us whatchyou got." Tim does not wait to hear it twice and immediately unzips his fly, ready to display his manly attributes. She eggs him on: *"Put it out, put it out and lemme see it!"*

"Uh, you wanna see it, you sure? You ain't gonna be disappointed, sweetheart, I tell you! You want it?"

"Put it out, lemme see what you got. I bet you ain't gonna put it out, cause the truth is, you ain't got nuthin' to show."

"Okay!" Tim pretends to extract his male member out of his half-open pants with a theatrical gesture that would lead one to believe that it is of exceptional size.

"Put it out and I'll give you a [inaudible]." She slides in close to him and suddenly puts her hand on his groin.

"Whoa! don't you touch it! *The last woman who put her hand on it, she hadda get a doggy bag to bring some back to her mama!"*

Unanimous howls of laughter from the friends and onlookers around them. Tim challenges the dancer again to touch it, which she's just about to do when he grabs her vigorously by the arm.

"Come on, let's go in the room next door there, we're gonna see who come out first."

"I ain't afraid of nothin' you can show me. You can't show me *nuttin'."*

"Alright then, come on in, we're gonna see who's comin' out *runnin'."*

The two of them disappear into the same storeroom that, barely two hours earlier, served as our dressing room, unleashing irrepressible laughter from Tim's buddy. His girlfriend, on the other hand, is livid! A long minute later, the half-naked dancer comes back out, walking proud and catlike, followed by a grinning Tim. The latter shouts out to the company at large: "See who came out first?" She retorts jeeringly: "But am I runnin'? *Am I runnin'?* You said who's gonna come out d'room runnin'. I ain't runnin'."

DeeDee chats for a while with a former middleweight champion, a member of the 1960 U.S. Olympic team with Ernie Terrell and Muhammad Ali. He introduces him to Liz and me. I take some pictures in the bar and sketch a few dance steps to Ashante's and Lamar's delight—they are bent on my doing "The Running Man" for them, my well-known impersonation of the rapper M. C. Hammer, on the dance floor.[33] DeeDee too starts strutting about in place, then he cuts in on Derrick and steals Wanda from him. They spin around, the two of them alone on the dance floor—I find her touching with her wide owl-like smile and her long red dress. It is past midnight now. There's almost no one left except the group from Woodlawn and Curtis's family. It's time to get going.

---

33. During an evening at a dance party at a club on the South Side, I had, without even knowing it, picked up this dance step "trademarked" by the rapper M. C. Hammer with such flair that the DJ asked the crowd to move back and leave the dance floor to me. This incident earned me the nickname "The French Hammer," tinged with irony in the context of the boxing gym, where it could have been taken to refer to my exceptional punching power.

"You Stop Two More Guys and I'll Stop Drinkin'"

We split up into different cars: Ashante zips up to the North Side with Ernie Terrell and two old-timers; Olivier, Fanette, Liz, Eddie, and the fat lady from 63rd Street with the plastic hips cram into my Plymouth Valiant; I head out with DeeDee and Curtis. But, as I step up into the Jeep, I discover that we have company: a black teenager, her hair braided and wearing a very flashy ruby-red tank top, is sitting in the back seat, huddled in the shadows. Curtis is about to take off when DeeDee suddenly becomes aware of the unexpected presence of this cutie and summons Curtis to account for it. And the two fire off into a long dispute about whether or not Curtis told the girl to come home with him and whether she got into the car before or after the old coach. The poor teenager keeps mum, terrified to be the cause of a violent verbal scrap that will drag on for a good part of the trip. DeeDee assails her with questions ("Who are you? Whose girl are you? How old are you? What you doin' there? Who told you to get in this car?") in an aggressive tone that is actually aimed at Curtis, who makes a show of singing at the top of his lungs along with the soul song playing on the car radio. This is DeeDee's way of letting Curtis know that he doesn't approve of this last-minute romantic invitation. During the entire trip, DeeDee and Curtis also quarrel over when and where Curtis should drop the girl off. DeeDee insists that Curtis take her to her place first, the subtext being no monkey business with her after you've dropped me off at my house.

The two cronies chew each other out in squalls. When we cross South Chicago Avenue, the old coach even threatens to get out of the car and return home on his own. In a hushed voice, I reassure the young girl: "Don't worry, they fight like this all the time, they're like an old married couple." She's mightily intimidated by DeeDee's palpable surliness. He and Curtis briefly return to the subject of the fight. The Woodlawn boxer defends himself from his trainer's criticisms. (I find that he tends to be too pleased with himself after a fight; he doesn't see his mistakes.) In spite of the stifling noise of the music, I manage to record the conversation. Selected excerpts.

DEEDEE: I'd sure like to know how she got in here.

CURTIS [feigning surprise]: Oh you don't know how she got in here?

DEEDEE [barely controlling his exasperation]: No, I did not see the lady!

CURTIS: Well she already there when you got into the car?

DEEDEE: Yeah!!

CURTIS [raising his voice in anger in an effort to reverse roles]: How did she get here then?

DEEDEE: She in there when I came when you got in the car.

CURTIS: Man you was the only one in the car, nobody jumped in the car like dat: she jumped in with Louie . . .

DEEDEE [calmly]: *Nope.*

CURTIS [turning around toward the girl]: Who'd you get in the car with?

GIRL [timidly]: By myself.

DEEDEE [incredulous]: By herself?

CURTIS [acting as if the case were closed]: That answer that, DeeDee, don't it? *Don' blame it on me:* I'm just like you, tha's all [implying "I attract girls and I just can't help it"].

DEEDEE: Uh-uh. No you ain't like me.

CURTIS: Naw I ain't like ya, that's true, 'cuz you a heathen. [He laughs lustily at his sally, and me with him.] I been checkin' you out all night. Tryin' to cut in on Derrick an' stuff [when he was dancing with Wanda]! [Curtis laughs all the more.]

DEEDEE [indignant]: Cuttin' on Derrick?

CURTIS: Yeah!

DEEDEE: Him and Wanda?

CURTIS [jovial]: Yeah!

DEEDEE: I been havin' a lil' fun. I wasn't havin' no [inaudible]. It wasn't for that drink [inaudible].

CURTIS [in a reproachful tone]: Why you always drinkin'?

DEEDEE [aggravated]: I don't have anything else to do.

A long and convoluted argument ensues over DeeDee's statutory right to kick back and indulge in some of the pleasures of life from time to time—those very pleasures that Curtis must deny himself— owing to his ripe old age, followed by a dispute over whether Curtis will drop off the girl before or after taking DeeDee and me home.

CURTIS [interrupting DeeDee by yelling to make himself heard over the music blaring through the stereo speakers]: Havin' fun? That ain't fun!

DEEDEE: An' then you gonna be droppin' Louie comin' back. Drop the lady off, *then* drop *me* off an' go in an' take Louie. I'm not *crazy.* [As

Curtis is feigning to not listen to him, he vociferates.] Okay, go pull off, an' I—pull here on the left an' stop right [inaudible] by the fence.

LOUIE: You can't here, this is South Chicago, you can't turn that way.

CURTIS: Look, DeeDee I told you about y'all stop that drinkin' man. I oughta put you out my car!

DEEDEE [getting angry for real]: Hell *I can get out!* Shit! I know how to go home.

CURTIS: Do you? Did you make it last time—

DEEDEE [interrupting him]: You make a right, yeah.

CURTIS: Somebody better slap him upside—

DEEDEE [interrupting him again]: Ain't nobody gonna slap me.

LOUIE [to the girl in the back, petrified with fear]: They always get into arguments like that. Not to worry.

The conversation winds around and returns to the evening's fight.

CURTIS: He allofa sudden throw a punch, he was so wild I can't just rip it on straight on or nuthin'. But it jus' caught me at the same time when I was gonna throw the punch. An' I wan—I had tried to set my feet straight. [Irritated by DeeDee's indifference, who obviously wants to hear nothing of his explanations.] At the same time—it wadden no knockdown! I'm tellin' ya, the referee counted it a knockdown *so I had to treat it like* a knockdown. [He raises his voice to keep DeeDee from cutting him off, but in vain.]

DEEDEE: You went down, an' every time you hit the canvas whether it's a flash knockdown [when the boxer jumps back up instantaneously] or a straight knockdown or whatever, it's not a slip. [Brief pause.] You don't al—you always get up an' knock them people out in the same round. [huffing] An' it don't make sense!

CURTIS: What don't make sense? *The fans savor it!* [Raising his voice by way of defense, but in a neutral tone.]

DEEDEE: Yeah I know, like, that old strong boy was overweight . . . [A reference to a fight held the previous year, during which Curtis was sent briefly to the canvas by an opponent who was ten pounds heavier than him.]

CURTIS: Yeah.

DEEDEE: He knocked you down, boop-boop! You got up an' had *him* down, know what I mean? [Pause] Yeah 'cos it take you too long to get your mind *jacked up.*

CURTIS: I mean when I fell down they started countin' it as a knock-down I knew I had to get busy.

DEEDEE: An' it takes you too long to get off *on the inside*. An' you *stronger* in there, but you gotta bend yo' knees. How many times you knocked 'im down?

CURTIS [turning around toward me with suppressed pride]: Louie, how many I knocked 'im down?

LOUIE: Uh, three times and once they called it a slip. [Pause] An' one time also you threw him, I mean you sort of pushed him into the ropes.

CURTIS [interrupting me]: He had his head up into my eye.

DEEDEE: Yeah I know it.

LOUIE: He almost went through the ropes and out the ring.

DEEDEE [laughing softly and shaking his head]: Hee, hee, hee, he was throwin' elbows too. It wasn't nuthin' wrong with that. He's a *veteran*, he's been in forty-some fights.

DeeDee announces that he's going to cap the evening off with one last drink at a tavern near his place. Curtis jumps at the chance to lecture him again.

CURTIS: *Man,* stop, you don't need to drink no more! [Raising his voice in mock anger.] You be, you know you trippin' boy! You jus' *trippin', trippin', trippin'.*

DEEDEE [snickering, as if he has found the perfect parry]: You win two more fights, *stop two more people an' I'll stop drinkin'*.

CURTIS: Yeah right! Louie, you heard that, you heard that right?

LOUIE: Yeah I heard that.

DEEDEE: Two mo', stop two mo' guys an' I'll stop drinkin'.

LOUIE: I'll be a witness.

DEEDEE [triumphant]: *An' smokin'!*

CURTIS [delighted to realize that DeeDee cares this much about him being successful in his career]: Did that scare you when he knocked me down?

DEEDEE [in an indifferent tone]: *Nope.*

CURTIS: Why not?

DeeDee [shaking his head]: Uh-uh.

Curtis [incredulous]: Why not? Why *not?*

DeeDee: Why? Because I looked the way you got up. [calmly] You didn't get up *James Brownin'* an' *wobbly.*

Curtis: So I got up like that, ooohlllyhaaa!

DeeDee [lets out a long belch]: If you'da got up saggin' an' James Brownin', [muttering under his breath] then I know we're through.

But I knew you ain't hurt.

When we get to Cottage Grove Avenue, Curtis announces pleased as punch that he's going to take me home first, take the girl home next, and DeeDee last. "An' don't think you gon' tell me where to drive. *The only place you tell me what to do is in the ring!*" The Jeep Comanche pulls up in front of my building, I hop out onto the sidewalk and we tell each other good night, see you tomorrow at the gym.

The next day the telephone rings a little after noon, while I'm in the midst of typing up my notes. It's DeeDee calling to catch up. He's still foggy from the third-rate whisky he drank the night before—he finished the evening in the company of Curtis and the girl at the tavern on the corner of 69th Street and Indiana. "I didn't stay, wasn't nobody there but me an' the bartender. I introduced that heathen Curtis to him." Then Curtis dropped him off at his place before taking the sweetheart who had been in the car with us home. Or so he says . . .

DEEDEE: I'monna get on his ass 'bout this girl. She got no business bein' in d'car no-how. She was younger than what she say. She's the girlfriend of Milkman an' he only sixteen so . . . She say she got in a' argument with 'im and left.

LOUIE: You sure scared her, DeeDee.

DEEDEE: Well, I used to *scare a lotta them away,* in the gym. There be girls comin' to the gym and I ask them: [in a steely cold voice] "What you doin' up in there?" Or one girl come see Curtis and I tell him, loud, "Curtis, *yo' wife called"* [burbling laughter]. He be pissed . . . I'm not gonna go to the gym, maybe I'll take a half day off.

It's true that we all need a good rest: it was a long day, from the weigh-in to the return from Studio 104, and even if DeeDee insists that he never worried about anything, the nervous tension that surrounds a fight is always trying. "Oh, I don't be nervous. Oh, shit, nuttin' make me nervous, Louie. *Nothin's d'matter.* It ain't no big deal. That fight was nothin'. I don't let nothin' bother me. Wha's gonna happen is gonna happen no-how. After fifty years of this shit, it don't bother me. Even when Curtis got knocked down, I looked at 'im, the way he got up, I knew he wasn't hurt. He knocked down Hannah that same round an' almost had 'im out. Same thing happen when he fought that big boy in Harvey: he got knocked down, he got up an' knocked *his* ass down, and he'd have knocked him out if he stayed on 'im too. I know what he be doin'. He pull that shit [staying passively against the ropes so as to let his opponent tire himself out punching into his gloves] in the gym. You do that a lot then you get too relaxed. It's *habit-forming* to do that a lot when you spar. He done it in d'gym with Keith, layin' there, then he's gonna lay there in d'fight. I know he know what he's doin'. People don't know but he know what he's doin' and I know he know it. But that come from the gym: he can't *get off* like he want in the gym when he work with Keith. He can't work hard with 'im. *It's not enough guys around* t'work hard with: Rodney and Tony ain't here and Ashante ain't ready yet." DeeDee is of the opinion that Curtis doesn't have anyone at the club with whom he can train all-out at his own level: he hits too hard and too fast, and he's not patient with his sparring partners.

The coach grouses again about old Papa Page, who called him this morning at daybreak: "He be tellin' me about Al Evans is in town: [in a voice faking excitement] 'Al Evans is in town, DeeDee!' *Who the hell is Al Evans: no-thin', no-bo-dy, he cain't do nothin'.* I say, 'Man, why you be tellin' me about that, I don't even wanna know. And you sound all excited, I thought Jesus Christ came to town!'" Evans is a second-tier local boxer whose sole claim to fame is to have kayoed Mike Tyson a dozen years ago during a small amateur tournament in which he shouldn't have even been participating given that he was too old (he was twenty-four and Tyson barely fourteen). Then he turned pro and picked up five losses in six fights. Today he gets "hired out" as a sparring partner in the training camps run by the big national promoters—they are always in need of a heavyweight to serve as punching bag for their protégés. He was at the event last night and the announcer from Studio 104 introduced him to the crowd. "He's a nice guy, he awright. But why in hell would I call you early in d'morning an' tell you Al Evans's in town? I never would have told it."

Maybe DeeDee will stay home to rest up and leave the gym closed today—if he does this would be the first time in the two years I've been going there. But then, with much reticence: "I don't know if Eddie gon' be there and then, Eddie, once he's through with Lorenzo an' Keith, he don't care too much about the other guys. It's always guys that are gonna show up. An' I don't like guys goin' in and pickin' up shit. Like I can't find some of the gloves. I asked Anthony do he have them, he say no. Maybe somebody walked into the gym an' took them."

He's got it under his skin, DeeDee, his gym.

"Busy" Louie at the Golden Gloves

Seven weeks of preparation. Fifty days of labor and sweat, of grimaces, of mingled doubt and enthusiasm, of "monastic devotion," as Joyce Carol Oates puts it so well.[1] Six miles gobbled up each morning, in the arctic cold of a Chicago winter; billions of gestures, sometimes minute, simple or complex but always painstakingly executed, assiduously repeated and polished; and oh so many punches— thrown, absorbed, taken in and dished out. Tonight, I'm stepping into the ring. The moment of truth. The Chicago Golden Gloves has arrived, the most prestigious amateur tournament in the city. Proud of its seventy-something years, carrying in its wake the legend of the glory days of the Sweet science, when Chicago Stadium vied with Madison Square Garden in New York City for the pugilistic limelight. Tony Zale, Ernie Terrell, Sonny Liston, Cassius Clay first honed their skills there, first wreaked havoc there. Anxiety, impatience. Come on, let's do it!

Becoming a boxer, training for a fight is a little like entering a religious order. *Sacrifice!* The word comes up time and again in the mouth of the old coach DeeDee, who knows what he's talking about: a half-century devoured pacing the backstage corridors of the rings of Chicago, Los Angeles, Osaka, and Manila, in the course of a life with as many ups and

---

1. Joyce Carol Oates, *On Boxing* (Garden City, N.Y.: Doubleday, 1987).

downs as a roller coaster. He learned his trade under the watchful eye of
Jack Blackburn, the trainer of Joe Louis, who used to do his daily roadwork in the same Washington Park where I go running every morning.
He knocked around from one gym to another on the South Side before
going into exile in Asia for several years to mend a broken heart. Back in
Chicago, in the poverty of the black ghetto, or what is left of it, after having
had his moment of glory, brief and intense: two world championships with
the Filipino Roberto Cruz and the American Alfonzo Ratliff. Forgotten before they were ever even known by the mainstream public. The boxing
gym of the Woodlawn Boys Club will be his last port of call. Today,
DeeDee gets by as well he can, keeps things together as best he can.
He opens the gym every day at one o'clock sharp, closes its twisted iron
gate at seven on the dot. "This damn gym, some days I cain't stand it."
But nothing could keep him away. This is where he *is;* it's as simple as
that. Including on those Sundays before a fight, when his boys perform
at Park West, at the International Amphitheater on the corner of Halsted
and 43rd Street, or in some suburban movie theater. His life is but one
long sacrifice to this science of bruising, to which he has given everything
and which has given him back so little and so much at the same time. "My
life's been one great big waste, but what a beautiful waste!" he says slyly
to me, smiling. He has no regrets. Or so he says.

   Sacrifice! The word bounces off the yellowish walls of the gym, rolls
along the peeling ceiling, slides off the heavy bags swaying at the end
of their chains, echoes inside the metal lockers where the regulars put
away the tools of their trade at the end of the day: well-worn gloves,
handwraps drenched with sweat, high-top shoes, headgear, faded
sweatsuits in once-daring colors. Training for a fight is subjecting oneself, day after day after day, to a ritual of mortification. I understand
better now why DeeDee always grumbles that "boxin's a job that keep
you busy twenty-four hours a day. You gotta have it on your mind every
minute. You cain't do nuthin' else if you do it right." Indeed, it's not so
much the brutality of the fights that leads pros at the end of their careers
to hang up their gloves as the uncompromising and inevitable rigors
of training, the wearing away of the will and of the body that it slowly
but surely produces. No one escapes time, especially not boxers, those
men who daydream of immortality.

   The life of a boxer in the ring resembles that "nasty, brutish and short"
existence of which Thomas Hobbes spoke when describing the state of
nature. By comparison, the life he leads in the gym seems woven with

langour and sweetness.[2] It has its own time, stretched out to infinity; its rituals stamped with precision; its rhythms that aim, paradoxically, as much to make the fighter forget the upcoming bout as to ready him for it. It feeds not on inflicted, unpredictable and feared violence, but on violence willed, planned for, self-inflicted, and consented to because it is controlled. Domesticated. Forget the ring: it's in the anonymous and prosaic obscurity of the training gym, both refuge and workshop, that a fighter is forged. The gym is first and foremost made up of sounds or, more to the point, a symphony of specific noises, immediately recognizable among a thousand others: the panting and hissing of the boxers, the slap of gloves on the heavy bag, the clicking of the chains, the rhythmic gallop of a jumprope, the inimitable "rat-tat-tat-tat-tat" of the speed bag. All of this in a giddy, staccato tempo. Next, it's the smells: pungent, tenacious smells. It's a microclimate, a dense atmosphere, nearly suffocating, intoxicating with its very monotony. These sounds, these smells, this atmosphere impregnate the body through every pore, penetrate it and shape it, invest it and excite it through every nerve ending, mold it for combat.

"You win your fight in the gym," the old-timers repeat time and again. Because *the gym is a factory*. Gray, closed in on itself, rudimentary, where the high-precision machineries that are boxers are manufactured, according to methods that appear archaic but are in fact so very time tested and nearly scientific. To work on the bag is to craft a product, as you would on a lathe, with the crude tools that are gloved fists. And the tool and the product meld into that same body that serves as weapon, shield, and target.[3] Finding your distance, breathing, feinting (with your eyes, your shoulders, your hands, your feet), sliding one step to the side to let the bag swing by, catching it again on the fly with a left hook right to the midsection. Not too high and not too wide, so that the move can't be seen coming. Double it up, to the head, with a short, sharp movement. Follow up with a straight right, taking care to turn the wrist over like a screwdriver in order to align your knuckles horizontally

---

2. It has frequently been pointed out—correctly, according to my experience—that boxers are often people full of gentleness outside the ring, as if eager to display the kindness forbidden to them in the ring; see, for example, George Bennett and Pete Hamill, *Fighters* (New York: Dolphin Books, 1978).

3. This work of corporeal fabrication of the pugilistic habitus is dissected in Loïc Wacquant, "Pugs at Work: Bodily Capital and Bodily Labor among Professional Boxers," *Body and Society* 1, 1 (March 1995): 65–94.

at the precise moment of impact. "The left hook and the straight right, they go together like husband and wife," explains Eddie, the assistant trainer of the gym. The back foot pivots slightly, transfering the weight of the body onto the other leg. The hips swivel back just enough to position your body at an angle that minimizes the area left open to your opponent. One step to the left and you follow with a jab, the straight punch with the forward arm around which everything revolves, as it serves alternately as foil (defense) and as gun sight (offense). "Pump that jab for me! Give 'im the stick! Make him eat some leather with your left! Double up on d'jab and follow up with a right, that's it."

Make no mistake about it: working on the bag is every bit as much mental as it is physical. The distinction itself dissolves in the acrid sweat that streams into my eyes. "Move yo' head, damn it! That's not a bag you got in front of you, Louie, tha's a man!" DeeDee's voice thunders. "How many times do I gotta tell ya that ya got to think? *Think! You box with your mind.*" And yet, everyone knows intimately, from having suffered it in his own flesh, that you hardly have time to step back and reflect in the ring, where everything takes place based on reflex, in fractions of a second. The head is in the body and the body is in the head. Boxing is a little like playing chess with your guts.

The gym is also a lair. Where you come to seek refuge, to rest up from the harsh, cruel light and looks you get from people outside your world: white people, cops, "bourzois" blacks (as my buddy Ashante calls them), bosses and supervisors, and all the respectable folks who veer out of your way with a shudder when you get on the bus. Being young, poor, and black in America is no bed of roses. So in the gym, you close in on yourself, in the company of others like you. You protect yourself. From the outside, from yourself. You bracket for a moment a life that you no longer even find unfair, because you're so used to it, so weary of it. Just hard, the way fists are hard. There are few words, few useless gestures in the gym. "This ain't no social club, you're not here to make conversation, get t'work!" Everyone strives to pull himself in, to distill, to the fullest extent possible, his entire being into a body—a seamless, armored, taut body. You never really let your guard down, even behind the door of the locker room, the ultimate sanctuary.[4] In that narrow little room with the greasy sheetrock walls recently repainted a shocking

---

4. See Loïc Wacquant, "Protection, discipline et honneur: une salle de boxe dans le ghetto américain," *Sociologie et sociétés* 27, 1 (spring 1995): 75–89.

blue, seated on the single wooden table that serves as a bench, we exchange—with a parsimony born of a sense of modesty—words, taps, laughter, and especially looks. We chat furtively, about boxing, women, streetfights, boxing, prison, football, rap music, boxing. And always and forever, boxing; the subject is inexhaustible. We comment on the sparring of the day: "You hurt me with that right, Cliff, I can still feel my jaw . . . Think of keepin' your left hand higher, Keith, when you're comin' out of a clinch. You still takin' too many punches." Ever since a hand injury interrupted his promising career, Butch has served as an unofficial technical adviser: "With a puncher who charges atchyou like Torres, you let 'im come to you an' you counter with sharp jabs. Sharp! Aim right at his neck and hit 'im like you're going to go right through him." Holyfield is favored three-to-one: the Jamaican "Razor" Ruddock can punch, for sure, but he has no defense. And Holyfield has come up a weight class, he's "too hungry."

The gym is the antidote to the street. Every hour spent behind the walls of the club is another hour snatched away from the sidewalks of 63rd Street. After ten years in the ring, sixteen wins and one draw as a pro, Lorenzo hopes to fight for the WBO welterweight world title soon. "If it wasn't for boxin'," he confides to me hesitatingly, "I don' know where I'd be . . . Prob'ly in prison or dead somewhere, you never know. I grew up in a tough neighbo'hood, so it's good for me, at least, to think 'bout what I do before I do it. To keep me outa the street, you know. The gym is a good place for me to be every day. Because when you're in d'gym, you know where you are, you don' have to worry about gettin' into trouble or getting shot at." What if the gym closed down? The rumor goes around and makes all shudder. The city has promised to tear down the Maryland Theater next door, a shell of brick and boards abandoned since the mid-seventies, when the prosperous white neighborhood of Woodlawn underwent its final, brutal metamorphosis into a black ghetto. Yes, what if the gym were closed down? Curtis doesn't even want to think about it. "It would be like takin' kids away from their own home. You got a lotta kids in d'neighborhood, you know, who hang out in d'street, they come to the gym just to get away from d'street. You got older guys who come here to quit drinkin' and to give up that reefer an' drugs an' stuff, who come to the gym to try to clean out their system. It's like—it's like taking somethin' away from the people around here, from the public. You can't do that. It mean a lot. For me too . . . You're talkin' about takin' away my livelihood, you're takin' away my children's Christmas, takin' the bread outa their mouths."

The gym is also—and above all—a dream machine. Dreams of glory, of success, and of money, of course. To make a million dollars in one night . . . It doesn't matter that the purses of so-called club fighters barely exceed two hundred bucks for a four-round bout, a thousand dollars for an enticing ten-round main event, a tad more if Telemundo, the city's Spanish-language television station, deigns to bring in its cameras. Who knows if, by dint of will, perseverance, sacrifice, and well-placed connections . . . one day, maybe . . . The story goes that Alfonzo Ratliff made it, that famed million dollars, before getting his face bashed by Mike Tyson in Las Vegas in two pitiful rounds. The truth is less glamorous: his biggest purse never exceeded thirty thousand dollars, and that is before subtracting the "cuts" for his managers, trainer, cutman, promoter, all the entourage that swarms and multiplies as soon as you start to rise up in the ranks a little. Way off the million-dollar mark. Curtis talks about rebuilding the corridor of hopelessness that is 63rd Street: "You see all those burned-out buildin's, all those vacant lots, people without jobs, doin' drugs? When I'm world champion, I'monna change all that. I'm goin' to open up stores with big neon signs, a detox center, a dry cleaner's, an' a youth club." When I'm champion of the world . . .

It doesn't matter, because in the meantime the gym is a machine that pulls you out of *in-difference,* out of *in-existence,* a machine running full-bore. One thinks of the soliloquy in the famous scene from *On the Waterfront,* where Marlon Brando plays an ex-boxer who says to his brother: "Don't you understand? I could have had some class. I could have been a contender. I could have been *somebody." To be somebody,* that's what it's all about! To escape from anonymity, from dreariness, if only for the space of a few rounds.[5] A boxer in the ring is a being who screams, with all his heart, with all his body: "I want to be someone. I exist." Who is dying to be seen, known, recognized, even if only, as a last resort, by people from the neighborhood, friends, or kids in the vicinity, like the ones who argue over who gets to carry Curtis's gym bag and who follow his comings and goings with admiring eyes. Being a "role model"—the antithesis of, and antidote to, the drug dealer

5. According to the paradigm offered by Billy Tully, the poignant main character in Leonard Gardner's novel *Fat City* (New York: Vintage Books, 1969), made into the film of the same name by John Huston. As Jean-François Laé writes: "The very fact of getting into the ring is itself a step up. Defeat is not a mark of dishonor, far from it. You don't fear it, you don't avoid it at all costs"; "Chausser les gants pour s'en sortir," *Les Temps modernes* 521 (December 1989): 129.

everyone knows and envies even as they despise him—is already a lot. But the Golden Gloves, that's so much more, it's a galaxy unto itself. "This tournament, y'know, it's a title that every man dreams of having, okay? It's the dream of a lifetime! Golden Gloves! You know it's on TV and everythin'? Man!" Curtis is frantically tapping Chears on the chest. "That Golden Gloves jacket, like the one I got here, you know what's so special 'bout it? I'll tell you what's so special: you can't buy it in a store, you have to earn it in d'ring." And, of course, from the Golden Gloves to Caesar's Palace would be but one step.

But the sacrifice neither begins nor ends at the door of the gym. "Trainin' in the gym, tha's only half the work. The other half is the discipline: you got to eat right, hit the sack early, get up in the mornin' to do your roadwork, leave the women alone an' everythin'—you know, takin' care of your body." Food, sleep, sex: the Holy Trinity of the pugilistic cult.[6] DeeDee has concocted for me a diet of fish, chicken breasts, and turkey cutlets, dressed with boiled vegetables and some fruit, washed down with tea and tap water. Avoid bread; sugar and sodas are like the plague. And what if I'm still hungry? He rages: "Hungry, that don't mean nuthin'! Tha's in your head, it don't exist—period." Especially since depriving yourself at the table is nothing compared to depriving yourself in the bedroom.

Women are the object of all desire and of all terror. Boxing people say, and absolutely believe, that you have to wean yourself off women for weeks on end leading up to a fight, because making love softens you up, makes you tender, and weakens you. And with good reason: "When you come, you lose blood from yo' spine." Ashante pulls me back in line: "You leave your girl alone now, Louie, we only got three weeks left 'til the fight." Little Reese is no less categorical: "That sex is a monster, man. It kills ya, I tell ya, 'cause I tried it." Fat Joe, who bragged last year about fornicating every night and then took a real beating in his first bout—the fallout everyone was expecting—this time has prepared himself with the seriousness of a pope: "I told my girlfriend: no way! Wait until after the tournament. I quit this three-hundred-dollar-a-week job to train hard an' win the title, so I'm not 'bout to waste it all just to get me some, right?" Fred, a bundle of nerves and bad temper who invariably gets winded by the second round, is another case in point: everyone deplores his lack of continence. Says Eddie: "It's a damn shame. Fred, he would make a

6. For historical illustrations, see the tales collected in Ronald Fried, *Corner Men: Great Boxing Trainers* (New York: Four Walls Eight Windows, 1991).

good boxer. He's strong as a bull, he hits hard an' he can take a punch. But he likes girls too much . . ."

Of all the sacrifices, sex is by far the most costly. Anthony is sitting behind DeeDee's desk, bare-chested, looking somber. "You know what, Louie? I'm tiiired. I've had it. Every day—box, sweat, box, sweat—*every single day!* I've really had it. Every day the same routine. That's not a life." His shifty eyes are glued to the ceiling. I don't know what to say, I've never seen him like this, he who is usually overflowing with energy and trains with a fervor that borders on hysteria. The problem is, he hasn't touched his fiancée going on five weeks and he's got another fight coming up in two weeks. "I won't make it, Louie, I won't make it." Worse, he's afraid that Bonnie, sweet Bonnie, might seek some all-too-natural consolation in someone else's arms. To sum up: "Don't talk to me about those ladies. I could give you a list of boxers buried forever by women so long it would break your heart."[7]

29 January: I wrap up my first month of intensive training with three frustrating rounds of sparring with Ashante. I can't find my timing or keep his attacks in check. My punches are wild, disorganized, hurried, and Ashante has no trouble getting through my guard to pepper my upper body with short hooks. He counters my every punch tit for tat, and nearly takes my head off with a combination flush in the face: bim-bam! My head flies back. I finish in a daze, half-groggy in the locker room, and leave the gym physically and emotionally drained. I tell myself that I'll never be a boxer, that I might as well give up right here and now.

5 February: an hour of running with my dog this morning, in a cold drizzle. This roadwork is real torture but I feel myself getting stronger. My body is gradually adjusting to the draconian regimen. I've lost nine pounds since Christmas and am halfway there. DeeDee's advice and reprimands are growing more intense and more emphatic as the fateful date approaches—which is a good sign. I am furious at Aaron, who spent our three rounds trying to take my head off. His overhand rights to the top of my skull made me see stars. I shook him up with a left to the temple but didn't follow up. I have to be meaner when I'm sparring or else I'll never get anywhere. While we're showering, Ashante calms me down and warns me that I'm going to panic at first: "In your first fight, you

---

7. Statement made by Patty Flood, Sugar Ray Leonard's trainer when he was an amateur, cited in Sam Toperoff, *Sugar Ray Leonard and Other Noble Warriors* (New York: McGraw-Hill, 1987), 32.

got two opponents: the guy in front of you an' the crowd. Sometimes, you're so overwhelmed that you dunno what to do. Tha's how I lost my first two amateur fights. I was so depressed afterwards that I wanted to quit everythin'."

D-Day minus ten. The gym is full and buzzing like a hive. For two hours straight, the ring isn't empty once. You have to stand in line to put on the gloves. The pros, "Machine Gun" Ashante, Lorenzo "The Stallion" Smith, good old Smithie, Big Earl, and even "Rockin'" Rodney Wilson have come specially to work with the candidates for the Gloves. The tension rises day by day. "Boxhead" John has become sullen: he looks like a miniature Marvin Hagler, with his shaved head and the hungry glare in his eyes. He's been waiting for this moment for ten years, ever since he left his home state of Alabama and put on his first pair of gloves in the army. "Mighty" Mark Chears is dripping with sweat underneath his hood, drunk with concentration. Rico wales away like a trooper on the uppercut bag. No one has seen Fred for a week, bad omen: he must be hanging around with his homies from the Disciples gang, somewhere on 73rd Avenue.

DeeDee lengthily weighs the optimal matchups for sparring. He first calls Rico, considers Anthony, makes Cliff cool his heels, appraises the various possible combinations before putting together the most harmonious pairs. I spar four rounds, two with Reese and two with Ashante, strenuous and pugnacious rounds. My punches snap, I can see better on defense. I finish up the session with three rounds on the heavy bag, three on the jab bag, three skipping rope and a killer set of situps. My body aching, I take a shower alongside Smithie: "The day before your fight, don't be standin' up, stay in bed or lie down on your couch as much as you can so your legs don't get tired. Be lazy, relax. It's super important: you're fulla energy now, you need to save it for the fight. Don't waste it."

D-Day minus one. A thunderbolt strikes in the sky of the gym: "You didn't hear the news, Louie?" O'Bannon, the good-natured mailman who is driving us to the weigh-in in his van, calls out to me. What news? Tyson got busted by "Buster" Douglas! What? The invincible "Iron" Mike Tyson—the same Tyson who seemed barely human he so terrorized his opponents before they even stepped into the ring—sent to the canvas, finished, washed up? Even those who saw the fight late last night on pay-per-view are having a hard time believing it. And yet there's no mystery: "Tyson got his ass whipped. That'll teach 'im a lesson: you don't mess around with the science of boxin'. See the fat he had on his back?

He wasn't ready, he didn't train seriously, he was chasing them girls."
Anthony squeezes my hand with delight, in one of those "soul shakes"
only he knows how to do: "Awright, Louie is fightin' tomorrow night!"
You'd think he's anticipating my match with as much impatience as
his own.

A few minutes later, Nelson Mandela emerges from twenty-three
years in captivity onto every television screen around the world. Erect,
magnificent, radiating with dignity. The living anthesis of Don King who
is gesticulating and shouting himself hoarse, all the way from Tokyo,
trying to convince an incredulous press corps that Tyson, humiliated according to the rules, was the victim of a mistake by the referee.

The weigh-in, in a school gym on the North Side, has an unreal and
comical quality to it. The scene is reminiscent at once of a circus, a freak
show, and a slaughterhouse: all this human meat pressed into lines,
milling around in a windowless basement, makes you shudder and smile
at the same time. Every size, every shade, every shape, every build, is
represented. There are little tough guys who have taken everything off
but their sunglasses and their shorts and are glaring angrily at their potential opponents. A tubby Puerto Rican with the face of a piglet, framed
by long sideburns and filthy hair, is walking around completely naked,
his tiny penis hanging out, to the great delight of his cronies who are
choking with laughter against the wall. A big ebony-colored heavyweight
is flexing his muscles, undaunted, while waiting to step up to the metal
scale. Two café-au-lait super lightweights, looking like accountants who
somehow wandered in by mistake, are chatting next to me, while a white
guy with a flabby belly sports a gigantic pair of briefs that would seem to
be concealing a large carpenter's square. Rico, James, and Mark have
already been weighed and put their clothes back on. My turn to step on
the scale. One hundred and thirty-seven pounds. Photo. On the way
back, in the car, I find out that Rico and Reese's parents are so poor
that there's often nothing to eat in the house. DeeDee is worried about
whether Rico will be able to fight on an empty stomach. I am ashamed
of myself for being among them and wanting to box out of scholarly curiosity and a sense of fun.

It's on Sunday afternoon that I get more and more anxious thinking
about my fight. I suddenly start to feel weak; a vague bellyache is nag-
ging at me. I pester Liz by constantly asking what time it is. I feel like I've
caught a cold: my neck hurts, my nose is running, my mouth is dry; I am
tired and have no strength. I take a long, hot bath and try to calm down

Big James steps on to the scale,
followed by Rico and Mark

"Busy" Louie stands in line and makes the weight

by gulping some chocolate mints, a few Pepperidge Farm cookies, and some ice cream. This only worsens my malaise because I know that all that isn't good for my body. My throat is in knots, a diffuse sense of distress comes over me.

Wake-up the next morning at eleven o'clock. I slept like a log and I have a very hard time believing that I'm going to climb into a ring that evening. Me? I force myself to ingest a chicken breast and a grapefruit around four o'clock. I feel at once serene and tense, and am brimming over with energy. Meet up at the gym to leave all together for Saint Andrew's Gym. Everyone greets me with a word of encouragement. Sober and without fanfare. Oddly, far from overwhelming and intimidating me, the idea of carrying the hopes of the Woodlawn Boys Club on my shoulders gives me peace of mind. "Hey Louie, the French Bomber, you're goin'to win tonight!"[8] As for DeeDee, as always, he acts as if nothing special is going on. "You ready, Louie, you got everythin'? Handwraps, trunks, mouthpiece?" He fishes around in his little doctor's satchel, digs out a small brownish vial, then takes two cotton swabs from a leather pouch. With the gestures of a surgeon, he delicately dips one of the Q-tips into the bottle and hands it to me: "Stick that in your nostrils, all d'way up there, an' dab it all around." The smell is strong but not unpleasant. The adrenaline cools down my nasal passages: this coating will keep my nose from bleeding too much, for a change. On the way out, I collect my last words of encouragement from Alfonzo, who is finishing getting dressed in front of his locker with the moves of a carnivore: "You're gonna kick someone's ass tonight, man." Or get my ass kicked.

There's a lot of traffic because of the snowstorm swooping down onto the city, and it takes us nearly an hour to get to Saint Andrew's Gym. The tidal wave of nerves rises as we get closer and closer. We reassure each other (and ourselves) as best we can, by laughing or exaggerating our fear. But once we reach the corner of Addison and Paulina, the wave recedes and an irrepressible desire to box takes over. We enter the big hall. Four dollars admission, a dollar for a hot dog or a beer. The guy selling Tyson T-shirts and patches is complaining behind his table: the value of his inventory has crashed along with the downfall of his idol in Tokyo. The good-natured, family-oriented crowd (maybe eight hundred people, counting the fighters and their always plentiful entourage;

8. An oblique reference to Joe Louis's nickname in the 1930s and 1940s, "The Brown Bomber."

relatively few blacks, large numbers of Hispanics, Mexicans and Puerto Ricans, and some poor-looking whites) has come to have fun or to see some good boxing. Because you watch the fights differently according to the division: novice boxers for comedy, their colleagues in the "open" division for technique and "heart." And when an "animal" comes onto the scene, you roar with laughter. The pros are the hardest spectators to please. As two mediocre fighters strike affected poses, Ashante yells out in his booming voice: "Come on, you bums! Get busy in d'ring!"

Verification of the license, simulacrum of a medical checkup, call to the officials' table to get a brand-new pair of gloves—everything is going by very quickly and I hardly have time to get nervous. I am boxing eighth, after Fred and Chears and before Big James. In the bare room that serves as a makeshift locker room, the boxers change their clothes in silence, a mask of anxiety on their faces that some of them try to hide under a thin layer of false confidence and bravado. I slip my

The one-minute medical exam

The anguished and anguishing wait in the dressing room

cup on, underneath my black bermuda shorts, then my red knee-high socks with white socks over them and the blue "Ringside" jersey that Ashante gave me. Smithie offers to wrap my hands with the blue Velcro wraps that DeeDee has entrusted to him. This he does with the precision of a very motherly nurse, making sure each time around that the fabric is neither too tight nor too loose. He wraps it around my knuckles again and again and enfolds each finger separately. "Close your hand now, how does it feel?"

It's already Fred's turn. Curtis pumps him up before he enters the ring: "Don't forget you're from Woodlawn, nigger!" Fred is horribly nervous but he immediately takes the fight right to his opponent, a stocky young Mexican whom he batters like a wildman for two rounds. In the third round, he runs out of gas and absorbs rights and uppercuts by the truckload. Curtis leans on the ringpost, bellowing at the top of his lungs: "Come on, *fight, motherfucker, fight!*" One last flurry of wild hooks and straight rights, and Fred wins by the skin of his teeth. DeeDee and Eddie gloat discreetly and all of Woodlawn with them.

I make the mistake of asking the official who is lacing up my gloves if my opponent is there. "Uh, Cooper? Yeah, that's him over there." Damn, he's a tall black guy with the musculature of a panther. He must be a good six foot one, with long arms, supple like vines, and slim legs that emerge, straight as posts, from his impeccably pleated white trunks.

Two sinister-looking black men, fiftyish and athletic, are rubbing down his shoulders while whispering in his ear who-knows-what cunning ring ruse. Right away, I tell myself: "Shit, that guy knows how to box! Look at the boots! The boots! They're worth at least sixty bucks, he wouldn't have boots like that if he didn't box for real. Shit, I'm gonna get killed!" But I get hold of myself immediately by thinking back on the hours of sparring in the gym: "That guy can't be better than Ashante or Lorenzo, can he?" I warm up, shadowboxing at the back of the gym, under a gigantic stars and stripes, still closely surrounded by my club mates. Eddie tells me again to relax, Ashante and Smithie stay right next to me, feeding me advice. I can't wait to get into the ring, the moment so hoped for and dreaded all these weeks has come. Don't disappoint!

From that moment on, everything speeds up and melts together in my mind. I can remember clearly only little chunks here and there that are difficult to put together. I'm too focused, too tense. Eddie washes off my mouthpiece with his water bottle and sticks it in my mouth, then shoots a stream of cold water into the back of my throat, which is horridly dry. This is it, it's my turn, this time it's for real! I've had such a rough time of it in that goddamn gym that I only want one thing: to get it on. I run into DeeDee at the foot of the ring. He envelops me in a gaze at once fond and paternal, stern but full of affection; not a single word slips from his lips, which are turned up in an impassive little smile. With my gloved fist, I tap the closed fist he holds out to me, from above and from below. That really warms my heart. I briskly saunter up the little set of steps while Eddie bends his plump chest to stretch the ring ropes out of my way.

The spotlights hanging above the ring are blinding. The voice of the announcer, John Bollino, a retired high-ranking army officer, proclaims the identity of the fighters with dramatic tremolos: "Busy" Louie Wacquant versus Larry Cooper. I feel like I am hallucinating when I hear my name, followed by a wave of thunderous applause rolling in behind me from the bleachers where the guys from the gym have congregated. I bounce around nervously in place, exhaling, my eyes fixed on the opposite corner, where my enemy-for-a-night is shaking out his long, thread-like limbs and windmilling the air with both fists. "Get to work, Louie!" Here I am, *alone in the ring*. The long weeks of waiting, of arduous work, to get here flash before my eyes. Maybe it's irresponsible of me but I don't feel the slightest bit afraid. I am focused, full of determination and quiet rage. Wasn't Cus D'Amato, the legendary trainer and "inventor" of Mike Tyson, fond of saying: "Boxing is a sport of self-control. You've got to understand fear in order to master it. Fear is like fire, you can make it

"Busy" Louie draws the salute of DeeDee
and the encouragements of Ashante
before stepping into the ring.

work for you"?[9] The referee, a potbellied Mexican with slicked-down hair, calls me to the center of the ring for our final instructions.

The whistle hisses, signaling the start of the round. I walk resolutely toward Cooper, who holds out both fists joined together so that we can touch gloves before I lunge at him. Jab, jab, jab, right. Cooper has the reach advantage and counters me sharply. Punches are raining from the get-go. I take a straight right smack in the face, which doesn't stop me at all from going into action "pumping" my jab. In a crazed rhapsody, the shouts of the crowd mix with the torment of the punches thrown and taken. With competition gloves on, which are lighter and less padded, fists cut through the air and punches hurt more—a lot more! And this

9. Cited in José Torres, *Fire and Fear: The Inside Story of Mike Tyson* (New York: Warner Communications Books, 1988), 60.

damn Cooper hits hard. *"Hands up, hands up,* Louie, get your hands up!" Smithie bellows. I unload a barrage of well-timed straight punches. Cooper backs up swiftly and weaves under my left hook, then catches me with a sledgehammer right on the nose, which stings all over. As soon as we clinch, he ties up my arms in the tentacles that pass for his arms, frustrating my attempts to work on his body. I attack once again, with a jab to his chest and suddenly, *boom!* Everything swings upside down, the ring pitches wildly, the ceiling lights blind me and . . . the next thing I know, I'm on my ass on the floor. I feel like a grenade exploded right in my face! I didn't see anything coming. I jump back up, the referee grabs my fists, wipes them off on his gray jersey, and makes me retreat to a neutral corner. He's annoying me, pushing himself up against me with his big, soft mouth counting in a sing-songy English: "Three, four, five . . ." Shit, he's giving me a standing eight count! I got knocked down. I'm really upset. "It's all right, it's all right, I'm okay, it's nothing." Out of the corner of my eye, I keep watch on Cooper who is breathing hard in his corner. I throw myself at him again, jab against jab, and I try several times to get past his guard. He ties me up and bangs away at my sides. I respond with a solid right to the solar plexus. *"Break!"* then *"Box!"* An exchange of jabs and straights. Tweeeet! The whistle interrupts our revels. Sustained applause.

I turn toward my corner, where Eddie has already slid out the stool. The most amazing thing about all this is . . . the fact that I'm not amazed at all! I feel like a tough ring veteran when Eddie takes out my reddened mouthpiece and rinses it off in a flash. "How you feelin'?" "Fine." I'm not even winded. I catch sight of DeeDee's head on my left, at the edge of the ring apron, with his big glasses and his black beret bolted down on his skull: "You're too far away, you need t'take two steps forward. Block his right an' move closer. Tighten your wrist good an' don't get tense, you're doin' good." I gargle, then spit the water out into the Budweiser bucket between my legs. The warning whistle blows, the cornermen get back out of the ring. Cooper is standing across from me again. Tweeet! Second round. We resume our maneuvers, only faster and harder. No time to think. My battered face is throbbing and dripping with sweat. I box on instinct, increasing the pressure on my opponent, as if in a high-speed film in which all the sensations are exaggerated. Cooper's fists seem like they've been dipped in steel when they bang on me. I attempt several left hooks behind my jab, without much success:

my punches cut through the air because their target has nimbly stepped back. But I stay on the offensive and throw three lefts that land right on target. "Be first! Don't wait! Combinations!" I remember clearly a wide left to the chest that knocked the wind out of me on the way out of a clinch. I slide along the ropes like a ballerina to try to get my bearings back and to avoid the straight right hands Cooper is launching one after the other. Tweeeet! End of round two, back to my corner. Same little scenario on my stool, where this time I'm trying to catch my breath. Eddie pulls on the waistband of my trunks to free up my stomach: "Take a deep breath, one mo' time. Come on, Louie, you win this round for us!"

This is the last straight line: I rush at Cooper and attack without letting up. I'm taking a lot of punches but I'm dishing out some of my own in return and the wild shouts of my supporters give me an extra boost of energy. We're both running out of steam and getting tired. Three minutes in the ring is an eternity! Jab, jab, right, double jab, I really am busy—at least I will have earned my ring name! When Eddie yells *"Thirty seconds!"* I turn into a windmill, throwing punches as fast as my arms will let me. Surprised, Cooper tries to fend me off by sticking his left arm out, palm open, like a pitchfork. Suddenly invigorated, I finally break through his guard and pin him up against the ropes, right next to my corner. Jab, hooks with both hands, to the body and to the head, over and under. *Bingo!* Everything is landing where it should. Woodlawn is hooting with joy. Cooper tries to push me off, then takes refuge behind his gloves. I pound on him as fast as I can: I need to score, quick, score! I want to knock him out. He struggles back, ties me up, takes his turn pounding on my body. Eddie and Ashante nearly jump into the ring, delirious: *"Both hands, both hands!* Underneath, underneath again!" I'm gasping for air and extricate myself with a furious jab, then lunge back at Cooper with a right that he catches in his gloves. Tweeeet! End of the third round and of the fight. I'm li-que-fied. We hug briefly, body against body, and slap gloves, before going back to our respective corners.

Eddie squeezes my shoulders feverishly and takes my headgear off with excited gestures: "You fought a helluva fight, Louie, a helluva fight!" DeeDee is all smiles, Ashante and Smithie hail me as the winner. Oooof! I'm wiped out, incredulous, delighted, drained, amazed, relieved—in a word, happy. A thousand emotions throb inside me. At the end of the day, I'm still in one piece, which is not so bad: that goddamn Cooper hit like a jackhammer. (I will later learn that he already had a record of nine wins and only one loss.) Everything happened so fast, too fast. More than anything, I am gratified by having done well by the gym, whose reputation is so envied by the other clubs. The referee calls us to the middle of the ring. Bollino reads the judges' verdict in his cavernous voice: "And the winner, by decision, in the red corner, from Bessemer Park, *Larry Cooooppeeeer!* Larry Coo-per . . ." The boos of the crowd drown out his announcement, there is whistling. "Boooo! Boooo! Bullshit!" Smithie and Eddie vociferate at the judges. I congratulate Cooper, who is glowing with satisfaction: "Good fight, man, good fight, good luck for the next one." The referee signals me to get out of the ring. An official promptly unties my gloves and hands me my passbook, which bears the still-wet inscription: "Defeat: Cooper, by decision." I have a crazy urge to laugh about it all. Liz, Eddie, Olivier, Ivan, Rico, Ashante, Aaron, Reese, Mark, old Scottie with the wine on his breath, all crowd around me: *"Man,* you won that fight, them bastards robbed you!" DeeDee main-

The Woodlawn Boys Club victorious: Big James and "Mighty" Mark proudly display their trophies, flanked by Eddie and DeeDee tains Olympian calm: "Far as I'm concerned, you won the fight, by a hair, with that flurry in d'last round. They shoulda given him a standin' eight count, he wasn' fightin' back." (I think that, more than anything, DeeDee's glad that I didn't get hurt. Ashante will reveal to me later that the old coach hesitated up until the last minute to let me step into the ring: "I don't want Louie to get hisself killed.") Liz hugs me, overcome with emotion: "Lo, Lo! You fought like a tiger, I couldn't believe my eyes." Me neither! I am flabbergasted that it all went by so quickly. Olivier and Eddie insist that I put some ice on my eye and on my nose, which are starting to swell up alarmingly. Liz runs to the concession stand to fill up a bag of it for me. DeeDee finally relaxes: "Boxin's never fun. You don't climb in d'ring to have fun. You have your fun after the fight."

Waking up the day after the fight is painful. I've slept like I was bludgeoned and can't remember anything about the fight. Was I dreaming? I feel numb, psychologically drained, like a squeezed lemon left with only the withered yellow skin. The mirror reflects the image of a hideously bruised face. My left eye, partially closed by the straight right that sent me to the canvas in the first round, is in the process of turning from an ocher red to purple. Not a pretty sight. The ridge of my pinkish nose has doubled in size; I touch it gingerly, to make sure that it's not broken again. A cut runs across my left eyebrow. I'm also sporting a swollen and purplish bottom lip and a bruise on the corner of my mouth, also on the left side. And I find it hard to breathe very deeply, because of my banged-up ribs. No, no doubt about it, I wasn't dreaming.

But all this hurting vanishes upon my triumphant return to the gym. I feel like a soldier going back to base camp after having been at the front lines, I'm so bombarded with high-fives, smiles, winks, pats on the shoulder, compliments, and commentary on the refereeing. "You done got robbed, Louie!" I surprised everyone at the gym—starting with my-self. From now on, I am fully one of them: "Yep, *Louie's a soul brother.*" Ashante is eagerly inquiring about my next fight when DeeDee shuts the party down: "There ain't gonna be no next time. You had yo' fight. You got enough to write your damn book now. *You* don't need to get into d'ring."

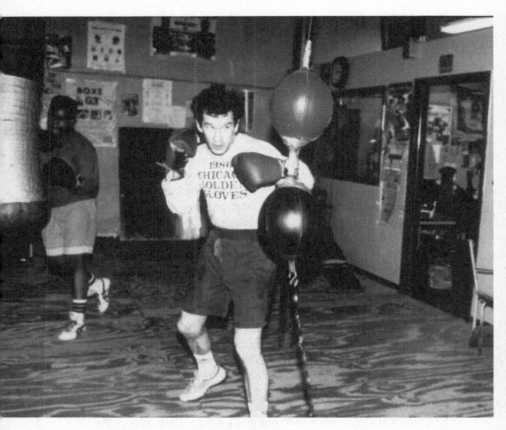

"One of DeeDee's Boys"

Forging the Pugilistic Habitus
Reflections on Becoming a Prizefighter

> All life is essentially *practical*. All mysteries which lead theory to mysticism find their rational solution in human practice and in the comprehension of that practice.
> —Karl Marx, seventh thesis, *Ad Feuerbach* (1844)

> It suffices to situate oneself *within* "real activity as such," that is, in the practical relation to the world, this pre-occupied, active presence in the world through which the world imposes its presence, with its urgencies, its things to be done and said, its things made to be said, which directly govern words or deeds without ever unfolding as a spectacle.
> —Pierre Bourdieu, *Le Sens pratique* (1980)

In this postface, I explicate the analytic agenda woven into the narrative fabric of *Body and Soul* to unpack its theoretical import and leverage its research implications. I recount how I took up the ethnographic craft, stumbled upon the Chicago boxing gym that is the main scene and character of my conversive ethnography of prizefighting in the black American ghetto, and designed the book so as to both deploy methodologically and elaborate empirically Pierre Bourdieu's signal concept of *habitus*. I draw out some of the biographical and intellectual connections between this research project on a plebeian bodily craft, the theoretical framework that informs it, and the macro-comparative inquiry into urban marginality of which it is an unplanned offshoot.[1] I sketch how the practicalities of firsthand observation led me from the ghetto as implement of ethnoracial domination to *embodiment as puzzle and springboard for social inquiry*. Through this reflection on becoming a

---

1. For a fuller account, see Loïc Wacquant, "Marginality, Ethnicity and Penality in the Neoliberal City: An Analytic Cartography," *Ethnic & Racial Studies Review* 37, 10 (2014): 1687–1711.

prizefighter as social phenomenon turned sociological experiment, I advocate for the use of fieldwork as an instrument of theoretical construction, the potency of carnal knowledge, and the imperative of epistemic reflexivity. I also stress the need to expand the textual genres and styles of ethnography so as to better capture the *Sturm und Drang* of social action as it is manufactured and lived.

The concept of habitus supplies at once the anchor, the compass, and the course of the ethnographic journey recapped in *Body and Soul*. It is the *topic* of investigation: the book dissects the forging of the corporeal, emotional, and mental dispositions that make up the proficient boxer in the crucible of the gym. But it is also the *tool* of investigation: the practical acquisition of those dispositions by the analyst serves as a technical vehicle for better penetrating their social production and assembly. In other words, the apprenticeship of the sociologist is a *social variant and methodological mirror* of the apprenticeship undergone by the empirical subjects of the study; the former is mined to dig deeper into the latter and unearth its inner logic and subterranean properties, and both in turn test the robustness and fruitfulness of habitus as a guide for probing the springs of social conduct.

Contrary to a commonly held view that habitus is a vague notion that mechanically replicates social structures, effaces history, and operates as a "black box" that obviates observation and confounds explanation,[2] it emerges that Bourdieu's sociological reworking of this old philosophical concept offers a flexible and powerful tool to steer social inquiry into the making of the social agent and to trace out operant social mechanisms at ground level. Properly used, habitus not only illuminates the variegated logics of practice springing from the mutual fabrication and reciprocal solicitation of cosmos and agent; it also grounds the distinctive virtues of deep immersion in and carnal entanglement with the object of ethnographic inquiry.

Pathway to the Ethnographic Craft

Since the notion of habitus proposes that humans are historical animals who carry within their bodies acquired categories, abilities,

---

2. By force of sheer repetition, these views have led generations of scholars to misread Bourdieu's phronetic theory of action as either rational conduct or mechanical execution of structural dictates, and thence to miss the radical historicism at the basis of his social ontology and epistemology.

and sensibilities that are the sedimented products of their past social experiences, it is useful to begin with how I came to ethnographic research and what intellectual interests and social expectations I brought with me to the South Side of Chicago. My initiation to fieldwork predates my entry into graduate school at the University of Chicago in 1985. To fulfill my military duties (as every French male had to do back in those days), by an extraordinary stroke of luck, I was assigned to do a stint of civilian service in the South Pacific as a sociologist in a research center of the Office de la Recherche Scientifique et Technique d'Outre-Mer (ORSTOM), France's former "bureau for colonial research." So I spent two years in New Caledonia, a French island located northwest of New Zealand, as part of a small research team—there were only three of us—around the time of the Kanak uprising of November 1984.

This means that I lived and worked in a very brutal and archaic colonial society, because New Caledonia in the 1980s was an imperial outpost of the nineteenth-century type that had survived virtually intact to the end of the twentieth century.[3] It was an extraordinary social experience for an apprentice sociologist to carry out research on the school system, urbanization, and social change in the context of a nationalist insurrection, under a state of emergency, and to observe in real time the struggles between the colonials and the independence forces. For instance, I was privileged to participate in a closed congress of the Kanak Socialist National Liberation Front in Canala at the height of the clash. I traveled all the way around the "Grande Terre" (the main island) and made several sojourns on Lifou island at the home of friends who were long-time Kanak militants. At the time, practically no one practically no one was moving about in the territory due to the combination of official travel restrictions, a strict curfew, and rampant fear of ethnopolitical violence to which the French state had responded by flooding the island with thousands of military troops and riot police. It was impossible, under these circumstances, not to reflect constantly about the power-knowledge nexus, the gap between bookish and

3. See Alban Bensa, *Chroniques Kanak: L'ethnologie en marche* (Paris: Ethnies, 1995); Michel Naepels, *Histoires de terres kanakes: Conflicts fonciers et rapports sociaux dans la région de Houaïlou (Nouvelle-Calédonie)* (Paris: Belin, 1998); Éric Soriano, *La Fin des indigènes en Nouvelle-Calédonie: Le colonial à l'épreuve du politique, 1946–1976* (Paris: Karthala, 2013); and David A. Chappell, *The Kanak Awakening: The Rise of Nationalism in New Caledonia* (Honolulu: University of Hawai'i Press, 2013).

field approaches to inquiry, and the civic role of social science in the unfolding conflict.

The New Caledonian crucible sensitized me to ethnoracial inequality and to spatial consignment as a vector of social control—the Kanaks were massively relegated to isolated rural reservations placed under "customary law," and to hypersegregated neighborhoods in the capital city of Nouméa. It also alerted me to the variegated workings of rigid hierarchies of color and honor in everyday life, and to the crucial place of the body as a target, product, and fount of asymmetric power relations. (I remember vividly the overt expression of scorn and suspicion on the faces of the local *caldoches*—descendants of the white settlers—in their routine city encounters with Kanaks dressed in their traditional *manou* and *popinée*). And it exposed me to extreme forms of deprecative racial imagery: the native Melanesians were typically pictured as "super-primitives" devoid of culture and history, even as they were rising to seize their collective fate through forceful political protest.[4]

All of this would prove immensely useful later, on the South Side of Chicago, where germane treatments of African Americans were current: during the 1983 election campaign that made Harold Washington the first black mayor of the Windy City, the white Republican candidate had run under the slogan "Epton: Before It's Too Late" and distributed bumper stickers that blared "Vote Right, Vote White"—and to good effect, as he garnered 81 percent of the white vote and nearly captured City Hall in an overwhelmingly Democratic metropolis.[5] It was in New Caledonia that I read the classics of ethnology: Mauss, Malinowski, Radcliffe-Brown, Raymond Firth, Margaret Mead, Gregory Bateson, and others (especially works on the South Pacific, as the Trobriand Islands were nearby), and that I kept my first field notebooks. The very first was scribbled among the Lifou tribe of Luecila, in the Bay of Wé, at Christmas of 1983, where I had been invited to attend a traditional wedding ceremony held by the clan of a prominent Kanak nationalist leader, about a year before the independentist uprising (the notebook's highlight was a section on going bat hunting and having to eat the roasted

4. Pierre Bourdieu and Alban Bensa, "Quand les Canaques prennent la parole," *Actes de la recherche en sciences sociales* 56 (May 1985): 69–85.
5. Paul Kleppner, "Race War, Chicago Style: The Election of a Mayor, 1983," in *Chicago Divided: The Making of a Black Mayor* (Decatur: Northern Illinois University Press, 1985).

Elders from the Unë clan, tribe of Luecila, Lifou Island,
New Caledonia

proceeds of our expedition at dinner that evening). Field notations found their way into my first publications on educational inequality, colonial conflict, and the transformation of Melanesian communities under the press of capitalist expansion and contested French rule.[6]

At the close of my Caledonian sojourn, I got a four-year fellowship to pursue my doctorate at the University of Chicago, the cradle of U.S. sociology and home to the main tradition of urban ethnography. When I arrived in Upton Sinclair's town, my firm intention was to work on a historical anthropology of colonial domination in New Caledonia, but I got unexpectedly derailed and detoured into America's dark ghetto. On the one side, the New Caledonian gates were abruptly shut after I filed a complaint against the mediocre bureaucrat who was my research supervisor in Nouméa and had forced his name as coauthor of a monograph on the school system that I had carried out by myself.[7] The directors of the institute in Paris hastened to cover up for the cheater, which effectively banned me from the island. On the other side, I found myself confronted day-to-day with the grisly reality of Chicago's ghetto, or what was left of it. I had been assigned the last student-housing unit available on campus, the one nobody wanted, and so I lived on 61st Street near Cottage Grove Avenue, at the edge of the poor black district of Woodlawn. The outermost "white telephone" marking the protected zone patrolled by the private police force of the university (the third largest in the Midwest) was right by my building's front door, which I and my fourth-floor neighbors, an African-American couple from Georgia, were the only ones to use; the other tenants studiously came in and out through the back door, oriented inside the safe harbor of Hyde Park.

It was a constant tremor and puzzlement to have right under my window this quasi-lunar urban landscape, with its unbelievable decay, misery, and violence, backed by a totally hermetic separation between

6. Among them, Loïc Wacquant, "La question scolaire en Nouvelle-Calédonie: Idéologies et sociologie," *Les Temps modernes* 464 (March 1985): 1654–1685; and "Communautés canaques et société coloniale: Notes complémentaires sur la 'question canaque,'" *Actes de la recherche en sciences sociales* 61 (March 1985): 56–64.
7. Loïc Wacquant, *L'École inégale: Éléments de sociologie de l'enseignement en Nouvelle-Calédonie* (Paris and Nouméa: ORSTOM with Institut Culturel Mélanésien, 1985); "The Dark Side of the Classroom in New Caledonia: Ethnic and Class Segregation in Nouméa's Primary School System," *Comparative Education Review* 33, 2 (May 1989): 194–212.

the white, prosperous, and privileged world of the university and the abandoned African-American neighborhoods surrounding it on three sides. Two incidents emblematic of the near-apartheid that organized the South Side at the time stick out in my mind decades later. On my very first day at the university, the department secretary handed me a campus map and proceeded literally to *black out* the areas south of 60th Street, west of Cottage Grove Avenue, and north of 47th Street with this ominous warning: "Don't ever cross into those areas if you care for your life"—which of course I did that very afternoon to satisfy the puzzlement this had caused me. One warm afternoon that fall, a skinny black teenager who had biked in from Woodlawn got run over by a car in front of the school of social service administration; he laid on the road bloodied and moaning in pain for nearly thirty minutes until a city firefighter's ambulance finally came to pick up him and truck him ten miles away to Cook County Hospital. It never occurred to the university police and staff present on the scene to take that kid two hundred yards to the university's glitzy hospital within sight right across the Midway Plaisance. Coming from Western Europe, where such levels of urban blight, material destitution, and ethnic segregation are unknown, this disquieted me profoundly on a quotidian level—existentially, intellectually, and politically. It was at this point that the second decisive encounter of my academic life took place, the one with William Julius Wilson. (The first was with Pierre Bourdieu, four years earlier, when I decided to convert from economics to sociology after hearing a perplexing public lecture by him on "Questions of Politics" at the École Polytechnique, followed by a luminous small-group discussion into the wee hours of the night in the student cafeteria).[8]

Wilson is the most eminent African-American sociologist of the second half of the twentieth century, and the foremost expert on the nexus of race and class in the United States—his analysis of "Blacks and Changing American Institutions" in *The Declining Significance of*

---

8. See Loïc Wacquant, "Taking Bourdieu into the Field," *Berkeley Journal of Sociology* 46 (2002): 180–186. The scene was recounted two decades later by the École Polytechnique student who had organized that conference. He reports that three participants to this late-night confabulation switched disciplines and went on to productive careers in social science, cf. Éric Brian and Marie Jaisson, "L'éducation structurale," in *Travailler avec Bourdieu*, ed. Pierre Encrevé and Rose-Marie Lagrave (Paris: Flammarion, 2003), 120–122.

Race set the parameters for that subfield of social research in 1978 and continues to shape it decades later.[9] He was one of the faculty who had attracted me to Chicago and, from our initial meeting, we "clicked" on both intellectual and personal levels: I found the analytic rigor and civic fervor that animated his investigations refreshing and fully consonant with his forthright persona; he seemed energized, if sometimes daunted, by my scientific curiosity and academic irreverence. So when he offered me to work with him on the big research project on urban poverty he had just started (roughly, the agenda marked out by his book *The Truly Disadvantaged*),[10] I jumped at the chance, and I quickly became his close collaborator and coauthor. This afforded me the opportunity to get straight to the core of the subject and also to get a close-up look at how this scholarly and policy debate operated at the highest level, especially in the philanthropic foundations and "think tanks" that shaped the resurgence of the problematic of race, class, and poverty in the so-called inner city during that decade.[11] That is how I started my investigations, first as an acolyte of Wilson and then by myself, on the transformation of the dark ghetto after the riots of the 1960s, by striving to break with the pathologizing vision that pervaded and distorted research on the question.

I owe a huge personal and intellectual debt to Bill Wilson, who was a mentor at once demanding and generous. He stimulated and supported me, and he also gave me the freedom to diverge from his analyses, and at times to go in a direction diametrically opposed to his. By example, he taught me intellectual courage: to pursue the big picture, to dig deep into the details, to ask the hard questions—even when this entails ruffling a few social and academic feathers along the way. Wilson also invited Pierre Bourdieu to speak to his research team on Bourdieu's Algerian research on urbanization and proletarianization from the early 1960s

9. William Julius Wilson, *The Declining Significance of Race: Blacks and Changing American Institutions* (Chicago: University of Chicago Press, 1978, 2nd ed. 1980, new expanded anniversary edition 2013).

10. William Julius Wilson, *The Truly Disadvantaged: The Inner City, the Underclass, and Public Policy* (Chicago: University of Chicago Press, 1987, new expanded edition 2012).

11. For a rich account, read Michael B. Katz, *The Undeserving Poor: America's Enduring Confrontation with Poverty*, revised and updated ed. (Oxford: Oxford University Press, 2013), chapter 5.

during a Chicago visit in the spring of 1987.[12] As it turns out, Bourdieu had tried to get *The Declining Significance of Race* translated into French in his book series with Éditions de Minuit a few years earlier. This meeting and the ensuing discussion solidified my sense that I could make a link between Bourdieu's early anthropological inquiries into the life paths of Algerian subproletarians and the contemporary predicament of the residents of Chicago's black ghetto that preoccupied Wilson. But I did not know yet just how. Relatedly, I was intrigued by the possibility of mating statistical and interpretive methods, as Bourdieu had done from the outset in his youthful Algerian forays, and by the challenge of bringing "high flying" theory to bear on mundane realities at ground level.

Ethnography played a pivotal role at that juncture, on two counts. On the one hand, I took more anthropology than sociology courses, because the Sociology Department at the University of Chicago was very dull intellectually, and because I was viscerally committed to a unitary conception of social science inherited from my French training. The courses, writings, and personal encouragements of John and Jean Comaroff, Marshall Sahlins, Bernard Cohn, and Raymond Smith pushed me toward fieldwork. (There was no one actively involved in ethnography in the Sociology Department in those days). On the other hand, I wanted to find a direct observation post inside the ghetto because the existing literature on the topic was the product of a "gaze from afar" that seemed to me fundamentally biased if not blind.[13] That literature was dominated by the statistical approach, deployed from on high by researchers who, most often, had no firsthand or even secondhand knowledge of what makes the ordinary reality of the dispossessed districts of the Black Belt, and who filled the gap between survey data and reality with stereotypes drawn from common sense, journalistic or academic. As I did not share that national common sense, and particularly the racial presuppositions it entails, I found that approach untenable. So I resolved to reconstruct the question of the ghetto from the ground up, based on a precise observation of the everyday activities

---

12. Pierre Bourdieu, Alain Darbel, Jean-Pierre Rivet, and Claude Seibel, *Travail et travailleurs en Algérie* (Paris and the Hague: Mouton, 1963; new expanded edition, Raisons d'Agir Éditions, 2020); Pierre Bourdieu, *Algerian Sketches* (Cambridge: Polity Press, [2008] 2013).

13. Loïc Wacquant, "Three Pernicious Premises in the Study of the American Ghetto," *International Journal of Urban and Regional Research* 21, 2 (June 1997, "Events and Debate"): 341–353.

and relations of the residents of that *terra non grata* and, for that very reason, *incognita*.[14]

I deemed it epistemologically and morally impossible to conduct research on the ghetto without gaining serious firsthand knowledge of it, because it was right there, literally at my doorstep (in the summertime, one could hear gunfire going off at night on the other side of the street and the occasional clunker rolling along on naked rims), and because the established works on the topic seemed to me to be full of implausible or pernicious academic notions. The first of these noxious notions was the *trope of "disorganization,"* spawned by the first Chicago School, which stipulates that inner-city areas or dispossessed districts more generally are, by definition, disorganized merely because their residents are short on social power or deviate from middle-class standards of conduct and aspirations. I refer here to the culturalist interpretations of the ideas of W. I. Thomas by Louis Wirth and Harvey Zorbaugh,[15] later codified into a static framework by positivist criminology based on the gang research of Clifford Shaw and Henry McKay that is now a central pillar of the sprawling "neighborhood effects" literature. Characterizing disorganization as "lack of social control," or by the triad of "socioeconomic disadvantage, ethnic heterogeneity, and residential turnover," ensures that most lower-class districts are *by mere stipulation* disorganized (and upper-class districts organized!), which prevents us from examining variations in the degree and type of organization they sport and their determinants. This inchoate notion, repeatedly invalidated empirically by the very research it has inspired, owes its remarkable academic staying power to the deep moralism and abiding anti-urbanism of American national culture, which casts the city as a cauldron of social disintegration and moral perdition.[16]

---

14. An early effort to restart from the street level while revoking the mutilating alternative between (liberal) structural and (conservative) cultural accounts is Loïc Wacquant, "Inside the Zone: The Social Art of the Hustler in the Black American Ghetto," *Theory, Culture & Society* 15, 2 ([1992] May 1998): 1–36.
15. Peter Jackson, "Social Disorganization and Moral Order in the City," *Transactions of the Institute of British Geographers* 9, 2 (1984): 168–180.
16. The historical roots and enduring hold of America's virulent anti-urbanism are unearthed by Morton Gabriel White and Lucia White, *The Intellectual Versus the City* (Cambridge, Mass.: Harvard University Press, 1962); and documented by Paul Boyer, *Urban Masses and Moral Order in America, 1820–1920* (Cambridge, Mass.: Harvard University Press, 1978).

Urban desolation on 63rd Street near Kimbark Avenue

The second intellectual obstacle to properly reconceptualize the postwar trajectory of the ghetto was the *scholarly myth of the "underclass,"* which was a veritable academic cottage industry in those years.[17] A genealogy of the term and its proliferating uses sufficed to trace its mutation from a structural construct in the work of the Swedish economist Gunnar Myrdal who coined it, to a pejorative behaviorist notion at the hands of policy researchers who adopted it through the initiative of philanthropic organizations eager to relegitimize their action in light of the abject defeat they had suffered in the "War on Poverty," to a neo-ecological concept in the work of William Julius Wilson, who sought in vain to mediate between these two poles before abandoning the term in the early 1990s. It demonstrated the logical circularity, empirical incoherence, unwarranted racial skew, and heavy moral baggage carried by the notion.[18] A reflexive return on this demonic trope showed how, by circling in and out of the social sciences, journalism, and the political-policy fields thanks to its semantic elasticity, the "underclass" effectively screened from view the collapse of the ghetto as an implement of ethnoracial control and its gradual replacement by a dual sociospatial structure composed by the bare hyperghetto, on the one hand, and segregated black middle-class districts, on the other.[19] It also worked to *dehistoricize and depoliticize* the predicament of the urban (sub)proletariat doubly marginalized by the fragmentation of wage labor at the bottom of the postindustrial employment scale and the planned retraction of the Keynesian social state leading to the virulent penalization of racialized poverty and its correlates fueling America's carceral boom.

Again, along with historicization, the antidote to the terministic contamination of the "underclass" was to turn to precise field observation

17. See Michael B. Katz, ed., *The "Underclass" Debate: Views from History* (Princeton: Princeton University Press, 1993); Herbert Gans, *The War against the Poor: The Underclass and Antipoverty Policy* (New York: Basic Books, 1995).
18. Loïc Wacquant, *The Invention of the "Underclass": A Study in the Politics of Knowledge* (Cambridge: Polity Press, 2022). The notion subsequently vanished overnight from public debate as a result of Clinton's 1996 "welfare reform", which prioritized pushing destitute black women in the urban core "from welfare to work," later supplemented, on the masculine side of the equation, by the bureaucratic charade and bandwagon of "prisoner reentry."
19. Loïc Wacquant, "A Janus-Faced Institution of Ethnoracial Closure: A Sociological Specification of the Ghetto," in *The Ghetto: Contemporary Global Issues and Controversies*, ed. Ray Hutchison and Bruce Haynes (Boulder, Colo.: Westview, 2011), 1–31.

guided by a set of clean analytic constructs forged through a comparative reading of the history of the ghetto. In short, I turned to ethnography not just to gain an "experience-near" grasp of the phenomenon to be investigated (its conventional usage, codified for American social science by Clifford Geertz)[20]; I also mustered it as an indispensable instrument of rupture with the preconstructions of urban sociology, a methodological sword wielded to pierce through the armor of ordinary, policy, and scholarly doxa.[21]

As a Frenchman raised in a provincial village near the Mediterranean, my formative social and intellectual experiences made me a complete foreigner to the black American ghetto and intensified the need I felt to acquire some practical familiarity with it. After a few aborted attempts, including walking the streets only to discover that this was both risky and unproductive (I would find out later that my mere presence there led people to suspect that I was either disoriented prey, a drug addict, or an undercover policeman), I found, by accident, a boxing gym in Woodlawn, at the back of a day-care center on the derelict thoroughfare of 63rd Street, some three blocks from my apartment. I signed up saying that I wanted to learn how to box, quite simply because there was nothing else to do in that setting. I had absolutely no curiosity about or interest in the pugilistic world in itself (but I did want to get good exercise)—as my ring compatriot Ashante wouldmuse later, "Louie, when you first came into d'gym, man, you couldn't tell a fish hook from a left hook." The club was to be a platform for observation inside the ghetto, a place to meet potential informants and to branch out into the ordinary institutions of the South Side. In a letter to Pierre Bourdieu dated 15 August 1988, I wrote:

Don't you laugh: I signed up in. . . a boxing gym in the ghetto (on 63rd Street). I can't believe it myself, but it's a good distraction and an excellent way to get in shape (I'm virtually paralyzed with aches and soreness on the days after

20. Clifford Geertz, " 'From the Native's Point of View': On the Nature of Anthropological Understanding," *Bulletin of the American Academy of Arts and Sciences* 28, 1 (October 1974): 26–45; reprinted in *Local Knowledge: Further Essays in Interpretive Anthropology* (New York: Basic, 1983; new ed. 2000).

21. In mobilizing ethnography thus, I simply implemented the rules for the construction of the scientific object laid out in Pierre Bourdieu, Jean-Claude Chamboredon, and Jean-Claude Passeron, *Le Métier de sociologue*, 2nd ed. (Paris: Mouton, 1973; trans. *The Craft of Sociology: Epistemological Preliminaries*, New York: De Gruyter, 1990).

training) and a unique pathway into the lives of young black men from the neighborhood. And coach DeeDee is a good storyteller. . . It's very interesting to note—and to feel first-*hand*, in the literal sense!—that the workout consists in a bodily training or taming effected purely through mimesis: you get the hang of the moves by watching others or yourself in the mirror. In short, it's a matter of habitus.

Habitus Comes to the Gym

But, very quickly, that gym turned out to be, not only a wonderful window into the daily life of young men in the neighborhood, but also a complex microcosm with a history, a culture, and an intense and rich social, aesthetic, emotional, and moral life of its own. In a matter of months, I formed a very strong, fraternal bond with the regulars of the club and with the old coach, DeeDee Armour, who became a manner of adoptive father to me. Gradually, I found myself attracted by the magnetism of the "Sweet science" to the point where I spent most of my afternoons in and around the gym. After about a year, the idea grew on me to dig into a second research subject, namely, the social logic of a bodily craft.

What is it that draws and thrills boxers? Why do they commit themselves to this harshest and most destructive of trades? How do they acquire the desire and the skills necessary to last in it? What is the role in all this of the gym, the street, and the surrounding violence and economic precarity, of masculine hubris and racial contempt, of self-interest and sensuous pleasure, and of the collective belief in personal transcendence? More abstractly still, how does one create a social competency that is an embodied competency, transmitted through a silent pedagogy of adept organisms in motion? In short, *how is the pugilistic habitus fabricated and deployed?* That is how I soon found myself working on two connected projects simultaneously—two problematics ostensibly very different from each other but in fact tightly linked: one a carnal microsociology of the apprenticeship of boxing as subproletarian bodily craft *in the ghetto*, which offered a particular "slice" of life and labor on Chicago's South Side from below and from inside; and the other a comparative and theoretical macrosociology *of the ghetto* as instrument of ethnoracial closure and social domination, providing a generalizing perspective from above and from the outside.[22]

22. Loïc Wacquant, *Urban Outcasts: A Comparative Sociology of Advanced Marginality* (Cambridge: Polity Press, 2008).

I had started writing a field diary after every training session from my first afternoon at the gym, initially to overcome the overpowering sense of being out of place in the pugilistic scene on so many levels (during my first training session, I had kept my eyeglasses on and felt "cray-white as a cadaver"), and not knowing really what, if anything, I would do with these notes. Now I shifted to taking systematic notes and exploring the various facets of the weet science. The notion of habitus immediately came to me as a conceptual device to make sense of my personal experiences as a boxing apprentice and as a scaffold to organize my ongoing observation of pugilistic pedagogy. I had read Bourdieu's anthropological works front to back during my New Caledonia years. Slowly working my way through *Le Sens pratique* (awkwardly translated into English as *The Logic of Practice*), a few pages early each morning and late at night, in my bare apartment of Nouméa, had been an existentially exhilarating and intellectually transformative experience. It felt as if my brain was being sociologically rewired line by line, synapse by synapse. The chapter on "Belief and the Body" and its treatment of temporality had made a particularly deep impression on me.[23] So I was fully familiar with Bourdieu's elaboration of habitus, intended to capture the phronetic character of human action as tactful social groping and to overcome the mutilating antinomy between an objectivism that reduces practice to the mechanical precipitate of structural necessities and a subjectivism that confuses the personal will and intentions of the agent with the motor of her action.[24]

As indicated in the genealogy of habitus drawn in the next chapter of this postface (*infra*, pp. 291–302), the author of *Outline of a Theory of Practice* had retrieved the notion from a long line of philosophers, stretching from Aristotle and Aquinas to Ockham and Husserl, to develop a dispositional theory of action recognizing that social agents are not passive beings pulled and pushed about by external forces, but skillful creatures who actively construct social reality through "categories

---

23. The exposition of Bourdieu's model of practice is more advanced theoretically in *Méditations pascaliennes* (Paris: Seuil, 1997; trans. *Pascalian Meditations* (Cambridge: Polity Press, 2000), see in particular chapter 4, "Knowing by Body." But *Le Sens pratique* is unmatched for its seamless integration of epistemological disquisition, empirical observation, and analytic audacity.
24. Pierre Bourdieu, *Le Sens pratique* (Paris: Minuit, 1980; trans. *The Logic of Practice*, Cambridge: Polity Press, 1990).

of perception, appreciation and action." But, against phenomenology, Bourdieu insists that, while being resilient and shared, these categories are not universal (or transcendental, in the language of Kantian philosophy), and that the generative matrix they compose is not unchanging. Rather, as the embodied sediments of individual and collective history, they are themselves socially constituted by historical action.

> As the product of history, habitus produces individual and collective practices, and thus history, in accordance with the schemata engendered by history. It ensures the active presence of past experiences which, deposited in each organism in the form of schemata of thought and action, tend, more surely than all formal rules and all explicit norms, to guarantee the conformity of practices and their constancy across time.[25]

Four properties of the concept of habitus suggested its direct relevancy for disclosing the social making of prizefighters. First, habitus is a set of *acquired* dispositions, and no one is born a boxer (least of all, me!): the training of pugs consists precisely in physical drills, ascetic rules of life (concerning the management of food, time, emotions, and sexual desire), and social games geared toward instilling in them new cognitive categories, kinetic abilities, and inner appetites specific to the pugilistic cosmos.[26] Second, habitus holds that practical mastery operates *beneath the level of consciousness and discourse*, and this matches perfectly with a commanding feature of the experience of pugilistic learning, in which mental understanding is of little help (and can even be a serious hindrance in the ring) so long as one has not grasped boxing technique with one's body.[27] Third, habitus indicates that sets of dispositions vary by social location and trajectory: individuals with different life experiences will have gained varied interlinked ways of thinking, feeling, and acting; their primary dispositions will be more or less distant from those required by the Sweet science; and thus they will be more or less invested in and adept at picking up the craft. This certainly accorded with my

25. Bourdieu, *The Logic of Practice*, 54, my translation.
26. Loïc Wacquant, "The Prizefighter's Three Bodies," *Ethnos: Journal of Anthropology* 63, 3 (November 1998): 325–352.
27. Loïc Wacquant, "The Pugilistic Point of View: How Boxers Think and Feel about Their Trade," *Theory & Society* 24, 4 (August 1995): 489–535.

Coach DeeDee conversating on the phone
in the backroom, timer in hand

personal experience and notations on the disparate behaviors of my
gym mates over time, as they tangled with the competing lure of the
street and the ring, adapted to the authority of our coach, and sought
to remake their self in accordance to the exacting demands of the
trade. Fourth, the socially constituted cognitive, conative, and emotive structures that make up habitus are malleable and transmissible
because they result from *pedagogical work*. If you want to pry into
habitus, study the organized practices of inculcation through which it
is layered: dissect the temporal, moral, and technical organization of
gestures, exercises, and organisms flowing in the specialized social
space devoted to its engineering.[28]

28. Loïc Wacquant, "Pugs at Work: Bodily Capital and Bodily Labor among
Professional Boxers," *Body & Society* 1, 1 (March 1995): 65–94, and idem,
"*Homines in extremis*: What Fighting Scholars Teach us about Habitus," *Body &
Society* 20, 2 (June 2014): 3–17. For a germane extension using videography, see
Jürgen Streeck, *Gesturecraft: The Manu-facture of Meaning* (Philadelphia, PA: John
Benjamins, 2009).

The "magical moment" of fieldwork that crystallized this theoretical hunch and turned what was initially a side activity into a full-blown inquiry into the social logics of incarnation was a rather inglorious one: it was getting my nose broken while sparring in July of 1989, about ten months into my novitiate. That fateful week, I had persisted in "gloving up" several days in a row, disregarding DeeDee's warning about wearing my body down; I had insisted on "mixing it up" with Anthony, a lanky middleweight with a zippy jab he was rightfully fond of likening to "a cobra bite"; and then I hid from my coach that my nose was bleeding badly after getting battered in the second round so I would get to go for a third. As a result, I was all black and blue that evening, my face throbbing with pain, with a discolored nose and eye socket, in addition to a bruised right ear, an aching left thumb, and a sore right shoulder. (On 20 July 1989, I wrote in my diary: "I'm bushed. The toughest is, after a training session like this, to wonder whether I should continue or call it quits because this time I really took it in the noggin . . . I also learned something else today: that a mouthpiece caked in dried blood smells like death." But the next morning, notwithstanding "a purple blotch under my right eye and a darkening patch on the left side of my nose" and general soreness, I mused: "Rough profession. And yet I can't wait to get to training tonight, to work the bags, to shadow-box, to feel my body in pugilistic motion").

A few days later, an alarmed Bourdieu insisted on the phone that I stop training for two months. He did not mince words: "This is an order of the faculty of medicine, not the faculty of social science." The order was easy to follow, as the pain soon grew to be downright disabling. The injury forced me to take an extended "time out" away from the ring, during which Bourdieu urged me to write a field report on my initiation for a thematic issue of *Actes de la recherche en sciences sociales* in preparation on "The Space of Sports." The result was a long article that showed me that it was both feasible and fruitful to convert the theory of action encapsulated by the notion of habitus into an empirical experiment on the practical production of prizefighters at the Woodlawn gym.[29] This article was soon amplified by more direct engagement with habitus on the theoretical front.

---

29. Loïc Wacquant, "Corps et âme: notes ethnographiques d'un apprenti-boxeur," *Actes de la recherche en sciences sociales* 80 (November 1989): 33–67, and idem, "Taking Bourdieu into the Field."

While I was carrying out my investigations on pugilism and on the vestiges of the "Black Metropolis,"[30] I was in constant contact with Pierre Bourdieu, who encouraged and guided me. Upon learning that I had signed up to learn how to box at the Woodlawn Boys Club, he had written me a note on a Collège de France card that said essentially, "Stick it out, you will learn more about the ghetto in this gym than from all the surveys in the world." Later on, as I got deeper into my immersion, he got a bit scared and tried to get me to pull back, in vain. When I signed up to fight in the Chicago Golden Gloves, he threatened to disown me, as he feared that I would get seriously hurt, before realizing that there was no need to panic: I was well prepared for this trial by fire.

Bourdieu came to Chicago thrice during this period; he visited the gym and met DeeDee and my boxer friends. I introduced him to them as "the Mike Tyson of sociology"; they welcomed him with a mix of curiosity and reverence. It was succulent to watch and listen to DeeDee and Pierre chatting casually at the foot of the ring during sparring, as two masters of their respective crafts (I learned then that a teenage Bourdieu had briefly tried his hand at boxing at his high school in southern France). During one of these visits, we hatched the project of a book that would explicate the theoretical core of his work, aimed at the Anglo-American readership, since it was on this front that there were the strongest distortions and obstacles to a fertile grasp of his models. We devoted over three years to writing that book across the Atlantic directly in English (by phone, fax, letters, and meetings every few months), titled *An Invitation to Reflexive Sociology*, in which we disentangle the nexus of habitus, capital, field, and symbolic power, and lay out the logics of their use.[31]

During those years, I led a sort of Doctor Jekyll and Mister Hyde existence, boxing by day and writing social theory by night. At noon, I would go pick DeeDee up and take him to the gym after sharing a cup of soup at Daley's, the last surviving restaurant in the vicinity, on the corner of 63rd Street and Cottage Grove Avenue. I would return home to read and write sociology, and then, in the late afternoon, I would trot to the gym, train dutifully, hang out with my ring buddies, and "conversate" on

30. St. Clair Drake and Horace R. Cayton, *Black Metropolis: A Study of Negro Life in a Northern City* (Chicago: University of Chicago Press, 1945, new ed. 1993).
31. Pierre Bourdieu and Loïc Wacquant, *An Invitation to Reflexive Sociology* (Chicago: University of Chicago Press, and Cambridge: Polity Press, 1992).

Trainer Eddie watching after his charges (from left to right, Reese, Aaron and Rico) working on the bags end with our coach in the back room before driving him home at closing time. And, much later in the evening, after having dutifully typed up my field notes, I would switch back to the manuscript with Bourdieu. It was in turns intoxicating, invigorating, and exhausting. But the daytime sessions as a hands-on student of pugilism offered both a respite from theoretical cogitation and powerful stimuli for thinking through the abstract issues tackled in the book in very mundane empirical terms. The sociology of the ghetto (which I had extended to encompass a comparison with the postindustrial transformation of the French urban periphery), the carnal ethnography of the skilled violent body, and theoretical work with Bourdieu: all these strands were elaborated together and at the same time, and they are all woven together.

The boxing project is an ethnography in a very classic mold in terms of its parameters, a sort of village study like the ones British anthropologists conducted in the 1940s,[32] except that my village is the boxing gym and its extensions, and my tribe the fighters and their entourage. I retained this structural and functional unity because it encloses the boxers and carves out a specific temporal, relational, mental, emotional, and aesthetic horizon that sets the pugilist apart, pushes him to "heroize" his lifeworld, and thereby raises him above his ordinary environs.[33] I wanted, first of all, to dissect the cloven relation of "symbiotic opposition" between the ghetto and the gym, the street and the ring, the secular plane of worldly pleasures and the sacred plane of manly ascesis. Next, I sought to show how the social and symbolic structure of the gym governs the transmission of the techniques and embodied ethics of the Manly art and the production of collective belief in the pugilistic *illusio*. And, finally, I wished to penetrate the practical logic of a corporeal practice that operates at the very limits of practice by means of a long-term apprenticeship in "the first person."[34]

32. Adam Kuper, *Anthropology and Anthropologists: The Modern British School, 1922–1972* (New York: Pica Press, 1977).
33. Loïc Wacquant, "Protection, discipline et honneur: Une salle de boxe dans le ghetto américain," *Sociologie & sociétés* 27, 1 (Spring 1995): 75–89. The attentive reader will have recognized here the constituent element of "primitive religion" according to Émile Durkheim and Marcel Mauss.
34. The merits and limits of apprenticeship in field research are discussed in Michael William Coy, ed., *Apprenticeship: From Theory to Method and Back Again* (New York: State University of New York Press, 1989). The rarity

THE 1990 GOLDEN GLOVES

ARE HERE

——PRELIMINARIES BEGIN——

FEB. 12-13-14 & 19

——SEMI-FINALS——

FEBRUARY 20 & 21

ST. ANDREWS

CORNER OF ADDISON & PAULINA

All Events Begin at 7:00 pm

FOR INFORMATION 294-2315 or 268-5104

DON'T FORGET THE FINALS

ROSEMONT HORIZON

MARCH 19

GET YOUR TICKETS EARLY!

For three years, I melted into the local landscape and got caught up in the game. I learned how to box and participated in all phases of the preparation of the pugilist, all the way to fighting in the big amateur tournament of the Golden Gloves. I followed my gym buddies in their personal and professional peregrinations. And I dealt on a routine basis with trainers, managers, promoters, and others who make the planet of boxing turn and share in the spoils of this "show-business with blood," to recall Budd Schulberg's expression.[35] In so doing, I got sucked into the sensuous and moral coils of pugilism, to the point where I seriously envisaged aborting my academic trajectory to turn professional. I was saved from the dangers of venturing further into the boxing jungle by DeeDee who, wisely anticipating that I would soon come to that fork on the pugilistic road, had forewarned me: "If I ever hear you're 'goin' downtown' [to get your professional license at the Illinois State Building in the Loop], Louie, *I'll bust your forehead an' break botha your kneecaps*, you hear me?" His humor carried a serious warning, and I heeded it.

But, as the foregoing should have made clear, the object and method of this inquiry were not of the classic mold. *Body and Soul* offers an *empirical and methodological radicalization of Bourdieu's theory of habitus.* On the one hand, I open the "black box" of the pugilistic habitus by disclosing the production and assembly of the categories, dexterities, and desires that together define the competence and appetence specific to the boxer. In so doing, I sweep away the conventional criticism that habitus is a murky notion that keeps us locked in conceptual obscurity and hampers empirical investigation. On the other hand, I deploy habitus as a methodological device; that is, I place myself in the local vortex of action in order to acquire through practice, in real time, the dispositions of the boxer, with the aim of elucidating the magnetism proper to the pugilistic cosmos. This allows me to disclose the powerful allure of the combination of craft, sensuality, and morality that binds the

of its use among anthropologists is unwittingly documented by R. M. Dilley, "Apprenticeship: Anthropological Aspects," in *International Encyclopedia of the Social and Behavioral Sciences*, ed. Neil J. Smelser and Paul B. Baltes (London: Pergamon, 2004), 604–607. Its transformative impact on the practice of fieldwork is documented by Jean Lave, *Apprenticeship in Critical Ethnographic Practice* (Chicago: University of Chicago Press, 2011).

35. Loïc Wacquant, "A Fleshpeddler at Work: Power, Pain, and Profit in the Prizefighting Economy," *Theory & Society* 27, 1 (February 1998): 1–42.

pugilist to his trade as well as impresses the embodied notions of risk and redemption that enable him to overcome the turbid sense of being superexploited.[36] The method thus tests the theory of action that informs the analysis according to a recursive and reflexive research design.

The idea that guided me here was to push the logic of participant observation to the point where it becomes inverted and turns into *observant participation*, making full involvement in the theater of action the means of parsing it. In the Anglo-American tradition, when anthropology students first go into the field, they are cautioned: "Don't go native." In the French tradition, radical immersion is admissible—think of Jeanne Favret-Saada's *Deadly Words*, not to mention Michel Leiris and his *Afrique fantôme*[37]—but only on condition that it be coupled with a subjectivist epistemology that gets us lost in the inner depths of the anthropologist-subject. My position, on the contrary, is to say, "go native," but "*go native armed*"; that is, equipped with your theoretical and methodological tools, with the full store of problematics inherited from your discipline, with your capacity for reflexivity and analysis, and guided by a constant effort, once you have passed the ordeal of the novitiate, *to objectivize this experience and construct the object*, instead of allowing yourself to be naïvely embraced and constructed by it. Go ahead, go native, but come back a sociologist![38] In my case, the concept of habitus served both as a bridge to enter into the factory of pugilistic know-how and methodically parse the texture of the work(ing) world of the pugilist, and as a safeguard against the lure of the subjectivist rollover of social analysis into narcissistic storytelling.

---

36. Loïc Wacquant, "Whores, Slaves, and Stallions: Languages of Exploitation and Accommodation among Professional Fighters," in "Commodifying Bodies," special issue, *Body & Society* 7, 2/3 (June 2001): 181–194.

37. Jeanne Favret-Saada, *Les Mots, la mort, les sorts* (Paris: Gallimard, 1977, trans. *Deadly Words: Witchcraft in the Bocage*, Cambridge, UK: Cambridge University Press, [1977] 1980); Michel Leiris, *L'Afrique fantôme* (Paris: Gallimard, 1934).

38. My position has evolved since to where I now question not just the movement of "going" (or not) but also the destination of "native": the ethnographer must not capture "*the* native point of view"—*pace* Malinowski and Geertz after him—but construct plural points of view vying for normative status in a hierarchized social space (cf. Loïc Wacquant, "For a Sociology of Flesh and Blood," *Qualitative Sociology*, 38, 1 (March 2015): 1–11, esp. 7–8).

For Epistemic Reflexivity: From Flesh to Text

Some of my critics, conflating the narrative form of the book with its analytic contents, and mistaking my work for an extension of the "study of occupations" in the style of the second Chicago School,[39] did not notice the double role that the concept of habitus played in the inquiry and even bemoaned the absence of theory in the book.[40] In fact, theory and method are joined to the point of fusion in the very empirical object whose elaboration they make possible.

Body and Soul is an *experimental ethnography* in the originary meaning of the term, in that the researcher is one of the socialized bodies thrown into the sociomoral and sensuous alembic of the boxing gym, one of the bodies-in-action whose transmutation will be traced to penetrate the alchemy by which boxers are fabricated. Apprenticeship is here the means of acquiring a practical mastery, a visceral knowledge of the universe under scrutiny, a way of elucidating the praxeology of the agents under examination, as recommended by Erving Goffman in a famous talk on fieldwork—and not the means of entering into the subjectivity of the researcher.[41] It is absolutely not a fall into the bottomless well of subjectivism into which "autoethnography" joyfully throws itself,[42] quite the opposite: it relies on the most intimate experience, that of the desiring and suffering body, to grasp *in vivo* the collective manufacturing of the schemata of pugilistic perception, appreciation, and action that are shared, to varying degrees, by all boxers, whatever their origins,

39. Everett C. Hughes, *On Work, Race, and the Sociological Imagination*, ed. Lewis A. Coser (Chicago: University of Chicago Press, 1994), chapters 1–6.
40. See my response to the (ambush masquerading as a) symposium on *Body and Soul* organized by defenders of the citadel of Chicago-style moral empiricism, Loïc Wacquant, "Shadowboxing with Ethnographic Ghosts: A Rejoinder," *Symbolic Interaction*, 28, 3 (Summer 2005): 441–447.
41. Erving Goffman, "On Fieldwork," *Journal of Contemporary Ethnography* 18, 2 (July 1989): 123–132.
42. Deborah Reed-Danahay, ed., *Auto/Ethnography: Rewriting the Self and the Social* (New York: Berg, 1997); Carolyn Ellis, *The Ethnographic I: A Methodological Novel about Autoethnography* (Orinda, Calif.: Altamira Press, 2003). The subjectivist involution of ethnography as scriptural gesture fastened onto the private person of the ethnographer reaches the point of absurdist solipsism with Norman Denzin, *Interpretive Autoethnography* (Newbury Park, Calif.: SAGE, 2013), complete with its avant-garde rhetorics glorifying the tired tropes of modernist romance (with life made up of "selves, stories, experience") as a brave new "interpretive, performative, poststructural, and politically transgressive methodology."

Busy Louie throws a left jab at Ashante during a
sparring session

their trajectory, and their standing in the sporting hierarchy.[43] The central character of the story, then, is neither "Busy" Louie, nor this or that boxer, and not even the venerable head coach DeeDee, in spite of his central position as pugilistic conductor: it is the gym as a social and moral forge, at once ensconced in and cut off from the material and symbolic structures of the hyperghetto and the surrounding metropolis. My intellectual guide here is not Carlos Castañeda and his Yaqui shamans, but the Bachelard of *Rationalisme appliqué* and of the materialist poetics of space, time, and fire.[44]

43. Loïc Wacquant, "Carnal Connections: On Embodiment, Membership and Apprenticeship," *Qualitative Sociology* 28, 4 (Fall 2005): 445–471 (response to the special issue on *Body and Soul* 28, 3, Summer 2005).
44. Carlos Castañeda, *The Teachings of Don Juan: A Yaqui Way of Knowledge* (New York: Washington Square Press, 1985, first pub. 1968); Gaston Bachelard, *Le Rationalisme appliqué* (Paris: PUF, 1949), and idem, *La Psychanalyse du feu* (Paris: Gallimard, 1938), and *La Poétique de l'espace* (Paris: PUF, 1957).

Indeed, I hold that, with this project, I did in an explicit, methodical, and above all *extreme* manner that which every good ethnographer does; namely, to give oneself a practical, tactile, sensorial grasp of the prosaic reality one studies in order to shed light on the categories and relations that organize the ordinary conduct and sentiments of one's subjects. Except that, usually, this is done without thematizing as such the role of "co-presence" with the phenomenon being studied, or by making (oneself and others) believe that this is a mental process, and not a bodily and sensual apprenticeship that proceeds at the pre-objective level before it becomes elaborated by language. *Body and Soul* offers a demonstration in action of the distinctive possibilities and virtues of a *carnal sociology* that fully recounts the fact that the social agent is a suffering animal, a situated being of flesh and blood, nerves and viscera, inhabited by passions and endowed with embodied knowledges and skills—by opposition to the *animal symbolicum* of the neo-Kantian tradition, refurbished by Clifford Geertz and the followers of interpretive anthropology, on the one hand, and by Herbert Blumer and the symbolic interactionists, on the other[45]—and that *this is just as true of the sociologist*. This implies that we must bring the body of the sociologist back into play and treat his intelligent organism, not as an obstacle to understanding, as the intellectualism drilled into our folk conception of scientific practice would have it, but as a vector of knowledge of the social world.

Body and Soul is not an exercise in reflexive anthropology in the sense intended by what is loosely called "poststructuralist" or "postmodern" anthropology, for which the return of the analytic gaze is directed either onto the knowing subject in her personal intimacy or onto the text that she delivers to her peers and the circuits of power-knowledge in which it travels, in a contradictory and self-destructive embrace of relativism.[46] Those forms of reflexivity, narcissistic and discursive, are rather superficial; they certainly constitute a useful moment in a research undertaking by helping us to curb the play of the crudest biases (rooted in one's identity and trajectory, affects, rhetorical effects,

45. Clifford Geertz, *The Interpretation of Cultures* (New York: Basic Book, 1973); Herbert Blumer, *Symbolic Interactionism: Perspective and Method* (Englewood Cliffs, N.J.: Prentice-Hall, 1969).
46. Kirsten Hastrup, *A Passage to Anthropology: Between Experience and Theory* (London: Routledge, 1995); George Marcus, *Ethnography through Thick and Thin* (Princeton: Princeton University Press, 1998).

etc.). But they stop the movement of critique at the very point where it should plow ahead, through the constant questioning of the categories and techniques of sociological analysis and of the relationship to the world these presuppose. It is this return onto the *instruments of construction of the object*, as opposed to the subject of objectivation, that is the hallmark of what one may call *epistemic reflexivity*.[47]

And here is another difference with the "egological" or textual reflexivity of the subjectivist anthropologists: epistemic reflexivity is deployed, not at the end of the project, *ex post*,[48] when it comes to drafting the final research report, but *durante*, at every stage in the investigation. It targets the totality of the most routine research operations, from the formulation of the initial problematic to the selection of the site and the recruitment of informants to the choice of questions to pose or to avoid, as well as the engagement of theoretical schemata, methodological tools, and display techniques, at the moment when they are implemented.

So *Body and Soul* is a reflexive book in the sense that the very design of the inquiry forced me to reflect constantly on the suitability of the means of investigation to its ends, on the difference between the practical mastery and the theoretical mastery of a practice, on the gap between sensorial infatuation and analytic comprehension, the visceral and the mental, the *ethos* and the *logos* of pugilism as well as of sociology. Likewise, *Urban Outcasts*, the companion book of macrosociology that draws up a comparison of the structure and experience of urban relegation in the black American ghetto and the French urban periphery, is a work of reflexive urban sociology because it ceaselessly interrogates the very categories it puts into question and into play—"underclass," "inner city," "*banlieues*," hyperghetto, anti-ghetto, precariat—to plumb the novel configurations of marginality in the city. And because it rests on a clear-cut demarcation between folk categories and analytic categories, which is for me the plinth of reflexivity.[49]

Epistemic reflexivity is all the more urgently needed by ethnographers, as everything conspires to invite them to submit to the preconstructions

47. Bourdieu and Wacquant, *An Invitation to Reflexive Sociology*, 36–46; Pierre Bourdieu, "Participant Objectivation: The Huxley Medal Lecture," *Journal of the Royal Anthropological Institute* 9, 2 (February 2002): 281–294.
48. Renato Rosaldo, *Culture and Truth: The Remaking of Social Analysis* (Boston: Beacon Press, 1987, expanded ed. 1993).
49. Wacquant, *Urban Outcasts*, esp. Prologue, 1–12, and "Revisiting Territories of Relegation: Class, Ethnicity and the State in the Making of Marginality," *Urban Studies*, 53, 6 (2017): 1077–1088.

of common sense, lay or scholarly. By methodological duty, they must be attentive to the agents they study and take seriously their "point of view." If they do their job well, they also find themselves bound to these agents by affective ties that encourage identification and transference.[50] Finally, the public image of ethnography (including, regretably, in the eyes of other social scientists) likens it to story-telling and diary-writing, if not to epic. It follows that the anthropologist or sociologist who relies on field-work must *double the dose of reflexivity*. This is what I tried to demon-strate in "Scrutinizing the Street" about contemporary trends and foibles in U.S. urban ethnography.[51] The considered target of my critique is not the three books on race and poverty that I subject to a meticulous analytic dissection (and still less their authors, who are here simply points in aca-demic space, or their political positions, to which I am utterly indifferent), but a certain epistemological posture of unreflective surrender to folk apperceptions, to ordinary moralism, to the seductions of official thought, and to the rules of academic decorum. This posture is the fount of serious scientific errors, as these errors are systematic and difficult to correct be-cause they have both ordinary and scholarly common sense on their side.

To enable the reader to experience the thrills of the apprentice boxer and to make palpable both the logic of the fieldwork and its end product required adopting a quasi-theatrical mode of writing. How to go from the guts to the intellect, from the comprehension of the flesh to the knowledge of the text? Here is a real problem of concrete epistemology about which we have not sufficiently reflected, and which for a long time seemed to me nearly irresolvable (notwithstanding the varied attempts at and discussions of formal innovation and poetic construction among anthropologists after the "Writing Culture" debates of the 1980s).[52] To

50. For an astute analysis of the methodological use of transference in *Body and Soul*, see Philip Manning, *Freud and American Sociology* (Cambridge: Polity Press, 2005); also Henderikus J. Stam, ed., "Special Section on Habitus in the Work of Loïc Wacquant," *Theory & Psychology* 19, 6 (December 2009): 707–777. For a model conversion of burning existential affect into cool social analysis, read Nancy Scheper-Hughes, *Death without Weeping: The Violence of Everyday Life in Brazil* (Berkeley: University of California Press, 1993).

51. Loïc Wacquant, "Scrutinizing the Street: Poverty, Morality, and the Pitfalls of Urban Ethnography," *American Journal of Sociology* 107, 6 (September 2002): 1468–1532.

52. James Clifford and George E. Marcus, eds., *Writing Culture: The Poetics and Politics of Ethnography* (Berkeley: University of California Press, 1986, new expanded ed. 2010). For more recent sorties, see Anand Pandian and Stuart J. McLean, eds. *Crumpled Paper Boat: Experiments in Ethnographic Writing* (Durham, NC: Duke University Press, 2020).

restitute the carnal dimension of ordinary existence and the embodied anchoring of the practical knowledge constitutive of pugilism—but also of every practice, even the least "bodily" in appearance, including sociological analysis—requires indeed a complete overhaul of our way of writing social science. In the case at hand, I had to find a style breaking with the monological, monochromatic, linear writing of the classic research account from which the ethnographer has withdrawn, and instead elaborate a multistranded prose mixing styles and genres, so as to capture and convey "the taste and ache of action" to the reader (as indicated in the original preface to the present book).

Body and Soul is written against subjectivism, against the narcissism and irrationalism that undergird "postmodern" literary theory, but that does not mean that we should deprive ourselves of the literary techniques and instruments of dramatic exposition that this tradition gives us.[53] That is why the book mixes three types of writing, intertwined with each other, but each given priority in one of the three parts, so that the reader slides smoothly from concept to percept, from analysis to aisthesis. The first part anchors a classic sociological style in an analytic mold that identifies at the outset structures and mechanisms so as to give the reader the tools necessary for explaining and understanding what is going on. The tone of the second part is set by ethnographic writing in the strict sense, that is, by a dense depiction of the ways of being, thinking, feeling, and acting proper to the milieu under consideration, where one encounters again these mechanisms but in operation, through the granular effects they produce. The experiential moment

---

53. I was inspired on this front by the bold but well-nigh forgotten book by Robert Nisbet, *Sociology as an Art Form* (New York: Oxford University Press, 1976). It is indicative of the collective lack of reflection and training on the formal and practical aspects of writing—not to mention aural, theatrical, visual, and cinematic techniques of capture and representation—that a meticulous manual for fieldwork fails to provide a panoramic engagement with issues of rhetorics in social science (Robert Emerson, Rachel I. Fretz, and Linda L. Shaw, *Writing Ethnographic Fieldnotes* [Chicago: University of Chicago Press, 1995, new ed. 2011]), while another "how-to" guide influential in American sociology reduces them to a simplistic alternative between realist, confessional, and impressionist "tales" set "in pursuit of culture" (John Van Maanen, *Tales from the Field* [Chicago: University of Chicago Press, 1988, new ed. 2011]), in full disregard of social structure, power, and the status of ethnography as multivalent discourse circulating in plural circuits of action and representation.

comes in the third part, in the form of a "sociological novella" that delivers felt action, the lived experience of a subject who also happens to be the analyst.[54]

The weighed combination of these three modalities of writing—the sociological, the ethnographic, and the literary—according to proportions that become gradually inverted as the book progresses, aims to enable the reader to understand rationally and to feel emotionally the springs and turns of pugilistic action. For this, the text weaves together an analytic lattice, stretches of closely edited field notes, counterpoints composed by portraits of key protagonists (providing competing and complementary views taken from strategic locations in the space of pugilism) and excerpts from interviews, as well as photographs whose role is to foster a synthetic grasp of the dynamic interplay of the factors and forms inventoried in the analysis, to afford the reader a chance to "touch" the beating pulse of pugilism. Here again, everything hangs together: the theory of habitus, the use of apprenticeship as technique of investigation, the place accorded to the sentient body as vector of knowledge, and formal innovation in writing. Indeed, there is no point in carrying out a carnal sociology backed by practical conversion if what it reveals about the sensorimotor magnetism of the universe in question ends up disappearing later in the prose, on the grounds that one must abide by the textual canons dictated by Humean positivism or neo-Kantian cognitivism.

Most social researchers view theory as a set of abstract notions that either float high up in the pure sky of ideas, disconnected from the nitty-gritty of the conduct of inquiry, or constitute responses to the empirical questions that the latter raises, to be discovered in the real world, as in the self-mystifying approach labeled "grounded theory."[55] This is a misconstrual of the relationship between theory and research, and of ethnography as embedded and embodied research in particular. Whether the investigator is aware of it or not, theory is always driving field inquiry because, as Gaston Bachelard taught us,

54. That clutching literary techniques to social scientific concerns can help us capture and convey the imponderable in fieldwork is shown by Kirin Narayan, *Alive in the Writing: Crafting Ethnography in the Company of Chekhov* (Chicago: University of Chicago Press, 2012).
55. Barney Glaser and Anselm Strauss, *The Discovery of Grounded Theory: Strategies for Qualitative Inquiry* (Chicago: Aldine, 1967).

"the vector of knowledge goes from the rational to the real,"[56] and not the other way around. And it must of necessity engage observation in order to convert itself into propositions about an empirically existing entity, propositions that in turn incite the ongoing reformulation of the very theory that generated them. This applies to habitus, which, like every good concept, is not an answer to a research question but an organized manner of asking questions about the social world so that the latter may answer intelligibly—in the case recounted here, a methodical plan for vivisecting the social fabrication of pugilists in their workaday world that can be fruitfully extended to plumb the making and *modus operandi* of the full diversity of social beings, be they prizefighters, painters, prophets, or professors.[57]

56. Gaston Bachelard, *Épistémologie* (Paris: PUF, 1971).
57. The analytic extension of the model and methodology applied here to pugilism to cover the gamut of human practice is sketched in the call "For a Sociology of Flesh and Blood,." *Qualitative Sociology 38*, 1 (2015): 1–11. See also the stimulative responses by Randall Collins, Victoria Pitts-Taylor, Randol Contreras, and Karen A. Cerulo (in the same issue).

A Concise Genealogy and Anatomy of Habitus

It is sometimes believed that Pierre Bourdieu is the inventor of the concept of habitus.[1] In fact, it is an old philosopheme, originating in the thought of Aristotle and of the medieval Scholastics, which the French sociologist retrieved and reworked after the 1960s. His aim was to forge a dispositional theory of action suited to reintroducing time and the inventive capacity of agents within structuralist anthropology, without for that falling back into the Cartesian intellectualism that skews subjectivist approaches to social conduct, from behaviorism and phenomenology to symbolic interactionism and rational choice theory. The notion plays a central role in Bourdieu's lifelong effort to develop a science of practice, and a correlative critique of domination in its manifold manifestations, based on the *triple historicization* of the agent (habitus), the world (social space and fields), and the categories and methods of the social analyst (reflexivity).

The roots of habitus are found in Aristotle's notion of *hexis*, elaborated in his doctrine of virtue in the *Nicomachean Ethics* (c. 350 BCE), meaning an acquired yet entrenched state of moral character that orients our feelings and desires, and thence our conduct. The term

---

1. This is asserted, for instance, by Hans Joas and Wolfgang Knöbl in their otherwise authoritative *Social Theory: Twenty Introductory Lectures* (Cambridge: Cambridge University Press, 2009).

was translated into Latin as *habitus* (past participle of the verb *habere*, "to have or hold") in the thirteenth century by Thomas Aquinas in his *Summa Theologiae* (1269), in which it acquired the added sense of ability for growth through activity, or durable disposition suspended midway between potency and purposeful action.[2] It was used sparingly and descriptively by sociologists of the classical generation familiar with the philosophy of the Scholastics, such as Emile Durkheim (who speaks of the Christian habitus in his course on *Pedagogical Evolution in France*, 1904–1905), his nephew and close collaborator Marcel Mauss (famously in the essay on "Techniques of the Body," 1936), as well as by Max Weber (in his discussion of religious asceticism in *Wirtschaft und Gesellschaft*, 1918).[3] It resurged in phenomenology, most prominently in the writings of Edmund Husserl, who designated by habitus the mental conduit between past experiences and forthcoming actions. Husserl also used as conceptual cognate the term *Habitualität*, later translated into English by his student Alfred Schutz as "habitual knowledge" (and thence adopted by ethnomethodology), a notion that resonates with that of *habitude*, as refined by Maurice Merleau-Ponty in his treatment of the "lived body" as the mute yet intelligent spring of social meaning and behavior.[4] Habitus also figures fleetingly in the writings of another student of Husserl, Norbert Elias, who muses on "the psychic habitus of 'civilized' people" in his classic study *Über den Process der Civilisation* (1939).[5]

---

2. Vernon J. Bourke, "The Role of Habitus in the Thomistic Metaphysics of Potency and Act," in *Essays in Thomism*, ed. R.E. Brennan (New York: Sheed and Ward, 1942), 103–109.

3. Émile Durkheim, *L'Évolution pédagogique en France* (Paris: PUF, [1924] 1990; trans. *The Evolution of Educational Thought: Lectures on the Formation and Development of Secondary Education in France*, London: Routledge, 1977); Marcel Mauss, "Les techniques du corps" (1936), in *Sociologie et anthropologie* (Paris: PUF, 1950; trans. "Techniques of the Body," *Economy & Society* 2, no. 1 ([1936] 1973): 70–88 (reprinted in *Essays in Sociology and Psychology: Essays*, London: Routledge, 1979); Max Weber, *The Sociology of Religion*, ed. Ephraim Fischoff (Boston: Beacon Press, 1963).

4. Edmund Husserl, *Experience and Judgment* (Evanston, Ill.: Northwestern University Press, [1947] 1975); Alfred Schutz, *Structures of the Lifeworld* (Evanston, Ill.: Northwestern University Press, 1973–1989); Maurice Merleau-Ponty, *Phenomenology of Perception* (London: Routledge, [1947] 1962).

5. Norbert Elias, *The Civilizing Process: Sociogenetic and Psychogenetic Investigations* (Malden, Mass.: Basil Blackwell, [1939] 2000).

But it is in the work of Pierre Bourdieu, who, as a keen early reader of Leibniz and Husserl, was steeped in these philosophical debates, that one finds a thorough sociological revamping of the concept designed to transcend the opposition between objectivism and subjectivism. In his hands, habitus is a *mediating construct* that helps us revoke the common-sense duality between the individual and the social by capturing "the internalization of externality and the externalization of internality"; that is, the ways in which the sociosymbolic structures of society become deposited inside persons in the form of lasting *dispositions*, or trained capacities and patterned propensities to think, feel, and act in determinate ways, which in turn guide them in their creative responses to the constraints and solicitations of their extant milieu.[6]

Bourdieu first reintroduced the notion denotatively in his youthful field studies of the nexus of honor, kinship, and power in the peasant society of his native Béarn in Southwestern France and in the Berber-speaking Kabyle settlements of colonial Algeria. In both settings, he activated habitus to capture the *discordance* between the culturally given capacities and proclivities of people and the requirements of the emerging social system, leading to historical rupture and societal upheaval—belying what would later become the rote academic tale of Bourdieu the high priest of "reproduction theory."[7] On the Béarn side, the greater ability of local girls to incorporate urban values conveyed by the school and mass media consigned the local men to bachelorhood, and thence the village society based on male primogeniture to a slow death; on the Algerian side, uprooted *fellahin* bore within them a contradictory mix of categories inherited from ancestral tradition and imported by colonization, and this "cultural sabir" (or split habitus) made them misfits in both the agrarian community and the urban economy, living supports of structural contradictions that propelled the country toward revolution.[8]

6. A lucid discussion of the ontological and epistemic status of dispositions as constituents of mind and matter, and whether they can anchor causal or functional explanations, is provided by Stephen Mumford, *Dispositions* (Oxford: Clarendon Press, 2003); for a broader panorama, see Gregor Damschen, Robert Schnepf, and Karsten Stüber,eds., *Debating Dispositions: Issues in Metaphysics, Epistemology and Philosophy of Mind* (New York: Walter de Gruyter, 2009).

7. Loïc Wacquant, "Following Pierre Bourdieu into the Field," *Ethnography 5*, 4 (December 2004): 387–414.

8. Pierre Bourdieu, "The Peasant and His Body," *Ethnography 5*, 4 ([1963] December 2004): 579–598 (also in idem, *The Ball of Bachelors*, Chicago: University of Chicago Press, [2002] 2008); Pierre Bourdieu and Adbelmalek Sayad, "Colonial

Bourdieu then elaborated habitus analytically at the turn of the 1970s through a dual critique of Sartre's phenomenology and Lévi-Strauss's structuralism in his *Outline of a Theory of Practice*. In this and subsequent writings, culminating a quarter-century later in *Pascalian Meditations*, he proposes that practice is neither the mechanical precipitate of structural dictates nor the spawn of the intentional pursuit of goals by individuals, but rather

> the product of a dialectical relationship between a situation and a habitus, understood as a system of durable and transposable dispositions which, integrating all past experiences, functions at every moment as a *matrix of perceptions, appreciations, and actions*, and makes it possible to accomplish infinitely differentiated tasks, thanks to the analogical transfer of schemata acquired in prior practice.[9]

As individual and group history sedimented in the body, social structure turned mental structure and sensorimotor engine, habitus may be thought of by analogy to Noam Chomsky's "generative grammar," which enables speakers proficient in a given language to produce proper speech acts unthinkingly according to shared rules in inventive yet predictable ways.[10] It designates a practical competency, acquired *in and for* action, that operates beneath the level of consciousness and is continually honed in the very movement of its deployment. But, unlike Chomsky's grammar, (i) habitus encapsulates not a natural but a *social* aptitude, which is for this very reason variable across time, across place, and most importantly across distributions of power; (ii) it is *transferable* to various domains of practice, which explains the rough coherence that obtains, for instance, across realms of consumption—in music, sports, food, and furniture, but also in marital and political choices—within

---

Rule and Cultural Sabir," *Ethnography* 5, 4 ([1964] December 2004), 444–486, and idem, *Le Déracinement: La crise de l'agriculture traditionnelle en Algérie* (Paris: Minuit, 1964; trans. *Uprooting: The Crisis of Traditional Agriculture in Algeria,* Cambridge: Polity Press, 2020).

9. Bourdieu, *Esquisse d'une théorie de la pratique* (Paris: Seuil, 1972, new edition 2000; rev. trans. *Outline of a Theory of Practice,* Cambridge: Cambridge University Press, 1977), 261.

10. Noam Chomsky, *Topics in the Theory of Generative Grammar* (Berlin: Walter de Gruyter, 1966).

and among individuals of the same class and grounds their distinctive lifestyles;[11] (iii) it is enduring but *not static or eternal*: dispositions are socially mounted and can be eroded, countered, or even dismantled by exposure to novel external forces, as demonstrated by situations of migration and specialized training; (iv) yet it is endowed with *built-in inertia*, insofar as habitus tends to produce practices patterned after the social structures that generated them, and because each of its layers operates as a prism through which later experiences are filtered and subsequent strata of dispositions overlaid (thus the disproportionate weight of the schemata implanted in infancy, among which the binary opposition between masculine and feminine); and (v) habitus thus introduces a *lag*, and sometimes a hiatus, between the past determinations that produced it and the current determinations that interpellate it:

As history made nature, [habitus] is what confers upon practices their relative autonomy with respect to the external determinations of the immediate present. This autonomy is that of the past, enacted and acting, which, functioning as accumulated capital, produces history on the basis of history and so ensures that permanence within change that makes the individual agent a world within the world.[12]

Against structuralism, then, the theory of habitus acknowledges that agents actively make the social world by engaging embodied instruments of cognitive construction; but it also insists, against constructivism, that these instruments are themselves made by the social world through the somatization of social relations. The situated individual "determines herself insofar as she constructs the situation that determines her," but "she has not chosen the principle of her choice," such that "habitus contributes to transforming that which transforms it."[13]

Habitus supplies at once a principle of sociation and individuation: *sociation* because our categories of judgment, sensibility, and conduct, coming from society, are shared by all those who were subjected to similar social conditions and conditionings (thus one can speak of

11. Pierre Bourdieu, *La Distinction: Critique sociale du jugement* (Paris: Minuit, 1984; trans. *Distinction: A Social Critique of the Judgment of Taste*, Cambridge, MA: Harvard University Press, 1984).
12. Bourdieu, *Le Sens pratique*, 56.
13. Bourdieu, *Méditations pascaliennes*, 177.

a masculine habitus, a national habitus, a bourgeois habitus, but also of an artistic habitus, a juridical habitus, a carceral habitus, etc., corresponding to specific institutions); *individuation* insofar as each person, by virtue of having a unique trajectory and location in the world, internalizes a unique combination of such schemata (even identical twins are separated by their order of birth and treated differently by their parents and others). Because it is both *structured* (by past social milieus) and *structuring* (of present perceptions, emotions, and actions), habitus operates as the "unchosen principle of all choices" guiding practices that assume the systematic character of strategies even though they are not the result of strategic intention and are objectively "orchestrated without being the product of the organizing activity of a conductor."[14] As a *multi-scalar construct*, habitus enables us to mate the study of the generic, capturing constituents shared across concentric circles of conditioning, with a focus on the specific, as it paves the way for a clinical sociology capable of entering into the depths of a given biohistory without reducing it into idiosyncrasies.

For this dispositional philosophy of action, in which "the socialized body is not opposed to society" but constitutes "one of the forms of its existence,"[15] the social actor is neither the isolated, egoistic individual of neoclassical economic theory, a computing machine seeking to maximize utility in pursuit of clear goals, nor a disincarnated manipulator of symbols somehow suspended above the pull of material forces, as in the neo-Kantian tradition of symbolic anthropology and the neo-pragmatist strand of Meadian interactionism. (Beyond their vitriolic opposition on the question of the ultimate supremacy of interest versus culture, these two conceptions of conduct are equally spontaneist, instantaneist, and intellectualist.) She is instead a sentient being of flesh and blood inhabited by historical necessity who is enmeshed in the world by an opaque relationship of "ontological complicity"—or enmity, as the case may be—and who is bound to others through the "implicit collusion" fostered by shared categories of perception, appreciation, and action.[16]

14. Bourdieu, *Le Sens pratique*, 256.
15. Pierre Bourdieu, *Questions de sociologie*, (Paris: Minuit, 1980; trans. *Sociology in Question*, London: Sage, 1994), 29.
16. Bourdieu, *Méditations pascaliennes*, 163.

Retracing the philosophical origins and initial usage of habitus by Bourdieu to account for the historical disjuncture wrought by the Algerian war of national liberation and the postwar modernization of the French countryside allows us to clear up four recurrent misunderstandings about the concept that the present study of the making of prizefighters further corrects. First, habitus is never the replica of a single social structure, since it is a *multilayered and dynamic set of schemata* that records, stores, and prolongs the influence of the diverse environments successively traversed during one's existence. It follows that

[a] genuine sociogenesis of the dispositions constitutive of habitus should strive to understand how the social order captures, channels, reinforces or thwarts psychic processes, depending on whether there is homology, redundancy or, on the contrary, contradiction and tension between the two logics. It goes without saying that mental structures are not the mere reflex of social structures.[17]

The malleability of habitus due to its "permanent revision" in practice is further spotlighted by Bourdieu's cardinal distinction, broached in his early research on education and class[18]—and dramatized by this author's learning of the categories, skills, and desires of the pugilist— between the *primary habitus*, acquired in early childhood through osmosis in the familial microcosm and its extensions, and the *secondary habitus*, grafted later onto the primary habitus by the specialized pedagogical labor of the school and other didactic institutions (a boxing gym, a painter's studio, a religious sect, a political cell, etc.). The result is a compromise formation that dynamically articulates generic and specific dispositions across the life cycle into an operative set of schemata.[19]

It follows, second, that habitus is *not necessarily coherent and unified*. Rather, it displays varying degrees of integration and tension,

17. Pierre Bourdieu, "Les contradictions de l'héritage," in *La Misère du monde* (Paris: Seuil, 1993; trans. *The Weight of the World*, Cambridge: Polity Press, 1998), 717.
18. Pierre Bourdieu and Jean-Claude Passeron, *La Reproduction: Éléments pour une théorie du système d'enseignement* (Paris: Minuit, 1970; trans. *Reproduction in Education, Society and Culture*, London: SAGE, 1977).
19. A stimulating study of the grafting of the generic (country-masculine) and specific (organizational) components of a concrete habitus is Matthew Desmond, *On the Fireline: Living and Dying with Wildland Firefighters* (Chicago: University of Chicago Press, 2007).

depending on the character and compatibility of the social situations that fashioned it over time. A sequence of congruent institutions and stable microcosms will tend to fashion a cohesive habitus whose successive layers reinforce one another and work in unison. Dissimilar organizations anchored by divergent values or entropic universes, by contrast, cultivate unstable systems of dispositions divided against themselves and are wont to generate irregular and inconsistent lines of action. Thus, a broken or splintered habitus was common among the Algerian subproletarians studied by Bourdieu in the early 1960s, as it was among the members of the black precariat of Chicago's hyperghetto encountered in the pages of this book.[20]

Third, habitus is no less *suited to analyzing crisis and change*, across multiple scales ranging from the individual to the largest macrocosm, than it is to analyzing cohesion and perpetuation. This is because habitus does not necessarily agree with the social world in which it evolves. Bourdieu warns repeatedly that one must "avoid unconsciously universalizing the model of the quasi-circular relation of near-perfect reproduction that is completely valid only in the case where the conditions of production of habitus are identical or homologous to its conditions of functioning."[21] That habitus can "misfire" and have "critical moments of perplexity and discrepancy" when it is incapable of generating practices conforming to the milieu constitutes a major spring of personal resistance, social innovation, and structural transformation.[22]

---

20. Pierre Bourdieu, *Algeria 1960* (Cambridge: Cambridge University Press, [1977] 1979); Wacquant, "The Craft of the Hustler." See also Bourdieu's dissection of the "cleft habitus" of Édouard Manet that "synthesized opposites," a conformist bourgeois side and a rebellious artsy side, and whose "astounding tension" propelled his artistic innovation: Pierre Bourdieu, *Manet: Une révolution symbolique* (Paris: Seuil and Raisons d'agir Éditions, 2014), 454–463 and 648–651.
21. Bourdieu, *The Logic of Practice*, 62–63.
22. Bourdieu, *Pascalian Meditations*, 191. This implies that there is no need to "supplement" the theory of habitus to cover "creative action" by contrast to reproduction (Hans Joas, *The Creativity of Action*, Chicago: University of Chicago Press, 1997), to capture the multiplicity of temporalities and structures (William H. Sewell Jr., *Logics of History: Social Theory and Social Transformation* (Chicago: University of Chicago Press, 2005, chapter 4), or to rediscover the "acting subject" alive to hidden historical possibilities (Sherry B. Ortner, *Anthropology and Social Theory: Culture, Power, and the Acting Subject*, Durham, NC: Duke University Press, 2006).

Last, and not least, it should be stressed that habitus is not a self-sufficient mechanism for the generation of action: like a spring, it needs an external trigger, and so it cannot be considered in isolation from the definite social worlds (and eventually fields) within which it operates. Moreover, the same habitus will yield different lines of conduct when called out by different strategic opportunities. The dissection of dispositions must thus proceed in close connection with the mapping of the system of positions that alternately excite, suppress, or redirect the inclinations of the agent. This two-way, dynamic, *mutual gearing of embodied and objectified social structures* is yet another source of potential transformation of both person and cosmos:

> When the objective conditions of its accomplishment are not given,
> a habitus continuously thwarted by the situation can be the site
> of explosive forces (as with ressentiment) that may await (nay
> look out for) the opportunity to exercise themselves and express
> themselves as soon as those objective conditions are offered (e.g.,
> the position of a petty boss). . . . In reaction against instantaneous
> mechanicalism, one is led to stress the "assimilative" capacities of
> habitus, but habitus is also adaptation: it constantly performs an
> adjustment to the world that only exceptionally takes the form of
> radical conversion.[23]

A full accounting of practice thus requires a triple coordinated elucidation of the social genesis and structures of habitus as historicized subjectivity, of the formation and dynamics of social space as a historical distribution of possibles, and of the situated specifics of their confrontation in the microdialectic of dispositions and positions.

For every situation, the social analyst must determine (i) the degree of *internal coherence* of habitus, that is, the extent to which its various components—cognitive, conative, affective—or its different temporal layers are compatible and integrated, or work in tension and at loggerheads with one another, and (ii) its degree of *external congruence* with the specific social world in which it is plunged.[24] These two orthogonal dimensions vary independently of one another and span a space

23. Pierre Bourdieu, *Questions de sociologie*, 135–136.
24. Loïc Wacquant, "Putting Habitus in its Place: Rejoinder to the Symposium," *Body & Society 20*, no. 2 (2014): 118–139.

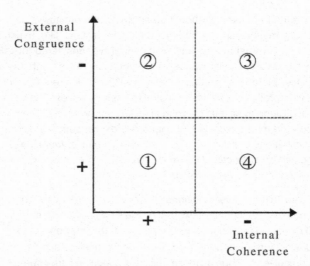

Internal coherence and external congruence of habitus:
mapping their combinations

of analytic possibilities described by the figure above. When a coherent habitus meets a congruent cosmos, the fit between mental structure and social structure, the meshing of embodied history and objectified history, is perfect and produces smooth reproduction (quadrant 1). This is illustrated by Bourdieu's study of kinship strategies guided by "The Sense of Honor" in traditional Kabylia or of the role of higher education in the perpetuation and legitimation of class inequality in 1960s France captured, appositely, by the famed title, *Reproduction*.[25] But this is only one of multiple configurations encompassed by Bourdieu's model. Quadrant 2 covers situations where a coherent habitus is discordant with the social world in which it operates: as we have seen, this is the case of the "empeasanted" peasant of Béarn who cannot keep pace with the changing taste of village girls and finds himself devalued on the

25. Pierre Bourdieu, "Le sens de l'honneur" (1967), reprinted in *Algeria 1960*) Bourdieu and Passeron, *La Reproduction. Éléments pour une théorie du système d'enseignement.*

marriage scene, causing a crisis of social reproduction and the dissolution of the village society.[26] This is also the case of every *social migrant* who travels across class, ethnic, or sexual borders to find themselves in a location where they are bereft of the proper categories of perception, such that they must learn anew the ways of being, feeling, and acting suited to their new milieu (as with the example of academics of working-class origins).

A third configuration arises when an incoherent, cleft, or torn habitus encounters an incongruent world, combining two sources of friction, disjuncture and contradiction (quadrant 3). This configuration is studied by Bourdieu in *Uprooting,* where displaced Algerian peasants bearers of a "cultural sabir" (embodying a disjointed combination of traditional values based on collective honor and capitalist values rooted in individual interest) were corralled in forced resettlement camps during the Algerian war, spawning cataclysmic social and cultural transformation.[27] The fourth combination (quadrant 4), of an incoherent habitus congruent with the social world, implies that this world itself is incoherent or splintered. The limiting case is that of social entropy caused by the double dissolution of subjectivity and cosmos, best approximated by situations of war or the aftermath of natural catastrophes. But Bourdieu suggests that this configuration also emerges in universes riven by contradictions where the agents bear these very contradictions within themselves: "Thus it can be observed that, to contradictory positions, which tend to exert structural 'double binds' on their occupants, there often correspond destabilized habitus, torn by contradiction and internal division, generating suffering."[28]

External congruence refers to the mutual compatibility between habitus and world and must be clearly distinguished from *hysteresis,* a term Bourdieu borrows from physics, which refers to the built-in lag between the forces that created habitus and their remanent effects in time.

---

26. Pierre Bourdieu, *Le Bal des célibataires. La crise de la société paysanne en Béarn.* (Paris: Points Seuil, 2002; tr. *The Bachelors' Ball,* Cambridge: Polity Press, 2006).
27. Bourdieu and Sayad, *Uprooting,* esp. chapter 6, "Town-Dwellers Without a Town."
28. Bourdieu, *Pascalian Meditations,* p. 190. Bourdieu and his associates plumb this configuration in *The Weight of the World.*

Congruence is historical and contingent; hysteresis is ontological and necessary, rooted in the makeup of every habitus. Bourdieu explains:

> Even if dispositions may weaken or waste away for lack of 'use' (linked, in particular, to a change in social position or condition), or as a result of an awakening of consciousness associated with a work of self-transformation (such as the correction of accents, manners, etc.), there is an inertia (or *hysteresis*) of habitus which have a spontaneous tendency (based in biology) to perpetuate structures corresponding to their conditions of production.[29]

To grasp the nature of hysteresis is critical to understanding how habitus always bears within itself the possibility of social disruption and change. Endowed with its own logic and dynamic, themselves the product of the sedimentation of individual and collective experience, "it is not mechanically subjected to an external causality" and thus "it gives a freedom with respect to direct and immediate determination by the present circumstances."[30] This is to say that, contrary to conventional interpretations, habitus is a vector of historicity in its own right, and its study opens the door to a *sociology of human freedom as a historical achievement* rooted in the double history of bodies entwined with institutions.

Although philosophers such as John Searle, Jacques Bouveresse, Charles Taylor, and Iris Marion Young have discussed Bourdieu's elaboration of habitus in relation to the philosophy of mind, language, and self, and neurobiologist Jean-Pierre Changeux has connected it to current developments in brain research, grounding it in our synaptic architecture,[31] it bears stressing that for Bourdieu the notion is first and foremost a stenographic manner of designating a *research posture*. Habitus puts at the heart of social analysis the genetic mode of thinking

---

29. Bourdieu, *Pascalian Meditations*, p. 190, my translation.
30. Bourdieu, *Pascalian Meditations*, p. 210, my translation.
31. John R. Searle, *The Rediscovery of the Mind* (Cambridge, Mass.: MIT Press, 1992); Jacques Bouveresse, "Règles, dispositions et habitus," *Critique*, 51 (1995): 573–594; Charles Taylor, "To Follow a Rule," in *Bourdieu: A Critical Reader*, ed. Richard Schusterman (Cambridge: Wiley-Blackwell, 1999), 29–44; Iris Marion Young, *On Female Body Experience: "Throwing Like a Girl" and Other Essays* (New York: Oxford University Press, 2005); Jean-Pierre Changeux, *L'Homme de vérité* (Paris, Odile Jacob, 2004).

as it directs us to excavate the implicit cognitive, conative, and emotive constructs through which persons navigate social space and animate their lived world. For the assembly and deployment of the socially constituted schemata that make an adept and appetitive agent are fully accessible to methodical observation and analytic parsing. Ultimately, the proof of the theoretical pudding of habitus must consist in its empirical eating.

DeeDee tries on his authentic Basque bérêt,
a Christmas gift from France

The Afterlives of Chicago Prizefighting Across Three Decades

> The only hearth at which we can warm ourselves morally is that
> formed by the company of our fellow men. The only moral forces
> with which we can nourish our own and increase them are those
> that others lend us.
>
> —Émile Durkheim, *Les Formes élémentaires*
> *de la vie religieuse*, 1912

In April of 1992, the Woodlawn Boys Club was closed by the United Way, its sponsor, ostensibly because the building that hosted it in the back as well as a day-care facility in the front was too decrepit to be maintained or repaired—but also because the new female director of the Boys and Girls Clubs for the city despised boxing as a youth activity. Coach DeeDee Armour and most of his fighters moved to the Fuller Park boxing gym, an anomic municipal facility at the heart of the historic Bronzeville. He continued to train fighters, amateur and professional, but things were never the same: Fuller Park was not *his gym*, and so he could not run it his way and impose the strict discipline he imparted to the Woodlawn club. His last distinguished pupil was the Puerto Rican Fres Oquendo, aka "The Big O," who won the WBC Latino heavyweight title on the way to a record of 37 victories and 8 defeats garnered from 1997 to 2014. DeeDee clocked in daily at the gym until the final months of his life. He died at the age of eighty after losing his bout with brain cancer. He was buried in February 2000 by a phalanx of heartbroken and loving boxers from the Woodlawn Boys Club at the Oak Woods Cemetery, only blocks from the gym.

What became of my gym mates over the three decades following the closing of the club and DeeDee's passing? How did their careers in the ring unfold and end? Where did their trajectories in social space take them? And what can we learn about the social and symbolic structures of prizefighting from an examination of their tribulations in and out of the squared circle? In this closing chapter, I tackle each of these questions in turn to flesh out the afterlives of professional boxing in Chicago into the twenty-first century.

What They Became after the Woodlawn Gym Closed

The alumni of Woodlawn have mostly stayed in touch with one another; some have remained buddies, train together into their fifties, know each other's children, and consort regularly in the gym. Others are loosely linked by the boxing grapevine even when they have moved away from the game. A few communicate intermittently via Facebook. When I contacted them to retrace their peregrinations over the past thirty years, they were uniformly excited to recap and reflect upon their life for this new edition of *Body and Soul* and joyful to reactivate the bonds of brotherhood we developed back then. Much as in the glory days of the Woodlawn Boys Club, ring talk and lore serves well to divert and distract us from the humdrum of everyday life.[1]

Trainer Eddie is pushing sixty-three and has continued to mold fighters nonstop to this day. He is currently heading the Davis Square Park gym in the Chicago neighborhood of Back of the Yards, working as an instructor for what he snidely calls the "Crooked Park District" (i.e., the Chicago Park District, renowned for its murky and convoluted patronage regime: "It's all about politics, it's all about who you suck up to"). He supervises high school and college students at his city park facility and works corners as a cutman for local professionals, a craft he learned from the expert Jim Strickland (see *infra*, p. 164). In the 1990s, after the U.S. Steel mill where he worked as a furnace operator closed, Eddie plied his craft at Fuller Park until he was hired in 1997 as a full-time trainer by Don King Productions, the country and the world's leading boxing firm, owned by the inimitable and controversial mogul

---

1. I was unable to track down one Woodlawn alumnus, and another one did not respond to my entreaties (communicated through an intermediary). When possible, I triangulated the responses of my gym mates in our interviews with information gleaned from their peers, former trainers, and promoters. I gathered factual information on their ring careers on the boxing registry Boxrec.com (see the presentation, *infra*, p. 366).

Don King.[2] He spent a decade working with top-ranked boxers and contenders from 8 a.m. to 6 p.m., six days a week, at King's training camp in bucolic Orwell (population 1,660) near Youngstown, Ohio, "a million-dollar camp" hosting two dozen top professional fighters and up to fifteen trainers at any one time, complete with two gyms, sleeping quarters, a spacious TV room, kitchen, and dining room.[3] There he got "to work with other trainers from all over the world"—in sharp contrast with Chicago, which "holds you back, because it's real political"—and he enjoyed the countryside, the food, "learning different cultures" from his fellow trainers, and "being around the Amish people" from a nearby settlement.

Eddie got to "live the life, five-star hotels, the best meals" when he "broke camp" to go on the road with fighters promoted by Don King, for whom he wrapped hands (a delicate operation and highly prized responsibility) and worked corners ("I took all my teachings from Woodlawn with me"). He traveled extensively to boxing venues around the country and made sorties to Berlin and Belfast. Eddie maintains that there is a good side to Don King that the public does not get to see: "He's a *businessman*, and he's real cool to be around, he's just a regular person. Then, Louie, all the *bad stuff* they write about him, I seen him save people from losin' their houses, losin' their cars. I seen it, I'm a witness to that. I done seen him feed homeless people, ex-fighters, that he had, he seen that they not doin' so good, he look out for them." Eddie stopped working for Don King in 2007, despite the "very decent" salary with all expenses paid, because the work was week-to-week and did not

2. King rose from the streets of Cleveland, where he ran the "policy game," to the top of the boxing world, amassing a fortune estimated to exceed $150 million. His checkered past includes two homicide convictions and stints in Ohio prisons, the production of "The Rumble in the Jungle" (the 1974 Ali-Foreman face-off in Zaire), and the sponsorship of myriad world champions in the 1980s and 1990s (including Mike Tyson, Evander Holyfield, Julio Cesar Chavez, and Roy Jones Jr.), from whom he is reputed to have stolen tens of millions of dollars. He has been the target of multiple federal investigations and criminal indictments related to his boxing business, but has always managed to avoid conviction (when necessary by buying off jurors). His flamboyant style, vertical hair, poetic tirades, manipulative skills, and financial misdeeds are the stuff of legend. He is the topic of several biographies, including Jack Newfield, *The Life and Crimes of Don King: The Shame of Boxing in America* (New York: Harbor Publishing, 2003), which was adapted into the Emmy-winning 1997 documentary movie, *Don King: Only in America*.
3. On the distinctive social, economic, and emotional makeup of training camps, see Thomas Hauser, *The Black Lights: Inside the World of Professional Boxing* (New York: McGraw-Hill, 1986).

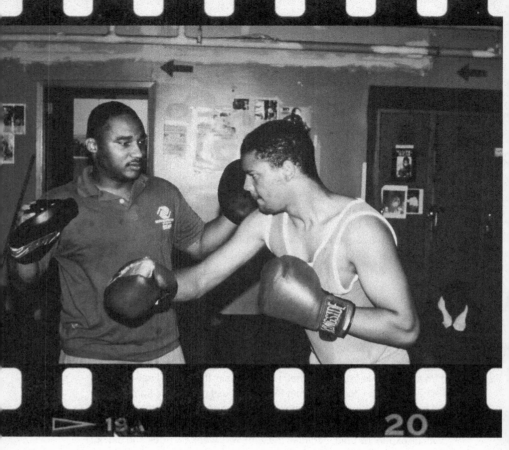

Eddie makes the young amateur Rico work on the pads

include medical insurance, and so he eventually returned to Chicago for the security of a municipal job with benefits.

Eddie has one son who owns a small trucking company; he did not teach him boxing because his son was into body-building. He is being considered for induction into the recently established Illinois Boxing Hall of Fame, but he is incensed that this local pantheon does not include DeeDee, and he would refuse to enter it before his long-time mentor— matchmaker Jack Cowen rues this oversight, confirming that this hall is "a joke, it's ludicrous, it's stupid, it's all their friends and relatives and whatever, DeeDee would have to go in" if only it was run properly. In his free time, Eddie studies old boxing films. He is full of wistful memories of his Woodlawn days and especially of coach DeeDee, whom he often evokes with other old-timers from the city's gyms: "Every time I pass on 63rd, man, the memories come back, me and DeeDee goin' down to

Daley's [restaurant], coming back to the gym. . . . He was like a second father, he mentored me in being the trainer that I am. He discussed with me how to deal with individuals in boxing, to work with attitudes, a boxer's physical abilities, to adjust to each boxer because everybody got a different style, you can't train every fighter the same way. . . I *loooved* Woodlawn. The steel mill and boxin', that was my life man! I loved the people there, the gym, learnin' the trade, and we was real busy, and *we showed unity*: wherever we went we showed unity. . . . And they took your fight at the Gloves, you beat that kid, man!"

Curtis fought live on national TV in the resort city of Deauville, France, in November 1990 against Jacobin Yoma, the French champion in the junior lightweight division; in Atlantic City against the no. 6 world-ranked South African November Ntshingila in April of 1991; and against Olympic champion and superstar-in-the-making Oscar De La Hoya in February of 1993 on ABC's Wide World of Sports (the video of the bout is on YouTube). He lost all three fights, two on points and the last by TKO due to a deep laceration over his right eye in the fourth round, after agreeing to fight an opponent five pounds over the weight limit for a bigger purse (a $5,000 bonus negotiated at the weigh-in the morning of the bout, a thousand dollars per excess pound, added to the purse of $20,000). Curtis went on to work for several years as a sparring partner at the training camps of world contenders and champions (among them Joe Gamache, Oscar De La Hoya, and Georgie "Go Go" Navarro) all over the United States, from Lake Tahoe, Nevada, and Portland, Maine, to Big Bear, California, and Las Vegas, Nevada, as well as in France and Germany: "No I didn't like bein' a sparrin' partner, but I know how to use my hands and it was keepin' money in my pocket—I had to make a livin' right?" The salary of $150 a week, all expenses paid, covered the bills; but the hope of being slotted on the undercard of televised fights never materialized, despite what Curtis recalls as dominant performances in training ("I'm whoopin' asses like I was the main fighter"). He hung up his gloves in 1999 at thirty-two after a thirteen-year stint with a record of 16 victories (10 by KO), 10 defeats (2 by KO), and 2 draws.

Curtis put an end to his ring career because "it was no use, it was going nowhere," and he was distraught by the passing of coach DeeDee, who was an anchor of his life. He soon returned to the gym in the 2000s to train his teenage son Christopher, who won the Chicago Golden Gloves before competing in the Olympics tryouts. But Curtis would not let him "turn pro" because "Chris wasn't real about it" and "he liked girls too much," so that he would not obey the occupational

KODAK 5076 28

▷ 27A 28

DeeDee gloves up Curtis for the day's sparring session

ethic of "sacrifice" needed to succeed between the ropes.[4] When his son stopped boxing, Curtis stopped going to gyms and tournaments. Reflecting on his boxing days, he muses: "I loved it because it was easy for me, it was fun, it was *a joy*, it was like a release. I never had no stress inside of me, cuz I know I'm gonna go to the gym and hit that speed bag, jump some rope, or get in there sparrin' and get out all my flustrations [*sic*] or any kind of anger that I had built inside." To this day he misses the gym: "I miss all the heathen friends I had, I miss all-of-y'all [he picks out the names of a half-dozen regulars]. It was the best gym in the world! I 'member when Muhammad Ali came to the gym. I mean shit, he was the reason I started boxin'. And then bein' in the ring with him!"[5]

Curtis does not regret putting on the gloves even though his professional venture did not bring him the material rewards he had hoped: "I'm supposed to be rich, I'm not s'posed to be livin' like this man. I'm s'posed to be famous an' shit. I mean, with all this talent that I had—you seen it withchyour own eyes. I shoulda been five times world champion" (later in our conversation he quips: "You seen I have the talent, why didn't you try to promote me in France?"). He maintains that he wasn't "built" and "moved" properly with opportunities to face adversaries of increasing grade to gain experience and progress in the professional rankings. He wasn't "kept busy" fighting regularly (he contrasts his fourteen victories to the hundred-odd wins of Marty Jakubowski, the Indiana titlist he clashed with in 1996). He has no doubt that he was mismanaged by Jeb Garney, who had money but no strategic knowledge or social capital in the fistic business. They parted without a word in the mid-1990s: "I just

4. The three tenets of "sacrifice" are strict prohibitions on food, social life, and sexual activity; see Loïc Wacquant, "Sacrifice," in *Body Language*, ed. Gerald Early (Saint Paul, Minn.: Graywolf Press, 1998), 47–59, and *supra*, pp. 67–68. These "negative rituals" aim to "actualize the state of separation" of the boxer from the profane world, "the system of prohibitions swelling and aggrandizing itself to the point of invading the whole of life." Émile Durkheim, *Les Formes élémentaires de la vie religieuse* (Paris: Presses Universitaires de France, [1912] 1985), 445.
5. Muhammad Ali owned a mansion in nearby Hyde Park-Kenwood and, in his late forties, sometimes came to the Woodlawn Boys Club to work out (he knew DeeDee from back in his amateur days), creating a joyful commotion in and out of the gym. The latter would quickly fill up with entranced people from the neighborhood told of Ali's presence by eyewitnesses to his coming. On his last visit, in September of 1990, a bus driver diverted his bus from Cottage Grove Avenue to come park in front of the gym and unloaded his ravished customers to come hail the GOAT (Greatest Of All Time). Jimmie Kitchen was there with his camera to immortalize the scene, including that of an elated Curtis shadow-boxing in the ring with Ali in his rubberized sweat suit (see page 312).

An elated Curtis shadow-boxing in the Woodlawn ring
with Muhammad Ali

walked away, he wasn't payin' me no salary anyhow, everythin' went
south." He does not know anything more about his former manager.

Curtis struggled to find and keep employment during the
1990s: getting a job is difficult in the city, he insists, because "it's all
politics, it's all about who you know." He bemoans the complication of
the application process, with its multiple forms, required resumes, background checks, and drug tests (even though he has no criminal record).
After the gym closed, the former heavyweight champion Ernie Terrell, a
lifelong friend of DeeDee's, hired him at his cleaning firm as a janitor for
the city's school district. But he was let go after a year when business

I

slowed down. He then worked on and off as a laborer on construction sites—where he met his second wife, Stephanie, who was a site coordinator (and whom he knew since sixth grade). Curtis married her in 1998, but when she suddenly passed away in 2007, he was distressed ("when you lose somebody you become a different person"), and he went back to live with his mother: "That was a thing I never thought I would have to do. I thought I prob'ly have my mom an' them [his brothers] livin' with me, *buy them* a home—'cause I was a world-class fighter." He worked for six months at the counter of a pizza outlet where the employees ribbed him mercilessly about his missed opportunities in the ring. His big break came in 2000 when, thanks to the personal recommendation of his priest, he landed a job as an assistant clerk for the Circuit Court of Cook County in the downtown Loop.

The job at the court is stable—Curtis has held it now for two decades—and it comes with benefits, but the pay is meager (in the mid-$30,000 range) and barely enough to make ends meet. "It keeps me going, I enjoy the commute with other people, I get to socialize with people and just the idea, wakin' up in the mornin', I have a responsibility to go to work and pay my bills," including a monthly rent of $950, a car note and expensive motor insurance, not to mention that he maxed out on his sole credit card. He shops at a nearby Dollar Store, buys household necessities in bulk, and stays frugal, spending his free time at home watching television. Still, he is living "paycheck to paycheck." So three years ago he bought a secondhand Chevy (for a down payment of $1,500) and started driving for Uber. When he finishes his day job at the court, he rushes home, washes up, and jumps into his car for up to eight hours of driving at night.

Curtis attends mass punctually every Saturday at St. Philip Neri Church, the same church he has gone to for all of his adult life. He credits his faith for keeping him on the straight and narrow through thick and thin: "I worship my Savior, we have a relationship. I ain't the best person in the world but I ain't the worsest. Every day I learn, he takes me through my trials and tribulations." He has used his faith as a bulwark against the temptations and dangers of the street: "I never introduced myself to that lifestyle: I don't do drugs, I don't mess with homosexuals and stuff . . . I'm not gonna sell no drugs, go out and rob nobody, kill nobody, go out there and carjack somebody, that's not even in my background, I'm a *alien* to that lifestyle . . . I don't know how to live on the street, I don't know how to hustle. I don't wanna lead that life, I'd probably get killed. . . . I'm already labeled as a bad guy because of my *pigmentation*, you know how it is Louie, how they treat African

Americans: from the day I came outa my mother's womb I was marked as a bad guy. . . . If I can't make it honestly, I don't do it."[6]

His three children—Chris (who finished high school and works as a birthday party organizer), Mimi (a stay-at-home mother with two years of community college), and Mercedes (who finished high school and runs a West Side grocery store with her boyfriend)—have eight kids of their own between them. They have all moved to the far suburbs to escape the seeping violence and failing public schools of the South Side. Curtis has shown his grandchildren, boys as well as girls, how to box, "so they don't get bullied at school." He is excited about the pugilistic potential of his nine-year-old grandson little Chris: "I'm gonna teach him how to fight way before he even start to wanta smell a female. He gonna be a awesome fighter, it's like he was born to do it, it's how good he is" when his grandfather drills him into throwing jabs and right crosses into the palm of his hands.

Curtis lives in a modest one-bedroom apartment near a shopping mall in East Side, a predominantly Hispanic neighborhood marred by high street crime at the southern edge of the city, near the Chicago Skyway. The first thing you notice upon entering his place is the boxing paraphernalia and mementos: "I sit back and I look at my trophies, my belt and my medals and my pictures, I got them on top of my mantle in my living room. When people walk in they see my trophies, I got one-two-three [he enumerates them aloud . . .] nine of them. And I got pictures of Joe Louis up there, I got my pictures with Ali, with [world featherweight titlist] Juan Laporte, [world super-welterweight champion] Terry Norris. . . I still got my gloves, I have my hand pads, my boxin' shoes, my shorts, my robe." More than the material accoutrement of his past trade, Curtis lives with the ghostly and loving memory of coach DeeDee: "DeeDee is the greatest person I ever known, he was my father. He taught me everything, how to be gentleman in and out of the ring. . . . He knew how to train me, how to keep my balance, how to step into my punches, shorten them up. Remember, *he birthed me*, he *designed me* to his likin'. . . . You know of all the fighters [at Woodlawn] I was the closest one to DeeDee . . . I was seventeen years old when he

---

6. The historical foundation for this prevalent sentiment is discussed in Loïc Wacquant, "Race as Civic Felony," *International Social Science Journal* 57, 183 (2005): 127–142.

took me from there on. I *loooved* him. I told my [second] wife, 'I want you to meet my father.' This man taught me so much, he was always there for me. Before they put me on employment with the Boys and Girls Club [as a janitor for the gym], DeeDee used to give me money and stuff. Cuz he seen that I was *persistent*, he seen that I had the *talent*, everythin' he told me to do I would do it, without hesitation . . . DeeDee was raisin' me, he was tellin' me, stay calm, stay out of trouble 'cuz if you have a bad name don't nobody wanta mess with you."

When he goes through a rough patch, Curtis is too proud to ask his children for financial support, but he gets occasional help from his sisters to cover his bills. He remembers with a touch of bitterness the days when he was (momentarily) flush with the monies from his fights and could show largesse toward his kin. "Everybody doin' good, no news is good news. But the guy that was promised to *go up* to make somethin' of his self, and that's me. Everybody had *high hopes* on me makin' it: I was gonna be the one to break the ceilin' an' stuff and bust out with all this money an' stuff, and be rich and famous and bring everybody along with him. And that didn't happen." Curtis wishes that I would come back to Chicago and set up a nonprofit to open a gym where he could be the head coach: "If I get my own gym, I know I can get some world champions."

In the fall of 1989, "Ashante" fought in Mabopane near Pretoria against an ascending South African boxer with a record of 10 wins and 1 loss to fulfill his lifelong dream of seeing "the mother country," for a measly purse of $5,000, the biggest of his boxing life. His career crashed after he lost two more close fights in a row against rising welterweights, fights that he took injured (a broken jaw suffered in sparring) or unprepared, solely for the money (another $5,000 for each fight). Following those defeats, Ashante worked as a sparring partner in Marseilles, France, in 1992, but he injured his left eye and he turned down later invitations to training camps in France and Germany because "you're like a punching bag." After the gym shut down, he had only one professional bout, closing out his eight-year career in 1993 with a record of 9 victories and 4 defeats, for a total of 65 rounds in the squared circle.

Ashante stopped fighting but he did not officially retire, and for years he kept thinking and talking animatedly about returning to the ring, insisting that his fight experience and personal maturity would put him in a favorable position. He credits boxing with nothing less than saving his life: "It gave me a *option*, I ain't gotta to be on the street *hustlin'*, I don't gotta *gang bang*." His main regret is that he did not follow DeeDee's

Ashante shadow-boxing in the ring

advice to stay in the amateur ranks for another year or two. At the time, the enthusiastic cheers of his buddies, the entreaties of would-be managers, and the lure of "gettin' my mother a house and a car" proved too strong and he turned professional prematurely. In addition, when Chicago matchmaker Jack Cowen asked him, "You want me to *build you up* or you want to *make some money?*," his answer was, "I got five kids, I wanta make some money." So, instead of being "fed" safe "opponents" to gain experience and accrue a record in the long run-up to lucrative fights, he took tough fights out of town for the quick purses.[7] Much to DeeDee's ire, he was even offered a bout against ring legend Julio Cesar Chavez at the peak of his form (87 victories and zero defeats) for a paltry purse of $10,000, but the fight fell through when Ashante broke his jaw in training for the second time. He is wistful about it: "Ten thousand dollars, man, that woulda been nice. I know if I don't win I'm gonna look good, somebody gonna see somethin' in me."

When his ring career tanked, Ashante fell back on a combination of insecure, short-term employment ("what I call slave jobs") and illegal activities in the street economy. He was hampered in his job search by his prior criminal convictions, which he had to hide in order to pass through the hiring stage, but which would automatically lead to his swift dismissal (on grounds of having lied on his application) whenever his employer ran a periodic background check of the workforce. The litany of precarious jobs ("temp-temp-temp") he has held include laborer in a bakery and in a pizza factory, material handler and loader in warehouses, security staff, janitor at O'Hare Airport and the downtown Navy Pier, hospice health aide, nursing home assistant, laundromat attendant, and the gamut of short-term, low-skill, degraded and degrading work (mostly warehouse, moving, and cleanup work) furnished by day-labor agencies.[8]

Most of these jobs lasted a few weeks to a few months; none of them came with benefits (health care, sick days, paid vacations, pension) and promotion prospects; they were not even covered by unemployment insurance. By far the best pay he received was twelve dollars an hour, and most work paid less than half that rate. Not to mention that he was the victim of systematic "wage theft": many of his employers paid less than the legal minimum and routinely underdeclared the number of hours he

---

7. By making quick money his priority and forgoing the route of "sponsored mobility," Ashante accepted that he would be offered bouts against superior opponents (especially out of town, where you may have to knock your adversary out to guard against a "hometown decision" on points) designed to "build" their career. The difference between sponsored and contest mobility in the boxing economy is discussed *infra*, pp. 346–347.

8. Day labor was the most accessible form of employment for ex-convicts during that period because, unlike the majority of low-skill employers in the city, they did not run criminal background checks. See Jamie Peck and Nik Theodore, "Carceral Chicago: Making the Ex-Offender Employability Crisis," *International Journal of Urban and Regional Research* 32, 2 (2008): 251–281; and Gretchen Purser, " 'Still Doin' Time': Clamoring for Work in the Day Labor Industry," *WorkingUSA* 15, 3 (2012): 397–415.

worked. In addition to harsh working conditions, Ashante's restiveness toward authority created difficulties with his supervisors as well as tension with his coworkers, whose pliability he despised: "They be Uncle Toms, boot-lickin' all day, I just can't deal with certain characters, certain type of personality." To pay the rent and raise his younger son (the oldest was staying with his mother after they split), Ashante dove back into the criminal economy, which he knew well from his younger days as a gang member who had "juice" on the street. But the freedom from supervision and easy money generated by illegal activity (he grossed over $8,000 a month) came at a high human cost: he served three stints in prison, on sentences of three and six years for narcotics offenses and two years for mail fraud (in addition to the six years of the twelve-year sentence he served for armed robbery prior to coming to the gym, during which time he earned his General Education Diploma and got initiated to boxing).

For the past decade, Ashante has spent the brunt of his free time at Trumbull Park, a city gym run by Woodlawn mate Rodney: "I'm livin' at the gym, it's *my sanctuary*. I love the gym." He trains a half-dozen amateurs for the love of the game, some of whom have won local tournaments: "I *love trainin'*, cuz the knowledge I got from DeeDee I'm passin' on to these kids. Make them do somethin' positive with their life, teach 'em discipline, teach 'em how to get in shape." He attends amateur tournaments about town but not professional cards due to the high cost of tickets ($35 for general admission, $120 for a ringside seat). He was not successful in teaching the Sweet science to his two sons: Shortman is tough (he recently got shot twelve times in a murder attempt and survived, barely), but he got caught up in the street life due to the nefarious influence of a gang-member uncle ("this is what I regret, not putting him in the gym like I should have"); Aaron showed promise as an early teen ("he was kickin' butt in the gym" when he was ten), but he soon fell in love with basketball instead ("he quit on me, he broke my heart: he told me he don't wanta get hit in the face, he's got pretty-boy complex"). The oldest left school in the tenth grade and toils in an Amazon warehouse while waiting to get disability pursuant to his near-death shooting; his other son graduated from high school and migrated to Hammond in nearby Indiana to escape the dangers of the streets; he stays at home to take care of his two daughters while his girlfriend works as a bank teller.

Ashante is nearly blind in his left eye, due to traumatic cataracts he attributes to the injury he suffered while working as a sparring partner in Marseilles thirty years ago. The promoter in charge of the training camp wanted to send him back to the United States when his eye got as big as a tennis ball, but Ashante needed the money so he "toughed it out" and continued sparring daily for over a week. He is due for surgery soon ("that will be a blessin' on me"). He also hurt his shoulder on one his many factory jobs, and his weight has fluctuated wildly over the years, from 160 to 250 pounds (he used to fight at 147 pounds on a 5'6" frame). Over the years, Ashante has shared lodging and its cost with brothers, nephews, and work mates "from the plantation" (the pizza factory where he toiled for a year) as well as young trainees from the gym in whom he sought to instill discipline ("you're going to school or you're going to work"). He has changed residence and come close to eviction thrice in the past decade.[9] He now resides alone in a room he rents out for $250 on 113th Street near State Street, on the city's far South Side, but the cranky old lady landlord who lives in the building is making his life impossible. More than ever, the gym is his real home: "It's *still* my sanctuary. I feel safe. It give me peace of mind and it give me a chance to interact with young black males like myself and put 'em on the right road. Them young kids, they need a big brother, they need a father, they need a uncle: *that's me.*"

Anthony "Ice" (who also fought under the ring moniker "Poison") had accrued 16 contests when I left the gym, for a record of 8 victories, 7 losses, and 1 draw in three years. He became a regular "opponent" on the national and international circuit—skilled enough to give a good account of himself without getting hurt, and defensively minded so that he would not threaten a superior adversary.[10] He went on to fight an extraordinary fifteen more years, retiring in October of 2006 at age forty-two with a final record of 32 victories (12 KOs), 78 defeats (5 KOs, all of them TKOs, where the referee stops the contest), and 6 draws, for an astronomical total of 821 rounds in the squared circle (for comparison, Mike Tyson finished his career with 50 wins and 6 losses but fought only 215 rounds). His fights were set up by matchmaker Jack Cowen— "he was Jack's number one 'opponent,'" reports one trainer—and he was managing his own career. Boxing allowed Anthony to travel widely, with forty-three fights overseas in Canada, France, Andorre, Mexico, Scotland, England, Germany, Denmark, Ireland, Puerto Rico, Italy, Hungary, Ukraine, and Finland. He also worked as a sparring partner

9. On the prevalence, causes, and destructive impact of housing eviction in the hyperghetto, see Matthew Desmond, "Eviction and the Reproduction of Urban Poverty," *American Journal of Sociology* 118, 1 (2012): 88–133.

10. In boxing lingo, an "opponent" is a serviceable boxer who is regularly "fed" to superior fighters in order to "build" the latter's record in pursuit of higher-level contests and purses. He is dispatched to boxing cards on the national and international

at training camps in Hamburg, Lyon, Moscow, Monte Carlo, Mexico City and Kingston, Jamaica. In these foreign lands, he made a point of visiting the best martial arts schools, rather than tourist sites ("I'm here for business, not pleasure").

Fighting overseas against local prospects or contenders allowed Anthony to collect purses in the thousands of dollars, with peaks in the $10,000 range; the highest purse of his career was the $15,000 he garnered for fighting the welterweight world titlist Jamaican Simon "Mantequilla" Brown (who was 35 and 2 at the time, while Anthony was 10 and 11) in Las Vegas in August of 1992. Matchmaker Jack Cowen reminisces: "He got robbed so many times! Anthony was a very very good boxer, but he threw very few punches, it wasn't hard to steal a fight from him. He enjoyed fighting, he always made fairly decent money, he never got hurt, never got beat up."[11]

Anthony leads an ascetic existence guided by his Muslim faith and works out daily in the gym at age fifty-six. He also teaches daily boxing classes and trains a half-dozen pro fighters at the Sam Colonna Boxing MMA and Fitness Club, the city's premier gym, where he has solidified his reputation as one of Chicago's top trainers. He has taught the game to his three sons, Antonio, Gazi, and Azziz, two of whom fought with distinction in the amateur ranks. With his accumulated ring earnings and the sage guidance of his second wife, who is a skilled money manager and a follower of Minister Farrakhan like him, he purchased and rehabilitated several buildings on the South Side of Chicago,[12] including

circuits with little if any hope of victory. He often travels without cornermen. To endure, opponents have to be reliable, fight hard, and give a good account of themselves in the squared circle (they are not "divers," "bums" or "tomato cans"), even as they take beat-downs and run up long losing records. At its lower edge, the category shades into that of "journeyman" (see *supra*, p. 195, and *infra*, pp. 346–347).

11. This remark is both self-serving and implausible: no matter how skilled the fighter, the sheer accumulation of punches received during 116 fights could not but take a severe physical toll (see *infra*, pp. 332–333).

12. Minister Louis Farrakhan is the fiery, enigmatic, and controversial leader of the Nation of Islam, at the crossroads of religion, black nationalism, and racial politics. He is viewed as a dangerous bigot and anti-Semitic demagogue by his detractors and as a prophet of black dignity and separatism by his followers. Arthur J. Magida retraces his extraordinary social, intellectual, and political trajectory in *Prophet of Rage: A Life of Louis Farrakhan and His Nation* (New York: Basic Books, 1996). A nuanced theological and ideological account of the Nation of Islam is Mattias Gardell, *In the Name of Elijah Muhammad: Louis Farrakhan and the Nation of Islam* (Durham, N.C.: Duke University Press, 1996).

ED 200

> 4A
Anthony in his corner between rounds during
a fight at the Aragon Ballroom

a two-story house and a half-dozen condominiums that he rents out. In 2008, Anthony and his wife, Sandra, founded a renovation and decoration company, which Sandra manages; it works with four subcontractors to refurbish derelict housing units for the Chicago Housing Authority and repaint schools for the city. It also has maintenance and service contracts with a number of city-run homes for the elderly. As a result, Anthony has achieved a level of material success that is the envy of his gym mates, and he is a veritable whirlwind of action, always busy, always on the go. Anthony and Sandra reside in a quiet condominium near Lake Michigan in the black bourgeois neighborhood of South Shore. He insists that he is in good health and in good shape: "I'm like a average person, I'm not beat up. I'm thankful, steady working, never stop." His existence is well encapsulated by the message on his answering service: "Peace be unto you, this is coach, brother Anthony, the contractor, please leave me a message, peace."

Alfonzo professional career in the cruiserweight division spanned the period 1980–1989. Thanks to his devastating punch, he ran up thirteen victories before losing to Tim Witherspoon, and another three victories before losing to Pinklon Thomas, both of whom went on to briefly hold world heavyweight titles. As a condition of "getting a shot" at the world title, Alfonzo was forced to sign with Don King's son as his manager and to fight a boxer also managed by Don King's son on a card promoted by Don King. This led to a split with DeeDee that was never repaired, to the eternal chagrin of both parties. Alfonzo did win the WBO cruiserweight world title from Carlos de Leon on a split decision in June 1985 in Las Vegas (for a purse of $150,000, half of which was skimmed by Don King; the fight is on YouTube), but he lost it only three months later to Bernard Benton on a unanimous decision. A year later he fought a young brash heavyweight by the name of "Iron" Mike Tyson (undefeated in 26 bouts with 24 KOs at the time, he would go on to win the world heavyweight crown in his next fight two months later). Like nearly all of Tyson's adversaries, Alfonzo "froze up" and lost by TKO in the second round (the fight can be viewed on YouTube). "I wasn't really ready when Don King presented that fight to me, but I had to take what was comin' my way, cuz I'm dealin' with gangsters. I broke my hand before the fight. . . . If I had two hands, Tyson would have never beat me, I would have to beat myself." The purse for the bout was $175,000 but Alfonzo took home only $35,000: Don King billed him for the costs of training camp and took his cut as promoter, while King's son took another cut as the manager of record. Alfonzo went on to win four of nine fights before hanging up his gloves for a final tally of 25 victories (18 KOs) and 9 defeats (6 KOs).

When the Woodlawn Boys Club closed, Alfonzo moved to Memphis, Tennessee, where he lived and labored for four years at a pharmaceutical factory for GlaxoSmithKline, before returning to Chicago to take care of his ailing parents. He married for the third time; his latest wife is a pastor who runs two churches, which Alfonzo attends regularly ("I forget their names, sometimes I forget my name"). After working as a

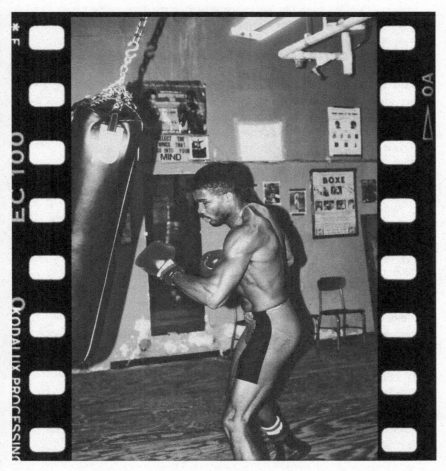

Alfonzo working on the hard bag

baker in a bread factory, a head coach for the gym attached to his wife's church, and a personal trainer and membership sales associate for the Chicago Health Club, Alfonzo found his economic niche as a carman for Amtrak Railroad, after being hired there as a cleaner ("it was a blessing from God"). He worked at this solid unionized job (making over $50,000 a year) for sixteen years and is now retired from the railroad at sixty-five. He has six children, including five sons, none of whom boxed because their mothers opposed them getting hit in the head.

Reflecting back on his boxing days, Alfonzo reveals to me a secret that only DeeDee knew (the old coach actually shared it with me back then): when he was nineteen, trying to stop a killing on the street, he was savagely stabbed in the arm; his injuries were so severe that the doctors envisaged amputating him. They saved his limb but he suffered permanent nerve damage and a claw hand such that he could not punch hard with his right hand. He spent all his years in the ring fighting as a one-armed boxer, unbeknownst to his opponents.[13] Alfonzo does not follow prizefighting any more, but he did get caught up in the local media uproar following the death of boxer Patrick Day in a Chicago ring in 2019 (an event to which I return in closing). "To me a boxer is *a noble person*. When I go in the ring an' that bell ring, I don't think I'm goin' out to hurt nobody, I don't think I'm gonna kill that man. I got a family and a wife and he do too. So when I hear 'bout fighters bein' bums it pisses me off."

Alfonzo keeps a special place in his heart for DeeDee's gym: "What I liked about the Woodlawn Boys Club is *the spirit* that was in that club, it's *like family*, it's just like goin' to the church. I came in Woodlawn as a boy and when I left I left as a man. DeeDee was like my daddy, I had a father but I never was as close to him as I was to DeeDee. When he took a likin' to you, he was all in for you." Alfonzo has no regrets about stepping into the square circle: "Nah-nah-nah-nah, *the gloves kept me alive*, without the gloves I wouldn't be alive today, they kept me out of trouble [prior to finding the gym, he had served four years of a twelve-year sentence for armed robbery]. I was the typa guy that I had a lotta energy and

13. Boxers fighting despite disabilities kept secret is part of the lore of the craft. Heavyweight world champion Joe Frazier was nearly blind in his left eye following a training accident early in his career. He hid his impairment to avoid getting his boxing license revoked and learned the eye chart by heart to pass the prefight physical examination. He adapted his distinctive attacking style of constant "bobbing and weaving" to keep his good eye fixed on his opponent. When pressed by his inner circle about the health risk he was taking in the ring, Frazier famously retorted: "I would rather be rich and blind than poor and blind." Mark Kram, *Smokin' Joe: The Life of Joe Frazier* (New York: HarperCollins, 2019), 244.

I didn't know how to channel it. When I was introduced to the gym it was the best thing that happened to me cuz I started somethin' that I really really loved. *I love boxin'*: it's man to man, techniques for techniques, skills for skills, will for will."

Lorenzo "The Stallion" T. ran up twenty straight victories and fought for the WBO junior welterweight world title in 1992 (he lost by TKO in the sixth round) and then for the WBO welterweight world championship a year later (he lost by unanimous decision in his opponent's "backyard"

Lorenzo getting ready to spar

of Belfast), for modest purses of $30,000 and $40,000, respectively—his former manager reports that he took those fights "on a low budget." He closed out his fifteen-year professional career in 2003 with a loss in a minor title bout (IBU world welterweight) and a record of 34 wins (14 KOs), 4 defeats (2 KOs), and 1 draw.

Lorenzo never realized his earnings potential in the ring because, according to a former friend, "he couldn't give up that street life, as the years went by he just didn't want to stop. Hey, can't tell a grown man what he gotta do." Unbeknownst to his gym mates, Lorenzo was leading a Doctor-Jekyll-and-Mister-Hyde existence, openly diligent in the gym and secretly embroiled in the drug economy on the street. This caused him to miss fight opportunities for big purses (he could have fought the Nicaraguan world champion in the middleweight division, Ricardo "El Matador" Mayorga, for a reported $150,000). Lorenzo broke with his trainer in 2002 and slowly sank into criminal activities, eventually serving five years in the penitentiary for narcotics trafficking. He is now suffering from a motor neuron illness similar to Lou Gehrig's disease (amyotrophic lateral sclerosis), likely caused by his clashes in the ring, even though he was stopped only twice on technical knockouts. Lorenzo's trajectory illustrates well the continued contradictory pull of the ring and the street in the career of boxers.

Ed Smith, better known as Smitty (or Smithie), fought as a professional from 1984 to 1990 and accrued a record of 8 victories (5 KOs), 4 defeats (all by KO), and 1 draw. He faced two world-ranked cruiserweights at Harrah's Casino in Atlantic City and lost both bouts (I accompanied him and DeeDee for the second one, which gave me a good insider's view of the casino fights). He put an end to his career due to a severe tendinitis in the left shoulder, which made it excruciatingly painful to throw jabs. Having previously been a professional football player in a minor league with the Chicago Blitz, he knew to listen to his body. It was time to exhale and move on to a different phase in his life: "I cut it out before it cut me out. I had a good career, I wasn't someone that was *punished* in the game, I knew what I didn't want to be a part of, I managed myself, and then I proceeded on with my life—I had my options. I fought the best and I defeated the best. I have nothin' but good feelings 'bout boxin'."

Smitty's ambition upon retiring from the ring was to found a gym, with the goal of "helpin' other people, developin' lives, so they can become into great people, developin' a positive talent," similar to the counseling he was doing on his job as a mental health technician (working in public hospitals,

Smitty in action during a
"main event" at Harrah's
Casino in Atlantic City

Butch skipping rope
in a meditative mood,
as always

private clinics, and correctional agencies). But he could not find the funding for it, so he tried his hand at promoting professional fights, investing his own money into the venture. He put on three shows in his hometown of Gary, Indiana, and assisted fighters for a few others, but the economics of the venture just did not pan out. Now that he is securely retired from his job after three decades in counseling, he keeps busy with his family (he has four daughters, none of whom he introduced to boxing—"they're too pretty for that"—and ten grandchildren), and he recently launched a business consultancy, called "Be Your Own Boss" (byoboss.org), aiming to promote inner-city enterprise via network marketing and motivational training.

Smitty has kept fond memories of his time in Woodlawn; he relished its camaraderie, its home feeling, and being a leader in the gym and a model for its younger members. "I remember your fight in the Gloves, I was yellin' like *I was in the fight*. You put forth, you came back and I think you won that fight. You worked hard, you believed in yourself and you went in there *with guts*, without question, with your vehicle of *determination*, you tore off your rearview mirror, you tore off your brake pedal, and put your foot to the gas. And you put forth the skills that you learned." He explicates the boxer's complex relationship to his craft and its lure with a trademark parable: "It's like bein' in an affair with a woman who *hates you*, but she's right there in life *with you*, and you have to watch her cookin' and you have to watch her attitude, and you gotta watch your back—but *you love her anyway* [chuckles]. You're fooled by how pretty she is, okay, and the lies that she tells you, and you know that they're lies, but guess what, you wanta believe them anyway. . . . It is a *love affair* that's givin' you a whole *buncha pain*, a whole *buncha agony*, but it looks *so good* to you, okay, and it lies to you *so well*. . . . But *guess what*: if I had to do it all over again, *I would*."[14]

Firefighter Wayne "Butch" Hankins boxed "pro" from 1985 to 1997 and compiled a record of 12 victories, 3 losses, and 1 draw. He fought for

14. I discuss the roots of this constitutive ambivalence of *libido pugilistica* in Loïc Wacquant, "The Pugilistic Point of View: How Boxers Think and Feel about Their Trade," *Theory & Society* 24, 4 (1995), esp. pp. 519–524. The feeling of a captive and nefarious love is conveyed by some of the essays in Carlo Rotella and Michael Ezra, eds., *The Bittersweet Science: Fifteen Writers in the Gym, in the Corner, and at Ringside* (Chicago: University of Chicago Press, 2017). The dualities of love and hate, euphoria and dysphoria, salvation and ruination, in pugilistic infatuation expresses the fundamental "ambiguity of the sacred," according to Durkheim. This ambiguity is rooted in the polarity between the sacred positive, which is auspicious, pure, and saintly, and the sacred negative, which is disastrous, impure, and sacrilegious, and the ever-present danger of the transmutation of the one into the other. Émile Durkheim, *Les Formes élémentaires de la vie religieuse*, Book III, chapter 5, 584–592.

the Illinois state light heavyweight title and for the WBO Intercontinental light heavyweight title but, to his eternal chagrin, lost both bouts: "All I wanted is one of those belts, Louie, and it didn't happen." He retired from firehouse duties at the end of the 2000s and opened a barber shop on 103rd Street. He still lives in the South Side home that his wife and he owned back in 1990. He is now an avid chess player, competing in tournaments all over Chicagoland.

"Rockin" Rodney ran up a record of 25 wins, 13 defeats, and 3 draws between 1988 and 2003, fighting five times in Las Vegas, twice in France, and once in Germany. His first defeat came at the hands of Olympian Kelcie Banks in his twelfth fight. He won the Illinois super lightweight title from his stable mate Curtis Strong in the summer of 1992, and again five years later against a local pug with a record of 17 victories and 19 defeats. During the last decade of his ring career, he supported himself working part time for Lakeside Maintenance Company cleaning office buildings downtown ("I always been a worker"). He was also employed as a sparring partner in the gyms of major promoters in Las Vegas; he is proud to have crossed gloves with world champions Donald Curry and Floyd Mayweather.

For the past twenty years, Rodney has been on the city payroll as head coach for the Trumbull Park boxing gym on the Far South Side (where Curtis used to train his son and Ashante hangs out). At any one time, he oversees a dozen amateurs and a handful of professionals as well as a rotating gaggle of kids from the neighborhood. He lives with his old trainer and the latter's daughter, to whom he is engaged. None of his four sons have boxed because "they ain't choosed to do it, they had no interest at all, they want the women"; the only one who had taken to his pugilistic teaching early was shot dead in a gang confrontation in his late teens. He was the only one of his children involved in the street culture. Rodney himself has never been in trouble with the law, because he had "a father that was a disciplinarian, he didn't play, I didn't wanna get in no trouble *with him*." As for boxing, it definitely enriched his life: "It keep me out of trouble, I traveled, I seen a lot of people, it gave me a chance to *see the world*, get out, away from the neighborhood. Hey, I have no regrets. I fought for twelve rounds in my life, I got three belts at home, I'm a four-time Golden Gloves champ. . . . I'm happy that I made it through without gettin' hurt or punch-drunk."

Little Keith ("Minicannon") competed in the professional ranks in the lightweight division for only three years, starting in 1989. With the financial support of his black manager Oscar (a self-made entrepreneur running a midsized tile company), he spent his last active

"Rockin' " Rodney after his third victory at the Park West, flanked by his managers Elijah and Oscar

Little Keith waiting for his bout to be called at the Park West

year in Las Vegas, where he worked out at the gym of famed trainer Roger Mayweather with fighters from around the country. It portended to be a good move for his career: sparring there was a lot more intense ("there is no goin' light" when partners do not know each other personally as they did in Chi-Town), boxing shows were more frequent, and preliminary bouts paid better ($200 a round as against $50 in Chicago). But chances to rise up the pugilistic ladder did not come to pass. In all, Keith won 7 contests and lost 3, including three fights on the night's undercard in Vegas (two against the same Salvadoran adversary who had 11 victories for 2 defeats only six months apart). In his last bout, Keith broke his hand in the first round and suffered a serious eye injury in the second, so that the contest was ended by the ring doctor in the third. When he received medical advice that he should no longer fight, he called it quits on the spot and took the first flight home from Vegas.

Landing in Chicago "poor and broke," Keith returned to the minimum-wage job he had held prior to his Vegas sojourn as a delivery driver for the *Chicago Tribune* newspaper. And he cut himself off from the boxing world entirely: "I ain't talked to nobody, I tried to get away from the sport as far as I could, cuz I was hurt" that prospects for professional success had not materialized (the biggest purse of his career was $800 for a four-rounder broadcast on ESPN, the country's leading sports cable network). He fell into a deep depression for three years that induced him to contemplate suicide until "the Lord re-came into my life." He moved on to work as a driver for a payroll company and a security guard. The latter job led him to a church where he apprenticed in the ministry, and in 2009 he became a pastor. Keith wedded Gladys, a dialysis technician, that same year, much to the glee of his former trainer: "When Keith was young, we never seen him with a girl, *never*. And when he got married, me an' the guys was shocked. *We was shocked but we was happy*." Together they subsidize a small church with a dozen members, the Harvesting Hearts Christian Center on 106th Street and South Wentworth, for which they recently found a building and whose community roots they hope to grow.

Four years ago, Keith got on Facebook and reconnected with some of his gym mates from Woodlawn. He reminisces: "DeeDee really was a *true trainer* and then he cared about me and us that was there. I 'member when I walked in the gym with my Mohawk, he holler, '*not you, kid!* I didn't expect this from you!' . . . I have no regrets at all [that

I boxed pro], I'm glad I did it, it was a great experience, you can't beat it, especially meetin' the people I met. And the sport itself is great. The injury is not a problem, I knew the risk that I was takin'. It could be serious injuries like brain damage, all of that was there—but *the reward outweigh the risk.*" Still, what tugs at him is that "I had the opportunity to achieve somethin' as opposed to come back to nuttin'. I went from bein' round people that had millions of dollars, bein' driven in a limo an' seein' all this fame out there to comin' back home to where I'm by myself havin' nuttin'." This disappointment was intensified by the feeling that he had let down his Chicago manager Oscar (who was footing the bills) and his Vegas trainer. Before Oscar sold his tile company to retire in his native Texas, Keith and his wife visited him at his mansion in the posh suburb of Country Club Hills: "I thanked him, I'm grateful for the opportunity he gave me to do somethin' with my life."

∎ A "practical gamble" in the ring

Prizefighting is like playing roulette with a body especially enskilled and inured for confrontation between the ropes. The odds of success are minimal, but for those enmeshed into the sensual and moral coils of pugilism, getting into the ring is what Erving Goffman calls a "practical gamble—the willful undertaking of serious chances"(1). The notion that "the rewards outweigh the risks" and that serious corporeal harm can be avoided by dutiful training and polished ring technique is a common view among Chicago pugs, who hold an instrumentalist conception of the body and are well apprised of the various injuries they risk, for the simple reason that they experience many of these ailments firsthand and commonly come across colleagues and old-timers who suffer occupational disabilities in gyms and at boxing shows (2). These injuries include crushed knuckles and broken hands, cracked ribs, bruised kidneys, pericardiac damage, dislocated shoulders, cervical spine fissure, facial lacerations, facial contusions and nerve damage, mouth and lips cuts, chipped teeth, fractured jaws, flattened and broken noses, cauliflower ears and punctured eardrums, shattered cheekbones and Adam's apple, eye and brain trauma, not to mention chronic neuralgia, carpal bossing, osteoarthritis, and the various ills associated with extreme weight loss to make the "fight weight" (boxing in a state of acute dehydration can cause blurred vision and mental disorientation as well as heat syncope and heat stroke, and it increases the likelihood of kidney damage, brain bleeding, and brain concussion) (3).

Injuries in the ring are a normal event in the life of the prizefighter, although estimates vary across sources. An examination of 524 fights in Nevada between 2001 and 2003 revealed that 17 percent of boxer-matches entailed an injury; an Australian retrospective study of some thousand professional bouts across the 2000s found an injury rate of 24 percent; a similar survey using medical records for 550 fights in Canada for the same decade turned up a prevalence of 50 percent, the most common injuries being contusions, concussions, and lacerations, with 44, 10, and 9 percent, respectively. Spectacular knockouts in fights understandably garner the most public attention (and indignation), but the sheer accumulation of punches across bouts as well as in training, causing "sub-concussive" head injury, is more insidious and concerning, considering that the force of a mid-sized professional boxer's punch is roughly comparable to being hit with a six-kilogram bowling ball travelling at 32 kilometers an hour (4).

The most serious long-term physical damage to pugilists is likely *inflicted not in the fight but in sparring in the gym*. The head-guard boxers wear in sparring is designed to protect the eyes and ears and to prevent facial cuts, while larger padded gloves cushion against hand injuries; but neither lessens the severity of the blows, whose impact is determined by the rotational acceleration of the brain upon impact (indeed, *ceteris paribus*, wearing a head-guard increases the number and velocity of the punches that connect, as it creates a larger target, shrinks the visual field of the boxer, and adds strain on the neck). Unlike other contact sports such as American football and rugby, the recent public concern over chronic traumatic encephalopathy (CTE) in boxing is not new but merely the rediscovery, under a new name, of the "punch-drunk syndrome" (*dementia pugilistica*) first identified in 1928 by the forensic pathologist Dr. Harrison Martland and well documented for a full century, not least in the stunning descent of the legendary Muhammad Ali into Parkinsonism (5).

The cumulative brain damage suffered by boxers depends on several pugilistic factors: the length of their careers (as measured by the total number of rounds fought more so than the number of bouts), the incidence of kayos and technical kayos suffered, the vigor and frequency of sparring in the gym, and most importantly their body make and correlative strategic style in the ring: "brawlers" or "sluggers" (who tend to be short and stocky) and "pressure fighters" (who constantly walk up to their opponent) are willing to "take punishment" to get close to their opponents, whereas "boxers" or "boxer-punchers" (who are mostly tall and lanky with longer arm reach) use movement and technique to avoid in-fighting and strike from a distance. The former have a much shorter ring life, but any boxer, no matter his style, can see his bodily capital sharply devalued, even annihilated, by a single ferocious fight, win, lose, or draw (6).

Two to three decades after they hung up the gloves, most of my gym mates from Woodlawn insist that they are in good health—indeed, they typically volunteer the information before I get to ask it, as if there was doubt already hanging over the matter. They maintain that they beat the odds, getting out of the trade before they got seriously hurt, and that they have kept their wits about them. But, by definition, a former boxer suffering from cognitive decline, one of the markers of chronic brain trauma, is the last person to be able to make a reliable self-diagnosis (and it would be unbecoming of the sociologist to record his subjective impressions on such a touchy topic).

1. Erving Goffman, "Where the Action Is," in *Interaction Ritual: Essays on Face-to-Face Behavior* (New York: Pantheon, 1967), 149–270, citation p. 181. Among "practical gambles," Goffman lists boxing as one of those "spectator sports whose performers place money, reputation and physical safety in jeopardy all at the same time" (174), and he notes: "Different individuals and groups have somewhat different personal base-lines from which to measure risk and opportunity; a way of life involving much risk may cause the individual to give little weight to a risk that someone else might find forbidding" (157–158).
2. The techniques of neutralization boxers deploy to submerge this awareness are discussed in Loïc Wacquant, "Pugs at Work: Bodily Capital and Bodily Labour among Professional Boxers," *Body & Society* 1, 1 (1995): 65–93, esp. "Risk, *illusio* and *collusio*," 82–89.
3. For a medical overview, see Robert C. Gambrell, "Boxing: Medical Care in and out of the Ring," *Current Sports Medicine Reports* 6, 5 (2007): 317–321; Henry Clausen,

Paul McCrory, and Vicky Anderson, "The Risk of Chronic Traumatic Brain Injury in Professional Boxing: Change in Exposure Variables over the Past Century," *British Journal of Sports Medicine* 39, 9 (2005): 661–664; and Mayur Jayarao, Lawrence S. Chin, and Robert C. Cantu, "Boxing-Related Head Injuries," *The Physician and Sportsmedicine* 38, 3 (2010): 18–26.

4. See Shaun Rudd, Peter Lewis, and Michael Wang, "Should We Ban Boxing?," *British Medical Journal* 267 (January 2016); also Gregory H. Bledsoe, Guohua Li, and Fred Levy, "Injury Risk in Professional Boxing," *Southern Medical Journal* 98, 10 (2005): 994–999; Barry D. Jordan, "Chronic Traumatic Brain Injury Associated with Boxing," *Seminars in Neurology* 20, 2 (2000): 179–186; and David M. Erlanger, "Exposure to Sub-Concussive Head Injury in Boxing and Other Sports," *Brain Injury* 29, 2 (2015): 171–174.

5. See Abhinav R. Changa, Robert A. Vietrogoski, and Peter W Carmel, "Dr. Harrison Martland and the History of Punch Drunk Syndrome," *Brain* 141, 1 (January 2018): 318–321; and Tris Dixon, *Damage: The Untold Story of Brain Trauma in Boxing* (Boston, Mass.: Hamilcar Publications, 2021).

6. In 1973, "Smokin'" Joe Frazier (who was the epitome of the "slugger," while archrival Muhammad Ali was the personification of the "boxer") lost his heavyweight world crown to a young and hard-punching George Foreman in two brutal rounds during which he was knocked down three times in each round. The bout was elected "Fight of the Year" by *Ring Magazine*. Frazier was never the same fighter or the same man afterward.

After leaving Woodlawn alongside Keith to train and fight in Las Vegas for two years at the Top Rank Gym (run by the eponymous promoter), Tony "The Rock" came back to Chicago in 1990. He ran up a string of four victories but decided to hang up his gloves in 1995, with a final record of seven victories and two defeats, because his ring career "didn't really work out the way we wanted it to." He never left the gym and transitioned to training amateur fighters, clocking in daily at the Trumbull Park city gym, run by his Woodlawn mate Rodney, where he also works out to this day and keeps in tip-top shape—he texts me a picture to prove it, and he is right.

Upon his return from Vegas, Tony worked for thirteen years as a truck driver for CSX, a rail-to-truck transport company, then four years as an armed security guard for Prudential Security on the far South Side (a solid job with medical benefits). At about the same time, he also picked up security work for the Chicago school district. At the high school he patrolled, Tony challenged the kids who got involved in tussles on the street to come with him to the gym: "If you really believe you can fight, *let's see you in the ring.*" For the past decade, Tony has worked for

Home Medical Solutions delivering and installing medical equipment (hospital beds, oxygen tanks, bariatric products) in nursing homes and private residences. Ironically, the job does not provide medical benefits. Tony is not married but has five children ages twelve to thirty-seven. He resides with the younger two in a small apartment in Englewood, a derelict neighborhood of the South Side with the highest homicide rate in the city: "*They* call it a war zone, but it's a typical way of life that I grew up with, so we look at it as just a regular neighborhood [we both chuckle]. You be dodgin' bullets. To stay away from a lot of that, I go in the gym." His three sons all graduated from high school but went no further; they played football in their teens and showed no interest in boxing, even though Tony was at the ready to teach them. "Boxing was something that was *in my blood*, that I truly loved and wanted to do. But I raised my sons to do whatever it is they wanted to do and I support them." The two older ones now work as a roofer and a sports physical therapist, while his oldest daughter is a legal secretary going to night school to become a paralegal.

Throughout the years, religion has been and remains his guiding light: "I coudn'ta done the things I've done without religion. I feel that the Man upstairs gave me the skills an' gave me the confidence to believe in me, to give me the strength, to keep me movin'—and if I kept movin', I could become champion of the world one day. [earnestly] I became a Park District champion, I became a Golden Gloves champion, I became a CYO [Catholic Youth Organization] champion, I became a Prairie State Games champion, so if I could become them kindsa champions, *hey*! *Who says* I can't become champion of the world one day? I just felt like this was my path. If God didn't direct me that way, I don't know where I would be. I'm proud of my life, of my teenage years, my adult years. I never been in and out of jail and nothin' like that. That's because I stayed in the gym from the time I was in high school till now. It kept me focused in a way."

Even though he did not reach his goal of being a professional champion, Tony is not bitter like his mate Keith. "When I look back on my boxin' career I don't have any regrets, 'cause I felt that I was good enough to end up in Las Vegas, boxin' at the Top Rank Boxing gym. I trained with Mike Tyson, I trained with Buster Douglas, I trained with Donald Curry, I trained with Roger Mayweather. I trained with a lotta professional fighters and champions, and it was an experience that *I wouldn't change it for anything in the world*." Similarly, he would take Woodlawn over any other club: "Woodlawn was the kinda gym, either you had to come in there tough or we *made you tough*. And if you didn't have what it took, we still tried to teach you and give you that confidence to box. Everybody was on the same accord, everybody help each other to be successful." The gym was also an island of safety in a sea of dangers: "The people who was comin' to the gym, we had the same thing on our minds an' we had the same goals, and they wasn't about the street life. And if they *were* about street life, they didn't bring it into the gym, and we didn't let that come into our gym. And we made sure that everyone that came was okay and safe. *Same thing with you Louie!*"

Tony is especially fond of the special pedagogy of the head coach of Woodlawn: "DeeDee was a fantastic trainer, he did not have to get up and train you: he can talk to you and tell you what you need to do, and then he'll sit there and *watch you*. And just like he talk to you, *you talk to the next person* and tell them what do to and how to do it. And he watched to see if we was doin' it right or doin' it wrong. He was the first trainer that I ever met and he was the best trainer I ever met." Even in the world-renowned gyms of Las Vegas, "couldn't nobody teach us the way DeeDee did. And he put confidence *in us*, that we can succeed. And if we do it in the gym, we could do it *outside of the gym*. And I will cherish that for the rest of my life, most definitely."

Veteran boxer Bernard Hightower had a record of 7 victories and 0 defeats in the cruiserweight division when he put an end to his pro career after only two years in 1987. He frequented the gyms for another decade to keep in shape and enjoy the company of pugs. He retired from his job as an X-ray and CAT-scan technologist at Cook County Hospital in 2013. He remained active on the pugilistic scene into the 2000s as a judge at amateur and professional shows (he officiated for eighty-nine professional bouts) and as an amateur referee. One of his two sons had a few amateur bouts but did not go further. Bernard himself opted out of pro boxing because fight opportunities were too few and far between: "I kinda felt like I was overtrained and underpaid. I would be in the gym every single day and I would get a fight every 5 or 6 months." At the same time, he was finishing his education as a radiology technician, so "here's a fork in the road: do you want to be paid every four–five months or every two weeks? I had somethin' to fall back on and typically a lotta the guys didn't."

Turning to the amateur fighters of the Woodlawn Boys Club, "Mighty" Mark gave up the uncertain dream of "turning pro" in 1993 for the safety of steady employment with a downtown bank, where he landed a job walking off the street and rose from lockbox clerk to wire investigator to customer service representative to portfolio manager. For

Chears wins the Golden Gloves title
in the super lightweight division

the past thirty years, he has been happily married to Laura, who works
as a secretary at an alternative school for troubled children. They reside in the black middle-class suburb of South Holland near the Indiana
border with their four children, three girls and one boy, ages fourteen
to twenty-two. Mark has taught them all how to fight and occasionally

spars with them ("they all got good hands"), but none of them boxes competitively. At age fifty-three, he works out three times a week at the Hammond boxing gym, where he also trains a dozen amateurs and five professionals who keep him plugged into the local boxing scene. Last but not least, Mark is an ordained minister ("I felt the call to spread the Gospel") who offers weekly marriage counseling at the Friendly Temple Church of God in Christ on 77th Street and State Street. He does not find it difficult to square his faith with boxing: "I'm on the Peter side of the Gospel. Boxing you're not supposed to use your skills outside the ring, boxing is more so of a game. I teach the same thing, don't fight out on the street, use the things you learn inside [the ring] to stay calm." Every so often he wonders: "What if I would have turned pro? What would my life be had I done that? But I won't say regrets because sometimes I see people who are *worse for the wear*. I think I did right to take the route that I did take. Who knows: I coulda been a champion but, then again, I coulda been in a wheelchair [chuckles]."

The two Harris brothers, Rico and Reese, did not turn professional either. They both joined the army and left Chicago; the former trekked to Los Angeles where he was stationed and his tracks get lost, and the latter became a policeman and married in Virginia. Ashante, who knew their mother well (their father was in prison) reminisces: "Reese was dangerous, he used to come to the gym with a gun, he was a *dan-ge-rous* lil' kid—I call him a time bomb, I'm glad he went into the army."

"Boxhead" John was working for Anthony's company as a laborer on housing rehabilitation sites when he died from a heroin overdose in 2008; his body was found, badly decomposed, in a back alley. There were no funerals in Chicago, as his family took his remains back home to Mobile, Alabama.

Matchmaker Jack Cowen (who steered club prizefighting in Chicagoland out of his Hyde Park home office on the 29th floor of a tower overlooking Lake Michigan) kept busy through the 2000s, putting together cards, recruiting boxers in the Midwest, and renting them out across the country and the ocean (in Western Europe and South Africa).[15] Until, shockingly, his license was revoked and he got banned from boxing in Illinois following accusations of financial mismanagement of the Chicago Golden Gloves. As a result, he wound down his operations and turned to his second passion, horse racing, which gets his heart pumping and on which he enjoys wagering small sums of money.

15. The complex craft and controversial character of the matchmaker in the boxing economy are elucidated in Loïc Wacquant, "A Fleshpeddler at Work: Power, Pain, and Profit in the Prizefighting Economy," *Theory & Society* 27, 1 (1998): 1–42.

Jack Cowen at work setting up fights in his home office

Looking back at his long career, what stands out to Jack is "the fact that I traveled and was able to make matches all over the world. It was intriguing to take two people and to make attractive matches, matches that are competitive." He could have done without the managers, many of whom were personally insufferable and ignorant about the game, or both; what he relished was the challenge of sizing up fighters to anticipate their ring trajectory: "You really never know. If a fighter can fight at all he should win his first half-a-dozen fights. And then comes a point in his career that you got to decide: is this a possibility of being a champion, is this a good main-event fighter, is this just a club fighter, just a guy maybe if he has a few fights he ought to quit? It's an individual thing once you get into it." Jack's fondest professional memory is making shows for South African promoter Cedric Kushner, with whom he traveled and grew to be close friends. His worst is dealing with fight cards down in Mississippi, where the boxing commission was perennially inept, the officials unreliable, and the fighters no less erratic. His favorite fight cities were New York City and Copenhagen, the latter because the people there treated him kindly and they all spoke English.

In his last decade on the pugilistic scene, Jack traveled regularly to foreign countries, to nurture his ties with local promoters, often alongside Anthony: "I never took my 10 percent from him, his purse wasn't cut in ten different ways. I liked Anthony, he always worked hard, he kept a job," and his wife managed his ring earnings conservatively: "He's a great guy, he came out with a little money." But the foreign market for American opponents shrunk as Western European promoters turned to recruiting pugilists from Romania, Bulgaria, and post-Soviet republics who competed for less money without the added expense of a costly transatlantic flight. Has the Muhammad Ali Act passed by Congress in 2000 to protect fighters from the corrupt practices of promoters had any impact on the game at the local level? Not that Jack noticed: "A couple of articles in the press, that's about the size of it." Particularly glaring was the failure to create a federal boxing commission capable of enforcing minimal economic, health, and safety standards on the patchwork of state commissions entrusted with licensing the game, which are often criminally inept.[16] The Illinois commission is "ran by somebody

---

16. J. Bradley Clair, "Why Federal Preemption is Necessary to Create Uniform Professional Boxer Safety Standards," *Brooklyn Law Review* 73 (2007): 1173–1208. Since 2000, the Muhammad Ali Act requires fighters to furnish a Federal Identification Card that includes a passport photo and bodily characteristics (including tattoos and scars) to prevent boxers from fighting under aliases and escape supervision. Boxers who are forbidden to fight due to medical reasons are put on a federal suspension list that a state commission is required to consult before licensing a bout.

who knows as much about boxing as I know about atomic energy," and in Wisconsin, "you could license your pet dog up there."

The growing availability and transparency of boxing information fostered by the Internet (discussed *infra*, pp. 366–367) have not eliminated the need for a deft middleman, conversant with both boxing and business, and capable of tailoring the supply of skilled bodies to the demand for fistic entertainment. To make suitable matches requires a precise and current knowledge of the record, stance, style, physical build, ring diligence, and reliability of individual boxers, and the worth of the fighters they faced: "Sometimes a guy's who's 20 and 0 is not as good as a guy that's 5 and 10, it all depends on who the opponents were. . . . You have guys, they don't even try to win, they just show up," and then others who do not even show up and have to be substituted at the last minute "by some guy they find on the street or in a bar, or one of the security guards."

The matchmaker does the "dirty work" of converting pain into profit by commercializing that most sacred of objects, the (masculine) body, so that consumers may enjoy a pugilistic spectacle, while taking his cut of the action.[17] For this reason, he is the object of suspicion, opprobrium, and sometimes aversion among boxers, regardless of his personal character and the scrupulousness of his transactions. Fighters commonly liken him to a pimp, a slave driver, or a racehorse owner. Privately, and with the distance of time, some Woodlawn alumni vituperate Jack, calling him the gamut of epithets from "crook" to "motherfucking rat." It is a rare boxer who gives him credit for helping their career in the ring, but one of them insists, "Jack has never mismatched a fight for me. All my fights, win or lose, I coulda won. I ain't never been overmatched. Oh, he's *exploitin' people, that's not the question*. [forceful] That's *life, that's the American way*. Gittin' what you can get off somebody's back: I don't fault him totally cuz if he wasn't doin' it, *someone else be doin' it*. Plus, the people *consent to it*: if nobody consent to it, Jack cain't be no matchmaker. So the fault is fifty-fifty."

Jim Strickland, pharmacist, civil rights activist, culinary expert, and trainer, manager, and cutman extraordinaire, sold his three pharmacies in 2000 and kept managing a couple of professional fighters in Chicagoland over the ensuing decades. He retired from the game in 2015, having worked as a cutman for twenty world champions (including Evander Holyfield) and seventy world title fights. He was inducted in the National

17. "Those pariahs who do the dirty work of society are really acting as agents for the rest of us." Everett C. Hughes, "Good People and Dirty Work" (1962), reprinted in *The Sociological Eye: Selected Papers* (New Brunswick, NJ: Transaction Books, 1984), 87–97, citation p. 93.

Boxing Hall of Fame in 2019 and passed away in 2020 at age ninety. Jimmie Kitchen, jovial ring photographer, wannabe trainer, and all-around swell guy, kept hanging around the city's gyms. In the 2010s he recovered from his long-time alcohol addiction and worked as a caretaker for an aging Ernie Terrell, the former world heavyweight champion and Chicago ring legend (who died in 2014). By everyone's account, "he got hisself together, he looked better, his skin had cleared up, it was a completely different Kitchen." He passed away quietly in 2019 in his late seventies.

On The Social and Symbolic Structures of Prizefighting

Several patterns emerge from the experiences of this admittedly small and particular sample of amateur and professional fighters (and their children), which confirm the analyses originally put forth in this book, challenge some of its predictions, and spotlight further features of the social and symbolic structures of prizefighting.[18]

First, two to three decades after their career between the ropes ended, none of the Woodlawn alumni regret "gloving up." To a man, they assert that boxing has been a positive force in their existence, even when they are disillusioned by its meager economic returns. The Manly art played a prophylactic role, keeping them away from the street and its dangers; it provided them with an encompassing and enduring framework for what Max Weber calls the "conduct of life" (*Lebensführung*);[19] it gave them a sensually vibrant stage on which to craft a gloried self and

18. On the uses of small samples and unusual cases for unearthing social mechanisms and suggesting theoretical hypotheses, see Mario Luis Small, " 'How Many Cases Do I Need?' On Science and the Logic of Case Selection in Field-Based Research," *Ethnography* 10, 1 (2009): 5–38; and Bent Flyvbjerg, "Five Misunderstandings about Case-Study Research," *Qualitative Inquiry* 12, 2 (2006): 219–245.

19. Max Weber, *The Protestant Ethic and the "Spirit" of Capitalism and Other Writings* (New York: Penguin, [1905] 2002), 5. The concept of *Lebensführung* (sometimes mistranslated as "lifestyle," for which Weber uses the term *Lebensstil*) implies a proactive and conscious structuring of one's behavior thus endowed with practical coherence: Richard Swedberg, *The Max Weber Dictionary: Key Words and Central Concepts* (Stanford, Calif.: Stanford University Press, 20005), 150–151. A compilation of moral teachings from pugilism by champions is John Oden, *Life in the Ring: Lessons and Inspiration from the Sport of Boxing* (Hobart, N.Y.: Hatherleigh Press, 2009).

gain social recognition (if only from their ring comrades); it enabled them to "get out of the neighborhood" to "see the world"; and it bound them to a select and honorific brotherhood. This is affirmed by the vividness of their memories from their gym days and their spontaneous evocation of shared moments in and around the ring (in our conversations, several mates recollected without prompting my one fight in the Chicago Golden Gloves). Yet the Woodlawn boxers also did not push their children to box, and when the latter learned the basics of the sport and competed in the amateur ranks, they did not take the fateful step into the professional world. "I'm fighting so my son don't gotta fight" was a common phrase by which prizefighters expressed the bounds of the skewed passion binding them to their craft back in the Woodlawn days.[20] The absence of occupational inheritance across generations validates it.

Second, the major obstacle standing in the way of the professional career of run-of-the-mill boxers is the sheer rarity of suitable ring contests. Because they were not backed by a promoter with the economic pull to slot them frequently on boxing shows in and around Chicagoland, the Woodlawn alumni typically fought an average of two to three times a year (four to five times early in their career). The spectacular outlier here is Anthony, who duked it out on average every other month for eighteen years because he became the chief "opponent" that matchmaker Jack Cowen dispatched nationwide and overseas; but he could do so only at the cost of running up a lopsided losing record (he was defeated in two-thirds of his 116 bouts) and because his extraordinary defensive skills allowed him to face superior fighters without getting knocked out or seriously hurt—except by the sheer wear and tear over time. Paradoxically, the more he lost (and lost bravely), the more valuable he became on the pugilistic market and the greater his opportunities to serve as a stepping stone in the career of other fighters. A second exception proves the rule: Alfonzo fought about every three months over a decade, but he rose in the international rankings only after cutting his ties to Woodlawn and signing an exclusive promotional contract with the nefarious Don King to "get a shot" at a world title (his first thirteen fights took place in Chicago, most of the next twenty-one were staged in Atlantic City, Las Vegas, and London).

20. Wacquant, "The Pugilistic Point of View," 523.

This confirms the coexistence of two divergent career tracks.[21] The *sponsored* track is one in which promoter and matchmaker join forces to keep their favored boxer "busy," "build" his record, and hone his skills by "feeding" him suitable (that is, weaker and variegated) fighters (of gradually increasing grade) until the time comes to face "serious customers" in more lucrative bouts, typically a ten-round "main event" or a title fight broadcast on sports cable television. On the *contest* track, by contrast, freelance boxers have to take whatever bout is offered to them on the local pugilistic scene, including on short notice (some pugs attend the weigh-in on the morning of shows to offer their services *illico* in case a contestant does not show up or fails to make the contractual weight), or to travel out of town to battle superior fighters "in their backyard" (exposing themselves to the predictable "hometown decision" if they do not win by kayo).[22] The latter is the track populated by "journeymen," skilled boxers who fight to win but mostly lose and never rise into the rank of "contenders," and also by the "bums," "tomato cans," and "palookas"—incompetent, out-of-shape, and washed-out pugs who get into the ring just for a quick payday.

The successful arc of the sponsored fighter (called the "protected fighter" or the "house fighter" in the pugilistic lingo), who typically made a name for himself in the amateurs (going to the Olympics is a big value booster), takes him through the stages of prospect, contender, challenger, and champion. The modal fate of the contest fighter is to remain a journeyman or a "trial horse" (an experienced pug of modest ability matched up with a prospect to test him out) until they retire or fall into the aforementioned variety of "bums," "stiffs," and "divers."[23]

21. I borrow the labels for this opposition from the classic article in the sociology of education, Ralph H. Turner, "Sponsored and Contest Mobility and the School System," *American Sociological Review* 25, 6 (1960): 855–867.
22. In 1995, for instance, Anthony fought ten times by traveling to Baltimore and Las Vegas stateside and in foreign lands to Paris and Cannes in France, Glasgow and London in the United Kingdom, Toronto and Waterloo in Canada, Frankfurt (Germany), and Aalborg (Denmark). He lost eight of these ten fights, all on points.
23. Note that DeeDee insisted that the term "bum" and its cognates were not to be used, as it is both insulting and ignorant: in the pugilistic code of honor, every fighter who "sacrifices" and steps into the ring deserves equal respect for doing so (*infra*, p. 205). For a vivid portrait of pugs toiling at the bottom of the boxing economy, read Rick Reilly, "You Can Count Them Out: Palookas, Tomato Cans, 'Opponents.' These

Every so often, a journeyman defies the odds and beats a prospect or a contender, tarnishing their record, but he does not for that change track. Paradoxically, an unexpected victory restricts his future fight opportunities, since it makes him a more risky adversary to face. It is a rare fighter who enters the game without a sponsor and manages to climb in the rankings and eventually headline a televised card or fight for a title. The structure of careers in prizefighting thus resembles a viscous caste regime more than it does a fluid class system allowing mobility based solely on bodily capital.

This bifurcated and slanted career structure suggests that, unlike amateur boxing, in which opponents typically face each other in an open tournament format, *professional boxing is a sport in name only*: it does not feature a level playing field in which athletes compete against each other based solely on sporting criteria to produce an uncertain outcome and a clear hierarchy of performers (as in judo or tennis, for instance, where competition involves matched pairs ranked by objective benchmarks). Neither is it a market-like structure in which price operates as a clearing mechanism and fluctuates according to the law of supply and demand. Prizefighting is more akin to a *bazaar economy* as characterized by the anthropologist Clifford Geertz in his classic study of the traditional marketplace of Moroccan towns. In a bazaar economy, personalized trading dominates, contracting is intensely relational, and mutual mistrust is rampant; "the level of ignorance about everything from product quality and going prices to market possibilities and production costs is very high, and much of the way in which the bazaar functions can be interpreted as an attempt to reduce such ignorance for someone, increase it for someone, or defend someone against it."[24]

are the Fighters Who Go Down So That the Hometown Heroes Can Go Up" (*Sport Illustrated*, 16 October 1989). Recently, the deprecatory label of "Uber driver" has come into usage.

24. Clifford Geertz, "The Bazaar Economy: Information and Search in Peasant Marketing," *American Economic Review* 68, 2 (1978): 29. For a broader discussion of the manifold social structures of the economy, see Pierre Bourdieu, *Anthropologie économique: Cours au Collège de France, 1992–1993* (Paris: Raisons d'agir and Seuil, 2018).

A boxing show at the Park West nightclub on the city's
North Side

How to "build" a "protected fighter": Curtis meets the "Golden Boy"

For a half-century commencing in the 1930s, prizefighting in
America was deeply enmeshed with organized crime: fights were
routinely fixed, judges and referees bought off, corrupt matches
set up for the benefit of bettors in the know, and a good chunk of
the earnings of top boxers and of gate proceeds, was skimmed by
mobsters (1). Nowadays, there is way too much money at the top
(where the tens of millions in financial profits come mainly from pay-
per-view fees) to permit the rigging of fights, and much too little at
the bottom of the boxing economy to motivate it. Most important,
there is no need to "fix" fights in professional boxing to slant the
contest in favor of a "protected fighter." All it takes is for that fighter's
promoter to *carefully match him with a suitably inferior adversary*
(based on record, style, body type, and recent performance) who

does not present a live threat to his effort to "build" his fighter's record and name. In some cases, the resulting fight is so lopsided on paper that it turns into a glorified sparring session or even target practice (2).

In addition to a favorable match, the protected boxer typically fights at home, with the benefit of crowd support and local judges inclined to give him a "hometown decision" if the contest is decided on points, while his out-of-town opponent has to travel, absorb the fatigue of the trip (and sometimes jetlag), settle in an alien environment on the eve or the morning of the bout, and tussle without the social and emotional support of his usual entourage. This is what happened to Curtis when he was offered to fight the rising all-world prospect Oscar "Golden Boy" De La Hoya in San Diego in February 1993 (3). As if this all was not enough, De La Hoya (who was 3 and 0 in the pros but drew on the experience of 234 wins in the amateur ranks, compared to 14 and 6 for Curtis on top of just 28 amateur fights) came in at the weigh-in five pounds overweight (which would translate into an advantage of a dozen pounds at fight time). Curtis could have refused to fight him and still got paid his purse, but the promoter offered him an extra $5,000 (one thousand per excess pound) to avoid canceling the bout set to be televised on ABC Wide World of Sports that afternoon. Working every angle to benefit his fighter, the promoter had also set up a small ring with soft padding to make it more difficult for Curtis to move and escape De La Hoya's power punches. Perhaps most remarkable about this set-up is that it was done completely above board. Indeed, the *planned one-sided* nature of the bout is best told in the words of the color commentators covering the bout on live television (4):

[Prefight segment.] ". . . If his opponent today, Curtis Strong, hangs in there for a few rounds, we may get to see the qualities that have some boxing people calling Oscar De La Hoya the fighter to carry the sport of boxing through the 1990s. . . . The people who managed De La Hoya have *invested more money in him* than in any fighter in the history of boxing, and the nice thing about the pros as against the amateurs is *you get to pick your opponent*: they have picked an opponent that *they consider safe*. The good news about Curtis Strong is, he's got a winning record, unfortunately—in terms of, if you want to see a competitive fight—he's lost four of his last five fights. But there are two things to remember: one, he's never been knocked out, and two, he does have a style of moving that will, *if Curtis comes to fight*, that will give us an opportunity to see how well Oscar De La Hoya can cut the ring off, which will be essential for him once he goes up in class."

[The "tale of the tape" is read as the fighters stand in the middle of the ring.] ". . . De La Hoya is younger, heavier, taller and rangier [by a full seven inches]—and despite the name, stronger."

[The bout starts. Within seconds Curtis suffers a flash knock-down.] "Curtis Strong is staying out of range. A wise decision. I think he'd like to be sitting with us right now. . . . Right now Curtis is in full survival mode. . . . Back to the smaller ring: is that a factor? Oh yeah, *Oscar's got everything going for him right now*: not only does he outweigh his opponent by five-plus pounds, he's got a 17-foot ring [instead of 20 by 20 feet] which tends to nullify Curtis Strong's movement, the ring padding itself is very mushy, which again will makes it harder for Curtis to run away from him. . . ."

[Fourth round.] "I don't think scoring the rounds here is crucial. What is, Dan, is watching how Oscar is taking care of an opponent who is giving him a little bit more than his previous opposition. . . . Curtis hasn't landed a hard punch, he has not shown much power in his career and it's one of the dangers for a young fighter like Oscar De La Hoya when you *consistenly go against outclassed opposition*, especially opposition that has no power: you get into bad habits."

The Pride of East LA opens a deep cut over the right eye of Curtis. To everyone's surprise, the ring doctor stops the fight to the benefit of De La Hoya, who salutes the crowd by climbing upon the four corners of the ring before he comes to lay a furtive kiss on the shoulder of Curtis as a mark of ring respect.

1. Jeffrey T. Sammons, *Beyond the Ring: The Role of Boxing in American Society* (Urbana: University of Illinois Press, 1988), chapter 6; Jeffrey Sussman, *Boxing and the Mob: The Notorious History of the Sweet Science* (Lanham, Md.: Rowman & Littlefield, 2019); Kevin Mitchell, *The Mob, the Garden and the Golden Age of Boxing* (Boston, Mass.: Hamilcar Publications, 2019).

2. One example will suffice: in 2005 in Indianapolis, the high-ranking middleweight prospect Quentin Smith was 20 and 0 when he fought Reggie Strickland, arguably the country's foremost "opponent" of that decade with an astonishing record of 66 wins and 269 losses. Smith won by a unanimous decision in eight rounds after a point was deducted from Strickland in the final round. The latter fought under three different names in the Midwest and Upper South (he fought only four times in foreign countries) over eighteen years, sometimes three or four times a month. A juicy account of "Mismatches" is Carlo Rotella, *Cut Time* (Chicago: U. of Chicago Press, ch. 3).

3. De La Hoya entered the professional ranks after winning a gold medal at the 1992 Olympics as a high schooler (fulfilling his mother's dying wish two years earlier). He was promoted from the get-go as the future of boxing, a cherubic and charismatic fighter capable of attracting large audiences (both American and Hispanic) and destined to realize "the American Dream" in the ring. He went on to win eleven world titles and is now a successful promoter of boxing and mixed martial arts fights. See Budd Schulberg, "De La Hoya: The Two Hundred Million Dollar Man," in *Ringside: A Treasury of Boxing Reportage* (Chicago: Ivan R. Dee 2006), 90–126; Tim Kawakami, *Golden Boy: The Fame, Money, and Mystery of Oscar De La Hoya* (Kansas City, Mo.: Andrews McMeel, 1999); and Oscar De La Hoya and Steve Springer, *American Son: My Story* (New York: It Books, 2008).

4. Transcript of the commentary of the De La Hoya-Strong fight, ABC *Wide World of Sports*, 6 February 1993 (available on YouTube). I have merged the lines of the two color commentators into a single text. The emphases are mine throughout.

Boxers, trainers, managers, matchmakers, promoters, venues hosting professional shows, boxing commissions and sanctioning bodies, and sporting media and television networks (for the top tier of the game) are enmeshed in murky, multiplex webs of relations, now collusive, now antagonistic, rife with conflicts of interests, and geared toward the staging of fights wherein skilled bodily capital and professional diligence are transmuted into streams of income and prestige, with a small element of chance and a high dose of privilege. Information uncertainty in a bazaar is reduced through "clientelization,"[25] or the repeated purchase of goods and services from the same purveyors based on informal personal connections and established going rates. In the case of the boxing bazaar, clientelization is supplemented by the formation of local monopolies at the bottom and (inter)national oligopolies at the top based on spatial aggregations of cliques striving to corner their sector of the pugilistic economy.

Periodic government efforts to regulate professional boxing flounder on the false assumption that prizefighting is either a sport or an industry driven by the laws of market economics. Two major pieces of federal legislation, the 1996 Professional Boxing Safety Act and the 2000 Muhammad Ali Boxing Reform Act (jointly known as the Ali Act), aiming "to promote honorable competition in professional boxing and enhance the overall integrity of the industry," have failed miserably, not just because of their lack of enforcement, but also because they ignore the distinctive structure and functioning of the pugilistic economy anchored by the dual tracking of boxers. In addition, rationalizing the paper economy at the top (e.g., forbidding coercive contracts, forced promotional options, and rigged rankings by self-proclaimed sanctioning federations at the world level) has no effect on the workaday world of "club fighters" in the middle and bottom tiers of the game, where oral contracts and informal agreements prevail in practice.[26]

A third notable characteristic of the careers of the Woodlawn fighters is the meagerness of their earnings, in absolute terms as well as relative to their economic expectations and the public image of the game as a fairy land of financial riches—based on the mega-fights that monopolize media attention in the "winner-take-all market" of prizefighting.[27] Upon entering the craft, boxers commonly daydream of gloving up for

---

25. Geertz, "The Bazaar Economy," 30–31.
26. The illusion of reform is entertained by Scott Baglio, "The Muhammad Ali Boxing Reform Act: The First Jab at Establishing Credibility in Professional Boxing," *Fordham Law Review* 68, 6 (2000): 2257–2259; John McCain and Ken Nahigian, "A Fighting Chance for Professional Boxing," *Stanford Law & Policy Review* 15, 1 (2004): 7–33; and Melissa Neiman, "Protecting Professional Boxers: Federal Regulations with More Punch," *Sports Law Journal* 15, 1 (2008): 59–97; a sobering assessment is Michael J. Jurek, "Janitor or Savior: The Role of Congress in Professional Boxing Reform," *Ohio State Law Journal* 67 (2006): 1187–1226.
27. Such a market results not from the distribution of talent, but from the uneven distribution of opportunities (in this case, the divergence between sponsored and contest tracks). Robert H. Frank and Philip J. Cook, "Winner-Take-All Markets," *Studies in Microeconomics* 1, 2 (2013): 131–154.

the mystical "million-dollar" bout, and, if successful, they hope to earn enough to buy themselves (and their mother) a car and a house, and perhaps open a gym or a business of their own. They quickly downsize their aspirations when they realize the low pay rate at the bottom and intermediate levels of the sport. As "preliminary fighters," my Chicago mates made $50 a round and a maximum of $1,000 for a ten-rounder on local cards (at a time when a minimum-wage job paid about $700 a month). Fighting three times in a year in a four- or eight-rounder meant grossing about $1,000 in the ring annually ($2,000 in today's dollars), hardly enough to envision abandoning your low-wage job or changing your standard of consumption.

If they agreed to go on the road to fight against the hometown favorite in a ten-round main event, Chicago fighters could earn up to $5,000 in one night, but at the cost of racking up losses, as happened to Ashante when he traveled to Lorain, Ohio, and to South Africa to clash with superior welterweights. Even Lorenzo, who rumbled for the world super lightweight belt after being carefully "groomed" to a record of 21 victories and 1 draw (having faced only two opponents with clear winning records until then), received a top purse of $40,000, well short of the monies needed to purchase a home or launch a business after paying one's trainer and manager. Again, Alfonzo is the only Woodlawn fighter to have reportedly gotten a six-figure purse *on paper*, but after the deduction of his promotional, managerial, and fight expenses (all going into Don King's pocket), he took home $60,000, leaving him about $45,000 after taxes to spend on himself and his eager entourage of family, friends, and hangers-on.

The meagerness and irregularity of their ring earnings suggest that, even when they insist that they are fighting to improve their economic condition, boxers step into the ring primarily because this is "where the action is"[28]—it is not the quarry so much as the chase that keeps them going. If the Sweet science did not offer day-to-day sensual rewards and moral benefits, an enveloping sociability anchored by the gym, and the periodic public affirmation of a higher-grade masculinity, it simply would not exist. In effect, *the symbolic economy of prizefighting* (for the many at the bottom) *sustains its material economy* (for the few at the top), and not the other way around, as commonly claimed by boxers, trainers,

28. "Action" refers to "activities that are consequential, problematic, and undertaken for what is felt to be their own sake." Erving Goffman, "Where the Action Is," in *Interaction Ritual: Essays on Face-to-Face Behavior* (New York: Pantheon, 1967), 149–270, citation p. 185.

19 ▷   20

Two light-heavyweights duke it out on the undercard
at the Park West nightclub

and managers, as well as boxing aficionados and analysts.[29] Combined with the uncertainty, unpredictability, and secrecy surrounding ring earnings—boxers never share information about their purses, even with their closest gym mates, and they wildly exaggerate their purses at every occasion—the fact that one of their club comrades had risen to battle for a championship belt, whether state, national, or world, sufficed to sustain the collective belief in the pugilistic *illusio*, the doxic notion, inscribed in flesh and reproduced by the day-to-day functioning of the gym, that the game is worth the candle and that the next fight just might be the one that opens wide the doors of fame and wealth.

Circuits of money in the "show business with blood"

Prizefighting is a paradoxical economy in that it is predicated on distrust, improbity, and the collective expectation of exaction—for which reason it has been dubbed "the red light district of sports." As one of my gym mates put it, "Everybody tryinna outdo everybody an' everybody tryin' to hurt everybody an' everybody don't trust nobody" (1). Like many other entertainment sectors, such as cinema and popular music, it is also a *dual economy*: at the top, a handful of mega-fights draw huge public attention for their extravagant promotion and astronomical purses (six or seven figures, occasionally more), based on the ability of the star contestants headlining the event to attract customers via pay-per-view; at the bottom, "club fights" and regional boxing cards draw modest gates barely covering the costs of the show, for which fighters collect purses in the hundreds of dollars (for thousands of hours of preparation in and out of the ring). But for many of these pugs the meager monies they chase after either offer a quick paycheck or carry the hope of climbing up the pugilistic ladder, and so they are discounted against an imaginary abacus of future riches (2). In the middle, we find the "casino fights" regularly staged in Atlantic City and Las Vegas, as well as shows in major boxing hubs such as New York City, Los Angeles, Detroit, Philadelphia, and San Antonio,

---

29. Hauser, *The Black Lights*; Jeffrey T. Sammons, *Beyond the Ring: The Role of Boxing in American Society* (Urbana: University of Illinois Press, 1990); Mike Silver, *The Arc of Boxing: The Rise and Decline of the Sweet Science* (London: McFarland, 2008).

for the benefit of sports cable television, offering purses in the thousands of dollars and providing a stepping stone between the bottom and the top tiers of the industry.

What novelist Budd Schulberg famously called a "show business with blood" *naturally tends toward monopoly* (3). The top tier of the game in the United States is controlled by a handful of bitterly feuding promotional companies; in the 1990s, this quatuor included Don King Promotions; Bob Arum's Top Rank Boxing; Main Events, run by rock promoter Shelly Finkel and veteran trainer Lou Duva; and the South African Cedric Kushner. Today, two companies run by the former star fighters Floyd Mayweather and Oscar De La Hoya have joined the fray. These promoters strike multi-event deals with boxing venues, television networks, and pay-per-view operators, on the one side, and sign exclusive contracts with a "stable" of top fighters, on the other. The bottom tier of prizefighting is typically controlled by the local matchmaker who helps resident promoters (or small-time managers eager to keep their boxers "busy") organize shows and populates their "undercard." He alone has specific knowledge of fight opportunities in the city and beyond, and he distributes them as he sees fit across the two divergent tracks of sponsored and contest mobility with their distinct occupational chances and temporal horizons (see *supra*, pp. 346–347).

The value of the fight purse is set in advance by contract and does not depend on the outcome of the bout. For "club fighters" such as my gym mates, it follows a *customary rate per round* which fluctuates somewhat across cities ($50 in Chicago circa 1990, $100 today, which means, considering inflation, that the rate has stayed constant over thirty years). A Chicago boxer then made $150 for a four-rounder opening the card, $300 for a six-rounder, $400 for an eight-rounder, and $500 to $1,000 for a main event in ten rounds. Fighting three to four times in a year on the undercard, he could hope to gross about $1,500, equal to $3,000 in today's dollars—a far cry from the median annual earnings of $51,370 calculated by the Bureau of Labor Statistics and circulating widely on the Internet (4). At the top level, the purse for a televised bout gets typically "cut" among parties as follows: 33 percent for the manager, 10 percent for the trainer, 2 percent (or a flat fee) for the cutman, 10 percent for the matchmaker, and the remainder for the fighter. For a world title challenge in the lower weight division with a hypothetical purse of $100,000 (and assuming that the promoter does not take an additional cut of 20 percent or more for expenses, which was common in the 1990s), the boxer got to take home $45,000, which translated into about $35,000 after income taxes and the cost of medical exams. It is common for the manager to forego his "cut" when the purse falls under a certain threshold ($1,000 back in my Woodlawn days), in which case the fighter also gives his trainer a couple of twenty-dollar bills and a twenty to the cutman (as Curtis did for DeeDee and cutman Jim Strickland after the fight at Studio 104).

1. Loïc Wacquant, "A Fleshpeddler at Work: Power, Pain, and Profit in the Prizefighting Economy," *Theory & Society* 27, 1 (1998): 1–42, and idem, "Whores, Slaves and Stallions: Languages of Exploitation and Accommodation among Boxers," *Body & Society* 7, 2–3 (2001): 181–194.

2. On the logics of multiple monies, see the classic study of Viviana A. Zelizer, *The Social Meaning of Money: Pin Money, Paychecks, Poor Relief, and Other Currencies* (Princeton, N.J.: Princeton University Press, 1994).

3. This was demonstrated long ago by Walter C. Neale, "The Peculiar Economics of Professional Sports: A Contribution to the Theory of the Firm in Sporting Competition and in Market Competition," *Quarterly Journal of Economics* 78, 1 (1964): 1–14. See, in particular, his discussion of the "Louis-Schmeling Paradox" (making reference to the legendary 1936 world heavyweight title bout pitting the black American Joe Louis, representing the Free World, against Max Schmeling, battling for Hitler's Nazi Germany).

4. Multiple boxing and financial websites cite this figure for boxers, but it actually pertains to all "athletes and sports competitors." The number of such jobs in the country was listed as 13,600 in 2019, suggesting that the Bureau of Labor Statistics does not in fact include prizefighters (who number about 5,000 in the United States), because boxing is not organized in a national league and boxers are not "on payroll" with "business establishments" (which is the source of the BLS survey).

Turning to the social front, most strikingly, the trajectories of my Woodlawn mates since their gym days turn out extremely dispersed, more so than I would have predicted based on their initial class position.

They settled across a wide spectrum of occupations, from subproletarian (intermittent day labor, security or warehouse work), to working class (delivery driver, factory and construction, train carman, boxing coach for the city), to petty bourgeois (barber, court clerk, building contractor). The gym members who had solid and skilled jobs at the start, as firefighter, radiology technician, and mental health counselor, kept them and retired securely from them, following relatively short or spotty careers in the ring (seven to fifteen professional fights). Most of the others navigated the lower reaches of the occupational structure until they landed stable if low-paid work with medical benefits (a major marker of social security and a criterion making city and county employment highly desirable). Two of eleven got entangled in the narcotics economy and paid for their involvement with prison sentences—a probability of about 20 percent, less than one-third the rate of lifetime incarceration for black men in their class category.[30] The Woodlawn amateurs similarly scattered across the social spectrum: while none of them turned pro, two enrolled in the army (and one later became a police officer) and one climbed from low-level clerk all the way to portfolio manager at his bank; the fourth died from a drug overdose while a laborer for the renovation company ran by a gym mate; the fifth was murdered by a gang member in a street confrontation while still a teenager in the gym.

How to explain this pattern of *dispersed mobility* that belies the conventional view that boxers are socially immobile if not downwardly mobile, going "from rags to even raggedier" as their career unfolds?[31] A two-step selection helps account for the relative success of the Woodlawn fighters in finding a steady place in the occupational structure. First, as argued originally (see *supra*, pp. 44–47), most boxers are recruited, not from the subproletariat but from the stratum of the working

---

30. Becky Pettit and Bruce Western, "Mass Imprisonment and the Life Course: Race and Class Inequality in US Incarceration," *American Sociological Review* 69, 2 (2004): 151–169.

31. Benita Heiskanen, *The Urban Geography of Boxing: Race, Class, and Gender in the Ring* (New York: Routledge, 2012), 27. This is a core theme of the social mythology of prizefighting, repeated *ad nauseam* by insiders and analysts of the trade, see Hauser, *The Black Lights,* 9–13; John Sugden, *Boxing and Society: An International Analysis* (Manchester, England: Manchester University Press, 1996), chapter 3; Joyce Carol Oates, *On Boxing,* expanded ed. (New York: Ecco, 2006); and Leger Grindon, *Knockout: The Boxer and Boxing in American Cinema* (Oxford, Miss.: University Press of Mississippi, 2011).

class on the cusp of economic integration, past the threshold of minimal material stability needed to have the capacity to organize their existence according to a rational plan, follow a stringent training regimen, and project their aspirations over a long time horizon.[32] Thus, the fathers of my Woodlawn mates held jobs as butcher, construction worker (for two of them), factory worker and foreman, boilermaker in a steel mill, truck and delivery driver, and telephone repair technician. Moreover, with one exception, their mothers all worked, in such occupations as mail carrier (for two of them), nurse, barmaid, cook, cleaner, steel mill worker, bank account manager, and psychiatrist. The initial economic and social conditions of formation of the pugilistic habitus help propel most boxers above the subproletarian condition later in their life course, irrespective of their ring earnings.

Prizefighters are a self-selected and gym-tested population that displays *above-average moral capital* (a subtype of embodied cultural capital or, what is the same, a dimension of their habitus); that is, they possess the incarnate qualities of patience, endurance, asceticism, abnegation, and courage required to launch and successfully navigate a professional career between the ropes. This moral capital allows the boxer to capture streams of money and aura converging on the ring; it is generally cultivated early in the family crucible (via the discipline imposed by the parents) and then preserved or increased by dutiful training routines, culinary habits, social frugality, and sexual abstinence, encapsulated by the core folk notion of "sacrifice," and by the constant succor of the gym entourage. It sustains boxers, not just in the squared circle, but also beyond it in their different life pursuits.

It is no surprise, then, that many professional fighters are durably attracted by another "greedy institution" resembling pugilism in its expectation of exclusive loyalty, ethical rectitude, and total commitment; namely, organized religion.[33] Keith and Mark have both become pastors and they minister to their own church in addition to working full time.

---

32. On the dialectic of material conditions of existence and the rationalization of life among (sub)proletarians, see Pierre Bourdieu, *Algérie 1960: Structures économiques et structures temporelles* (Paris: Minuit, 1977).
33. Lewis A. Coser, *Greedy Institutions: Patterns of Undivided Commitment* (New York: Macmillan, 1974). The omission of religion as an institution imparting social regularity and moral guidance suited to sustaining a boxing career is a serious flaw of my initial study.

Alfonzo is married to a pastor. Curtis is close to his priest, who helps him navigate his daily tribulations. Anthony and his wife are devotees of the Nation of Islam and attend prayer at the mosque every Friday. Ashante likens the gym to a "sanctuary." Bernard, whose cousin's son is an evangelist, writes in a text message: "Religion gives me a sense of belief, power, control, and guidance. It has given me a sense of purpose. Just as boxing has given me a sense of purpose. God bless!" The occupational morality practically learned in the gym translated into a *taste for discipline and group attachment* that has outlasted its social conditions of formation and inclines former boxers to seek out the special sociability and collective effervescence that religious institutions offer to their members.[34]

Boxing life on the internet and death in a Chicago ring

The boxing economy is highly cyclical, going through ups and downs, linked to waves of immigration and the periodic irruption of charismatic fighters (especially in the heavyweight division), set along an overall trajectory of long-term decline linked to the improvement of the social condition of the working class, challenges to traditional masculinity, the profusion of other forms of popular entertainment, and the diffusion of cultural sensibilities averse to interpersonal violence.[35] In recent years, the Chicago boxing scene has slowed down to a crawl. "We've had no hero, so to speak," observes Jack, "you've got to have a boxer that will bring people to shows." As for the amateurs, their ranks have thinned out as youths are increasingly opting to go into team sports integrated within the high school framework that are less taxing on the body: "Hey you don't have to get hit in the head to make five million dollars playing baseball or basketball."[36] What is more, "if you don't have good coaches,

34. The three components of morality according to Durkheim are the spirit of discipline, group attachment and the autonomy of the will. Émile Durkheim, *L'Éducation morale* (Paris: Presses Universitaires de France, [1902–1903] 1963).
35. Silver, *The Arc of Boxing*; David L. Hudson, *Boxing in America: An Autopsy* (New York: Praeger, 2012); Kasia Boddy, *Boxing: A Cultural History* (London: Reaktion Books, 2019); Kenneth G. Sheard, "Aspects of Boxing in the Western 'Civilizing Process,'" *International Review for the Sociology of Sport* 32, 1 (1997): 31–57.
36. For many boxers, pugilism is a *negative sporting vocation* born of the inability to play another sport due to their physical limitations: they were too small for football, too short for basketball, and not agile enough for baseball.

how are you gonna have fighters? You have to have the coaches that take interest in the kids, and most of those guys with the Chicago Park District it's just a job for them, they wind up being boxing coaches because they couldn't make them janitors."

The hopeful prediction that the rising population of Latinos, most of them from Mexico, a country where boxing is considered a religion and fighters are potent symbols of national pride, would boost the trade did not come to pass. Meanwhile, the explosive popularity of mixed martial arts has also taken some wind out of the sails of prizefighting.[37] The conspicuous and growing entry of women into the ranks of both amateur and professional boxers (correlated with the boom of professional women's sport at the turn of the century) has combined with the popularity of white-collar pugilism to change the face of gyms, but they have failed to stave off the long-term marginalization of the Sweet science as avocation and entertainment.[38] Three raw empirical indicators of this decline: the rarity of fights televised on the national networks (banished to minor cable channels after HBO discontinued its long-time sponsorship of the Manly art); the disappearance of boxers from the cover page of *Sports Illustrated*; and the fact that no world champion has made it as a household name with the general public, as was the case as late as the 1980s.[39]

In recent years, the game has declined to such a level and professional shows have been so few and far between in Chicago that the promoters who put them on do not even pay the contestants, except for the main event. Instead, they *sell slots on the undercard* to local managers or fighters who want to get on the show to stay active and build a record. Those boxers (known as the "A fighter") effectively fight gratis and their managers pay the purse of their opponent (known as the "B fighter") as well as cover the cost of transportation, food, and

37. Stephen D. Allen, *A History of Boxing in Mexico: Masculinity, Modernity, and Nationalism* (Albuquerque: University of New Mexico Press, 2017); Dale C. Spencer, *Ultimate Fighting and Embodiment: Violence, Gender and Mixed Martial Arts* (New York: Routledge, 2013); David L. Hudson, "The Future of Boxing and the Threat of MMA," in *Boxing in America: An Autopsy*, 119–132.
38. Lucia Trimbur, *Come Out Swinging: The Changing World of Boxing in Gleason's Gym* (Princeton, N.J.: Princeton University Press, 2013); Malissa Smith, *A History of Women's Boxing* (Lanham, Md.: Rowman & Littlefield, 2014), esp. chapters 9–11.
39. Jerry Izenberg, *Once There Were Giants: The Golden Age of Heavyweight Boxing* (New York: Skyhorse Publishing, 2021).

lodging (which can run up to $2,500 for a six-rounder). When the balance of power between promoter and boxer-manager capsizes in this fashion, prizefighting takes on the characteristics of an "economic world reversed" in which the pugilist must invest his bodily capital at an immediate loss in the faint hope of financial returns several bouts and years down the line.[40]

The pugilistic landscape from the days of my apprenticeship has long vanished. All four main gyms for professionals of the early 1990s have shut down. Windy City Gym, run by coach Colonna, closed in 2007 and was reopened, revealingly, as the Sam Colonna Boxing, MMA, Fitness Gym in a different location—but with the same old fight posters. It is a thriving center of training, geared mainly to recreational customers ("white-collar boxers" who want to boast to their friends that they "box," but "those are the guys who pay the bills"), which offers personalized lessons with "certified trainers" at $50 per session, with classes scheduled from 6 a.m. to 8 p.m. A dozen pros and three dozen amateurs train there daily, in addition to some fifty white-collar boxers, including women, who are said to be "more consistent than the men." Fuller Park city gym also closed and was consolidated with the nearby Stateway gym, also run by the city, and Sheridan Park no longer has professionals. As for venues for boxing cards, Studio 104 went bankrupt around 2000. The Park West nightclub stopped featuring live boxing, much to the chagrin of trainer Eddie ("I miss them Park West days, man, it was consistent and they booked our guys"). The cavernous International Amphitheatre on Halsted and 42nd Street was demolished in 1999. And then the killer: "The Golden Gloves is awful now, man, it's not what it used to be. It's only one ring and nobody hardly at the concession stand." The waning popularity of boxing has diminished the supply of amateur fighters in the city and made it hard to recruit commercial sponsors to stage tournaments. The regional center of prizefighting activity has now moved from the Windy City to neighboring northwest Indiana, where the

---

40. The logic of this economy is parsed by Pierre Bourdieu, "The Field of Cultural Production, Or: The Economic World Reversed," *Poetics* 12, 4–5 (1983): 311–356. This pattern of investment is similar to fashion modeling, where novice models are paid in "promise and prestige," "trade" (the clothes they wore at work), and "freebies" (gratis haircuts at chic salons, discounted gym memberships, and complimentary dinners and drinks at nightclubs), and commonly run into debt with their booking agency. Ashley Mears, *Pricing Beauty: The Making of a Fashion Model* (Berkeley: University of California Press, 2011), 45–55.

Horseshoe Casino in Hammond and the Majestic Star casino in Gary put on regular boxing cards drawing halfway decent crowds.

As with every domain of social life, the rise of the Internet and the popularity of social media have impacted boxing in multifarious ways. Vince Hudson, a former professional fighter and member of the Woodlawn gym in the 1970s, has used Facebook to launch the Chicago Boxing Brotherhood, a loose association of retired and active boxers from the city, amateur and pro, which held its first annual dinner at the Montell Griffin gym in 2011. "It's like a family reunion" where old pugs mingle and catch up with one another and plaques are awarded to trainers from the olden days, because "a lotta them they were father figures more than just trainers" and "they got us to where we are." It started out as a small get-together of five friends and has grown to a joyful assembly of some seventy participants (video from the 2018 edition is on YouTube). It features food, music with a deejay, and guest speakers drawn from the ranks of boxing personalities, all for a donation of ten dollars. The older boxers get a chance to informally impart some of their wisdom to the new generation, so "they don't make the same mistakes we made," including falling into the traps of drugs and financial distress (by "flashing money" when they have it), and failing to plan for their life after the ring.

Another effect of the Internet has been to spawn high-impact "white-collar fights" between digital celebrities. Consider the three ring kerfuffles featuring KSI, a misogynist British musician, gamer, and Internet personality (ranked second by the *Sunday Times*'s list of the top 100 UK influencers). He first went toe-to-toe with rival YouTuber Joe Weller, who had "dissed" him on Twitter, in a packed London arena; the grotesque clash was reportedly viewed live by 1.6 million and by 20 million over the next day. KSI then duked it out twice with the top American YouTuber, Vine vlogger, and podcaster Logan Paul (whose channel, like KSI's, has 20 million subscribers), first in the amateur format (garnering one million viewers paying $10 a connection for access to the live stream), and next as professionals making their ring debut in a crammed Staples Center in Los Angeles, headlining a show featuring two world title bouts *on the undercard*. The *New York Times* found it fit to reprint the California boxing license application of the two contestants to assuage the disbelief of its sports readers, while the *Independent* deemed the event "a ridiculous slugfest that was as wild as the Amazon rainforest and as sophisticated as a *Keeping Up with the Kardashians* boxset."[41] This development would not bear mentioning here if not for the fact that some boxing promoters see in such streamed celebrity fisticuffs a fleet vehicle for reaching big new audiences of young and diverse millennials who know nothing about prizefighting, even as many fight people express disdain and outrage at the degradation of the craft it entails.[42]

To be fair to the YouTubers, they are not the first to turn boxing into a circus act: boxers went there first in the continuing quest for publicity stunts aimed at bolstering the game's dissipating popularity. At the zenith of his career, Muhammad Ali himself agreed to face wrestlers in the ring, including the top Japanese wrestler Antonio Inoki in 1976 in a surreal Tokyo clash billed as the War of the Worlds.[43] In 2002, Fox broadcast two episodes of *Celebrity Boxing*, a reality-TV show featuring pitiful tussles between aging B-list singers and minor entertainment figures involved in media scandals (such as Tonya Harding, the evil lady of Olympic skating, against Paula Jones, renowned for suing President Clinton over sexual harassment), complete with top ring referees, ring announcer, and commentators.[44] One headliner was a melee between William "The Refrigerator" Perry, a 400-pound former football lineman, and Manute Bol, a 7′7″ former NBA basketball player, while the second featured an intergender clash between infamous sex criminal Joey Buttafuoco and pro wrestler Joanie "Chyna" Laurer. But the recent multiplication of celebrity and hybrid fights broadcast online heralds a new stage in the *growing commercial entanglement of boxing, reality TV, and*

41. Kevin Draper, "Logan Paul. KSI. YouTube. Fight. Logan Paul. KSI. Boxing," *New York Times*, 8 November 2019; Luke Brown, "KSI vs Logan Paul Fight Result: Londoner Wins YouTube Boxing Rematch on Points after Ridiculous Slugfest," *Independent*, 10 November 2019. The bout was reported on by myriad websites and social media threads.
42. When the commercial pole of the pugilistic field overwhelms the pole of the craft, boxing is more wont to descending into a *festival* of the grotesque than to playing out as a Bakhtinian *carnival*, as argued by Kath Woodward, *Boxing, Masculinity and Identity: The "I" of the Tiger* (London: Routledge, 2007), pp. 107–114.
43. A juicy behind-the-scene accounts of this absurdist performance (if such is the word) and its painful aftermath is in Thomas Hauser, *Muhammad Ali: His Life and Times* (New York: Simon & Schuster, 1991), pp. 336–338.
44. About which, read the funny short poem by Glen LeMesurier, "Celebrity Boxing Match," *Queen's Quarterly* 102, no. 3 (1995): 792.

YouTube, as evidenced by the announcement of a forthcoming "exhibition bout" featuring retired boxing legend Floyd "Money" Mayweather (the top fighter of the past decade) and Logan Paul, whose brother Jake Paul, meanwhile, has thrown the media gauntlet by way of a slew of sexual insults to mixed martial arts star Conor McGregor. The wedding of boxing and social media stardom only reinforces the bifurcation of the fistic economy, since, by definition, only those fighters who are already ring celebrities can hope to share in the digital wealth.

The Internet and social media have not only facilitated pugilistic sociability and spawned circus fights aiming to stave off the continued decline of boxing; they have also upended the traditional economy of prizefighting at the preliminary level, pushing it from a murky "bazaar economy" in which "information is poor, scarce, maldistributed, inefficiently communicated, and intensely valued,"[45] such that boxers must rely blindly on intermediaries (manager and matchmaker) to get slotted for fights, to a more open system of exchange in which rich information about adversaries from around the world is immediately accessible to all at no cost. The game changer here is the site BoxRec. com (Boxing Records Archive), an Internet platform inaugurated in 2000 giving open access to a database covering 2.3 million bouts from around the world (filed by volunteer editors in three dozen countries). It contains the complete records of every professional fight and fighter in the United States since the 1960s. For each boxer, it lists their age, nationality and residence, height, weight and reach, career dates, division, stance, record, percentage of KOs, as well as basic information for each bout (date, venue, official weights, number of rounds, knockout time, etc.).[46]

The exhaustive compilation and democratic diffusion of pugilistic intelligence have roiled the organization of preliminary fights and the time-honored manner of "building" boxers in the early phase of their career. The veteran trainer and gym owner Sam Colonna explains: "The fighters nowadays, they're way different, they want easy fights. Those fighters then [in the 1990s] were more *hungry* than the fighters now. . . . Lemme tell you what screwed everything up, it's *social media, BoxRec,*

45. Geertz, "The Bazaar Economy," 29.
46. In 2018, the Association of Boxing Commissions (which regulate professional fights at the state level) recognized BoxRec.com as its official record keeper. BoxRec provides information free of charge, unlike the rival site Fight Fax Inc. (FightFax.com), which charges information by the minute and forbids the copying of records.

YouTube: you click and you know what the guy eats, what he drinks, who's his girlfriend, who trains him, how many rounds he does, how many miles he runs. Back then you didn't have *all that shit*: you're fightin' him, you can't find out nuttin' about the guy. Now [in a mock scared voice] 'Oooh, that guy lifted 500 pounds, I'm not fightin' him,' 'Oooh he just sparred ten rounds, I'm not fightin' him.' You wanna know somethin', just Google it, and it pops up. . . . You can find out how many times a day he takes a shit, 'cos everybody's postin' everything. This is *ruinin' boxing*, 'cos nowadays these fighters are afraid of fightin' each other. It's hurtin' it *big time*. It's killin' everythin'. . . . BoxRec, it's good, [but] it should be limited only to trainers and to matchmakers, and promoters, *that's it—not the fighters*. The fighters go on there, [worried] 'Aw man, Sam, you sure you want me to fight this guy? Look, two months ago he fought at 150 and I'm only 140.' Shit! That means the guy was over-weight or the Commission put that down because they don't want a guy 140 fighting a guy 150, so they jacked up the other guy's weight. I know the game, they don't know the game! Again, social media, BoxRec killed that fight. . . . How are you gonna develop a guy? It's hard to build fighters nowadays 'cos everybody wants to fight a guy that's 1 and 5, instead of guys that's 2 and 2 or 3 and 0: they don't wanna fight. Look at this guy, he was a junior champion in Russia or some bullshit, and they can *find that out in a minute on their phone!* It's crazy. . . . The 1990s, those were my favorite days, now it's not the same. The love of the sport is different now: these guys are not as *hungry*, they're not as ambitious to come to the gym. It's killin' the sport."

The recent event that created a commotion, albeit a silent one, among the city's fight people is the October 2019 title bout held in Chicago between former Olympian and blue-chip prospect Charles Conwell (14 and 0) and New York's Patrick Day (17 and 3), in which Day was knocked down twice by mid-fight and then knocked unconscious in the tenth and last round. He was evacuated from the ring on a stretcher and underwent emergency brain surgery that night, only to fall into a coma and die four days later—the second fight-related death of a boxer in three months in the country.

Trainer Eddie extemporizes somberly: "That kid got killed in the ring, somebody wasn't doin' they job, the physical or somethin'. It was a lot of things happenin' in the gym too: his sparrin', how many times was he gettin' hit, was he was gettin' knocked down, was he in fight shape—see all that need to be observed *on up to the fight*. Was he makin' his

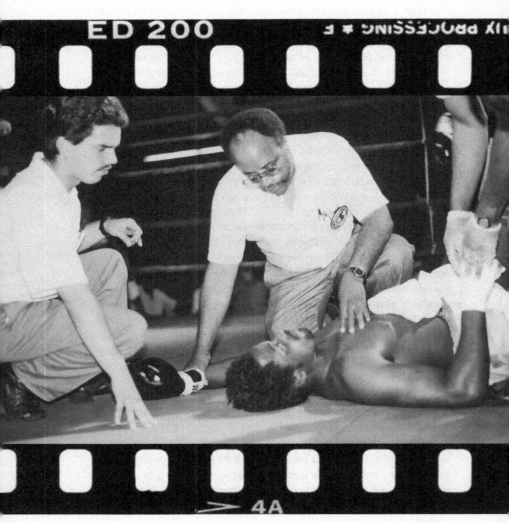

The ringside physician examines a boxer knocked unconscious in the ring on a show at the Photon Arena in Harvey.

weight, was he trainin', did he have oxygen in his body:[47] All that adds
up. Somebody wasn't doin' what they supposed to do." Curtis reacts
along the same lines: "That's coz they don't teach them guys how to
slip and move like DeeDee did. You know DeeDee taught us to slip and
move, block the punches, see what I mean, instead of just stand there,
you-hit-me I-hit-you you-hit-me—naw, *that ain't no fightin'*. [So it's the
fault of the fighter who got killed?] No it was the fault of the trainer an'
them that train him, coz while he was preparin' for that fight he probably
was *at war* with his sparrin' partners an' stuff: you-hit-me I-hit-you, let's
see who can hit the hardest! That ain't how you train a fighter. The name
of the game is hit and *don't-get-hit*. That's how the game go."

The belief that ring fatalities are caused by reckless incompetence,
improvidence, or failure to follow proper protocol or master the requisite
technical skills is necessary to persist in an occupation where a routine
day "at the office" can turn into fatal tragedy in a split second.[48] It stands
as a somber reminder that every time they step into the squared circle,
pugilists put their life on the line *and know it* (even as they work hard
collectively to submerge that awareness), which is the true measure of
their passion for the craft.[49]

47. Eddie refers here to the practice of extreme and sudden weight cutting in the
lead-up to the bout. Boxers commonly "dry out"; that is, they reduce their food
intake and stop drinking for days before a fight and deploy extreme heat methods
(training, running, and jumping rope in rubberized "sweat suits"—like the one worn
by Muhammad Ali when he visited the Woodlawn gym, see picture on page 312) to
make the required fight weight (typically well below their "walking-around weight"
and even their training weight). The practice is harmful to the body and fighting
in a state of acute dehydration can itself be life-threatening. But "drying out" is
also an ascetic rite of purification marking the boxer's entry into the sacred (and
homoerotic) space of the ring, where he clashes with another (near-naked) man
who has undergone a similar process of purification, thereby allowing *both* to attain
a higher grade of masculinity, *regardless* of the outcome of the contest. On the role
of the "negative cult" in elevating and consecrating its believers, see Durkheim, *Les
Formes élémentaires de la vie religieuse*, Book III, chapter 1.
48. Firefighters for the U.S. Forest Service react in the same way to the death of
one their own to an inferno, in order to maintain the organizational tenet that fire
is safe and controllable and that harm on the fireline can be averted by dutifully
following technical precautions. Matthew Desmond, "The Incompetent Dead," in
On the Fireline: Living and Dying with Wildland Firefighters (Chicago: University of
Chicago Press, 2008), 224–264.
49. A detailed insider account of killing in the ring and its complex moral and
emotional aftermaths is Elliot Worsell, *Dog Rounds: Death and Life in the Boxing*

Post Scriptum: On Pugilistic Piety

Writing about prizefighting and reconnecting with my gym mates three decades after my novitiate in the Manly art has brought back mostly happy and nostalgic memories. It has plunged me into a cottony mood of pugilistic remembrance and motivated me to return to my field materials. I gingerly reopened the dozen dusty black binders containing my typed field notes and surfed giddily across the 1,556 files distributed in thirty-eight folders created at the time in my computer for that research project. I excavated from piles of documents lost pictures and a hand-drawn map of 63rd Street recording every vacant lot, abandoned building, storefront church, and commercial establishment sprinkled along the desolate mile connecting Cottage Grove Avenue to Stony Island Avenue that instantly evoked in me myriad events and emotions, both public and intimate.[50] I digitally scanned the thousand-odd slides I shot in and around the gym over three years, rediscovering urban landscapes, ordinary scenes of training, fretful sorties at amateur tournaments and professional shows, and assorted personal encounters. And I unearthed more unfinished texts, raw notes to myself, outlines of planned articles, and thematic drafts laid fallow than I care to count or dare mention.

Ring (London: Blink Publishing, 2018). A historical repertory is provided by Hudson, "Death in the Ring," in *Boxing in America: An Autopsy*, 119–132; and Eben Pindyck, "An Obsessive Chronicle of Deaths in the Ring," *New Yorker*, 22 December 2015. An account of the death of the Korean lightweight Duk-Koo Kim at the hands of Ray "Boom-Boom" Mancini live on national television in November 1982, which led the American Medical Association to call for the sport to be banned, is in Ralph Wiley, *Serenity: A Boxing Memoir* (New York: Holt, 1989), 113–149. A literary rendition is Norman Mailer, "The Death of Paret," in *The Greatest Boxing Stories Ever Told*, ed. Jeff Silverman (Guilford, Conn.: Lyons Press, 2002), 235–240. A fascinating nineteenth-century case study where a boxer was charged with manslaughter following the death of his opponent in the ring is Kevin B. Wamsley and David Whitson, "Celebrating Violent Masculinities: The Boxing Death of Luther McCarty," *Journal of Sport History* 25, 3 (1998): 419–431. For a medical point of view, see Lissa C. Baird, C. Benjamin Newman, Hunter Volk, Joseph R. Svinth, Jordan Conklin, and Michael L. Levy, "Mortality Resulting from Head Injury in Professional Boxing: Case Report," *Neurosurgery* 67, 2 (2010): E519–E520.

50. On the uses of pictural and scriptural forms in the imaginative logic of ethnographic discovery, see Michael Taussig, *I Swear I Saw This: Drawings in Fieldwork Notebooks, Namely My Own* (Chicago: University of Chicago Press, 2011).

How does this biographical "revisit" of the Woodlawn Boys Club through the life trajectories of its key members complicate or alter the portrait of the Manly art I drew back in 2000?[51] Readers can assess for themselves the empirical congruence and analytic consistency between the earlier forward-looking account of the fabrication of the pugilistic habitus and the later retrospective supplements on its deployment in and beyond the ring. Regardless, one source of difference lies squarely with the author and his viewpoint as a view taken from a point in social space. I wrote *Body and Soul* very quickly, almost in a trance, to capture and convey the sensual and moral magnetism of prizefighting by enwrapping the reader inside its social microcosm, thereby mirroring in the very structure of the book the irresistible *phenomenological closure and engulfment* that boxers themselves experience as they progress in their moral and professional career.[52]

Even though I was a decade removed from my Chicago days, I had continued training intermittently (at the Somerville Boxing Club near Boston, the Times Square Gym in New York City, and King's Boxing Gym in Oakland, near the Fruitvale BART station) and, in the feverish months of writing, it was easy for me to become entranced again by the world I was painting—which I take to be a necessary condition for fleshing out (literally) the full carnal account I put forth. Also, in assembling the book, I reworked texts that had been written contemporaneously with my apprenticeship and were therefore soaked in that experiment.

Three decades later, not only do we get a reckoning of the *via dolorosa pugilistica* perceived, not through its enchanted promise at the start, but from its utterly prosaic end points. The author is also socially and existentially much further removed from the pugilistic cosmos as well as from his former gym comrades. Living the privileged and monkish life of the scholar—which, Pierre Bourdieu never tires of reminding us, comes from the Greek *skholé*, meaning leisure—no doubt changed my perspective on the fistic vocation, its immediate allure, and its pressing determinants. I have now resided for decades in

51. For stimulative reflections on the pitfalls and profits of revisiting a field project, read Michael Burawoy, "Revisits: An Outline of a Theory of Reflexive Ethnography," *American Sociological Review* 68, 5 (2003): 645–679.
52. This was the rationale for backgrounding the structural analysis of class, race, and space in the black American (hyper)ghetto, which is taken up in the companion volume to grow out of this project, Loïc Wacquant, *Urban Outcasts: A Comparative Sociology of Advanced Marginality* (Cambridge: Polity Press, 2008).

an "emotional community"[53] that sacralizes bodily integrity and whose threshold of tolerance for pain and displays of interpersonal violence is at a historical nadir, and thus at complete loggerheads with the affective profile of prizefighting.

I became aware of this chasm when, while drafting this post-face, I took to watching old fights from the 1970s and 1980s on YouTube, starting with the titanic battles of the "golden generation" of heavyweights: Ali, Frazier, Norton, Foreman, and Holmes. Late at night, eying my tablet, I was *shocked* and nearly *sickened* by the *brutality* of their clashes—I keep stumbling over the word "brutality," because it is fundamentally antithetical to the pugilistic point of view of craft, honor, and morality as I constructed and experienced it myself, but I cannot find a better one to express my hushed revulsion at the methodical and willful mutual battering of huge muscular (black) men in the ring.[54] I kept thinking of the physical damage thus inflicted upon, and indeed of the impairment suffered by, many of my Woodlawn mates decades after their rumblings in the ring. And, *at the same time*, truth be told, part of me is viscerally admirative of the skill, cunning, and courage of those same men. And so I have kept on watching, but with a turbid sense of disquiet that suggests that, in shifting from touch to sight in my primary mode of sensory entanglement with the trade, I may well have lost my pugilistic piety.[55]

Paris and Berkeley, February 2021

53. I borrow this notion from the medieval historian Barbara H. Rosenwein, *Emotional Communities in the Early Middle Ages* (Ithaca, N.Y.: Cornell University Press, 2006), who stresses the plurality of such communities in any society and the resulting tensions between differing sets of "norms of emotional expression and value" (2).
54. Wacquant, "The Pugilistic Point of View." This emotive reaction became clear to me during my weekly dominical conversations with Chris Muller, whom I thank for pushing me to share this postscriptural reflection.
55. This is in keeping with the theoretical arguments of both Émile Durkheim (in *The Elementary Forms of Religious Life*) and Norbert Elias (in *The Civilizing Process*, Cambridge: Basil Blackwell, [1939] 1994), for whom particular standards of cognition and emotion are anchored by distinctive social structures: remove those structures and the corresponding standards will appear shocking, improper, or downright nonsensical.

Coach DeeDee closes up the gym at the end of the day

List of Illustrations

prosperous neighborhood of Hyde Park, haven of the University of Chicago.

23 Three unemployed men linger in front of an abandoned store: pandemic unemployment sentences over half of adult males in Woodlawn to idleness.

23 In the landscape of urban desolation on 63rd Street, a storefront church ("Welcome to the New City Temple") and a former youth club ("Concerned Young Adults") lie in ruins.

45 "No school, no future": a billboard on a ghetto street (in Fuller Park, northwest of Hyde Park); in the distance, the buildings of the Robert Taylor Homes, the single largest concentration of urban poverty in the Western world at the time, ninety-nine percent black.

51 "Rockin'" Rodney Wilson enjoys a rare moment of feminine company, sitting aside the ring.

61 *Daily workout at the Woodlawn gym*

"Floorwork": Tony "The Rock" Jackson hammers the heavy bag while Anthony "Ice" Ivory warms up shadow-boxing in front of the wall mirror; in the background, the window of the office from which DeeDee monitors the floor.

62 *"Ringwork"*: Lorenzo "The Stallion" Smith works on the pads with trainer-in-second Eddie Davis (wearing a black T-shirt "Iron Mike Tyson, King of the Ring").

"Tablework": Curtis Strong does sit-ups lying on the table, under the attentive gaze of his cousin (holding his legs) and his son Christopher (seated on the chair). On the wall at left, hang portraits of Harold Washington, the first black mayor of Chicago, and of Martin Luther King, Jr.; at right, posters of boxers and advertisements for local cards are tacked on the wall.

Ed Smith (a.k.a. Smithie or Smitty) and Anthony wrap up their training session with three frenetic rounds of jump-rope in front of the door to the kitchen of the Boys Club.

80 His eyes glistening with concentration, Curtis, decked out in his Everlast head guard, throws a jab at his partner Ashante (real name Gary Moore) during a sparring session.

92 "Fat" Joe and Smithie at work in the ring. Joe, who boxes "southpaw" (with his right shoulder in front), holds his left fist half-open in order to block Smithie's jab (his back to the camera).

Fight Night at Studio 104

(*bottom*) Seated on the floor of the weigh-in room, Jack Cowen (*at left*) and his production assistant sort through the gloves and other accessories for the night's fights.

172 "If I wear a hat like that an' I'm walkin' around on d'streets, Louie, what'd you think?" A Woodlawn character poses under the "El."

182 A spectator and his girlfriend decked out in their best threads: sumptuous rings and opulent gold-plated medallions for him, a Fendi knock-off bag for her.

194 *Opening bout: Keith "Minicannon" Rush versus Sherman Dixon, in four rounds*

The ring, set up outdoors on the parking lot of the restaurant, is surrounded by about 300 people when the fights get under way at nightfall.

Keith marches resolutely on his opponent at the outset of the bout.

Eddie wipes the sweat off Keith's face between rounds (during another fight at Studio 104 the month before) under the watchful eye of Elijah, Keith's manager and cornerman.

The crowd claps and laughs at the spectacle in the ring; Wanda, Curtis's sister, raises her arms in intermingled excitement and outrage.

202 DeeDee (wearing his blue toga embroidered "Curtis Strong") wraps the hands of his charge in the storeroom-turned-dressing-room, in the midst of cartons of Baccardi, piles of posters, and other restaurant supplies. At left is the black leather doctor's bag in which the old trainer keeps his instruments: hand wraps, gauze, medical tape, scissors, Vaseline, Q-tips, a metal enswell, and vials of chemical products.

210 Curtis gets up in the ring in his white fight robe under the hurrahs of the crowd and the gaze of Pete Pogorsky, the referee for the evening's last bout.

214 *The main event: Curtis Strong versus Jeff Hannah, in eight rounds.*

From the get-go, Hannah bullies Curtis into the corner and pummels him after having sent him to the canvas, much to the astonishment of the crowd.

From the third round on, Curtis imposes his rule in the ring and punishes his opponent with stinging uppercuts from both hands.

'Busy' Louie at the Golden Gloves

250 At the foot of the ring, "Busy" Louie draws the solemn salute of DeeDee and the encouragements of Ashante and Olivier (a.k.a. The Doc) seconds before stepping in for the fight. Photo by Ivan Ermakoff.

252 *"Busy" Louie in action*

In the squared circle: Busy Louie goes on the attack after having been sent to the canvas in the opening minute of the fight. Photo by Jimmy Kitchen.

A view of the ring from Busy Louie's corner: one minute of rest and tactical advice. Photo by Jimmy Kitchen.

"Busy" Louie pins his opponent against the ropes with combinations with both hands at the close of the third and final round. Photo by Jimmy Kitchen.

254 The Woodlawn Boys Club victorious: Big James and "Mighty" Mark Chears each win their division and proudly display their trophies, flanked by Eddie and DeeDee.

256 "Busy" Louie polishes his moves on the double-end bag, under the stern eye of DeeDee (at right, seated at the front of his desk in the back office). Photo by Jim Lerch, courtesy of the *Chicago Sun Times.*

Forging the Pugilistic Habitus

261 Elders from the Unë clan, tribe of Luecila, Lifou Island, New Caledonia (December 1983). The women wear *popinées*, the traditional dress introduced by the Protestant missions in the late 19th century.

267 Urban desolation on 63rd Street under the tracks of the "El" (elevated train line).

273 Coach DeeDee conversating on the phone in the backroom, timer in hand.

276 Trainer Eddie surveilling his charges working on the bags.

278 Poster for the Golden Gloves tournament in which Busy Louie fought.

282 Busy Louie throws a left jab at Ashante during a sparring session.

A concise genealogy and anatomy of habitus

The Afterlives of Chicago Prizefighting across Three Decades

327 Butch skipping rope on the gym floor, an exercise done at the end of the day's training session which has a meditative quality to it.

330 "Rockin'" Rodney Wilson after his victory against Ricardo Luna (0 and 2) on a unanimous decision in four rounds at the Park West nightclub on the city's north-side posh neighborhood of Lincoln Park (August 1989). His manager Elijah (owner of a chain of laundromats, standing) and Oscar (head of a tile company) get in on the picture in the ring.

330 Little Keith waiting for his bout to be called at the Park West (August 1989). He lost that fight to John "The Steel City Shark" Lark (5 and 1) by a unanimous decision in four rounds. Lark went on to battle for the IBF world lightweight title seven years later.

336 Tony (Enoch) "The Rock" Jackson poses for a picture to use in an advertising poster before a show at the Park West

339 "Mighty" Mark Chears rejoices upon winning the Golden Gloves title in the superlightweight division at the Rosemont Horizon in March of 1990.

341 Matchmaker Jack Cowen at work setting up fights in his home office in Hyde Park. His work instruments: two telephone lines with four receivers, a fax machine, and yellow legal-size notepads on which he scribbles the information gleaned and the deals struck through the day.

348 A boxing show at the Park West night club in the upper-class white neighborhood of Lincoln Park. The upscale audience enjoys the fight while sipping fine wines and liquors.

354 Two light-heavyweights duke it out on the undercard at the Park West night club. Adolpho Washington, on the left was 5-and-0. Ron Lewis, on the right, was 4-and13. He finished his career a decade later with 5 victories and 20 defeats.

360 The entrance of the day-care center at the front of the gym on 63rd Street. The windows are protected by plywood and wire mesh and the door closed with a metal gate at the end of the day.

368 The ringside physician examines a boxer knocked out unconscious during a heavyweight fight at the Photon Arena in Harvey, a small black working-class suburb of Chicago.

373 Coach DeeDee closes up the gym at the end of the day.

Unless otherwise indicated, all photos were taken by the author.

A Note on Acknowledgments and Transcription

Like boxers, sociologists are the product of a long-term work of collective assembly that requires not only personal sacrifice and group discipline but also material sustenance. In the present case, essential support was provided by four institutions whose generosity I am happy to acknowledge here.

The University of Chicago brought me all the way from the other end of the world (Nouméa, New Caledonia) and awarded me a Century Fellowship to come to the Windy City to indulge in my passion for sociology for four years. My teachers there, especially Bill Wilson, Jim Coleman, Jean and John Comaroff, Adam Przeworski, and George Steinmetz, challenged and stimulated me on 59th Street, even as I kept them unapprised of my parallel life on 63rd Street. Bill Wilson's Urban Poverty Project supplied both the initial impetus for venturing into the ghetto and my first personal computer, a stolid IBM-PC loaded with XyWrite II-plus, without which I could not have typed and stored my field notes nightly.

The Society of Fellows at Harvard University enabled me to spend eighteen exhilerating months immersed among my Woodlawn mates and to realize that I had barely begun to loosen the knot of boxing, life, and labor on the South Side during the previous eighteen months of fieldwork. The House on Mount Auburn Street supplied fine food and still finer conversation that helped me surmount the deep depression I went through after leaving the gym.

The Fellows Program of the MacArthur Foundation stepped in next to relieve the constraints placed on research by research universities that have become triste shadows of their former glorious selves and afforded me the freedom to work on other projects until the time was right and ripe, on intersecting personal and intellectual planes, to write up this book.

Oxford University Press deserves high praise for bringing out the English-language edition of *Corps et âme* with just the right mix of diligence, patience, and all-around intelligence. I am especially thankful to Dedi Felman and Niko Pfund for delivering on every promise they made, demonstrating that probity and professionalism have not entirely vanished from the troubled world of publishing.

Numerous colleagues, students, friends, and loved ones in Chicago, Cambridge, New York City, Berkeley, Los Angeles, Rio de Janeiro, Paris, and Montpellier helped make this human experiment and sociological report possible. To list them all would require an extra chapter so I will thank them instead collectively and anonymously. Likewise, there are no words to explain what this book owes to Pierre Bourdieu and to Megan Comfort so I will not try to do so here, other than to say that this flight over a pugilistic nest could not have taken off without the former and landed without the latter. But there are two words suited to express my feelings toward my Woodlawn comrades and our coach: love and gratitude. This book is dedicated to DeeDee Armour in thankfulness for all he taught me about prizefighting, sociology, and, most important, life. Earning his trust and affection was my championship belt and I will always wear it proudly. I wish to extend my appreciation beyond Woodlawn to all the Chicago boxers and trainers who welcomed me into their midst, and to the cornermen, managers, matchmakers, promoters, referees, judges, and assorted "fight people" in many cities who together tutored me in the subtleties of the Sweet science. The names of a few individuals and locations as well as incidental details of events have been disguised when necessary to ensure confidentiality.

A note on translation and transcription is in order. This book was originally written in French, a linguistic detour that enabled me to achieve increased emotional distance from and analytic clarity about the materials. Along with the time lag, viewing my field notes from an external cultural vantage point helped to "estrange" myself from my own visceral experiences and first-hand accounts. Having to explicate the social relations and practices observed to a foreign audience that does not partake of the (national) doxic understandings shared by agents on the scene encouraged me to be more precise and concise in my depictions as well as more explicative in my analyses. But translating one's own work can be a tortuous and even a torturous endeavor. The five months of hard labor expended to convert the French text into English (based on a provisional draft produced by Christopher Rivers and edited by William Rodarmor) easily rank as the most grueling I spent on this entire project. In this more so than in the other foreign editions, I chose to stay close to the French original at the cost of the occasional turgidity or oddity of style, considering that, had I written this account in English, it would be a different book altogether (as *Passion of the Pugilist* will be).

I was alerted early on to the salience of language among lower-class urban African-Americans and so I sought, in keeping with the strand of folklore and sociolinguistics inaugurated by Roger Abrahams, William Labov, and Thomas Kochman to retain the linguistic specificities of the milieu studied. To better capture the idiom of the street, I relied particularly on William Labov, *Language in the Inner City: Studies in the Black English Vernacular* (Philadelphia: University of Pennsylvania Press, 1973), and John Baugh, *Black Street Speech: Its History, Structure, and Survival* (Austin: University of Texas Press, 1983). The result is uneven due to the heterogeneity of the verbal materials reported. Aside from the intrinsic difficulties of transcription, which are not unlike those of translation, the utterances, conversations, and quotes contained in the book (sometimes in the same scene) passed through three different filters: some were taped and transcribed later from the audio recording; others were written down in my field notebook on the spot or shortly after I heard them; and still others were recalled later during my nightly note-taking sessions. This, coupled with the fact that I became a more adept note-taker of language over time, creates an inescapable irregularity in the transliteration from oral to written communication. Imperfect as they are, I am nonetheless confident that the verbal materials presented in this book are less inaccurate that those produced by the standard practice of artificially converting the Black English vernacular into standard English.

I am grateful to Javier Auyero, Jenae Carpenter, Matt Desmond, Khoi Quach, Chris Muller, Alan Sica, and Michael Zanger-Tishler for their sharp and timely analytic and editorial suggestions on this postface as it was being written.

Index